Bryan Perrett served for nineteen years in Regular and Territorial regiments of the Royal Armoured Corps. His many popular books, widely read on both sides of the Atlantic, include *Last Stand!*, *Iron Fist*, *Seize and Hold*, *The Taste of Battle*, *Against All Odds!*, *At All Costs!*, *Impossible Victories*, *Heroes of the Hour* and a biography of Admiral Sir James Gordon, said to be the model for C. S. Forester's Horatio Hornblower, *The Real Hornblower*.

By Bryan Perrett

Desert Warfare
Tank Tracks to Rangoon
Canopy of War
The Czar's British Squadron
A History of Blitzkrieg
Knights of the Black Cross
Liverpool: A City at War
Last Stand!
At All Costs!
The Battle Book
Seize and Hold
Iron Fist
Against All Odds!
Impossible Victories
The Real Hornblower
The Changing Face of Battle
Gunboat!
Heroes of the Hour
For Valour

FOR VALOUR

Victoria Cross and
Medal of Honor Battles

Bryan Perrett

CASSELL

Cassell Military Paperbacks

Cassell
Wellington House, 125 Strand
London WC2R 0BB

First published in 2003
by Weidenfeld & Nicolson
This Cassell Military Paperbacks edition 2004

Distributed in the United States by
Sterling Publishing Co. Inc.
387 Park Avenue South
New York
NY 10016-8810

British Library Cataloguing-in-Publication Data.
A catalogue record for this book is available
from the British Library.

ISBN 0 304 36698 6

Printed in Great Britain by
Cox & Wyman Ltd

www.orionbooks.co.uk

Contents

Introduction   I

The Crimean War 1854–56

The Battle of the Alma   *20 September 1854*   13
The Battle of Balaklava   *25 October 1854*   25
Inkerman   *5 November 1854*   34

The Indian Mutiny 1857–58

The Delhi Arsenal   *11 May 1857*   45
The Siege of Delhi   *8 June – 20 September 1857*   49
The Storming of Delhi   *14–20 September 1857*   54
The Second Relief of Lucknow   *16 November 1857*   62

China · North America · Southern Africa
North-West Frontier · Cuba 1860–1900

The Taku Forts   *21 August 1860*   73
The Great Locomotive Chase   *12 April 1862*   78
Gettysburg   *1–3 July 1863*   83
Mobile Bay   *5 August 1864*   98
The Sioux War of 1876   104
Rorke's Drift   *22–23 January 1879*   115
The Storming of Nilt Fort   *2 December 1891*   128
San Juan Hill/El Caney   *1 July 1898*   135
Colenso   *15 December 1899*   144
The Boxer Rising   *1900–1901*   152

The First World War 1914–18

Mons, Le Cateau and The Aisne *August–September 1914*   167

Gallipoli *1915*   182

Jutland *31 May – 1 June 1916*   201

The Somme *1 July 1916*   208

Zeebrugge and Ostend *22–23 April and 9–10 May 1918*   217

Over There – Belleau Wood and The Argonne
June–November 1918   229

The Second World War 1939–45

Tobruk – Operation Crusader *18 November – 7 December 1941*   243

The St Nazaire Raid *28 March 1942*   252

Dieppe – Operation Jubilee *19 August 1942*   267

First and Second Alamein *July and October 1942*   273

Guadalcanal *7 August 1942 – 7 February 1943*   287

Bloody Sunday – The Ploesti Raid *1 August 1943*   303

Anzio *January–June 1944*   309

Kohima, Imphal and the Second Chindit Incursion
April–July 1944   327

Market Garden *17–25 September 1944*   344

Iwo Jima *19 February – 26 March 1945*   352

Epilogue   365

Appendix   366

Bibliography   367

Index   371

Introduction

Medals are a public statement of a serviceman's record. They tell us not only where he has served, but also acknowledge any exceptional acts of bravery that he has performed. They are an accepted facet of life in every army, navy and air force throughout the world; yet for all that, the modern system of gallantry awards and campaign medals is, historically speaking, a comparatively recent introduction. It is, of course, true to say that the Roman army rewarded outstanding acts of courage on the part of its soldiers with various insignia that could be worn with their armour. However, following the demise of the Roman Empire, the large standing professional army vanished from history for over a thousand years and with it the custom of rewarding individuals with visible devices in recognition of their courage.

It was the gunpowder revolution that restored to the battlefield the importance of ordinary soldier and seaman. The new weapons demanded new skills and new tactics that could only be executed by trained professionals, which, of course, involved the creation of national standing armies and navies. Commemorative medals were struck for such major events as the defeat of the Spanish Armada, and for many other battles, but these were for distribution only to the more important participants and it was not the intention that they should be worn as part of uniform. During the dynastic wars of the seventeenth and eighteenth centuries several European monarchs recognised that the rewarding of individual acts of courage by conferring insignia that could be worn with uniform would benefit the overall morale of their troops. One such example is the Pour le Mérite, better known as the Blue Max, established by Frederick the Great of Prussia in 1740. Better known, perhaps, is the Légion d'Honneur, founded by Napoleon Bonaparte in 1802 as a general military and civil order of merit conferred irrespective of rank, birth or religion, for acts of extraordinary military bravery and service in time of war, or twenty years of civil achievement in peacetime. Those admitted to the Legion for war services automatically receive France's highest military decoration, the Croix de Guerre.

During this period the British service offered little in the way of visible reward. In the army, if an officer performed an act of exemplary valour in action, he might receive promotion which, in the days of commission and advancement by purchase, was of considerable financial benefit to him. Promotion might also be the reward for selected non-commissioned ranks. Rarely, after a hard-fought action, one or more sergeants might be offered a commission, the recipients sometimes being chosen by a ballot of their peers. Some small progress, however, was made towards uniform decorations. In 1795 the Royal Navy introduced the Gold Medal for successful actions at sea, but only admirals and captains were eligible to receive this. The award was discontinued in 1815. Two years earlier the Prince Regent had approved the award of Army Gold Medals to commemorate victories on land during the Napoleonic Wars, these being similarly restricted to general officers and officers commanding regiments and battalions.

In passing, it is worth mentioning that the issue of commemorative campaign medals had already been initiated, not by the British government but by a commercial organisation, the Honourable East India Company, which was responsible for preserving British trade and other interests in India and the Far East. To perform this task the Company maintained its own army and navy, both of which were frequently in action. Recognising the importance of maintaining morale, as well as contributing to the prestige of its soldiers in local communities where the concept of 'face' was a matter of great moment, the Company began a general issue of commemorative medals in 1784. The first British campaign medal, as we understand the term, was the Waterloo Medal, issued in 1816. The precedent having been set, further campaign medals were issued as the need arose. Curiously, the numerous actions throughout the Napoleonic Wars that had preceded the Battle of Waterloo went unrecognised for many years. This omission was rectified by the issue of the Naval General Service Medal 1793–1840 and the Military General Service Medal 1793–1814, both authorised in 1847, and the Army of India Medal 1799–1826, authorised in 1851. These all carried bars listing the engagements at which the recipient had been present. Naturally, many of those who would have been eligible for the awards had died before they were authorised. The government was therefore able to save itself a little money by issuing medals only to those who were still living and able to claim them.

Still, no awards for gallantry existed and, once again, it was the Honourable East India Company that led the way by introducing the Indian Order of Merit in 1837. The award was made for acts of courage above and beyond the call of duty and its recipients were entitled to a higher pension on their retirement. So prestigious did the award become that, despite its commercial origins, it was granted official status when the Crown assumed responsibility for the Company's armed services after the Indian Mutiny. After Independence, the government of India continued to maintain the award under a different title.

As far as British servicemen were concerned, the Crimean War proved to be a major turning point. It is well known that, thanks to mismanagement and bungling at the highest levels, the troops were forced to endure their first winter in the Crimea without adequate shelter, clothing and rations, and that the army's medical services left a great deal to be desired. The scandal was widely reported in the popular press, with the result that the government of the day was brought down. Also reported was the exemplary fortitude and stoicism displayed by the troops in the face of all adversity, as well as numerous examples of supreme courage and self-sacrifice. All of this was followed closely by Queen Victoria and her husband Prince Albert, who decided that such acts of gallantry must receive a visible award. In 1856 the details were finally settled. The award, named after the Queen herself, consisted of a simple bronze cross, inscribed *For Valour* on the front and engraved with the recipient's name, rank, number, unit and the date of the action on the reverse. It was, and still is, made from the metal of a pair of ornamental Chinese cannon captured at Sevastopol, and was originally worn with a blue ribbon for the Royal Navy and a deep red ribbon for the Army. It was ordained that 'The Cross shall only be awarded for most conspicuous bravery, or some daring or pre-eminent act of valour or self-sacrifice or extreme devotion to duty in the presence of the enemy,' without barrier of colour, creed, sex or rank. The award could, and remains, subject to royal assent and whenever possible it is personally presented by the Sovereign. It was also decided that it should be made retrospective to the beginning of the Crimean War, for which 111 VCs were awarded. The first presentations were made to sixty-two officers and men by Queen Victoria at a parade in Hyde Park on 26 June 1857. In 1867 the award was extended to colonial forces throughout the Empire, save for the officers and men of the Indian Army, who became eligible in 1911.

From 1854 until the time of writing, the Victoria Cross has been awarded only 1,354 times, its very rarity making it the most highly prized decoration for gallantry any subject of the Commonwealth can earn. Inevitably, over the years there have been changes in the circumstances of the award. For example, between 1858 and 1881 the original warrant was amended to allow it to be granted 'under circumstances of extreme danger.' In certain circumstances, where an act of gallantry was performed by a group of men rather than an individual, recommendation for the award has been accepted by ballot. For many years posthumous awards were not sanctioned in circumstances where the potential recipient was killed during or died shortly after the qualifying action, his family having to be content with an announcement in the *London Gazette* to the effect that had he survived he would have been recommended for the VC. In fact, the original warrant made no recommendations on the subject. However, in 1900, during the Second Boer War, the authorities were presented with a *fait accompli*. At the Battle of Colenso, Lieutenant the Hon. Frederick Roberts, son of Field Marshal Lord Roberts, VC, was mortally wounded while attempting to bring out a battery of stranded guns under heavy fire and was granted the award posthumously after he died the following day. The war saw a further six posthumous awards, leaving the War Office no alternative other than to grant the award retrospectively to the earlier cases. Despite this, it was not until 1920 that an amendment to the warrant officially sanctioned the posthumous award of the Victoria Cross.

Again, the original warrant contained a provision to the effect that if a recipient of the VC was found guilty of discreditable conduct his award would be forfeit. There have been eight such cases of forfeiture, the crimes ranging from petty theft to bigamy. Many, not least King George V, found this stuffy attitude intolerable. On 26 July 1920 his Private Secretary, Lord Stamfordham, wrote an extremely pointed letter to the War Office, commenting: 'The King feels so strongly that, no matter the crime committed by anyone on whom the VC has been conferred, the decoration should not be forfeited. Even if a VC were to be hanged for murder, he should be allowed to wear his VC on the scaffold.' The forfeiture clause was quietly shunted to one side.

The award of the Victoria Cross brought with it some small financial reward. Initially, a pension of £10 per annum was granted to non-commissioned ranks. This was obviously insufficient to keep the wolf from the door for those who, on leaving the service, found themselves in dire financial straits. In fact, a number of early recipients went to unmarked graves, or, worse, shared a grave with fellow paupers. This was obviously not the end intended for such men and as the nineteenth century drew to a close, provisions were made for a discretionary increase to £50 per annum, subsequently increased to £75 per annum. In 1959 the pension was awarded irrespective of rank and increased to £100 per annum. A review in 1995 saw this increased to £1,300 per annum. Local privileges accorded to a recipient of the VC might include the courtesy of being saluted by all save recipients of higher rank. Since 1918, when the Royal Air Force was formed, the ribbon has been deep red for all three services.

The Distinguished Conduct Medal was also introduced as a result of the Crimean War, to be awarded to other ranks for less extreme acts of courage than those qualifying for the VC. Since then, further gallantry awards have been introduced. It can, of course, be argued that some of the early recipients of the VC would have been eligible for one of these rather than the supreme award. On the other hand, having read their citations, few would question their courage, let alone welcome being placed in similar circumstances. It will, too, be appreciated that because of the turmoil of battle the VC was earned many more times than it was conferred, and it was to allow for such unrecorded acts of self-sacrifice and supreme courage that the award was bestowed upon the tomb of the nation's Unknown Warrior in Westminster Abbey. Today, it is necessary for a minimum of three witnesses to make sworn statements on the precise circumstances of the act, and for the act to have a decisive bearing on the outcome of the engagement, before recommendations for the award can be considered. It is a matter of record that several VCs would have been conferred had not one or more witnesses been killed before their statements could be made, or that in preparing despatches on an engagement the decisive nature of the act has been obscured by the overall detail. Of those qualifying acts that conform to the modern criteria and result in an award being made, it has been calculated that the survival rate is one in ten.

The United States' Congressional Medal of Honor has a similar standing to the Victoria Cross, although its introduction was less straightforward. In 1782 General George Washington authorised the issue of a badge to recognise 'any singularly meritorious action' on the part of an individual soldier. The badge was heart-shaped and edged in lace. Only three such awards were made and the custom seems to have lapsed with the ending of the Revolutionary War. It was revived in 1932 by the then Army Chief of Staff, General Douglas MacArthur, in the form of a heart-shaped medal including a portrait of Washington on a purple ground, suspended from a purple and silver ribbon. Initially an army award, it was conferred on those who had been wounded during World War I or who possessed a Meritorious Service Citation Certificate. In 1943 eligibility was broadened to include navy, marine corps and coast guard personnel, and was later extended to include any civilian national who sustained wounds while serving with the armed forces.

Important as is the Purple Heart, military merit and wounds are not necessarily synonymous with acts of supreme courage and self-sacrifice. The latter went unrecognised by awards during the pointless War of 1812 with the United Kingdom, although during the 1847 Mexican-American War soldiers who distinguished themselves were awarded a certificate of merit. During the early days of the Civil War, however, it was suggested to General Winfield Scott, the army's General-in-Chief, that a medal for individual valour should be instituted. Scott, who was regarded as something of a father figure, rejected the idea as being un-American. The navy had no such reservations and on 9 December 1861 a Medal of Honor, 'to be bestowed upon such petty officers, seamen, landsmen and Marines as shall most distinguish themselves by their gallantry and other seamanlike qualities during the present war.' Naturally, the army was not inclined to be left behind and, despite Scott's opinions, its own Medal of Honor, to be awarded 'to such non-commissioned officers and privates as shall most distinguish themselves by their gallantry in action, and other soldierlike qualities, during the present insurrection,' was signed into law on 12 July 1862. Army officers did not become eligible for the medal until 3 March 1863, although the award was to be made retrospective to the beginning of the war. This provision was pointedly ignored, for although three officers did receive the medal shortly after the war ended, their awards were for acts performed during their service as enlisted men. This seems to have reflected the slightly priggish views of a small section of opinion, also present in the British service, that officers should not require the incentive of decorations to perform their duty; in fact, officers of the US Navy did not become eli-gible for the award until 1915. Be that as it may, in the years following the war the Grand Army of the Union, a veterans' organisation with considerable political influence, began lobbying for the award to be made to officers who had performed appropriate acts during the Civil War. When, in 1890, General Arthur MacArthur, the father of Douglas, successfully lodged his claim for the medal, others followed suit, so that between 1891 and 1896 there were sixty-seven awards of the CMH for gallantry during the Civil War, forty-five of the recipients still being on the active list. Strange as it may seem, some enlisted men were unaware that they had been awarded the medal until long after the event, which explains anomalies in the citations indicating the passage of years be-tween the act itself and receipt of the decoration. The Union Army's Confederate opponents in the war did not receive gallantry awards from their government, although the actions of brave men were supposed to be read out on parade, entered in the official records and reported in the press.

It was inevitable that in an army which expanded as rapidly as did the Union Army during the Civil War that a wide variety of interpretations should have been placed upon the qualifications required for the award of the new decoration. The result was that many inappropriate awards were made, none more so than in the case of the 27th Maine, whose 864 officers and men had enlisted for nine months and were due for discharge on 30 June 1863. The crisis culminating in the Battle of Gettysburg was then at its height and on 26 June the regiment was asked to remain in being as part of the garrison of Washington. It refused point blank, although 309 men agreed to stay when offered the CMH. The successful outcome of the battle resolved the crisis and on 4 July they were released without having had to fire a shot. In due course the Governor of Maine received a consignment of 864 medals but declined to distribute more than 309; the remainder were stashed in his barn, from whence they were stolen. In 1916 Congress revoked 911 inappropriate awards of the Medal of Honor, including all those conferred on the 27th Maine.

On 26 June 1897 new regulations were introduced, setting much stiffer criteria for the award of the CMH. Potential recipients were no longer permitted to enter their own claims. All recommendations had to be accompanied by the statements of eyewitnesses and had to be made within one year of the act, although in the event a degree of flexibility was permitted on the latter point. Like the Victoria Cross, the Medal of Honor therefore became increasingly difficult to earn. However, unlike the VC, at the time it could not be conferred on foreign nationals, exceptions being the CMHs conferred on the tombs of Allied Unknown Soldiers, including that of the British Unknown Warrior in Westminster Abbey, as part of a reciprocal gesture in which a VC was placed on the grave of America's Unknown Soldier in Arlington National Cemetery. The Medals of Honor for the navy (including the marine corps and coast guard), the army and the air force differ slightly in detail but retain the form of a five-pointed gilt star suspended from a watered silk sky-blue ribbon embellished with stars, worn around the neck. Earlier navy and army Medals of Honor were worn on the chest, suspended from a red, white and blue ribbon. Altogether, a total of 3,459 Medals of Honor have been conferred, nineteen of the recipients being awarded the decoration a second time.

It is, of course, impossible to predict what type of man will earn a Victoria Cross or a Congressional Medal of Honor. The recipients come from every conceivable background and possess widely differing temperaments. It is only after they have received their award that some form of commonality seems to appear. In 1984, General Mark Clark, who had commanded the Allied Fifth Army in Italy during World War II, observed in an article written for a local newspaper, 'During the war I found that men who won the Medal of Honor – and survived – were so conscious of the distinction that when they returned to combat they showed even greater courage, took greater risks and were far more likely to be killed than their comrades.'

It is a curious truth that some battles produce numerous VC and CMH awards, while others produce few or none. For example, the Battle of Britain, for all its desperate and decisive nature, saw only one award of the Victoria Cross, to Flight Lieutenant Eric Nicolson. On 16 August 1940 Nicolson was engaged in an air battle over Southampton when his Hurricane was set on fire by a burst from a Messerschmitt Me 110. Wounded in the foot and eye, he was on the point of baling out of his stricken aircraft when a second Me 110 crossed his line of vision. Dropping back into the cockpit, he opened fire on the intruder, continuing to fly the blazing Hurricane until he was satisfied that he had done the enemy mortal damage. He then baled out and, though landing safely, was unable to undo his parachute harness because his hands were so badly burned. Nicolson, who won the Distinguished Flying Cross in another action, was also the only pilot of the RAF's Fighter Command to be awarded the Victoria Cross during World War II. Tragically, he was to be killed in action over the Bay of Bengal on 2 May 1945. It is inconceivable that in six years of intense warfare more VCs were not earned by Fighter Command, if not conferred. A possible explanation is the individual nature of fighter combat, in which, once action is joined, pilots are totally committed to their own personal life and death battles and witnesses are few. On the other hand, some battles are remarkable for the crop of awards for supreme courage that they produce and the purpose of this book is to examine a representative selection of these.

The reason I have chosen to include both Victoria Cross *and* Medal of Honor battles is that they represent an historical progression. It was the German Chancellor Otto von Bismarck who remarked that one of the salient facts of the nineteenth century was that Great Britain and the United States spoke the same language. The remark was prescient, for at the time Britannia ruled the waves and the American expansion was only regaining momentum after the temporary check of the Civil War. It was inevitable that, sooner or later, the United States would outstrip the United Kingdom in terms of population, wealth and industrial capacity, achieving the status of a great international power. The process would be accelerated by two world wars, and in the final year of World War II it was clearly apparent that leadership of the English-speaking world had passed to America. That world, springing from the same roots and possessing the same ideals, the same principles of common law and similarly stable systems of government, has for two centuries proved to be a dominant influence in global events, to the extent that English is now the most commonly spoken language of all. Expansion and the defence of freedom are often painful processes involving the sacrifice of lives and treasure, for there are occasions when neither can be achieved without force of arms. As the reader will discover, one notable aspect of this progression is that the Victoria Cross and the Medal of Honor have on occasion been awarded for acts on the same battlefield.

THE CRIMEAN WAR
1854–56

The Battle of the Alma
20 SEPTEMBER 1854

The proximate cause of the Crimean War was the desire of Tsar Nicholas I of Russia to obtain unfettered access to the Mediterranean through the Turkish-controlled Bosporus and Dardanelles, an end he was prepared to achieve by dismembering the crumbling Ottoman Empire. Neither Great Britain nor France were prepared to tolerate a disturbance of the existing balance of power in the Mediterranean, and following the outbreak of hostilities between Russia and Turkey on 28 March 1854 they declared war on the former. British and French expeditionary forces sailed to support the Turkish army, but by the time they reached the war zone international pressure had forced the Tsar to abandon his invasion of Turkey's Romanian provinces. It was nevertheless decided that he must be taught a lesson, and his punishment was to be the destruction of the heavily fortified naval base of Sevastopol, on the south coast of the Crimean peninsula. Comparatively little thought was given to the difficulties involved in such an undertaking.

The British army had not fought a continental opponent for forty years. It had considerable experience of fighting in India and elsewhere, but the troops at home have been fairly described as an agglomeration of regiments, albeit of good quality, consisting of long-service professionals. The infantry had recently been re-armed with the new Minié rifle, which had far greater range, accuracy and penetrative power than the old Brown Bess musket. Unfortunately, the army's administrative, supply, transport and medical branches were in a hopeless bureaucratic tangle. Even worse was a critical shortage of trained staff officers. Worst of all was the choice of general officers to command divisions and brigades. Most of the former had last seen active service against Napoleon and were set in their ways, while some of the latter were so inexperienced they were unable to judge the amount of space required in which to deploy their brigades.

Having landed in the Crimea at Calamita Bay on 13 September, the Allies spent several days consolidating their position, then began marching south towards Sevastopol in gruelling heat. On 19 September they reached the River Alma, where the Russian army commanded by General Prince Menshikov could be seen drawn up on the high ground beyond. Menshikov, who had 37,000 men at his disposal, had chosen his ground well. Near the sea, the ground rose steeply from the river to the summit, but east of the village of Burliuk the slope was gentler yet still impressive as it provided an open glacis devoid of cover. The position was further strengthened by the erection of what became known as the Greater Redoubt, bristling with guns, on the forward slope of Kurgane Hill, and a smaller work, the Lesser Redoubt, covering the eastern approaches to the summit of the hill. Everywhere the Allies could see the solid grey blocks of the Russian infantry deployed to protect the redoubts, punctuated by numerous field batteries. Menshikov also had skirmishers in position along both banks of the river. He was so confident that he could hold the position indefinitely that he had a platform constructed on Kurgane Hill so that the ladies of Sevastopol society could picnic while they watched the repulse of the keenly anticipated Allied attack.

The British commander, Field Marshal Lord Raglan, had 27,000 men at his disposal, while his French counterpart, Marshal Armand de Saint-Arnaud, had 25,000. There were also some 8,000 Turks present. It was agreed that the Russian position would be assaulted on 20 September, although the plan was simply a broad statement of intent that the French and Turks would attack on the right, supported by the guns of the fleet, while the British would attack Kurgane Hill once the French attack had drawn off sufficient reserves from the Russian centre. The British advance would be made on a two-division frontage, with 2nd Division on the right and the Light Division on the left, supported respectively by the 3rd Division and the 1st Division. Each of the infantry divisions consisted of two brigades containing three battalions. The open left flank of the advance was screened by the cavalry of the Light Brigade. As the armies deployed the 2nd Division found itself jostled by the left-hand French division and took ground to its left, where it in turn overlapped the frontage of the Light Division. The latter compounded the difficulty by advancing obliquely to its right and, despite being ordered to do so, failed to conform to the general direction of the advance. In the circumstances it was a foregone conclusion that the regiments bordering the theoretical divisional boundaries would become intermingled.

On the extreme right the French attacked prematurely and succeeded in securing a small lodgement on the high ground at the mouth of the river. Their main attack, however, stalled under heavy fire below the steep slopes of the escarpment. The British, meanwhile, had been advancing towards the river but were halted by Raglan until he could ascertain whether the French assault had produced the required results. As the halt was made within range of the Russian artillery the regiments were ordered to lie down. With cannon balls, visible for most of their flight, bounding through and over the prone ranks, and shells bursting overhead, this would have been a testing ordeal for veteran troops. Few of those present had been in action before but the men endured their ordeal stoically and even joked among themselves about the performance of individual Russian guns. After approximately an hour and a half, at about 15:00, a French staff officer arrived with a wildly exaggerated report of French losses accompanied by an urgent request that the British should commence their own attack. Raglan gave the order to advance and with a great sense of relief the regiments rose to their feet. At this moment the Russians, seeing the scarlet lines moving forward, set fire to Burliuk, the houses of which had been stuffed full of combustible materials. The village contained the principal river crossing and lay directly in the path of the 2nd Division, the left-hand brigade of which was forced by the impenetrable flames to veer even further to the left, causing yet more intermingling with the Light Division, while the division's right-hand brigade bypassed the village to the right, a route which deviated from the main thrust-line of the assault.

When the regiments reached the Alma, therefore, those in the centre were already mixed together and in some disorder. The river itself was fordable but there were wide variations in its depth. Some men barely got their feet wet, others were forced to wade chest-deep with their rifles and ammunition pouches held above their heads, while others fell into unseen potholes and drowned and those who were hit by the enemy's fire vanished beneath the surface. The far shore consisted of a wide shelf backed by a steep bank. In the lee of this, officers vainly tried to sort out the units which had become mixed together. As groups scrambled over the bank, the priority became to maintain the momentum of the advance. 'Never mind forming, for God's sake!' was the cry. 'Come on! Come on anyhow!' The result was a ragged line, uneven to the point that in places it was sixteen men deep. Ahead lay several hundred yards of steep slope, broken regularly by lines of deep vineyard pits that would further disorder the ranks, up which the Russian skirmishers were retiring. Once the skirmishers had reached their own lines, the Russian artillery reopened fire.

At this point Brigadier General George Buller, commanding the Light Division's left-hand brigade, seems to have lost his head. One of his regiments, the 77th (later the 2nd Bn The Middlesex Regiment), had already wheeled left to provide a flank guard for the main attack, but for some reason Buller believed he was about to be attacked by cavalry and ordered his two remaining regiments, the 88th (The Connaught Rangers) and the 19th (The Green Howards), to form square. The 88th did so, reluctantly, but the 19th, closer to the Russian batteries, believing that the threat was exaggerated and aware that to comply under the muzzles of the enemy guns would be tantamount to suicide, declined the order and, veering to the right, attached themselves to the neighbouring brigade.

This, commanded by Brigadier General W. J. Codrington, originally consisted of the 7th Royal Fusiliers, the 33rd (Duke of Wellington's) Regiment and the 23rd Royal Welch Fusiliers. It was now swollen by the addition of the 19th and a large portion of the 95th Regiment (later the 2nd Bn The Sherwood Foresters) which belonged to the left-hand brigade of the 2nd Division but had become intermingled during the river crossing. This accidental reinforcement was, in a way, a blessing in disguise as the burden of this phase of the battle would fall on Codrington's men. As they continued to mount the long, bare slope they were so lashed by roundshot, shell and grape that one soldier of the 33rd later recalled that he 'never expected to live another minute.' As it was, every step of the brigade's way was marked by a trail of dead or wounded, stretching back to the river. The 95th's Colour party lost every ensign and five sergeants as well. For their part the Russians, who relied on heavy columnar tactics, were unsettled by the steady, disciplined advance of the untidy scarlet line.

On the right of the Light Division's advance the 7th Royal Fusiliers were counter-attacked by a two-column battalion of the Kazan Regiment. The distance closed to the point at which details of the enemy's uniform and features became apparent. The Russians were wearing ankle-length, yellowish-grey greatcoats and tall spiked helmets beneath which were curiously vacant white faces. A protracted firefight took place at murderously close range. To some extent this nullified the advantage in range possessed by the British; on the other hand, the greater penetrative power of the Minie bullet ensured that it punched its way through the leading ranks of the dense Russian formation and into those beyond. Again, the Russians were armed with the old smooth-bore musket, ineffective much beyond 100 yards, and only those at the front of the column could use them. They were, therefore, at a serious disadvantage but, while their advance was brought to a standstill they stood their ground, taking heavy casualties and inflicting serious loss in return. This stubborn killing match was to continue throughout the critical phase of the battle.

In the centre the Royal Welch Fusiliers closed in remorselessly on the Greater Redoubt, disregarding the blasts of grapeshot that cut through their ranks. Suddenly the battery fell silent as, in obedience to the Tsar's *diktat* that not a gun should be lost, the gunners began limbering up as their teams entered the position at a gallop. Sensing victory, the Fusiliers surged forward. Lieutenant Henry Anstruther, barely eighteen, rushed up the redoubt's breastwork and triumphantly planted the Queen's Colour on the summit. Shot dead immediately by fire from nearby Russian infantry, he fell, bringing down the Colour on top of him. Another member of the Colour party, Sergeant Luke O'Connor, was hit at the same time, but loosened Anstruther's grip on the stave and held the riddled silk aloft, yelling for the men to come on. They swarmed over the breastwork and into the redoubt, being rewarded by the sight of Sevastopol's gentry fleeing for their lives, shedding parasols, shawls and opera glasses in the process. Captain Edward Bell, spotting a Russian gun team in difficulties, ran forward and clapped his pistol to the driver's head, telling him to clear off. He did so, immediately. At this point the divisional commander, Major General Sir George Brown, appeared. This Peninsular War veteran was heartily disliked throughout the army, to the point that one of his junior officers described him as 'an old wretch'. True to form, Brown had no praise to offer Bell, and instead angrily ordered him back to his company. Before he did so, Bell turned the team's head and, slapping the lead horse on the rump, sent the gun bouncing down the slope towards the river. Nearby, a second gun was captured by Captain Heyland of the 95th.

As any good commander knows, attacking troops are at their most vulnerable just after they have taken an objective. They are usually disorganised, as was the case here, they are relieved that they have achieved what they set out to do, and they tend to relax. Fully aware of this, the Russians launched the Vladimir Regiment in a counter-attack, the regiment's advance being supported by field batteries firing into the now congested area of the Greater Redoubt from higher up the hill. The Vladimir came on in a dense column with bayonets levelled, proudly displaying an embroidered banner of their patron, St Sergius. Far from being intimidated, Codrington's brigade had begun shooting away the head of the column when one of the strangest incidents of the whole battle took place. A wild-eyed staff officer galloped along the line, shouting, 'Don't fire! For God's sake, don't fire! The column's French!' The officer was not recognised, nor has he been identified since. The possibility therefore arises that this was an unusually subtle Russian ploy, although the theory cannot be substantiated. It might just as well have been for the effect it had. The officer's claim, of course, was impossible, as the French were fully engaged downstream. Be that as it may, he rode up to a bugler of the 19th and ordered him to sound the Cease Fire. The man obediently did so and the call was taken up by other buglers along the line. Despite the shouts of regimental officers who knew the truth, firing died away. The officer then ordered another bugler to sound Retire, which was again taken up. Confused, the troops looked round, expecting to see the 1st Division climbing the slope behind them. In-stead, all they saw were their own casualties, stretching to the water's edge and beyond. At this moment the Vladimir opened fire, killing Colonel Chester of the 23rd just as he was reassuring his men that the column was Russian. With the exception of the Royal Fusiliers, still locked in their deadly struggle with the Kazan Regiment, the entire line began retiring sullenly down the slope, pausing frequently to fire at the ponderous column as it relentlessly followed. If the advance up the slope had been confused, the retreat down was far worse. In the 23rd, two men were responsible for stopping it becoming a rout. Sergeant O'Connor, who had declined suggestions that he should go to the rear and have his wound attended to, refused to surrender his Colour to anyone and in response to his shouts for the men to rally round it they did so. So heavy were casualties among the officers that Captain Bell was the senior survivor. Once he was aware of this he assumed command and was able to restore some sort of order to the regiment's line and control its movement.

Meanwhile, what of the 1st Division, which was supposed to be providing close support? The divisional commander was the thirty-five-year-old Duke of Cambridge, a cousin of Queen Victoria. Never having been in action before, the duke was acutely conscious not only of his lack of experience but also that he was responsible for the fate of the Guards and Highland Brigades, regarded by many as the best formations in the army. Having observed the disruption caused by the vineyards to the ranks of the Light Division, he hesitated in ordering the advance of his own brigades until sharply ordered to do so by General Richard Airey, Raglan's principal staff officer. The division forded the river with the Guards on the right and the Highlanders on the left. Within the Guards Brigade the Grenadier Guards were on the right, the Scots Fusilier Guards in the centre and the Coldstream Guards on the left. The Scots were over first and were forming up when the brigade commander, Major General H. J. W. Bentinck, received a request from Codrington for urgent assistance.

The situation now was that the Vladimir Regiment had recaptured the Greater Redoubt and had halted briefly to throw out skirmishers on its flanks before resuming its advance down the slope. To its front was the thin line containing the remnant of the 23rd Royal Welch Fusiliers and men from other regiments who had taken part in the first assault. The Grenadiers and Coldstream were emerging from the river and dressing their ranks. Bentinck, none too bright, reacted prematurely to Codrington's plea, bellowing at the Scots Fusilier Guards, 'Forward! Forward, Fusiliers! What are you waiting for?' Obediently, the regiment, its ranks still not properly formed, began ascending the slope. The Colour party set a cracking pace, so that the companies on either flank began to trail, producing an irregular arrowhead formation. Needless to say, a yawning gap appeared in the centre of the Guards Brigade.

Having reoccupied their former position, the Russian infantry and artillery opened a heavy fire on the troops below. As the Scots Fusilier Guards closed up to the ragged line of the 23rd the dense column of the Vladimir came swarming over the breastwork of the Greater Redoubt. At this point the mysterious galloping staff officer put in a second appearance. There was a shout of 'Retire! Fusiliers, retire!' This could have applied to the 23rd, or the 7th or the Scots Fusilier Guards. The 23rd, their ranks decimated by a further volley from the Vladimir, took it to apply to themselves and hurriedly withdrew through the ranks of the Scots Fusilier Guards, knocking over several men in the process. The latter were also beginning to feel the effect of the Russian fire so that the temporary check coincided with the regiment's first serious casualties. The Queen's Colour went down, its pole smashed and the silk shot through in twenty places. Brandishing his revolver, Sergeant James McKechnie dashed forward to retrieve it, rallying men around it despite receiving a wound in the process. It had now been accepted by the regiment's senior officers that the command to retire applied to them, too, and the order was given. The retirement was rapid, untidy and pressed so hard by the Vladimir that several casualties were subsequently found to have been stabbed in the back. Captain Robert Lindsay, Sergeant John Knox and Private William Reynolds all led parties in desperate but successful attempts to extricate the Colours which, it will be recalled, had been some way ahead of the battalion's main body, and thereby provided a rallying point upon which the ranks eventually reformed. The Vladimir pursuit was halted short of the river, its success prompting Prince Gortschakoff to lead two more Russian battalions down from the summit to complete the apparent rout of the British.

By now, the Grenadiers and the Coldstream had begun their advance up the slope. Since it was considered disgraceful for Guardsmen to turn their backs on the enemy, they were less than sympathetic to the Scots Fusilier Guards as they fell back between them, taunting them with shouts of 'Shame! What about the Queen's favourites now?' Once more, the galloping staff officer appeared with his warnings not to fire on the 'French' and his instructions to retire. This time, the truth was so brutally obvious that he was ignored. Dressing back their left flank, the Grenadiers opened a devastating fire with their Minié rifles into the flank of the Russian columns at less than 100 yards, to such good effect that, as one junior officer noted, 'They dropped by dozens, another and another volley and we cut them down in crowds as they came on.' Prince Gortschakoff's horse was shot under him and after landing on his head he limped back up the hill. His successor in command, General Kvetzinski, shared a similar fate and had to be carried off the field, sorely wounded. From the left, the Coldstream joined, shooting the closely packed ranks to tatters. It was more than flesh and blood could stand. Slowly and sullenly, the Russians gave ground. Notwithstanding their having sustained the loss of 171 men killed or wounded, including eleven officers, the Scots Fusilier Guards had completed their rally quickly and came up to take their place in the centre of the brigade. The entire Guards Brigade then advanced steadily in well-dressed lines, firing alternately by ranks, until they were within 40 yards of the Greater Redoubt, when the order to charge was given. They went in with a tremendous cheer heard a mile away. The Russians gave way but retired in reasonable order and continued to fire from a distance. They were not yet routed, and for that to happen one further act in the drama was required.

The Highland Brigade had forded the Alma upstream of the Guards, with the 42nd (The Black Watch) on the right, the 93rd (later the 2nd Bn Argyll and Sutherland Highlanders) in the centre and the 79th (The Queen's Own Cameron Highlanders) on the left. In command was Major General Sir Colin Campbell, who had first seen action as a boy fighting against Napoleon. For all his sixty-one years, Campbell retained all his abilities and vigour and was a sound, not to say canny, tactician who knew how to get the best out of his Highland soldiers. The Duke of Cambridge had also splashed across and encountered Buller, whose 77th Regiment was engaged with Russian infantry on the left while the 88th still stood uneasily in its square. It was at this moment that the remnant of Codrington's brigade finally gave way, followed by the Scots Fusilier Guards. Inexperienced as he was, the duke, a likeable man, could see only death and disorder at every hand, little realising that this was the normal state of affairs in battle. 'What am I to do?' he plaintively asked. Buller, aware that he was speaking to a member of the royal family, chose his words carefully: 'Why, your Royal Highness, I am in a little confusion here – you had better advance I think.' Unconvinced, he trotted over to Campbell, who, as a fiercely patriotic Scot, was disgusted by the apparent retreat of the Scots Guards. The duke suggested that a disaster would ensue if the 1st Division was not withdrawn. Campbell replied bluntly that a disaster was certain if it *was*, then went on to outline his plan for his brigade to mount an attack up the eastern shoulder of Kurgane Hill, taking in the Lesser Redoubt. Most reluctantly, the duke gave his permission, commenting sadly, 'We shall be tried for this, Sir Colin.' Yet, for all his diffidence, he was a brave man and, riding across to join the renewed assault of the Guards Brigade, was one of the first into the Greater Redoubt.

Aware that a considerable body of uncommitted Russian troops lay on the left, Campbell decided that his advance would be carried out echeloned to the rear from the right. As the Highlanders began moving forward, sarcastic shouts were directed at Buller from the Irishmen of the Connaught Rangers, a regiment noted both for its wildness in barracks and its formidable fighting record: 'Let the Scotsmen – they'll do the work!' Passing close by, Campbell tartly ordered them to stop standing about and form a line alongside the 77th.

The logic of Campbell's method soon became apparent. Seeing the advance of the Highland Brigade, the Russians launched the four battalions of the Sousdal Regiment, as yet untouched by the fighting, in a counter-attack against its flank. The first two battalions, hoping to enfilade the Black Watch, were themselves enfiladed by the 93rd, advancing in echelon to its left rear. The next two battalions, accompanied by some cavalry, then tried to enfilade the 93rd, but were in turn enfiladed in the same manner by the 79th. Alternately firing and cheering, the Highlanders advanced steadily. The Russians, outflanked, were unable to withstand the terrible hail of Minie balls. The arrival of two horse artillery batteries discomfited them still further, until they retreated whence they had come. Seeing how matters lay, the enemy hastily withdrew his own guns from the Lesser Redoubt. The High-landers' advance took them to the top of the hill. It was the sight of their tall, feathered bonnets breaking the crest that convinced Prince Menshikov that the battle was lost and that he must sanction a general withdrawal. Incredibly, the cost of the Highland Brigade's superb advance came to just fifteen men killed and eighty-three wounded.

Only one detail remained. We left the 7th Royal Fusiliers locked into their stubborn firefight with the Kazan Regiment. This had continued unabated, with the Kazan suffering the greater punishment and the out-numbered Fusiliers becoming steadily more exhausted. Like two fighters at the limit of their endurance, they continued to hang on to each other, fearing that if they let go they would collapse. The end, however, was nigh. At last, General Sir George de Lacy Evans's 2nd Divi-sion had worked its way round the burning village of Burliuk and crossed the Alma. Coming up on the right of the 7th, the 55th Regiment (later the 2nd Bn The Border Regiment), wheeled on to the flank of the Kazan and virtually destroyed it with a series of volleys.

The Battle of the Alma was over. From start to finish the British attack had taken just thirty-five minutes. British casualties amounted to 362 killed and 1,621 wounded. The French loss probably came to less than 500 killed and wounded. Russian losses included 1,800 men killed and an estimated 3,700 wounded. Whatever admiration the British may have felt for foes such as the Kazan Regiment was tempered when some of the Russian wounded made a point of shooting the very men who tried to ease their suffering. With grim humour, the British called them Resur-rectionists, took greater care, and shot or bayonetted any who displayed similar inclinations. This Russian custom was of long standing and was still being practised during World War II.

For reasons explained in the Introduction, many months were to pass before awards of the Victoria Cross were considered for acts during the battle. Sergeant Luke O'Connor of the 23rd Royal Welch Fusiliers, who was born at Elphin in County Roscommon, Ireland, on 21 January 1831, is officially recognised as being the first man in the army to perform an act resulting in the award.* When the Redan, one of Sevastopol's

* The first act resulting in the award of the Victoria Cross took place on 21 June 1854. HMS *Hecla* was bombarding the Russian fortress of Bomarsund in the Baltic. A live shell landed on the deck, its hissing fuse indicating that it was about to explode. Without hesitation, Mate Charles Lucas picked up the shell in his bare hands and hurled it overboard. It exploded as it entered the water. Lucas's act undoubtedly averted casualties and prevented serious damage to the ship. His commanding officer promoted him to lieutenant on the spot and in due course he rose to the rank of rear admiral.

principal defences, was assaulted on 8 September 1855, he again displayed exemplary gallantry despite being wounded in both thighs. Subsequently commissioned, he served in the Indian Mutiny and in the Ashanti War. He rose to the rank of major general and received a knighthood. A greatly respected figure, he became Honorary Colonel of the Royal Welch Fusiliers. He died in London on 1 February 1915.

Captain Edward William Derr Bell of the same regiment also received the Victoria Cross for his part in the battle, and in addition was awarded the Légion d'Honneur by the French. He, too, rose in rank to become a major general.

The Victoria Cross was also conferred on four officers and men of the Scots Fusilier Guards (now simply the Scots Guards), namely Sergeant James McKechnie, Captain Robert James Lindsay, Sergeant John Simpson Knox and Private William Reynolds. Little is known of McKechnie save that he died in Glasgow on 5 July 1886 aged sixty. Lindsay was additionally awarded the Légion d'Honneur. During the Battle of Inkerman (q.v.) he gathered a few men together and counter-attacked a larger party of Russians, killing one himself. He subsequently rose in rank to brigadier general and became Lord Wantage. He was one of the founders of the British Red Cross Society and served as Lieutenant Colonel Commandant of the Honourable Artillery Company and as Lord Lieutenant of Berkshire. John Knox was another who was additionally rewarded with the Légion d'Honneur. He clearly possessed great powers of leadership for shortly after the battle he received a lieutenant's commission in the prestigious Rifle Brigade. On 18 June 1855 he volunteered to command a ladder party during an assault on the Redan, acted with great gallantry in pressing home the attack, and refused to leave the field until he received a second wound. William Reynolds, too, received the additional award of the Légion d'Honneur and was later promoted to corporal. Little is known of his subsequent career save that on leaving the army he settled in London, died in 1869 in his early forties and is buried in Brookwood Cemetery, Surrey.

The seventh Victoria Cross awarded for the Battle of the Alma went to Sergeant John Park of the 77th Regiment which, it will be recalled, had protected the left flank of the British advance. The award was of a periodic nature, reflecting exceptional conduct during a number of engagements. Park, an Ulsterman, must have been a remarkable young soldier, for he was only nineteen years of age yet had already achieved the rank of sergeant. He demonstrated both his courage and leadership at the Alma, at Inkerman, was badly wounded on 19 April 1855 during an attack on some Russian pits in the defences of Sevastopol, and took part in both assaults on the Redan. Sergeant Park died at Allahabad, India, on 18 May 1863.

The Battle of Balaklava

25 OCTOBER 1854

After spending two days clearing the Alma battlefield, the Allies resumed their march on Sevastopol. In so doing their tracks crossed that of the Russian field army which, after leaving a garrison in the fortress, retreated into the Crimean hinterland. For a while, the possibility existed for the Allies to occupy the largely undefended north side of Sevastopol roadstead, a course of action that would have rendered the town itself, located on the opposite shore, vulnerable to direct artillery fire and therefore untenable in the long term. The accepted wisdom, however, was that the besiegers would require supply ports and they therefore crossed the Tchernaya River and marched round to the heavily defended south side. The French had much the better of the bargain with easy access to the small harbours of Kamiesch and Kazatch. The British supply port was the village of Balaklava, lying at the head of a long, narrow inlet that was quite incapable of handling the immense volume of traffic that would pass through it.

From Balaklava, a track passed through a gorge to the village of Kadikoi, then climbed 700 feet up the Sapoune Heights and on to the siege lines, a total distance of seven miles. To the north-east of Kadikoi was a plain that extended as far as the Fedioukine Hills, subdivided into the North and South Valleys by a shallow ridge named Causeway Heights because along its crest ran the Woronzoff Road, so called because it connected Sevastopol with the estates of Count Woronzoff to the east. Along the ridge six redoubts had been built, manned by Tunisian troops drawn from the Turkish contingent. At the western end of the ridge was the camp of the British Cavalry Division, providing a link between the siege lines and Balaklava as well as a base from which patrols could operate along the Tchernaya. This constituted Balaklava's first line of defence and was intended to do no more than buy time until reinforcements could be brought up from the siege lines. The main defence of the port was entrusted to Major General Sir Colin Campbell's Highland Brigade and an artillery battery stationed at Kadikoi, and a second battery manned by Royal Marines on the hills above Balaklava to the east of the track. It was unfortunate that by the last week of October the demands of the siege had reduced Campbell's brigade to a single regiment, the 93rd Highlanders.

The Russians were not fools and it was obvious to them that if the British could be deprived of Balaklava the Allies would themselves become besieged in an awkward coastal salient, trapped between the Russian field army and the Sevastopol garrison, which was being reinforced and supplied by a bridge of boats across the roadstead. Before dawn on 25 October, therefore, a force consisting of 22,000 infantry, 3,400 cavalry and seventy-eight guns, commanded by General P. P. Liprandi, assembled for this very purpose beyond the Tchernaya.

As dawn broke, the sound of gunfire came from the most easterly redoubt and a patrol came spurring back along the South Valley to report to the Cavalry Division's commander, Lord Lucan, that three infantry divisions had crossed the river. One was climbing the Fedioukine Heights, the second was approaching Causeway Heights and the third was already attacking No. 1 Redoubt. Lucan wasted no time in passing this on to Lord Raglan, the Army Commander, who ordered his 1st and 4th Divisions, commanded respectively by the Duke of Cambridge and Major General Sir George Cathcart, to march at once from their camps to the Balaklava plain. It would take some time for them to arrive, but the French, who had less distance to travel, were fortunately aware of the problem and despatched two infantry brigades and two cavalry regiments, which reached the edge of Sapoune Heights first.

The Tunisians held on longer than had been expected but by 08:00 had been driven from the first four redoubts. A large body of Russian cavalry, consisting of lancer and hussar regiments deployed in six blocks, entered the North Valley. Suddenly, four squadrons detached themselves from the main body and trotted over Causeway Heights into the South Valley, heading directly for Kadikoi. At this moment the 93rd, lying in a fold of ground to protect themselves from the fire of Russian guns that had unlimbered on Causeway Heights, were invisible to them. When the Russians were only 900 yards distant and had increased their pace to an easy canter, Campbell ordered the regiment to stand and dress ranks in line rather than square, which was the usual method by which infantry defended themselves against cavalry. Campbell, however, had a low opinion of the Russians and intended employing the regiment's maximum firepower. The 93rd were to become immortalised as the original Thin Red Line, although the phrase actually used by William

Howard Russell, the *Times* correspondent, was 'that thin red streak tipped with steel'. Some of the Turkish fugitives from the redoubts who had attached themselves to the regiment fired an ineffective volley and fled into Balaklava. At 600 yards the 93rd fired their first volley, emptying a few saddles. At 350 yards they fired their second volley. A number of men and horses went down, although many more were hit as, to the Highlanders' amazement, the Russians wheeled and rode back to Causeway Heights.

The Cavalry Division, formed up at the end of the North Valley, could see nothing of this because it was hidden by Causeway Heights. At this point Lucan received an outdated order from Raglan to detach eight squadrons of dragoons towards Balaklava to support the Turks. As the Turks had already abandoned the redoubts, Lucan could only interpret the order as being that he should cover the approaches to the port and he instructed Brigadier General the Hon. James Scarlett, commanding the Heavy Brigade, to proceed accordingly. The brigade began moving castwards into the South Valley in open column of troops, the 5th Dragoon Guards leading, followed by the Royal Scots Greys, the 6th Inniskilling Dragoons and the 4th Dragoon Guards, leaving behind two squadrons of the Royal Dragoons. Of necessity, the move was carried out at a walk as the horses had to pick their way through the division's camp, which had been struck and then looted by the Turks. The main mass of the Russian cavalry was now also heading for the South Valley over Causeway Heights, so that a clash between the two became inevitable.

The first warning the Heavy Brigade had of the enemy's presence was a line of lance points breaking the crest to their left, some 500 yards distant. The Russians, who clearly outnumbered the brigade by a wide margin, came ponderously on but halted at a dry ditch, pushing forward their outer wings so as to envelop their less numerous opponents. Scarlett immediately decided to charge and wheeled his regiments left into line, simultaneously taking ground to the right in order to clear the cluttered campsite. Once he was satisfied that his lines were properly dressed, he placed himself several horse lengths ahead of the centre, with his aide, trumpet major and orderly, then gave the order for the Charge to be sounded.

The brigade began to move forward slowly, gathering pace as it covered the 400-yard upward slope separating it from the enemy. It smashed into the Russians with a cheer, its impetus carrying it five ranks deep into the mass. Slashing and stabbing at those around them, the men used their bridle hands to grab the throats of their enemies on the left, pitching them over their cruppers. In such a mêlée it was every man for himself, and the dragoons, being big men on big horses, had a natural advantage over their smaller light cavalry opponents. It was soon discovered that the thick Russian greatcoats were proof against the British sabre, so resort was made to vertical and horizontal cuts to the head. In this context the British again had the advantage, for their weapons had been sharpened whereas those of the Russian hussars were blunt and often did no more than inflict a painful bruise. Furthermore, the unwieldy weapons of the Russian lancers, who performed best against broken troops in the open, were almost useless in this kind of close-quarter combat. The Greys in particular met determined opposition. Sergeant Major John Grieve, who must have been a powerful swordsman, saw that one of his officers had been surrounded by the enemy and was barely holding his own. Barging his way through the press, he decapitated one assailant and dispersed the rest. Near by, Sergeant Henry Ramage of the same regiment saved the life of a private surrounded by no less than seven Russians, laying about him to such effect that the enemy sheered off.

It was the Russians' attempt to envelop the Heavy Brigade that finally proved to be their undoing. Scarlett had already despatched his brigade major to bring up an Inniskilling squadron which had been moving in the direction of Kadikoi. This smashed into the Russian left wing just as it was completing its inwards wheel, taking its men on the vulnerable bridle hand or from behind. Simultaneously, the 4th Dragoon Guards smashed into the opposite flank, followed by the Royal Dragoons, whom Lucan had brought up at a gallop. The combined effect was similar to that of a series of controlled explosions bringing down a cliff. Under this succession of shocks the Russians lost their cohesion. They began shredding away at the left rear and suddenly the whole mass turned and bolted back across the crest into the North Valley, pursued for a short distance until Scarlett had the Recall sounded. Russian casualties were estimated at approximately 200, mostly wounded, while those of the Heavy Brigade were but a fraction of this. Rallied, the brigade returned to its original position at the end of Causeway Heights, forming up on the right of the Light Brigade. After a while, seeing that the enemy had no further intention of advancing on Balaklava, Lucan moved the Cavalry Division back into the North Valley.

Liprandi's imaginative plan had been foiled by the stand of the 93rd, by the charge of the Heavy Brigade, and, by no means least, by the bumbling of his cavalry commanders. He seemed uncertain what to do next and in that moment lost the initiative. From his position high on Sapoune Heights, Raglan could see the entire battlefield spread out below him. At the far end of the North Valley the routed Russian cavalry were sorting themselves out behind a battery of guns. There were more enemy guns and infantry around the captured redoubts on Causeway Heights, as well as on Fedioukine Hills to the left. He could also see what Lucan, Scarlett and Cardigan could not see because it was hidden to them by rolling ground, namely that Russian horse teams seemed to be dragging the captured guns out of the redoubts and towing them away. Having served under the Duke of Wellington, who had never lost a gun, he was mortified by the sight and instructed General Airey to order Lucan's division to recapture them. Airey's scribbled order has gone into history as a masterpiece of imprecision:

> Lord Raglan wishes the cavalry to advance rapidly to the front – follow the enemy and try to prevent the enemy carrying away the guns. Troop Horse Artillery may accompany. French cavalry is on your left. Immediate.

Worse still, the aide chosen to carry the order was Captain Lewis Nolan, who was volatile, short-tempered, arrogant, and despised Lucan. When the latter received the order he was nonplussed, as the only guns he could see were at the far end of the valley, and it was quite contrary to tactical doctrine for cavalry to mount a frontal attack on a battery. To his request for clarification Nolan merely retorted, 'Lord Raglan's orders were that the cavalry should attack immediately!'

'Attack, sir? Attack what? What guns, sir?' asked Lucan.

Nolan's duty at that point was to offer a full and complete explanation. Instead, he flung out his arm in the general direction of the Russian battery at the far end of the valley, remarking insolently, 'There, my lord, is your enemy! There are your guns!' For his part, Lucan should have used his discretion and declined the order pending more precise clarification from Raglan himself, but he was not a man to reason clearly when agitated and accepted Nolan's unintentional designation of the wrong objective at face value.

Cardigan and Scarlett accepted the order philosophically, knowing that they were about to embark on a death ride. As the Light Brigade's frontage was constricted, Cardigan redeployed it into three lines with the 13th Light Dragoons and 17th Lancers in the first, the 11th Hussars in the second behind the Lancers, and the 8th Hussars and 4th Light Dragoons in the third. When all was ready Lucan's divisional trumpeter sounded the Advance. With perfect dressing both brigades began moving along the North Valley at a steady walk that soon became an impatient trot. Among the Russian gunners, one-and-a-half miles distant, disbelief turned to grim satisfaction as they prepared their weapons for the coming slaughter. As the division entered the killing ground the pace increased to a canter.

The Heavy Brigade, its horses tired from their earlier exertions, fell steadily behind. Suddenly, artillery fire from both flanks and ahead began slicing through the Light Brigade, inflicting every conceivable injury on men and horses. 'Close in! Close in on the centre!' were the repeated cries as each swathe was cut down. For Lucan, riding between his two brigades, the dreadful trail of dead, dying and maimed men and horses was too much. Glancing round, he saw that the Heavy Brigade had also come under fire and had, in fact, already sustained more casualties than in its encounter with the Russian cavalry. Having reached a decision quickly, he ordered his trumpeter to sound the Halt, remarking to his adjutant, 'They have sacrificed the Light Brigade – they shall not have the Heavy if I can help it!' The dragoons reined in and wheeled back out of range. In the Light Brigade the call went unheard or unheeded.

The story has been told in many places how the Light Brigade, its ranks ripped apart but its men driven to insane rage by their losses, tore through or past the battery at the end of the valley in successive waves, spearing or cutting down the gunners, and went on to attack the already discomfited Russian cavalry beyond. Then, there was nothing to be done but return whence they had come, their way back along the littered valley still under fire from both flanks. Some, still mounted and in groups, fought their way through Cossack squadrons that had wheeled out in a half-hearted attempt to cut them off. Others, wounded, were herded to the rear by the unsparing Cossack lance points. Everywhere, there seemed to be little knots of dismounted lancers, hussars and light dragoons staggering along with the burden of their wounded. A nightmare quality was added by the screams of wounded and riderless horses, some with legs shot off, vainly stumbling across the battlefield in search of their masters. The ordeal would have been much worse had not at that moment the French Chasseurs d'Afrique executed a charge along Fedioukine Hills, forcing the Russian batteries there to limber up and head for safety.

Yet, if the collective discipline, dash and courage of the Light Brigade was to earn it immortality, there were, too, in that Valley of Death, many supreme acts of individual bravery that were the hallmark of this entire engagement. Trumpet Major Crawford of the 4th Light Dragoons was thrown heavily, stunned and lost his sword when his horse went down. He was being set upon by two Cossacks when Private Samuel Parkes of the same regiment intervened. Parkes, six feet two inches tall, an unusually big man for a light dragoon, had also had his horse shot under him. He promptly attacked the Cossacks, who made off looking for easier prey, and was joined by Private Edden, another 4th Light Dragoon, and Private Wightman of the 17th Lancers. The group were assisting Crawford as they made their way back down the valley when six more Cossacks appeared. Edden and Wightman cut their way out but Parkes and Crawford became prisoners when a shot deprived the former of his sword. Later, when General Liprandi visited the Light Brigade prisoners, he noticed the towering figure of Parkes and jokingly asked him, 'If you are a light dragoon, what sort of men are your heavy dragoons?'

Elsewhere, Sergeant John Berryman of the 17th Lancers had two horses shot under him. Recovering from his second fall, he looked up to see Captain Webb of his regiment unable to ride because of a shattered leg. He was joined by Sergeant John Farrell, also of the 17th, and two 13th Light Dragoons, Sergeant Joseph Malone and Private James Lamb. Still under fire from the artillery, now joined by that of the Russian infantry, they carried Webb back along the valley. Pausing for a rest, they realised that none of them possessed a water bottle, so Lamb retraced his steps to search among the dead horses until he found a calabash from which they were able to drink. Despite his repeated orders to leave him, Berryman and Farrell then carried their injured officer so safety while Malone and Lamb went to the assistance of another wounded man. Sadly, Captain Webb was to die of his wounds.

Captain William Morris had commanded the 17th Lancers during the charge. He had ridden straight through the battery at the enemy cavalry beyond and received the satisfaction of driving his sword into the body of a Russian officer. Unfortunately he was unable to withdraw the weapon and, defenceless, was severely wounded and forced to surrender. In the confusion he managed to escape, was dragged by a riderless horse he tried to mount, then caught another. This was shot under him as he rode back down the valley. He was lying helpless and bleeding badly under heavy fire when Corporal Charles Wooden, also of the 17th, came to his assistance. Wooden's efforts to staunch the flow proved unavailing, but he decided to remain with the officer. Meanwhile, the Heavy Brigade was cheering every small party of survivors to the echo as it came in, but not a few were so moved by the sight that they broke ranks to give whatever help they could. Among them was Surgeon James Mouat of the 6th Inniskilling Dragoons, who rode down the valley to Morris and Wooden. He managed to stop the severe haemorrhage and, assisted by Wooden, bandaged the wound sufficiently for Morris to be carried to safety. Near by, Sergeant Ramage of the Greys, who had already distinguished himself earlier in the day, rode to the aid of a badly wounded trooper who was reeling in the saddle and carried him in.

From start to finish, the Charge of the Light Brigade took just twenty minutes. Of the 678 men who took part, only 195 answered the roll call. Later, as more survivors trickled in, the brigade's losses were put at 247 killed or wounded. Of the horses, 500 were killed or were so severely injured that they had to be put down. For the moment, therefore, the Light Brigade was finished. Nevertheless, the ferocity of both British cavalry charges provided a severe shock for the Russians, whose own cavalry fought shy of similar encounters for the rest of the war. Allied casualties at Balakava amounted to 615 and those of the Russians to 627.

Sergeant Major John Grieve of the Royal Scots Greys was awarded the Victoria Cross. He was promoted to lieutenant and adjutant and died at Inveresk, Scotland, aged forty-three.* The award was also made to Sergeant Henry Ramage of the same regiment, who died in Ireland five years after the battle. The third of the VCs won by members of the Heavy Brigade went to Surgeon James Mouat, who also received the Légion d'Honneur. He subsequently rose in his profession to become the army's Surgeon General and receive a knighthood. In the 17th Lancers, the VC was awarded to Sergeant Major John Berryman, Sergeant John Farrell and Corporal Charles Wooden. Berryman went on to serve in the Indian Mutiny and the Zulu War, being commissioned and rising to the rank of major. After a full life, he died in 1896. Farrell rose to become quartermaster sergeant, dying at Secunderabad, India, in 1865. Wooden, a German by birth who never quite lost his accent, had an interesting career that was to end in tragic circumstances. He was promoted to

---

* It is a remarkable fact that in a surprising number of cases members of the same family have won the VC or CMH. John Grieve was the great uncle of Captain Robert Cuthbert Grieve of the 37th (Victoria) Bn Australian Imperial Force, who won the VC on 7 June 1917 at Messines, Belgium. His citation reads: 'During an attack on the enemy's position, and after his company had suffered very heavy casualties, Captain Grieve located two hostile machine-guns which were holding up his advance. Under continuous fire from the two guns, he succeeded in bombing and killing the two gun crews, then reorganised the remnants of his own company and gained his original objective. Captain Grieve set a splendid example and when he finally fell, wounded, the position had been secured.'

sergeant immediately and in 1860 he became regimental sergeant major. He was then commissioned as lieutenant and quartermaster in the 6th Inniskilling Dragoons. He was called as a witness for the prosecution during the Crawley Affair, one of the Victorian army's greatest scandals, then transferred to the 5th Lancers and finally to the infantry. On 24 April 1876, while serving in the barracks at Dover, he shot himself while the balance of his mind was disturbed. Sergeant Joseph Malone of the 13th Light Dragoons (later the 13th Hussars) also received the VC and in 1858 was commissioned lieutenant and riding master to the 6th Inniskilling Dragoons when they left for India, where he served alongside Wooden for a while. Choosing to remain with the regiment, he achieved the rank of captain before he died at Pinetown, South Africa, in 1883. Private Samuel Parkes of the 4th Light Dragoons (later the 4th Hussars) survived his captivity and returned home to learn that he had been awarded the VC. He does not seem to have remained in the army for long and died in London shortly after the tenth anniversary of the battle.

It might be thought that Private James Lamb of the 13th Light Dragoons also deserved an award for his part in the action, but the truth is that many similar acts of courage were performed that autumn morning and at the time no lesser award existed by which they could be honoured. Nevertheless, for any man to have ridden as one of the Six Hundred was to guarantee him the profound respect of his community for the rest of his days.

Inkerman

5 NOVEMBER 1854

Although disappointed by the results of Balaklava, Prince Menshikov was determined to break the Allied siege of Sevastopol. By the beginning of November his field army had been sufficiently reinforced for him to plan a much larger operation intended to smash through the British right flank, which his spies had correctly informed him was weakly defended. That flank rested on Inkerman Ridge. Before proceeding further it is necessary to examine the terrain over which the battle would be fought, as this was to influence the outcome of events.

Inkerman Ridge was roughly triangular in shape, the base of the triangle being the upper reaches of Sevastopol roadstead to the north. The western arm of the triangle was marked by a steep valley known as Careenage Ravine, which was extended by an even narrower valley, The Wellway. The eastern arm ran parallel to the Tchernaya, then followed the ridge round to form an apex with The Wellway. Approximately halfway along this arm a winding re-entrant, Quarry Ravine, gave access to the ridge, as did the smaller St Clement's Ravine, a way to the south. The summit of the ridge consisted of a long, narrow saddle between two features, Shell Hill in the north and Home Ridge to the south. Much of the ridge, and all the ravines, were boulder-strewn and densely covered with scrub, consisting mainly of stunted oak trees about three feet high. The camp of the British 2nd Division lay just south of Home Ridge, with that of the Guards Brigade approximately 1,000 yards to the south and that of the Light Division a little further to the south-west.

Lord Raglan's headquarters had been repeatedly warned that in view of the close proximity of the expanding Russian field army, steps should be taken to fortify the ridge. Very little was done, the excuse being that the troops were stretched to the limit by their duties in the siege lines, picket duty and the need for carrying parties to bring up supplies from Sevastopol. This was absurd, as good use could have been made of the 11,000 Turks idling their time away near Balaklava. The problem was that, unfairly, no one felt that they could rely on the Turks. Such work as had been completed was of mixed value. On a spur overlooking St Clement's Ravine was the Sandbag Battery, consisting of a rampart nine feet high pierced by two embrasures. It had been erected to deal with a Russian gun that was harassing the siege lines, but once that problem had been dealt with, its own guns were withdrawn. As no fire step for riflemen had been constructed within, it was militarily useless. Some 700 yards to the west a stone redoubt known as The Barrier had been constructed at the head of Quarry Ravine. On Home Ridge was a trench 100 yards long with a breastwork just two feet high, resembling little more than a drainage ditch. Such, advance pickets apart, were the total defences of Inkerman Ridge.

On 26 October the garrison of Sevastopol had mounted a sortie that had reached the summit of the ridge before being repulsed with heavy loss. Coupled with the rebuff the Russians had sustained at Balaklava the previous day, this engagement, which would become known as Little Inkerman, engendered a feeling of false security among Raglan's staff. In fact, Little Inkerman had been a reconnaissance in force, as a result of which the enemy had learned the precise range of the British lines for artillery positioned on Shell Hill. Warnings from as far afield as Berlin that Menshikov was planning a major operation, the arrival of more and more troops, and a personal visit by the Tsar's sons, the Grand Dukes Nicholas and Michael, all failed to arouse the staff's suspicions. For his part, Raglan is said to have brushed aside warnings of the impending attack with the comment, 'Nonsense! They will never dare come again.'

Although it could have been improved upon, Menshikov's plan was sound enough. Under the command of General Soimonoff, 16,000 men and thirty-eight guns of the Sevastopol garrison were to cross the Careenage Ravine and occupy the western spur of Shell Hill. Simultaneously, 16,000 men and ninety-six guns drawn from the field army and commanded by General Pauloff, would cross the Tchernaya and then divide, part to climb the northern slopes of the ridge to Shell Hill, and part to attack up the Quarry and St Clement's Ravines. Once both forces had reached the crest, they would come under the command of General Dannenberg and take the remainder of the ridge, thereby breaking through the British right flank and thus raising the siege. Diversionary attacks would be made opposite Sapoune Heights by 22,000 men and eighty-eight guns under Prince Gortschakoff, the intention being so to tie down the French that they would be unable to send assistance, and by the rest of the Sevastopol garrison against the siege lines. The flaws in the plan were that it required precise timing and co-ordination, which would be difficult to achieve on steep, broken terrain unfamiliar to the new arrivals. Furthermore, it was not appreciated that the saddle of the ridge was too narrow and the slopes on either side were too steep for the Russians to deploy more than a fraction of their strength. Nevertheless, Menshikov issued orders that the great attack would commence at dawn on 5 November.

Inkerman was the last battle to be fought by the British Army in full dress, although the term is relative and for many it was a come-as-you-are occasion, far removed from the spit and polish of peacetime soldiering. It is more commonly known as the Soldiers' Battle, in which senior officers could do no more than feed reinforcements into the mêlée, the outcome of which was decided by regimental officers, NCOs and private soldiers. Today, jargon is a much favoured currency of discussion, so that what was once referred to as hand-to-hand fighting has become the ICQB, or infantry close-quarter battle. In 1854, and for long after, there was no palliative acronym to conceal the savage, brutal business that it is, involving the bayonet and butt, fist and boot, and the stark choices of kill or be killed. Thousands of such combats took place at Inkerman, the course of the battle being so fragmented that it cannot be described in detail in the space available. Added to this, much of the fighting took place in a dense autumn mist so that it was impossible to tell what was taking place more than a few yards distant. Indeed, for the British, even the term regiment had little meaning as companies were detached to meet fresh threats and vanished into the fog, and stragglers from many units attached themselves to any officer or NCO who would lead them.

It is, however, possible to give a broad outline of what took place. It rained heavily on the night of 4 November, so that by dawn a heavy mist blanketed the entire battlefield, muffling the sound of the Russians' advance. The mist was an important factor in determining the nature of the fighting, since it prevented the Russians from seeing how few their opponents were, and concealed from the British the overwhelming strength with which they were being attacked. At first, Soimonoff's column did well, overrunning the British pickets and establishing its artillery on Shell Hill. These guns, which outreached and threw a heavier weight than the British field batteries, quickly opened fire on Home Ridge and the 2nd Division's camp. The division counter-attacked, repulsing repeated Russian advances. Field batteries fired case shot at close quarters into the oncoming grey masses. There would then be a fierce fight around the guns, which might be lost but which were recovered by a local counter-attack. Soimonoff was killed. By now Pauloff's column had entered the struggle. The number of guns on Shell Hill rose to approximately one hundred. Simultaneously, reinforcements from the other British divisions were being fed into the battle. Extremely bitter fighting took place on the saddle and at The Barrier. Most hotly contested of all was possession of the useless Sandbag Battery, which changed hands repeatedly throughout the battle. A curious feature of the fighting was that the Russians, instead of exploiting local successes, frequently halted as though uncertain what to do next. One Russian source mentions the loss of almost all the regimental and battalion commanders engaged, providing a probable explanation. Early in the battle, Raglan, seeing that his artillery was fighting at a crippling disadvantage, had given orders for two long 18-pdr guns to be brought up from the siege park to Home Ridge. Weighing three-and-a-quarter tons each, these required 150 men to haul them uphill over the difficult terrain, so that it was not until 09:30 that they began to make their presence felt. Although, initially, the gun crews suffered severely from the enemy fire, they soon had the range of the massed batteries on Shell Hill and began knocking them about, destroying guns, limbers and blowing up an ammunition wagon. The French, meanwhile, had recognised that Gortschakoff's attack was simply a diversion and began entering the battle in increasing numbers. By noon, the Russians had started to fall back and, covered by the fire of fifty British and French guns, a flanking attack on Shell Hill was under way. At 13:00 Dannenberg ordered a general withdrawal and within two hours the whole of Inkerman Ridge was again securely in Allied hands. The victory, nonetheless, had not been cheap. The British had sustained 2,573 casualties, including 635 killed, while the French lost 175 killed and 1,568 wounded. The Russian losses amounted to a staggering one-third of the 35,000 men actually engaged on Inkerman Ridge, 4,400, including six generals, being killed and 7,559 wounded.

Nothing more graphically describes the nature of the fighting at Inkerman than the acts of the sixteen officers and men awarded the Victoria Cross. Private Thomas Beach of the 55th Regiment (later the 2nd Bn The Border Regiment) was on picket duty when the Russians attacked. Seeing a wounded officer being robbed by several of the enemy, he charged them, killing two and driving the rest off. He then remained with the officer until help arrived.

Private John Byrne of the 68th Regiment (later The Durham Light

Infantry) was awarded a periodic VC. At Inkerman, although his regiment was ordered to retire, he went forward under fire and at great personal risk brought in a wounded comrade. On 11 May 1855, during a Russian raid on the siege lines, he engaged one of the enemy in personal combat, killed him and captured his weapons. He was later promoted to corporal.

Lieutenant the Hon. Henry Clifford of the 1st Bn The Rifle Brigade had collected a number of stragglers from various regiments when a large body of Russians emerged from the fog, only 15 yards distant. Clifford immediately gave the order to charge with the bayonet, killed one of the enemy with his sword, disabled another and saved the life of a soldier. All of his party save himself and two men were killed or wounded during the fight. In addition to the award of the Victoria Cross he received the Légion d'Honneur. Later in life he was knighted and rose to the rank of major general.

Sergeant Andrew Henry, Royal Artillery, was commanding the left-hand gun of G Field Battery when a large party of Russians broke out of an area of scrub to his left. He must have been a powerful man, for while continuing to defend himself with his sword, he used his left hand to snatch the rifle and bayonet from one of his assailants, then fling the man to the ground. Soon only he and Gunner Taylor, fighting back to back, were the sole survivors of the detachment. Taylor was killed but Henry fought on, being bayoneted in the chest, back and arms. Weak through loss of blood, he fell to the ground, where the enemy continued to stab at him. When the position was retaken by a counter-attack he was found to be unconscious but alive despite the twelve wounds he had received. Happily, he recovered and went on to retire with the rank of captain.

Private John McDermond, a Scot serving with the 47th Regiment (later The Loyal North Lancashire Regiment), rushed to the rescue of an officer who had been wounded and was lying helpless on the ground, surrounded by the enemy. He killed the man who had inflicted the wound, drove off the others and was responsible for saving the officer's life.

Lieutenant Frederick Miller, Royal Artillery, was commanding a division of P Field Battery, when the Connaught Rangers, heavily outnumbered by a Russian column, retired through the battery. Miller just had time to fire one round of case shot before the Russians were on him. As Lieutenant Colonel A. H. Burne was later to comment in *The Royal Artillery Journal*: 'Miller, in the last resort bade his gunners draw swords and charge, and he himself under a shower of bullets rode straight at the nearest of the advancing Russians. As though bewildered, these men stopped short in their onset. Then there followed a conflict of a singular kind between on the one hand a great weight of advancing infantry and, on the other, a few score of artillerymen, wildly striving to beat back the throng from their beloved gun with swords, with rammers, with sponge staves and even with clenched fists.' The odds were too great and those gunners who survived were pushed back beyond the guns, which were recovered shortly after by a counter-attack. Miller also received the Légion d'Honneur and eventually retired as a lieutenant colonel.

Not every man is a hero and those who have recently emerged from the traumatic experience of one bout of hand-to-hand fighting do not necessarily welcome the opportunity to take part in another. At one period of the desperate struggle for the Sandbag Battery the position had just been taken by the Russians. Brevet Major Sir Charles Russell of the Grenadier Guards called for volunteers to help him eject them. Only Private Anthony Palmer and two men followed him. Russell, a small man but a doughty fighter, wrenched the rifle and bayonet from the grasp of one Russian but was knocked to the ground by another and was on the point of being bayoneted when Palmer shot his assailant dead. Several times the little party seemed to be on the point of being overwhelmed by numbers, and indeed one man was killed, but the skill of the others with the bayonet was too much for the enemy, who bolted, pursued by the rest of the Grenadiers, save for the Colour party and a small escort. At this point a second Russian force approached the position from a different direction. For a moment there was a real possibility that the Colours would be captured, but Palmer led the small party in another ferocious bayonet charge that stabilised the situation, enabling the returning Grenadiers to conduct an orderly retreat. Russell retired from the army with the rank of lieutenant colonel, taking a practical interest in the development of the Volunteer movement that would evolve into the Territorial Army. Little is known of Palmer's subsequent career save that he retired to Manchester, where he died at the age of seventy-three.

During one of the many counter-attacks made on the Russians, Colonel the Hon. Henry Percy of the Grenadier Guards found himself with a number of men from various regiments who had charged too far and were now short of ammunition and in danger of being cut off. Although wounded himself, he took advantage of the mist and confusion to lead fifty of them through the Russians, attracting considerable fire in the process. Once the party had reached safety, it was able to replenish its ammunition and rejoin the fighting. Percy, who was to become Lord Henry later in life, also received the Légion d'Honneur. He subsequently achieved the rank of lieutenant general, served as Member of Parliament for North Northumberland 1865–8, and Colonel of the 89th Regiment (later 2nd Bn The Royal Irish Fusiliers) from 1874 until his death three years later.

Captain Hugh Rowlands of the 41st Regiment (later The Welch Regiment) was commanding a picket when the Russians attacked and held his position until compelled by overwhelming numbers to withdraw. Later in the battle he personally rescued the commanding officer of the 47th Regiment, who had been wounded and was surrounded by the enemy. Rowlands was also awarded the Légion d'Honneur. During his subsequent career he was knighted and became a general and at one point was Lieutenant of the Tower of London. He died in 1909, aged eighty-one, at the place of his birth, Llanrug, Caernarvon.

At one point during the battle, part of the 30th Regiment (later The East Lancashire Regiment) was directed to defend The Barrier, against which two battalions of the Borodino Regiment were advancing up the Quarry Ravine. The 30th's commanding officer, Colonel J. T. Mauleverer, told his men to lie down until the enemy were a only a few yards distant, then ordered a counter-attack. This was led by Lieutenant Mark Walker, who climbed upon the wall and exhorted his men to charge with him, despite the odds. This they did, smashing into the startled front ranks of the Borodino, forcing them back on those behind. Both enemy battalions recoiled in disorder, some running back down the ravine while others escaped in the direction of Shell Hill. Later in life Walker was to achieve the rank of lieutenant general and receive a knighthood.

Elsewhere during the confused fighting Sergeant George Walters of the 49th Regiment (later the 1st Bn The Berkshire Regiment), went to the rescue of a brigadier general who had been surrounded by the enemy, bayoneting one of the Russians and dispersing the rest. On leaving the army, Walters joined the London Police Force. He died at Marylebone in 1872.

As mentioned earlier, Russian activity also included diversionary attacks on the Allied siege lines. One position which came under severe attack was the Lancaster Battery on Victoria Ridge, to the west of Careenage Ravine, so named because it contained several of the new rifled Lancaster guns as well as three 68-pounders. Casualties within the battery were heavy but, seeing the Russians closing in, five seamen from the Naval Brigade mounted the parapet and, using muskets loaded for them by the wounded men below, kept up a rapid and sustained fire, picking off man after man until the Russians finally withdrew. Two of the five were killed, but the survivors, Seaman James Gorman, Seaman Thomas Reeves and Seaman Mark Scholefield, all received the Victoria Cross. Gorman was up-rated to Captain of the After Guard and later emigrated to Australia, where he died near Sydney in 1882. Reeves was up-rated to Captain of the Foretop but died at Portsea in 1862. Scholefield was promoted quartermaster and then petty officer; he did not long survive the battle, dying at sea on 15 February 1858. Nor were these the only Victoria Crosses won by the Royal Navy at Inkerman. Corporal John Prettyjohn of the Royal Marine Light Infantry was sent with a squad to clear some caves that were being used by troublesome Russian snipers. While completing the task the squad used up most of its ammunition. It was then noticed that more Russians had begun to climb the hillside towards the party, moving in single file. Prettyjohn told his men to collect large stones and conceal themselves in ambush. When the first of the enemy appeared, Prettyjohn used a wrestling hold to pick up the man and hurl him on to those below. The rest of the Russians, subjected to a rain of rocks, turned and fled. As commander of the squad, Prettyjohn received the award and in due course was promoted to colour sergeant.

Following the battle, Inkerman Ridge was thoroughly fortified. Ironically, the labour was willingly provided by those same Turkish troops that the generals had despised to use earlier. After its costly repulse on this sector, the Russian field army never seriously challenged the British in the open again, although on 16 August 1855 it was engaged with French and Sardinian troops at Traktir Ridge in a final but futile attempt to raise the siege of Sevastopol. The siege itself lasted from 8 October 1854 until 8 September 1855, ending when the Russians withdrew across the harbour after the French had stormed a key defensive feature, the Malakoff. Indirect pressure had been applied both to the Russian field army and the Sevastopol garrison by a squadron of gunboats which penetrated the Sea of Azov and severely disrupted the enemy's principal supply route to the Crimea.* The war itself was formally concluded in March 1856.

A total of 111 Victoria Crosses were awarded during the Crimean War. Apart from those won during the battles already described, some were

---

* The astonishing adventures of this squadron, and the remarkable number of VCs won by its members, are described in the author's book *Gunboat!*

gained in the Baltic or the Sea of Azov, but the great majority were awarded for acts of exemplary courage during the long and bitter siege of Sevastopol, which involved bombardment and counter-bombardment, sorties, counter-attacks, trench raids and two gallant but costly and abortive attacks on an important defensive bastion known as The Redan.

THE INDIAN MUTINY
1857-58

The Delhi Arsenal
11 MAY 1857

The British presence in India stemmed originally from trade, the conduct of which rested in the hands of the Honourable East India Company. As a result of a series of wars, treaties and alliances, the Company became responsible for huge areas of the subcontinent. To protect and maintain control of these it raised its own troops, both native and European, which were supported in the field by contingents of the British Regular Army. By the middle of the nineteenth century the Company's role in India had become administration on behalf of the British government.

At this period the Company maintained three armies, based respectively in its Bengal, Bombay and Madras Presidencies. The native troops of the Bengal Army were, even in the opinion of their comrades in the other armies, unduly sensitive on the questions of caste and religion, and over a period of years their grievances, real and imagined, achieved such importance in their eyes that mutiny seemed to represent the only way out of their difficulties. The situation was further aggravated by elements in Indian society whose vested interests had been harmed by the Company's imposition of law and order. For example, a system of land tenure was introduced where none had existed before, and such customs as *thagi* – ritual murder by strangulation in honour of the goddess Khali – and *suttee* – the burning alive of widows on their husbands' funeral pyres – were outlawed. This, coupled with missionary activity, created an underlying suspicion among the sepoys that a serious attempt was being made to convert them to Christianity by stealth, thereby placing their immortal souls in jeopardy. Unfortunately, in the years following the Sikh Wars, the relationship between their British officers and themselves had become somewhat distant. Some officers did not care what their men thought, and while others reported the growing unrest in the ranks, the Company's elderly generals, who had been much closer to the sepoys in their own youth, simply refused to believe that the latter were capable of disloyalty, let alone mutiny. There were, too, strange undercurrents in Indian life that should have been noted. Many recalled the prophecy that on the hundredth anniversary of the Battle of Plassey (1757) British rule in India would end, a belief encouraged by well-publicised British shortcomings in the Crimea. Likewise, there was the mysterious arrival of *chappatis* in villages, delivered at night by runners whose only message was that more *chappatis* should be baked and delivered to other villages, all of which seemed to signify to simple minds that momentous events were about to take place. The detonator that triggered the explosion was the issue of cartridges that an agitator falsely claimed were greased with a mixture of pig and cow fat. As the pig was an abomination to Muslims and the cow was sacred to Hindus, sepoys of neither religion were prepared to accept them. Unwisely, the authorities imposed draconian punishments. The sepoys, faced with what they believed to be a choice between defilement and unbelievably punitive discipline, felt they could take no more.

What became known as The Great Mutiny broke out among the Meerut garrison on Sunday 10 May 1857. In their fury, the mutineers committed horrific atrocities against British officers and their families, then, with their Colours flying and regimental bands playing, they marched to Delhi. The mutiny spread like wildfire, the mutineers receiving active support not only from disaffected members of the civil population, but also from princely rulers who had grievances against the Company. Beyond their general but ill-defined aims of escaping from their own hideous dilemma and ending the Company's rule, little thought had been given to what might follow. There was, however, general agreement that the movement needed a figurehead, and that chosen was the aged King of Delhi, Shah Bahadur II, a descendant of the magnificent Moghul emperors, who now lived as a Company pensioner in the crumbling Delhi palace known as the Red Fort, surrounded by his decadent family.

As soon as the Meerut mutineers reached Delhi on 11 May they were joined by the city's garrison and the disreputable elements of its population. A savage massacre of Europeans, including women and children, followed, accompanied by the looting and burning of their property and the desecration of Christian places of worship.

One of the mutineers' principal targets was the city's arsenal, which contained a large quantity of ammunition and other ordnance stores. In command at the arsenal was Lieutenant George Willoughby, Commissary of Ordnance, assisted by Lieutenants William Raynor and George Forrest, both of the Bengal Veteran Establishment, Deputy Assistant

Commissary John Buckley, Conductor Scully and four other warrant officers. Under their command was a guard consisting of sepoys of uncertain temperament. Realising that the mutineers would waste no time in trying to lay hands on the contents of the arsenal, Willoughby closed and barricaded the gates, inside which he placed two 6-pdr guns, double-shotted with grape. A loaded 74-pdr gun was also positioned in the courtyard, in front of the office building. As his sepoys were sullen, Willoughby laid trains of powder to the magazine and gave orders that these were to be lit if the gate was rushed.

Almost immediately, soldiers from Shah Bahadur's palace guard arrived. They began hammering on the gates demanding that the arsenal should be surrendered in the king's name. One of their officers then shouted that the king was sending scaling ladders so that the mutineers could scale the walls. The ladders arrived with a great mob of mutineers, but were first used by the sepoys of the arsenal's garrison to make good their escape. The mutineers then scaled the walls and opened fire on those within. As they were in a wildly excited state, most of their fire was inaccurate. For five hours the nine British officers and warrant officers replied to better effect with their cannon, rifles and pistols, until their ammunition ran out. By then, Forrest had been wounded in the left hand and Buckley in the right arm. Recognising that the end of the unequal contest was only minutes away, Willoughby gave the order for the powder trains to be lit. Although the chances of surviving the explosion were almost nil, the decision was accepted by everyone, not in a spirit of heroism, but because this act was simply seen as a matter of duty. Conductor Scully volunteered for the task.

The tremendous explosion was heard in Meerut, 40 miles away. The high walls surrounding the arsenal were blown flat. Several hundred mutineers were killed instantly by the blast or buried under tons of fallen masonry. Incredibly, virtue proved to be its own reward in some cases. With singed hair, scorched faces and uniforms blown to tatters, Willoughby, Buckley, Forrest, Raynor and one other staggered from the burning ruins and made their way to the city's Kashmir Gate, where other European fugitives had gathered and from which they were able to escape that night.

For their actions at the arsenal, the Victoria Cross was awarded to John Buckley, George Forrest and William Raynor. Buckley survived the Mutiny and returned home to die at Tower Hamlets in 1876. Forrest and Raynor were both promoted to captain but did not long survive the Mutiny, dying in India respectively in 1859 and 1860. Willoughby and

Scully would almost certainly have received the Cross had it been awarded posthumously at the time, but Willoughby was murdered by villagers a few days after his escape and Scully was killed by the explosion.

The loss of the munitions contained in the Delhi arsenal was undoubtedly a serious blow to the mutineers. Unfortunately, a second arsenal, located three miles outside the city, was handed over intact by its native guard, and this contained 3,000 barrels of gunpowder, which was sufficient for them to maintain their efforts for a considerable period.

The Siege of Delhi

8 JUNE – 20 SEPTEMBER 1857

Despite their early success, and the fact that regiments of the Bengal Army continued to mutiny across a wide area, the mutineers in Delhi lost their vital early chance to destroy British power in northern India when it was at its most vulnerable. Divided counsels, personal intrigues among their leaders, the unaccustomed lack of pay and inevitably relaxed discipline all conspired to loosen the strong regimental bonds that had once united them. There were, too, many who feared that the frightful atrocities that had been committed would provoke a terrible retribution once British counter-measures began to take effect.

The British Commander-in-Chief in India was General Sir George Anson, a seventy-year-old veteran of Waterloo. He recognised immediately that possession of Delhi was the key to the situation, and that once the mutineers had been deprived of this focal point they could be defeated in detail. Collecting together as many troops as possible, his Delhi Field Force began marching south on 17 May. Ten days later he died from cholera and command passed to General Sir Harry Barnard. At Baghpat, Barnard was joined by Colonel Archdale Wilson with the remnant of the Meerut garrison, bringing his strength up to nearly 4,000. The mutineers, aware of his approach, sent out some 30,000 men and thirty guns to oppose him at Badli-ke-serai, six miles north of the city. Without hesitation, Barnard attacked against odds of ten-to-one and, after a short fight, sent his opponents streaming back to Delhi. Continuing his advance he occupied a two-mile-long feature known as The Ridge, running from north to south, to the north-west of the formidable city walls. The Ridge, consisting almost entirely of rock from which it was impossible to construct fortifications, was only 40 feet higher than the surrounding terrain. Between it and the walls were several large buildings and an area of lush vegetation, gardens and walls which would provide excellent cover for rebel sorties.

To speak of a force consisting of 600 cavalry, 2,300 infantry and twenty-two field guns, holding a precarious position on a barren ridge, besieging a 40,000-strong rebel army equipped with hundreds of artillery weapons and holding secure fortifications, is to stretch credulity to its limits, yet such was the respective mind-set of the contenders. The story of the following months was one of repeated rebel sorties to break the British hold on The Ridge, and of the desperate defensive actions required to defeat them. Barnard died of cholera on 5 July. His successor, General Thomas Reed, was already ill and handed over to Archdale Wilson, who was granted the temporary rank of major general. Wilson decided simply to hold his ground until reinforcements and a siege train arrived. Even this proved to be a difficult strategy to implement, for while reinforcements did reach the Delhi Field Force, continual battle casualties coupled with the effects of disease meant that the number of effectives rose so slowly that by the beginning of July its nominal strength still amounted to only 6,600 men.

More reinforcements, however, were on the way from the Punjab, where the warlike Sikhs had decided to throw in their lot with the British. In command was a remarkable thirty-five-year-old officer whose temporary rank was brigadier general, although he was actually a substantive captain. His name was John Nicholson and he was a dour, humourless soldier in the Cromwellian mould, who fought in God's name to punish the wrongdoer. Curiously, he detested India and disliked Indians, although he inspired intense loyalty among them because of his personal deeds in the wild mountains of the North-West Frontier. In the Punjab he had commanded a highly mobile force known as the Movable Column, disarming potentially mutinous Company regiments and hunting down bands of mutineers in arms, blowing away their ringleaders from the mouths of his cannon.

In August, the Chief Commissioner in the Punjab, Sir John Lawrence, felt sufficiently secure to despatch Nicholson to Delhi with the latter's own Movable Column, three Punjabi cavalry regiments and seven Punjabi infantry battalions, followed by a heavy siege train drawn from the arsenals of Phillaur and Ferozepur. The arrival of Nicholson's cavalry and infantry doubled the size of the Delhi Field Force. The mutineers, however, aware that the much slower, elephant-drawn, siege train was still on the road, sent out a force of some 6,000 men to intercept it. Wilson despatched Nicholson with 2,500 men and sixteen guns in pursuit. On 25 August he found the mutineers drawn up at Najafgahr, 16 miles from Delhi. An hour's fighting cost the rebels 800 killed plus all their guns and baggage; British losses amounted to twenty-five killed and seventy wounded.

Nicholson's presence, the victory at Najafgahr and the arrival of the siege train proved to be just the tonic that the morale of the sorely tried Delhi Field Force needed. While the siege batteries began battering breaches in the city's walls, Nicholson and Wilson discussed the possibility of mounting an assault. Their debates became progressively more ill-tempered as Nicholson demanded an attack at the earliest possible moment, while Wilson urged delay and caution. Many historians have favoured Nicholson's viewpoint, but the burden of responsibility lay heavily upon Wilson's shoulders and he was conscious that a failed assault would enhance the mutineers' prestige and affect the overall situation throughout northern and central India. In the final analysis, the debate hinged upon the available resources. Wilson's chief engineer, Colonel Baird Smith, pointed out that the strength of the Delhi Field Force had reached its probable peak and that delay would inevitably see this eroded by daily wastage resulting from casualties and disease. On the night of 13 September a reconnaissance confirmed that the breaches could be stormed and it was decided to mount the assault the following day.

Before describing this, it should be mentioned that no less than sixteen awards of the Victoria Cross were made to members of the Delhi Field Force during the period that it fought its way through to The Ridge, held it against repeated enemy sorties, achieved control of the no man's land between The Ridge and the city, and prepared for the final assault. The majority of these were made for the rescue of wounded comrades in desperate circumstances, several being elected by ballot. Lack of space prevents details of all these acts being given, but the following two may be taken as representative.

It was the rebels' custom that as fresh regiments from mutinied garrisons reached Delhi they were required to prove their worth by attacking the British on The Ridge before they were allowed to enter the city. On 19 June it was the turn of the Nussereebad regiments, supported by a field battery and some cavalry. They attacked in the gathering dusk through the suburb of Subzi Mundi, lying close to the northern end of The Ridge, taking full advantage of broken ground cluttered with gardens and trees. Their attack was met by Colonel Hope Grant's cavalry brigade, with artillery in support, and a confused fight took place, the issue being decided by a charge of the Guides' Cavalry. At one stage during the mêlée Grant found himself in difficulty when his horse was shot under him. 'I must not fail to mention the excellent conduct of a sowar (Indian cavalryman) of the 4th Irregular Cavalry, and two men of the 9th Lancers, Privates Thomas Hancock and John Purcell, who, when my horse was shot down, remained with me throughout,' he wrote in his report. 'One of these men and the sowar offered me their horses, and I was dragged out by the (tail of) the sowar's horse. Private Hancock was severely wounded and Private Purcell's horse was killed under him. The sowar's name was Roopur Khan.' The attack was repulsed, leaving Grant's men in possession of two of the enemy's guns and several ammunition wagons. Hancock and Purcell received the immediate award of the Cross from the GOC Delhi Field Force, as permitted by Rule 7 of its governing regulations. It was as well that the award was immediate, for whereas Hancock was later promoted corporal and survived until 1871, Purcell died during the storming of Delhi.

The second incident involved the 2nd Troop, 1st Brigade, Bengal Horse Artillery, one of the Company's European units. The troop, which also took part in the action described above, had a fine fighting record and a reputation for efficiency that reflected the personality of its commander, Major Henry Tombs. On 9 July two of the troop's guns, under the command of Lieutenant James Hills, were positioned in support of a piquet guarding the camp at the northern end of The Ridge. Shortly after dawn, they were attacked by a large body of rebel cavalry. The piquet, manned by inexperienced troops, mistook the mutineers' uniforms for those of a loyal cavalry regiment serving with the Delhi Field Force. Discovering their mistake too late, they panicked and fled. Lieutenant Hills promptly ordered his guns into action and single-handedly charged the rebels to gain time for his gunners to load. He cut down one man, slashed another, and then his horse was ridden down. Scrambling to his feet, he found himself surrounded by three men, two of whom were mounted. He shot the first with his pistol, which he then dropped, grabbed the lance of the second, whom he wounded with his sword, but was then bowled over and disarmed by the third. Tombs had himself now reached the scene and, seeing Hills lying at the mercy of his opponent, shot the man dead. The two officers were then attacked by a fourth rebel, wielding a sword and brandishing Hills's own pistol. This man proved to be a tough customer who managed to cut Hills across the head before Tombs ran him through. Meanwhile, some of the rebel cavalry had broken into the camp in a vain attempt to persuade men of a loyal native artillery battery to join them, but after counter-measures came into effect they were driven off. Tombs and Hills, who subsequently changed his name to Hills-Johnes, were both awarded the Victoria Cross. Later in their careers both were knighted and retired with the respective ranks of major general and lieutenant general. In addition, for this and other actions during the Mutiny, the Royal Artillery Honour Title of Tombs's Troop was conferred on their unit.

If it is wondered why the fighting during the Mutiny possessed a quality of savagery absent in other wars, the answer is simple. The atrocities committed by the mutineers against women and children, especially at Cawnpore, where they were hacked to death and thrown down a well, had generated an implacable hatred within the British soldier that was foreign to his nature. In other circumstances, he would have been content with victory and borne no personal ill-will. Now, he sought only to kill and would show no mercy. For their part the mutineers, recognising that they could not expect quarter, fought the harder for their own survival. Nevertheless, the arrival of Wilson's siege train prompted the mutineers' leaders in Delhi to seek some sort of end to the matter. On 30 August they sent an envoy to Wilson's headquarters, suggesting terms subject to certain conditions. Their proposal was rejected out of hand. Both sides now recognised that the fight would be to the death.

The Storming of Delhi

14–20 SEPTEMBER 1857

Brigadier General John Nicholson, deputed by Wilson to lead the assault, was well aware that he had only 5,000 men with which to attack over 30,000 mutineers behind prepared defences, yet he did not contemplate failure. He formed five columns of assault, each of which reflected the composition of the Delhi Field Force. No. 1 Column (75th (Gordon) Highlanders, 1st Bengal Fusiliers (European) and 2nd Punjab Infantry), which he would lead personally, was to storm the main breach at the Kashmir Bastion.

No. 2 Column (8th (The King's) Regiment, 2nd Bengal Fusiliers (European) and 4th Sikhs) was to storm a smaller breach near the Water Bastion simultaneously. No. 3 Column (52nd (Oxfordshire & Buckinghamshire) Light Infantry, the Kumaon Gurkha Battalion and 1st Punjab Infantry) would be led by a 'forlorn hope' party that would blow in the Kashmir Gate, then penetrate as far as the huge Jumma Musjid mosque in the city centre. Having achieved their objectives, Nos 1 and 2 Columns would fight their way along the city walls to their right until they reached the Kabul Gate, where No. 4 Column (the Sirmoor Gurkha Battalion, the Guides Infantry, Dogras and Kashmiris) would be admitted after advancing towards the gate through the suburb of Kishengunj. No. 5 Column (61st (Gloucestershire) Regiment, 4th Punjab Infantry, a Baluchi battalion and a contingent supplied by the Rajah of Jheend) was initially to be held in reserve and committed as required. Most of the cavalry and the horse artillery was to form up on the right of the assault to prevent enemy sorties through the Lahore Gate that might threaten the attackers' rear. Almost all of the Delhi Field Force's active strength was committed to the assault, The Ridge and the camps being guarded by a handful of cavalry, such artillerymen as were not employed in providing gunfire support for the columns, and the sick. No attempt was made to cut the mutineers' line of retreat, for Nicholson recognised that if the enemy realised he could no longer escape through the southern gates of the city he would fight with the desperation of the trapped.

The columns advanced through the pre-dawn darkness behind a screen of 200 skirmishers from the 60th Rifles. When it was discovered that the mutineers had erected sandbag barricades across the top of the breaches, a halt was called while the siege guns blew these apart. By the time the advance was resumed it was light and the defenders could be seen, several ranks deep, lining the ramparts, which were ablaze with musketry. Most of the ladder parties were shot down, but the ladders were snatched up by others and carried forward to the ditch. Here the horrifying discovery was made that they were too short unless placed on the berm, which was too narrow to hold them. Casualties mounted rapidly while, under a rain of masonry blocks from above, rubble and bodies were piled into heaps on which the ladders could be placed. Mounting the ladders or scrambling up the debris of the breaches, the attackers closed with the rebels, driving them off the walls in savage hand-to-hand fighting.

Meanwhile, the 'forlorn hope' party leading No. 3 Column was rushing across the bridge towards the Kashmir Gate. The party, consisting of Bengal Sappers and Miners, was commanded by Lieutenants Duncan Home and Philip Salkeld of the Bengal Engineers. Salkeld, in fact, had made his escape from this very spot by climbing down a rope made from sword belts when the mutineers seized Delhi in May. The plan was that Home and three men would each place a 25lb sack of gunpowder against the gate, leaving the fuses exposed. Salkeld and six men would then tamp down the charges with sandbags and light the fuses. Attached to the party was Bugler Robert Hawthorne of the 52nd, who was to sound the Advance when the gate was blown in.

The odds against the survival of any of the party were enormous. However, when Home's group broke cover, the rebels on the walls above were taken by surprise so that they actually reached the gate unharmed. A heavy fire was opened on them from above and through a wicket gate, killing Sergeant Andrew Carmichael and seriously wounding Havildar Madho. Home had already dumped his bag and Sergeant John Smith picked up the other two and put them in place, coolly checking the position of the fuses as he did so. Salkeld and his group were already running across the bridge with their tamping bags. Salkeld was about to light the fuses when he was hit in the arm and leg. He fell from the bridge into the ditch, where Home and Hawthorne had already jumped to give the others room to work. Corporal Burgess snatched up the portfire and, believing that it had gone out, asked Sergeant Smith for a box of matches. Smith was in the act of handing these over when Burgess was shot through the body. Havildar Tillock Singh was mortally wounded as he helped him off the bridge and Sepoy Ram Heth was killed. Now alone, Smith was in the act of striking a match when the portfire burst into life again. Seeing that the fuses were burning too quickly, he jumped into the ditch, but before he hit the ground there was a tremendous explosion that showered those below with shattered timber and broken brickwork. As the dust and smoke cleared, it was apparent that the right-hand gate had been blown off its hinges. At Home's order, Bugler Hawthorne sounded the Advance three times. No. 3 Column charged forward across the bridge and through the gate, where most of the defenders had either been killed or stunned by the explosion, some of them sprawled around a loaded cannon within the archway. Beyond the gate lay a wide square known as the Main Guard, from which the mutineers had fled. Here the first three assault columns rallied and were joined by their reserves before moving into the second phase of the operation, which involved clearing the city's maze of narrow streets. So far, all was going to plan, despite the heavy casualties that had been incurred.

Of the 'forlorn hope,' subsequently described as 'the bravest deed ever performed in India by Engineers or Sapper and Miners', Home, Salkeld, Smith and Hawthorne all received the Victoria Cross. Home was killed by a premature explosion while demolishing a captured enemy fort at Malagahr, only eleven days after Delhi had fallen. Salkeld never recovered from his wounds and died on 10 October 1857. Smith was commissioned into the Bengal Engineers and continued a successful career, dying in 1864. Hawthorne left the army in 1861 and was employed as a porter by a respectable banking house in Manchester; on his death in 1879 he was accorded a full military funeral. The party's surviving Indian officers and soldiers received either the Order of British India or the Indian Order of Merit.

Meanwhile, despite coming under fire from rooftops and loopholed houses, No. 3 Column continued to make rapid progress into the heart of the city. It came within sight of the Jumma Musjid mosque, all entrances to which had either been bricked up or barricaded with sandbags. The column commander, Colonel George Campbell, now faced a difficult decision. He lacked demolition charges and British guns had not yet been brought forward into the city, so any assault on the mosque was likely to prove costly if not abortive. He had no idea how the other columns were progressing, but he suspected that he was so deep in enemy territory that he was in danger of being cut off. He therefore reluctantly decided to abandon some of the ground won. The mutineers, scenting success, pressed the column hard as it retreated first to the Queen's Garden, which was held for thirty minutes under heavy fire, and then to the area of St James's church, where the enemy was halted. In this sort of street fighting, with quarter being neither asked nor given, to abandon the wounded was to guarantee their deaths. As the column withdrew across the Chandi Chouk, the city's principal street, it was flayed with musketry and grapeshot from three sides. Lance Corporal Henry Smith of the 52nd Regiment, seeing a comrade lying wounded, risked almost certain death to bring him in. He received the immediate award of the Cross. Later in his career he was promoted to sergeant, but died of cholera in India in 1862.

In another incident the temporary dressing station being used by Surgeon Herbert Reade of the 61st Regiment came under direct fire from mutineers who had taken possession of nearby rooftops. Drawing his sword, Reade rounded up the nearest ten soldiers and counter-attacked to such good effect that the enemy were forced to abandon their positions. Such was the ferocity of the fighting that two of Reade's party were killed and five or six wounded, but if the attack had not been made those in the dressing station would almost certainly have been massacred.

Elsewhere, Nos 1 and 2 Columns had fought their way westwards as far as the Kabul Gate, where a pause was made so that the men could refill their cartridge pouches from a stack of ammunition boxes that had been brought forward by native bearers. For some unknown reason three of the boxes exploded and two more caught fire, causing confusion in the crowded area. Appreciating that if the rest of the stack should explode there would be heavy loss of life, Sergeant James McGuire and Drummer Miles Ryan, both of the 1st Bengal European Fusiliers, rushed into the fire and, seizing a burning box apiece, threw them over the parapet into the Delhi Canal, which entered the city walls at that point. Both were awarded the Victoria Cross. The case of McGuire was a sad one, for after the Mutiny he returned to farming in his native Ireland and was convicted of stealing a cow from his uncle, whom he said owed him money. On 12 December 1862 Queen Victoria signed the warrant declaring that his award was forfeit; ten days later he was dead, possibly by his own hand in a moment of shame and humiliation. Of Ryan almost nothing is known save that he was born in Londonderry in 1826, probably remained in the army, and may have died in India in 1887.

It will be recalled that at this point No. 4 Column was to have been admitted to the city through the Kabul Gate. Unfortunately, almost everything had gone wrong for the column from the very start. The guns that were to have supported its advance through the fortified suburb of Kishengunj did not arrive. Then, the raw Kashmiri contingent, mistakenly believing that the mutineers had begun abandoning their positions, launched a premature attack. This was a grievous error, for whatever else they were, the mutineers were still trained professional soldiers. The Kashmiris were routed and fled. Encouraged, the rebels began pouring through the Lahore and Kabul Gates, both of which were still in their possession at this stage, and attacked the main body of the column. At this critical moment Reid was wounded and the contradictory orders issued by his successors threw the column into confusion. Fortunately, not everyone lost their heads. Captain Robert Shebbeare, originally of the mutinied 60th Bengal Native Infantry, had led the Guides Infantry in two abortive attacks against a heavily loopholed building when the crisis developed. When the column began to fall back towards The Ridge, Shebbeare found himself on the wrong side of the Delhi Canal. One-third of the European officers were dead or wounded, but he managed to pull together a rearguard that successfully covered the withdrawal across the canal despite one bullet passing through his cheek and another carving a furrow across the back of his head. Nevertheless, the rebels, elated by their repulse of the column, swarmed on towards The Ridge. They were held in check only by the guns of Tombs's Troop and the thin screen of cavalry. During the protracted fight that followed the gunners fired until the barrels of their weapons glowed, but the cavalry, unable to charge because of the tangled gardens to their front, and unwilling to retire because that would expose the guns to capture, were forced to endure a hail of musketry and gunfire and suffered severely. The situation eased when No. 2 Column stormed the Moree Bastion and the Kabul Gate from inside the city walls, enabling them to fire into the mutineers' flank. The rebels were finally driven back with a counterattack by the rallied Guides Infantry, reinforced by the Baluchi Battalion from No. 5 Column. Shebbeare received the Victoria Cross for his part in the engagement. He is recorded as having died at sea off the China coast in 1869.

As the day wore on, Nicholson decided to continue the advance as far as the Lahore Gate. The way forward lay along a narrow lane with the city walls to the right and flat-roofed houses with parapets, held by the mutineers, to the left. In the lane, which was also covered by guns on the Burn Bastion, were two cannon, about 100 yards apart. The 1st Bengal

European Fusiliers tried to fight their way along the lane twice and were repulsed with heavy losses. Nicholson was attempting to lead them into a third attack when he was mortally wounded by a shot from a sepoy on the roof of one of the houses.

During the afternoon, General Wilson moved his headquarters into the despoiled St James's church, where he took stock of the situation. Despite the reverse sustained by No. 4 Column, the enemy's defences had been penetrated and about a quarter of Delhi was now in British hands. Against this, approximately one-quarter of those involved in the assault were now dead or wounded. The inescapable projection was that by the time the entire city had been captured the Delhi Field Force would all but have ceased to exist. The news that Nicholson was dying added further gloom to the proceedings. For a while Wilson toyed with the idea of abandoning the assault, then reached the conclusion that such a course would do more harm than good. To add to his troubles, the troops, having discovered the abandoned warehouses of the city's wine merchants, began to drink themselves insensible. On The Ridge they had endured months of hell under the scorching sun of the Indian summer, and during the day they had been involved in another kind of hell as they and their opponents slaughtered each other without pause, so it was understandable that they should seek some sort of mental anaesthetic. For thirty-six hours the Delhi Field Force was incapable of further action, yet during that time the mutineers made no attempt to mount a counter-attack. Some die-hards remained, but the majority's will to fight had been broken.

When, bleary-eyed, the Delhi Field Force renewed its advance on 16 September, its progress was steady and sustained. Kishengunj was found to have been abandoned during the night. Siege guns had now been brought into the city and began battering a breach in the repaired walls of the arsenal. This was stormed by the 61st Regiment and the Baluchi Battalion, one of the first into the defences being Herbert Reade, the 61st's fighting surgeon, who, together with a sergeant, spiked one of the enemy's guns. For this and his earlier deed he was awarded the VC. Reade, a Canadian by birth, went on to enjoy a distinguished career, becoming the army's Surgeon General and Hon. Surgeon to Queen Victoria. He died in 1897.

Within the arsenal were no less than 171 guns and howitzers and a large quantity of ammunition. Realising the enormity of their loss, the mutineers mounted a serious counter-attack, covered by musketry fire from the roofs of nearby buildings. They set fire to the thatched roof of a shed containing explosives. With musket balls cracking around him and in imminent danger of being blown apart, Second Lieutenant Edward Thackeray of the Bengal Engineers extinguished the blaze. Simultaneously, Lieutenant George Renny of the Bengal Horse Artillery, climbed the arsenal's wall and flung several shells with lighted fuses into the midst of the attackers. The carnage caused by the explosion of these put an end to the attack. Both officers were awarded the Victoria Cross. Thackeray, a cousin of the novelist William Makepeace Thackeray, later achieved the rank of colonel, was knighted and commanded the Bengal Sappers and Miners 1879–85. He was also Chief Commissioner of the Order of St John of Jerusalem 1893–8 and became a Knight of the Order of Grace. The last of the Delhi VCs to survive, he died at Gerassio, Italy in 1927. Renny subsequently rose to the rank of major general and died in 1887.

One by one the mutineers' remaining strongpoints, the Burn Bastion, the Lahore Gate and the Jumma Musjid mosque, fell during the days that followed. Finally, the gates of the Red Fort were blown in by Duncan Home on 20 September. Within, a few fanatics sold their lives to no purpose, but the king himself had gone. For a while, women had been permitted to leave the city through the British lines, provided they unveiled; sometimes the veil concealed the face of a rebel sepoy, who was despatched on the spot. As Nicholson had hoped, the surviving mutineers made good their escape to the south or across the river.

The drama had one act to run. On learning that the king was hiding in a mausoleum some miles outside the city, Wilson sent Major William Hodson, a noted swordsman who enjoyed fighting for its own sake, with fifty of the latter's irregular cavalry regiment to bring him in. On reaching the mausoleum Hodson's small party was surrounded by thousands of disbanded but still armed and dangerous mutineers. Facing them down, Hodson persuaded the king to surrender and returned with him and the queen to Delhi. He then made a second and even more dangerous visit to the mausoleum during which he obtained the submission of two of the king's sons and one of his grandsons who were known to be guilty of atrocities against European women and children. When, as they were approaching Delhi, the mob showed signs of attempting a rescue, Hodson personally shot all three princes dead, thereby depriving the mutineers of their last remaining figurehead.

The capture of the city had also deprived the rebels of their focal point. It had cost the Delhi Field Force 992 killed, 2,795 wounded and thirty missing, a total of 3,817 of whom 1,677 were Indian soldiers. No one knows how many mutineers were killed, but the number was far greater. Delhi had become a stinking ruin of unburied dead and gutted buildings. Looting continued for several days, recovering the Colours and mess silver of the mutinied regiments as well as priceless hoards of gold and jewels. Much had already gone by the time the official Prize Agents began their work, but even so they managed to accumulate property for distribution valued at £750,000.

The Delhi Field Force was divided into pursuit columns that harried the broken mutineers until their groups became little more than armed gangs roaming the countryside, although some preserved their discipline a little while longer. On 28 September, for example, they made a determined stand at the fortified town of Bolandshahr, from which they were only driven after what Home described as a 'tolerably sharp action' in which six VCs were earned, three of them going to men of the 9th Lancers.

The Second Relief of Lucknow

16 NOVEMBER 1857

While Delhi had been the symbolic centre of the Mutiny, its greatest strength lay in the region of Oudh, lying to the south-east of the capital. Once an independent kingdom, Oudh had been so misgoverned by its rulers that in recent years it had been annexed by the Company, a development that was bitterly resented by those of its inhabitants who had vested interests in preserving the status quo. As Oudh was also home to many of the high-caste Hindus who formed a large proportion of the Company's Bengal Army it was inevitable that it would provide widespread support for the mutineers.

The capital of Oudh was Lucknow, a sprawling, labyrinthine city bounded on the east by the River Gumtee and to the south by a canal. Its most important buildings, including palaces, temples and mosques, often enclosed by high walls and separated by gardens, lay beside the river. To the north of these was the British Residency, situated within its own enclosure on a small plateau. On all save the northern side the buildings of the city pressed close against the enclosure's walls, and in some cases overlooked them.

The Chief Commissioner for Oudh, Brigadier General Sir Henry Lawrence, was one of comparatively few senior officials who had seen trouble coming. In May 1857 he began to fortify the Residency, establishing a defensive perimeter with gun positions, laid in sufficient supplies of food, forage and ammunition to withstand a protracted siege, and made arrangements for the city's European population to be withdrawn into the defences. On 30 May the native regiments of the garrison mutinied but were driven out of the city by the understrength 32nd Regiment (later the Duke of Cornwall's Light Infantry) and 4/1 Battery Bengal Horse Artillery, a European unit. However, by the middle of June it was clear that every other British outpost in Oudh had fallen and, that being the case, the tiny garrison of the Residency was entirely alone in the enemy's heartland with no prospect of relief.

Curiously, the mutineers left Lucknow alone until 29 June, when an enemy force was reported to have reached Chinhut, some 10 miles distant. The size of the force was grossly underestimated, so that when the garrison sallied forth to meet it the result was a disastrous defeat involving the loss of 200 casualties and five guns, followed by a difficult withdrawal into the defences. Elated by their success, the mutineers and their supporters closed in from every direction and laid close siege to the Residency. The number of rebels in and around Lucknow varied between 50,000 and 100,000, and it was estimated that at any one time no less than 8,000 of them were firing into the defences with cannon and muskets. Nowhere within the perimeter could be considered safe. The banqueting hall, situated in the centre of the main building, had been turned into a hospital, yet even here several of the sick and wounded were killed by the enemy's fire. The rebels also resorted to mining under the defences, with mixed results, for many of the Cornishmen present had been tin miners and were often able to destroy their galleries before they could set their charges. When, on 2 July, Lawrence was mortally wounded by a bursting shell, command of the embattled garrison devolved upon Colonel J. E. W. Inglis of the 32nd Regiment, who was later promoted brigadier general. Inglis pursued an aggressive defence, mounting repeated sorties that wrecked the enemy's forward posts and spiked their guns.

The siege of the Lucknow Residency began to assume immense importance for both sides. For the rebels, the patched and tattered Union flag, flying from the Residency's highest tower, became a hated symbol that they longed to tear down. For those at home, outraged by the dreadful atrocities committed at the start of the Mutiny, the relief of the garrison and its fugitive women and children became a matter of the utmost urgency. Unfortunately, the military authorities in India could not make bricks without straw and, although reinforcements from England, including many Crimean veterans, were already at sea, for the moment their resources were concentrated on the capture of Delhi. On 25 September, however, a column under Major General Sir James Outram and Brigadier General Sir Henry Havelock was able to reach the Residency, having fought its way from Cawnpore and beyond against impossible odds and in intense heat. Sometimes referred to as the First Relief of Lucknow, the event was actually a reinforcement for, encumbered as it would be with numerous non-combatants and the sick and wounded, the combined force was too weak to fight its way out. By now, too, the original garrison had become seriously affected by cholera, dysentery, smallpox and heatstroke. Against this, the fact that the rebels had been unable to halt the relief column, coupled with the news that Delhi had fallen, did nothing to improve the enemy's morale. It was, nevertheless, apparent that final relief could only be effected by a much stronger force.

This, under Brigadier General Hope Grant, began its advance at the end of October and was joined by a column under General Sir Colin Campbell, now Commander-in-Chief India. The force included units that had fought at Delhi, troops recently arrived from England, Sikhs from the Punjab and a 250-strong naval brigade consisting of 250 sailors and marines from HMS *Shannon*, equipped with six formidable 24-pdr guns for use in street fighting or to batter breaches in the walls, plus two 8-inch howitzers and a rocket detachment. On 12 November the column reached the Alambagh, the summer palace of the former kings of Oudh, a few miles from Lucknow, where Outram and Havelock had left a garrison during the First Relief. The combined force then advanced on the city and, after a day's ferocious fighting on 17 November, in which the Residency garrison attacked the mutineers from behind, broke through the enemy's defences. Then, since Lucknow itself was of no military value, on 22 November Campbell executed a model evacuation in such secrecy that the enemy were still firing on the British trenches hours after they had been abandoned. If the mutineers felt some sense of satisfaction that, at last, they were able to occupy the ruins of the Residency, this was short-lived, for Campbell left Outram, with 4,000 men and thirty-five guns, to hold the Alambagh while he attended to matters elsewhere. The real lesson of the two reliefs was that Lucknow would fall to the British when they considered the time was right. That moment came on 21 March 1858 when Campbell, now at the head of a 20,000-strong army, routed the last of the mutineers from the city, to be dispersed and hunted down piecemeal.

More Victoria Crosses were won during the fighting in and around Lucknow than anywhere else in the Mutiny. Of these, the events of 16 November 1857 produced the greatest number ever won during a single day. Before describing the actions resulting in these awards, it is worth mentioning one other, namely the award made to Thomas Henry Kavanagh, since it was the first to be made to a civilian acting under military jurisdiction. Kavanagh was a thirty-six-year-old clerk, the father of fourteen children whose upkeep had led him into debt. During the siege he was employed on counter-mining tasks, for which he demonstrated a real ability. On 9 November Outram, learning of Campbell's approach, was anxious to inform the latter of the enemy's dispositions and advise him as to the best route to the Residency. The task of carrying such a message through the mutineers' lines was tantamount to suicide, but Kavanagh volunteered. Although he was to be dressed as a native, he was an unlikely candidate, as he was much taller than the average Indian and had a head of fair hair. Nevertheless, he stained his skin with a mixture of oil and lampblack, concealed his hair beneath a turban and, accompanied by one of Outram's native spies, slipped out during the night. The two were quickly picked up by an enemy patrol but managed to bluff their way through. They next lost their way and were forced to flounder across a swamp, finally reaching Campbell's outposts the following morning. Kavanagh then accompanied the relief column's advance, providing valuable intelligence as to the terrain and the rebels' positions. After some discussion as to whether he was eligible for the Cross, it was decided that circumstances justified the award. Kavanagh also received a grant of £2,000, which he used to discharge his debts, and a post in the Civil Service.

Campbell's force consisted of one cavalry and three infantry brigades of varying strength, plus supporting artillery and the guns of the naval brigade. Within the three infantry brigades, Brigadier General Greathead's contained the remnants of the 8th (The King's) Regiment, the 2nd Punjab Infantry and a composite battalion formed from detachments of units besieged in Lucknow; Brigadier General Russell's contained the 23rd (later Royal Welch) Fusiliers and part of the 82nd (later the South Lancashire) Regiment; Brigadier Adrian Hope's brigade, the strongest and intended as the spearhead of the relief, contained the 93rd (later Argyll & Sutherland) Highlanders, half of the 53rd Regiment (later The King's Shropshire Light Infantry), the 4th Punjab Infantry and a weak composite battalion formed from detachments. Campbell's plan was to advance as close to the river as possible, thereby avoiding the alleys of the city in which the first relief force had sustained heavy casualties. The difficulty was that this would involve the capture of several large, walled, fortified palaces along the way, all of which the rebels could be relied upon to defend tenaciously.

The first of these was the Secundrabagh. For ninety minutes two 18-pdr guns focused their fire on a small section of the wall at what would have been suicidally close range had not the combined fire of the 93rd kept down the heads of the rebels lining the wall. The Highlanders, still wearing their feathered bonnets, scarlet and tartan, had not been in India when the mutineers committed the worst of their atrocities, but they knew all about them and were after blood. Campbell's intention was that once the guns had created a large enough hole, part of the 93rd would storm through it and open the nearby gates, admitting the rest of the brigade. The hole that eventually appeared was only 4 feet square at best, but Campbell understood the Highlanders' temperament and gave the order for the regiment to attack. With the pipes whipping them into berserk fury, the men surged forward with a terrifying yell of rage. First through the gap was Captain Burroughs, slashing at those beyond with his broadsword. Close behind came Lance Corporal John Dunlay, then Lieutenant Colonel Ewart and his fourteen-year-old drummer, James Grant, then more and more kilted figures. In the rush to open the gate Burroughs was felled by a sword-cut to the head. His feathered bonnet cushioned the blow, but he was stunned and would certainly have been killed had not Dunlay defended him until the fight surged past. The struggle at the gates was savage in the extreme, but Highland ferocity carried all before it and they were flung open. The rest of the brigade charged in with the 53rd's Grenadier Company, led by Lieutenant Alfred Ffrench well to the fore. Another soldier of the 53rd who was among the first to enter the building was Private Charles Irwin, one of the regiment's incurable hard cases whose charge sheet contained a long list of serious military crimes. Be that as it may, he was shot through the right shoulder during the assault yet remained up with the attackers, displaying conspicuous courage. At this point some of the mutineers seem to have launched a counter-attack. Private J. Smith of the 1st Madras European Fusiliers, serving with the composite battalion, had also been one of the first through the gate. He was immediately surrounded, receiving a sword-cut to the head, a bayonet wound in his left side and a blow from the butt of a musket. Fighting his way clear, he too refused to seek medical attention and remained in action for the rest of the day.

When the mutineers broke, they were hounded into the courtyard, along passages, up stairways and from room to room. In this frenzied, hacking, stabbing struggle it was the bayonet and the sword that came into their own, for there was little time to reload firearms. Lieutenant Colonel Ewart of the 93rd personally killed eight of the enemy, including two native officers from whom he took a Colour, but was then wounded and set upon by five more mutineers. Private Peter Grant, also of the 93rd, rushed to his rescue and, depriving one of the enemy of his sword, killed all five with it. Two more members of the regiment who distinguished themselves during the fighting were Private David Mackay and Colour Sergeant James Munro. Mackay, who was to be severely wounded later in the day, captured another Colour after a hard fight.

Munro went to the assistance of the badly wounded Captain Welch of his regiment, thereby saving his life, and carried him to a place of safety, only to join him shortly after, having been seriously wounded himself. When all was over, not a rebel was knowingly left alive in the Secundrabagh. Over 2,000 of them were later carried out, but many more must have died, for a subsequent photograph of the palace's interior shows that vultures and other scavengers had left it little better than a boneyard.

It might be thought that there had been fighting enough for one day, but Campbell, determined to smash through the hard edge of the enemy's defences before dusk, ordered the 93rd and the composite battalion to attack the Shah Najaf, supported by the heavy guns of the naval brigade. This was a tougher nut to crack than the Secundrabagh, for the domed mosque lay within an enclosure surrounded by a loopholed wall, the entrance to which had been blocked with masonry, while the roof of the mosque itself was crowned with a parapet. Furthermore, any advance on the Shah Najaf would be enfiladed from the left by fire from a circular structure generally known as the Mess House, although some accounts refer to it as the barracks. The plan was that Captain William Peel, VC, RN, who had received the award for several courageous acts in the Crimea, would bring the heavy guns of his naval brigade to point-blank range and blast a gap in the perimeter wall, covered by the fire of the 93rd and the composite battalion, who would then storm the enclosure and the mosque. It was hoped that the fire of the 53rd and the Punjabis would neutralise that of the Mess House, but even as the 93rd began to deploy it came under fire from two field guns sited near the building. Gathering a small party together, Captain William Stewart attacked and took the guns, which could otherwise have caused serious loss. While the 53rd and the 93rd opened a furious firefight with the defenders of, respectively, the Mess House and the Shah Najaf, Peel's heavy guns were being trundled forward. 'It's no use unless we are close up,' said Peel. 'We must bring the whole place about our ears and then get to close quarters.' So close to the walls were the guns that, despite the efforts of their marine escort and the 93rd, the mutineers were not only able to snipe at the gun crews but also fling grenades among them. The walls proved to be remarkably tough, and it did not help that four of the guns had switched their fire against a large crowd of rebels firing from a nearby collection of mud huts. So galling was the fire from the walls that Lieutenant Nowell Salmon, Leading Seaman John Harrison and an able seaman climbed a tree, the branches of which were actually touching the wall, and began to pick off the snipers and bomb throwers. The able seaman was killed and Salmon was shot in the thigh, but their action probably saved the gun crews firing at the wall from complete annihilation. As it was, all save Lieutenant Thomas Young and Able Seaman William Hall were killed or wounded, and these two continued to load and fire a gun together. Even so, after three hours and with evening approaching, the walls remained unbreached. As a last resort, Peel brought up his rocket cart, which sent salvo after salvo of the screaming missiles, trailing flame and smoke, through the crowd of rebels lining the wall.

This may have been the last straw for them, as they cannot have failed to notice that no survivors had emerged from the Secundrabagh, or that the Residency garrison had taken several important buildings, or that Peel's guns had done more damage than was apparent from the outside. Whatever the reason or combination of reasons, at dusk their buglers could be heard blowing the Advance, followed by the Double. Imagining that the enemy was on the point of making a sortie in strength, Brigadier General Hope prepared his regiments to meet it. The bugle calls, however, were simply a ruse to cover the rebels' withdrawal. As firing died away, Sergeant John Paton of the 93rd, suspecting the truth, went forward on his own initiative. Skirting the perimeter wall in the gathering darkness, he discovered that the enemy were escaping through a break at the rear, but not before he was detected and shots were sent cracking past his ears. Returning, he led the regiment forward and the now deserted Shah Najaf was promptly occupied. Only the Mess House and a large building known as the Moti Mahal now separated the attackers from the Residency garrison, and these were stormed the following day, enabling Campbell to plan the evacuation of the combined force and its dependants.

Six members of the 93rd Highlanders were awarded the Victoria Cross: Lance Corporal John Dunlay (sometimes spelled Dunley), Private Peter Grant, Private David Mackay, Sergeant James Munro, Sergeant John Paton and Captain William Stewart. Lieutenant Colonel Ewart, Captain Burroughs and Lieutenant Cooper were recommended for the award but did not receive it. Paton later emigrated to Australia, where he died in 1914. Three members of the 53rd also received the award for actions on 16 November: Lieutenant Alfred Ffrench, Private Charles Irwin and Private James Kenny. Ffrench was subsequently promoted to captain. A fourth member of the regiment, Sergeant Major Charles Pye, received the award for his actions the following day, when he brought up ammunition under heavy fire during the attack on the Mess House. In

1862 he emigrated to New Zealand, where he served as a captain with the local defence force during the Maori Wars, and finally settled in Australia. Private J. Smith of the Company's 1st Madras European Fusiliers also received the award.

The award was also made to Major John Guise and Sergeant Samuel Hill of the 90th Regiment (later the Cameronians) for acts on 16 and 17 November when, together, they saved the life of an officer at the storming of the Secundrabagh and rescued two wounded men the following day. Guise later rose to achieve the rank of lieutenant general. Periodic awards for continuous conspicuous gallantry between 14 and 22 November were made to Lieutenant Hastings Harrington, Rough Rider Edward Jennings and Gunners Thomas Laughnan, Hugh McInnes and James Park, all of the Bengal Artillery. Harrington was later promoted to captain but was killed in action at Agra on 20 July 1861. All the awards quoted above were elected by ballot among the units in which the recipients were serving. An exception to this was that made to Lieutenant Robert Aitken, originally of the 13th Bengal Native Infantry and a member of the Residency garrison, for various acts of gallantry between 30 June and 22 November, which resulted from recommendation. Aitken later achieved the rank of colonel and retired to Scotland, where he died in 1887.

In the naval brigade, the award of the Victoria Cross for actions on 16 November was made to Able Seaman William Hall, Leading Seaman John Harrison, Lieutenant Nowell Salmon and Lieutenant Thomas Young. Hall, a Canadian born in Nova Scotia, was the first coloured man to win the VC. He later rose in rank to become quartermaster and petty officer, dying in 1904. Harrison became a boatswain's mate and petty officer. Salmon enjoyed a long and distinguished career during which he was knighted. As Commander-in-Chief Portsmouth he commanded Queen Victoria's Diamond Jubilee Review of the Fleet, subsequently retiring in 1905 as Admiral of the Fleet. Young later achieved the rank of captain.

Of those mentioned above, seven were of Scottish and seven of Irish birth, reflecting both the scale of the 93rd Highlanders' involvement in the fighting and the fact that during this period the British Army recruited heavily in Ireland. It is, perhaps, worth mentioning that when Lucknow was finally taken from the mutineers the following year, so great a quantity of loot was amassed that it has never been possible to value the total; suffice it to say that a number of heavily mortgaged English and Scottish estates cleared their debts shortly after.

CHINA
NORTH AMERICA
SOUTHERN AFRICA
NORTH-WEST FRONTIER
CUBA
1860–1900

The Taku Forts

21 AUGUST 1860

The Third China War, which was actually an extension of its predecessor, stemmed from the refusal of the Imperial Chinese government to implement the provisions of various treaties to which it had agreed, albeit under duress. The Western powers, notably Great Britain and France, were not prepared to tolerate further intransigence and in May 1858 a squadron of British and French gunboats was despatched to enforce the treaties. Having fought its way past the forts guarding the mouth of the Pei-ho River at Taku, the squadron proceeded upstream to Tientsin, only 80 miles' march from Peking. There, representatives of the Imperial government readily agreed to every one of the Allied demands and the squadron was withdrawn.

Unfortunately, the Chinese had no more intention of being bound by the Treaty of Tientsin than they had by earlier agreements. The following year, a squadron of British gunboats under Admiral Sir James Hope was sent to remind the Imperial government forcibly of its obligations. Arriving at the mouth of the Pei-ho, Hope was immediately aware that the Chinese had spared no effort to strengthen their defences. There was now a large fort on each bank of the river close to the estuary, and two smaller forts, one on each bank, some way upstream. Furthermore, the narrow channel between the mudflats at the river's mouth had been obstructed by lines of iron posts, a cable and log boom, and tethered rafts. The forts themselves bristled with hundreds of guns, clearly indicating that Chinese firepower outmatched that of the gunboats by a very wide margin. Nevertheless, when the mandarin commanding the area declined to permit the squadron passage, the over-confident Hope decided to batter his way through. The attempt, made on 25 June, ended in disaster, for several of the gunboats were sunk, the rest were seriously damaged, casualties among the crews were heavy, and a landing party was easily repulsed with serious loss. As a result of this, the force was compelled to withdraw. At home, the public was so outraged by this rare failure on the Royal Navy's part that neither decorations nor promotions were awarded to the participants, although numerous acts of suicidal courage by individuals among the gunboat crews would certainly have resulted in the award of several VCs.

The matter could not be allowed to rest there. When, predictably, the Chinese emperor declined to reply to a note demanding an apology for firing on British ships and his government's failure to act on the provisions of the Treaty of Tientsin, a combined British and French naval and military task force was despatched to enforce compliance. This, consisting of 11,000 British and Indian troops under Lieutenant General Sir James Hope Grant and 6,700 French under Lieutenant General Cousin-Montauban, began assembling at Hong Kong in May 1860. As the Taku defences were reported to have been strengthened even further, on 30 July the troops disembarked at Peh-tang, some miles to the north of the Pei-ho estuary. On 12 August they began marching across country towards the Pei-ho with the intention of attacking the forts' landward defences while the gunboats provided covering fire from the river mouth. Cousin-Montauban was for attacking the Large South Fort first, but Grant, who was in overall command, pointed out that this would involve crossing the river, thereby separating the troops from their supply base, whereas capturing the Small North Fort first would enable its guns to be turned on the weaker faces of the other forts, compelling their surrender. With a bad grace, Cousin-Montauban gave way.

The defences of the Small North Fort were formidable. In succession was a deep dry ditch; an open space obstructed by an abatis; a flooded ditch 45 feet wide and 15 feet deep; a 20-foot-wide belt of sharpened bamboo stakes; another flooded ditch; and another belt of bamboo stakes leading to the 15-foot-high crenellated and loopholed mud walls of the fort itself. Swamps on either flank restricted any advance on the fort to a narrow frontage on which a bridge over the outer wet ditch had been destroyed and a drawbridge over the inner wet ditch had been raised.

In overall command of the assault was Major General Sir Robert Napier. By the evening of 20 August he had emplaced forty-four guns and three heavy mortars. The assault itself, commanded by Brigadier General Reeves, consisted of 2,500 men drawn mainly from the 44th (later the 1st Essex) Regiment and the 67th (later the 2nd Hampshire) Regiment. Cousin-Montauban, apparently still sulking, contributed only 400 men, although they were better equipped for the work in hand as they brought light bamboo ladders carried by coolies, whereas the British relied on Royal Marines carrying awkward pontoons for use in crossing the wet ditches.

The guns opened fire at 05:00 on 21 August, knocking the abatis and mud walls apart, as well as landing shells inside the fort itself. One of the latter must have penetrated a magazine as there was a deafening explosion. For a moment the fort was lost to view in a dense cloud of smoke, dust and falling debris. The will of the Chinese defenders, however, seems not to have been affected, for after a brief pause they continued to man their guns. Meanwhile, the warships at the river's mouth had also opened fire on the Large North and South Forts. A second heavy explosion inside the Large South Fort indicated that they, too, were finding their mark.

At 06:00 Napier gave the signal for the assault to begin. The attackers surged forward with such élan that, as one witness put it, they clearly 'meant to get in.' The Chinese, however, could be seen crowding on to the battlements, blazing away with their guns, muskets and gingals. Nevertheless, the British and French were quickly across the dry ditch and through the smashed abatis. The Royal Marine pontoon carriers became a special target and sustained such losses that the pontoons had to be abandoned. Thus, at the first of the wet ditches, the British had to swim or flounder across, whereas the French coolies leapt in and, standing up to their necks in water, supported the ladders while the soldiers ran across. Brigadier General Reeves was himself seriously wounded and handed over command of the assault to Lieutenant Colonel MacMahon of the 44th Regiment.

Meanwhile, following in the wake of the assault was fifteen-year-old Hospital Apprentice Andrew Fitzgibbon of the Indian Medical Establishment, attached to the 67th Regiment. Having paused to bind the wound of an Indian dhoolie (stretcher-bearer), he disregarded the enemy's heavy fire and ran forward across the bullet-swept ground and attended to other casualties, being severely wounded in the process.

The second wet ditch was crossed in the same manner as the first, save that some of the British used the French ladders. On reaching the walls, the French erected more ladders, only to have them thrown down by the defenders. One of the first across was a Major Anson, serving on Grant's staff. Grabbing an axe from a pioneer corporal of the 67th, he severed the ropes holding up the drawbridge. When the bridge fell, two howitzers opened fire on the gates beyond from the edge of the dry ditch, to which they had been brought forward by General Napier when the assault began. In due course, these created a narrow breach leading into the fort's interior, but by then the issue had been decided in the most dramatic fashion.

The troops, whose units had inevitably become intermingled, were crowded together at the base of the wall, being pelted with grenades, cannon shot, jars of quicklime and 'stinkpots' that gave off clouds of choking smoke. Desperate measures were needed urgently if the assault was to succeed. Close to the gate was Lieutenant Nathaniel Burslem, formerly of the Military Train, which had been founded in the aftermath of the Crimean War to remedy the army's transport difficulties, but now a member of the 67th. With him was Private Thomas Lane, an Irishman serving with the same regiment. Together, the two scrambled up to a narrow embrasure, which they proceeded to widen with a pioneer's pick. Both sustained serious wounds but continued to enlarge the opening until it was wide enough to permit entry. Not far away were Lieutenant Robert Rogers and Private John McDougall of the 44th Regiment, who had swum the wet ditches, together with Lieutenant Edmund Lenon and Ensign John Chaplin of the 67th, the latter carrying the Queen's Colour of the regiment. Lenon pushed his sword deep into the mud wall, supporting the hilt while Rogers used it as a step, fighting his way into the embrasure above. More men pushed their bayonets into the wall, creating a ladder up which Lenon, Chaplin, McDougall and others clambered to join Rogers. At about the same time Burslem and Lane broke through their embrasure on to the ramparts. Men from both regiments now swarmed through the embrasures to pitch the defenders into the courtyard below. Simultaneously, the French, led by a drummer named Fauchard and the Colour bearer of their 102ème Regiment of the Line, also secured a lodgement. The fighting inside the walls began to take on a different character as troops from both nations sought to be the first to plant their flag on the fort's central tower, which was crowded with the enemy. The British won, fighting their way at the point of the bayonet up the tower's approach ramp, enabling Chaplin to plant his Colour on the summit, although he sustained three wounds in the process. The will of the Chinese, who until this moment had fought stubbornly, suddenly collapsed. Some jumped over the walls to escape, many being impaled on their own bamboo stakes or drowned in the wet ditches, while others sought hiding places from which they were winkled out. It was estimated that of the fort's 500-strong garrison, 400 were either killed or wounded.

Observing the outcome of the assault, the garrison of the Small North Fort promptly made off. The Large North Fort surrendered to the French without a shot being fired. The 2,000 Chinese within, certain that they were about to massacred, were simply disarmed and told to go home, which they did. The Large South Fort surrendered the following day. No fewer than 600 guns were counted in the two South Forts alone.

For their part in storming the Small South Fort the Victoria Cross was awarded to Lieutenant Rogers and Private McDougall of the 44th Regiment, and to Lieutenants Burslem and Lenon, Ensign Chaplin, Private Lane and Hospital Apprentice Fitzgibbon of the 67th Regiment. Rogers rose in the service to become a major general. Little is known of McDougall save that he died in his native Edinburgh in 1869. Burslem achieved the rank of captain. He sold his commission and in 1865 emigrated to New Zealand where he was tragically drowned in the Thames River the same year. Lenon and Chaplin retired from the army with the respective ranks of lieutenant colonel and colonel. Lane had a troubled history, becoming one of only eight men to forfeit the award, for on leaving the army he joined the Kimberley State Police Force in South Africa and in 1881 was convicted of desertion on active service and theft of a horse, arms and accoutrements. Andrew Fitzgibbon remained in the Indian Medical Establishment and later achieved the rank of apothecary. He shares with Drummer Thomas Flinn of the 64th (later the North Staffordshire) Regiment the distinction of being the youngest recipient of the VC, both being aged fifteen years and three months. Flinn won his award during the Indian Mutiny when, though wounded himself, he took part in a charge against an enemy battery at Cawnpore and personally engaged two of the rebel gunners in hand-to-hand combat.

Following the capture of the Taku Forts the Allies occupied Tientsin and advanced on Peking, twice defeating a Chinese army which attempted to bar their progress. The Imperial government then offered to negotiate but treacherously kidnapped the Allied negotiators, hoping that by holding them hostage it would discourage a further advance on the capital. When the ploy failed the Chinese capitulated, agreeing to every one of the Allied demands, including the payment of an indemnity and the ceding of Kowloon on the mainland opposite Hong Kong. It was then discovered that the captured negotiators had been so savagely tortured that half of them had died. In reprisal Grant ordered that the Yuen-Ming-Yuen, a group of palaces set in beautiful gardens, should be burned to the ground. The Imperial Summer Palace, lying outside the city walls, was also thoroughly looted. After this, apart from a brief undeclared war with France in the 1880s, the Imperial government more or less kept its word for the next forty years.

The Great Locomotive Chase
12 APRIL 1862

The American Civil War was fought on the issue of whether individual states had the right to remove themselves from the rule of the Federal government in Washington. Many in the southern states that were to form the Confederacy believed that slavery was an essential element in their economy, and that if it was abolished, as northern politicians insisted that it should be, they would face ruin. There were, too, those in the south who, while not actively supporting slavery, were adamant that Washington's authority did not extend to the internal governance of states which considered themselves to be sovereign entities, and that if the Federal government attempted to impose its will on those states they had the right to secede from the Union. There were also those in the north who supported this latter view, and some in the south who did not, so that the principles involved divided not only north and south, but also communities and families. Thus, the Federal north fought to put down what it believed to be a rebellion and so preserve the Union of the United States of America, while the southern states of the Confederacy fought for what they believed to be their independence and international recognition by the world powers.

The war itself was the first of the modern era, for the huge armies raised by both sides could never have been maintained in the field had it not been for the comparatively recent advent of the railway. In this respect the Confederacy was at a disadvantage as its industrial base was far smaller than that of its opponents. Rails themselves were in short supply and locomotives were so precious that one commander even declared that each of them was worth a division to him. It was natural, therefore, that the Federals should seek to exploit this weakness to the full. Early in 1862 a plan to wreck large sections of the Western and Atlantic Railroad was approved by Major General Ormsby Mitchel, who was responsible for Union spies in the Confederacy, although some sources suggest that the idea originated with Major General Don Carlos Buell, whose army would benefit most from the operation. This would be achieved by infiltrating a small body of troops in civilian clothes deep into Georgia. What followed was not a battle in the usual sense, although the threat posed to Confederate communications in the western theatre of war was just as severe as if it had been.

In command of the raid were two of Mitchel's spies, James Andrews and William Campbell, who were both civilians from Kentucky. Of the two, Andrews was designated the leader of the expedition. The rest of the party consisted of twenty men drawn from the 2nd, 21st and 33rd Ohio Infantry, all of whom had some sort of railway experience. The detailed planning required the hi-jacking of a locomotive that would be driven north along the Western and Atlantic Road, stopping periodically so that the raiders could destroy track, telegraph lines, bridges and tunnels, and finally enter the Federal lines at Huntsville, which it was agreed would be captured a day before the raid took place.

For some weeks before the raid took place Andrews had gained the confidence of the Confederate outposts by playing the role of a sympathiser who arranged for medical supplies to be smuggled across the lines. As a result of this, he and his raiders experienced no difficulty in making their way into Georgia. Having studied the operating schedule, they decided to seize the early morning northbound train from Atlanta when it made a halt for breakfast at Big Shanty. Andrews had chosen the site with care as the small station at Big Shanty did not possess a telegraph office, which meant that it would be some time before warning of the theft could be transmitted.

The train itself pulled out of Atlanta at 04:00 on 12 April 1862, drawn by *The General*, a typical wood-burning 4-4-0 locomotive of the period, complete with wide spark-arresting chimney, cow-catcher and bell. The train made a scheduled stop at Marietta, where it was boarded by Andrews and his men. Some miles to the north it halted again at Big Shanty, where the passengers and crew disembarked and made their way to the Lacey Hotel for breakfast, suspecting nothing. Accompanied by two other men, Andrews and Private William Knight, who had been a locomotive driver before the war, suddenly boarded *The General* while the rest of the raiders took up positions along the train. Andrews opened the throttle and the train began to move, gathering speed steadily.

So far, all had apparently gone according to plan, although luck was not to ride with the raiders that day. Railwaymen everywhere regarded themselves as an elite and took their duties very seriously. Conductor William Fuller, whose responsibilities included the safety of the train, was no exception. Enraged by the theft of his train, he set off in pursuit, running along the track accompanied by driver Jeff Cain and machine foreman Anthony Murphy. After covering two miles they reached Moon's Station, where they found a flat hand trolley. On reaching Acworth aboard this, they were joined by two track gangers who helped them propel the trolley along the gradual downgrade towards Etowah.

Meanwhile, Andrews had made several halts, during which his men dismounted to remove rails from the track, obstruct it with sleepers and cut telegraph wires. Some of the local people, used to the railway's scheduled traffic, asked him why *The General* was being manned by a strange crew. He replied that he was taking a special gunpowder train through to the Confederate army at Corinth – an entirely plausible explanation as only days earlier this army had fought the bloody battle of Shiloh. Curiously, Andrews did not destroy the railway bridge over the Etowah River, which was one of his primary objectives, nor did he obstruct the track between Etowah and Kingston. He probably felt that he had already spent too much time damaging the track and wanted to catch up with his own timetable, but the decision was to have baleful consequences.

Fuller's first thoughts were that his train had been stolen by deserters on the run. However, when he came across the series of obstructions he recognised that he was confronted by something far more sinister and better organised. Nevertheless, with some effort the hand trolley was manhandled across the gaps in the line. It rattled into Etowah, where he commandeered a small shunting locomotive, the *Yonah*, and set off for Kingston. At this moment Andrews had no idea that he was being pursued, but he was galled by having to slow down because of north-bound trains on the track ahead of him. As a result of this, Fuller was able to close the gap on his quarry until the two were only ten minutes apart.

Arriving in the Kingston marshalling yard, from which lines went off to the north and west, Fuller was informed that *The General* had passed through and was heading northwards. Exchanging the little *Yonah* for the larger *William R. Smith*, he again set off, only to find that Andrews had again begun tearing up the track some way short of Adairsville. It was, of course, impossible for the locomotive to cross the gap. Fuller abandoned it and, accompanied only by Murphy, began walking to Adairsville. The gap between pursuers and pursued began to open once more.

In Adairsville station Fuller found a stationary southbound freight train drawn by a locomotive named *Texas*. He had it uncoupled and

THE GREAT LOCOMOTIVE CHASE

driven on to the main line, then continued the chase with the *Texas* travelling full speed. A mile or two south of Calhoun a solitary figure was seen walking along the track in the opposite direction. Fuller recognised him as Edward Henderson, a seventeen-year-old telegraph operator from Dalton. Henderson told him that as the telegraph line to Atlanta was dead, he had been sent to find the break. Fuller took him on board and dictated a message to the commander of the Confederate troops in Chattanooga.

Shortly after the *Texas* had passed through Calhoun the crews of the two locomotives spotted each other's smoke. Andrews ordered Knight to halt while the rest of the raiders struggled to lift a rail, but the attempt was abandoned when it was seen that the *Texas* was coming up fast. A number of sleepers were then dropped from the rear of the train in the vain hope that these would derail the pursuing locomotive. Next, Andrews ordered the two rearmost freight cars to be uncoupled. The crew of the *Texas* took them in their stride, pushing them along until they could be shunted into the next siding. Observing that the pursuit was gaining again, Andrews halted inside the covered wooden bridge spanning the Oostanaula River. Here he uncoupled the train's passenger carriage, setting it on fire in the hope that the flames would consume the bridge as well. Again, he was unlucky, for recent wet weather had rendered the wood too damp to burn. The *Texas* came up and pushed the burning car as far as the next siding.

The chase continued with all of Andrews's raiders now riding on *The General*'s tender. In Dalton, Fuller slowed down sufficiently for Henderson to jump off and send his telegraphic message to Chattanooga, where measures were promptly taken to despatch troops down the line to Ringgold. No interception took place, for *The General* had run its course. The tender was almost empty of fuel but, worse still, the boiler had consumed most of the available water. As the locomotive climbed the grade towards the top of the Ringgold Gap, less and less steam began reaching the cylinders until, just short of the summit, *The General* stalled. Andrews and his men quickly made themselves scarce so that when Fuller arrived all he found was a badly overheated locomotive.

Some of the fugitives managed to get as far as Alabama, but all were eventually rounded up. As civilian spies and saboteurs, Andrews and Williams could expect no mercy and were hung. Legally, the soldiers were in little better case, for in carrying out the raid in civilian clothes they were acting contrary to the accepted rules of warfare and were also, therefore, liable to execution as spies. Six of them were hung, although how their actions differed from the rest is obscure. Of the remainder, eight escaped from prison in October 1862 and six were exchanged in March the following year.

While, thanks largely to Fuller's implacable pursuit, the raid inflicted only a fraction of the damage intended, the concept of its being carried out 200 miles inside enemy territory caught the public imagination. At this stage of the war, the Union needed heroes and the military participants received the first Congressional Medals of Honor to be awarded. In order of presentation the first recipients were Corporal Jacob Parrott of the 33rd Ohio, Privates William Bensinger and Robert Buffum and Sergeant E. A. Mason, all of the 21st Ohio, Corporal William Pittinger of the 2nd Ohio and Private William Reddick of the 33rd Ohio. The remaining raiders, Private William Knight of the 2nd Ohio, Privates Wilson H. Brown, Mark Wood, John Alfred Wilson and John Porter, all of the 21st Ohio, Privates Daniel Dorsey, Martin Hawkins and John Wollom, all of the 33rd Ohio, were presented with their medals some months later. Although a majority of the survivors were born in Ohio, Wood was born in England, Buffum in Salem, Massachusetts, Mason in Wayne County, Indiana, Dorsey in Waterford, Virginia, Hawkins in Mercer County, Pennsylvania and Reddick in Alabama. The six soldiers who were hung, Sergeant Major Marion Ross and Privates George Wilson and Perry Shadrack, all of the 2nd Ohio, Private John Scott of the 21st Ohio and Privates Samuel Robertson and Samuel Slavens, both of the 33rd Ohio, were awarded the medal posthumously. The medals were presented to their families, save for those awarded to Wilson and Shadrack, none of whose family members ever came forward to receive them.

Gettysburg
1–3 JULY 1863

It had never been the intention of either side that a major battle should be fought at Gettysburg. In the summer of 1863 the American Civil War was being contested on two major fronts. In the west the Union was making slow but steady progress and, save for the fortress of Vicksburg, besieged since May by Major General Ulysses S. Grant's Army of the Tennessee, it had almost seized control of the Mississippi along its entire length, all but isolating those Confederate states to the west of the great river. In the east, however, the Confederates were apparently more than holding their own. The previous year General Robert E. Lee's Army of Northern Virginia had invaded the north, hoping that by inflicting so serious a defeat on the Union Army of the Potomac, Great Britain and France would recognise the Confederacy as an independent state and induce Washington to make peace. These hopes had been dashed at the bloody but inconclusive battle of Antietam on 17 September. Lee had withdrawn into Virginia, but since then he had inflicted a sharp defeat on the Army of the Potomac at Fredericksburg on 13 December, and again at Chancellorsville in a battle lasting from 1–6 May. Overall Confederate strategy now demanded that he should mount a second invasion of the north, partly to ease the pressure on Vicksburg, but mainly with the intention of causing such alarm in the increasingly war-weary north that President Lincoln's government would be unable to resist popular demands for a negotiated peace. Lee's own plan involved marching up the Shenandoah valley into Pennsylvania, where he would disrupt vital rail communications with the western theatre of war, after which he would turn his attention to the capture of Philadelphia, Baltimore or Washington, according to the prevailing circumstances.

Lee's belief in his troops' ability to win battles was equalled only by the affection and respect in which he was held by them. What they did not know was that for some time the general had been suffering from pericarditis, the effects of which include painful discomfort and a general slowing down of the system, including the decision-making process. Furthermore, at Chancellorsville his trusted subordinate, Lieutenant General Thomas (Stonewall) Jackson, had been killed and he did not possess the same instinctive rapport with any of his three corps commanders, Lieutenant General James Longstreet (I Corps), Lieutenant General Richard S. Ewell (II Corps) and Lieutenant General Ambrose P. Hill (III Corps).

The Army of Northern Virginia began marching north on 3 June. Major General Joseph Hooker, commanding the Army of the Potomac, advised Washington of the fact and was ordered to conform, keeping his army between Lee and the capital. An unfortunate misjudgement by Lee's cavalry commander, the redoubtable Major General J. E. B. Stuart, kept the Confederate Cavalry Division on the wrong side of Hooker's marching columns, which were set a cracking pace. The result was that Stuart, now separated from the Army of Northern Virginia, was unable to keep Lee informed of Hooker's movements and could only rejoin him by marching directly north through Maryland into the proposed area of operations. The Federal troopers, however, operated under no such disadvantage and were able to supply Hooker with details of Lee's progress, if not his intentions. Nevertheless, all was far from well with Hooker. He was simply the latest in a line of generals commanding the Army of the Potomac, none of whom were apparently capable of getting the better of Lee, and the authorities in Washington had not forgiven him for being defeated at Chancellorsville. The lack of regard was evidently mutual, for when the latter refused to let him supplement his army with the 10,000-strong garrison of the Union arsenal at Harper's Ferry, he tendered his resignation, which was accepted. On 28 June Major General George C. Meade was appointed the army's new commander. Meade was steady and experienced, having commanded the army's V Corps at Fredericksburg and Chancellorsville, although some thought him unimaginative. Interested in neither place-seeking nor politics, he did not want the new appointment but could hardly refuse at a time when a major crisis was boiling up.

On the day that Meade received his appointment the Army of Northern Virginia was within striking distance of its first objective, the Pennsylvania Railroad at Harrisburg. Ewell's II Corps, in the lead, had one division at Carlisle and another at York, while Longstreet's and Hill's corps were in the area of Chamberstown, where Lee had established his temporary headquarters. Stuart's whereabouts still remained unknown to the army commander, as was that of the enemy. However, during the evening a Confederate spy reached Chamberstown, bringing with him news of Meade's appointment and that the Army of the Potomac had already reached Frederick, Maryland, and was still marching north. This being too close for comfort, Lee decided to suspend operations against Harrisburg and issued orders for his corps commanders to concentrate their troops at Cashtown in preparation for a major engagement.

Many Confederate soldiers were now marching barefoot, so that when rumour had it that there was a footwear warehouse in Gettysburg, eight miles east of Cashtown, it was considered to be worth investigating. On 30 June a brigade was despatched there, but found the town in the possession of Union cavalry. Both sides observed the other, but no engagement took place. However, the two armies were now aware of each other's presence and began to converge on Gettysburg, Lee with 75,000 men and Meade with 97,000 men organised in seven corps and a cavalry corps. In passing, it is worth mentioning that within the Union Army the term regiment might mean anything from less than 200 to well over 400 men. This stemmed from the fact that, for the sake of prestige, most states continued to raise the maximum number of regiments possible from their available manpower resources without giving thought to reinforcing those already in being. Consequently, the strength of the older, more experienced regiments dwindled to the point that they had become mere shadows of their former selves, the result being that some were little stronger than two conventional companies while others almost equalled the size of neighbouring brigades. Confederate regiments did not suffer from the problem to such an extent and had the added advantage of being brigaded together with regiments from the same state. Having said that, the enthusiastic amateurism that had characterised both sides during the early days of the war had long since given way to a tough professionalism generated by the cruel realities of the battlefield, although the belief in their respective causes remained as profound.

Gettysburg was a sleepy little town situated in pleasant, rolling countryside. It contained a Lutheran seminary but was otherwise unremarkable save that it was the meeting place of ten roads. The Gettysburg and Hanover Railroad entered the town from the east but had not been laid beyond that point, although work on the embankments and cuttings had been completed. The ground over which the decisive actions of the battle took place lies to the south of the town and consists of two low parallel ridges, approximately two-thirds of a mile apart and running from north to south, that to the west being known as Seminary Ridge and that to the east as Cemetery Ridge. At the northern end of

Cemetery Ridge is Cemetery Hill, from which the ridge extends south-wards, gradually losing height until it ends in a steep-sided valley through which a stream called Plum Run flows on a north-east to south-west axis. Across the mouth of the valley is the Devil's Den, an area of huge, smooth, tumbled boulders left behind by a retreating Ice Age glacier. The southern wall of the valley is formed by two hills named Little Round Top and Round Top, connected by a saddle. The summit and western slopes of Little Round Top consist of granite outcrops and scattered trees, but the eastern slopes, the saddle and the whole of Round Top are densely forested. Round Top is the higher of the two hills, although the close timber denies a view from the summit. However, from the summit of Little Round Top, the whole of Cemetery Ridge is visible and within range, rendering it untenable because of the enfilade fire that could be brought to bear along its entire length.

The battle itself began on the morning of 1 July when Hill's III Corps, approaching Gettysburg from the west along the Chambersburg road, was confronted by a Union cavalry screen. The cavalrymen, armed with Sharps carbines, with a rate of fire three times that of the rifled musket, offered the most dogged resistance imaginable, but were nonetheless pleased when they were joined by the Army of the Potomac's vanguard, consisting of Major General John F. Reynolds's I Corps. Seizing the initiative, Reynolds's divisions halted Hill's advance. In one counter-attack a Confederate brigade was all but destroyed when it was outflanked and driven into a railway cutting where the survivors of the 2nd Mississipi surrendered. All might have been well, for although Hill was feeding troops into the battle as they came up, this was balanced by the arrival of the Union XI Corps, under Major General Oliver O. Howard, which extended I Corps' line to the right. However, coming down from the north was Ewell's II Corps, which had been ordered to redirect its march to Gettysburg. The appearance of formed bodies of rebels in this direction caused Howard to deploy his centre and right to face the new threat. In effect, both Union corps were now within an uncomfortable salient and under fire from two directions. I Corps was forced back, defending each rolling crest in turn, until it was pushed off Seminary Ridge. XI Corps, forced to conform, had no such terrain advantages but fought a bitter rearguard action as it withdrew. In some confusion, elements of both corps were driven through the streets of Gettysburg to the south-east, where, during the afternoon, they rallied on Cemetery Hill and the northern end of Cemetery Ridge.

On balance, the day's fighting seemed to favour the Confederates, who had nevertheless sustained the considerable loss of, perhaps, 8,000 men killed, wounded or missing. The Federals sustained 12,000 casualties, including Reynolds, shot dead by a sniper. On the other hand, the Federals now held a stronger position than that in which they had begun the day and were rapidly being reinforced by the rest of the Army of the Potomac. To some extent, the fighting on 1 July also determined the course events would take during the next two days.

Although often eclipsed by what followed, the courage and determination shown by both sides during the day were not surpassed. Given that the armies were not yet fully engaged, a remarkable number of Medals of Honor were awarded, especially to personnel of I Corps. Among the recipients were Second Lieutenant George G. Benedict of the 12th Vermont, who passed through a murderous fire of grape and canister to deliver orders and rallied troops at a critical moment; Private Casper R. Carlisle of the Pennsylvania Light Artillery who, despite the fact that most of the horses had been killed and the drivers wounded, brought out a gun of his battery under heavy musketry fire; Sergeant Jefferson Coates of the 7th Wisconsin who, having had both eyes shot out, continued to encourage his men until led from the field; First Sergeant Edward Gilligan of the 88th Pennsylvania, who assisted in the capture of the Confederate flag by knocking down the sergeant carrying it; Lieutenant Colonel Henry S. Huidkoper of the 150th Pennsylvania who, while repelling an enemy attack, received a severe wound in the right arm but instead of retiring remained at the front in command of his regiment; Corporal J. Monroe Reisinger, also of the 150th Pennsylvania, awarded under an Act of Congress dated 25 January 1907, for 'Specially brave and meritorious conduct in the face of the enemy'; Sergeant James M. Rutter of the 143rd Pennsylvania who, at great personal risk, went to the assistance of a wounded comrade and, while under fire, removed him to a place of safety; Major Alfred J. Sellers of the 90th Pennsylvania, who voluntarily led the regiment under a withering fire to a position from which the enemy was repulsed; and Corporal Francis A. Waller of the 6th Wisconsin, who captured the Colour of the 2nd Mississippi. Awards of the Medal to men of XI Corps included those made to Captain Francis Irsch of the 45th New York for gallantry in flanking the enemy and capturing a number of prisoners, as well as holding a part of the town of Gettysburg while the corps was rallying on Cemetery Hill; and to Musician Richard Enderlin of the 73rd Ohio. Enderlin's award covers the first two days of the battle and is unusual in that as a musician he could not be made to fight as a soldier, yet chose to arm himself and serve as one. He is also on record as having voluntarily and at great personal risk penetrated the Confederate lines at night and, under a sharp fire, rescued a wounded comrade.

During the night more troops reached the battlefield until, by the morning of 2 July, the formal battle lines had been established. The Union position, offering as it did a refused right flank to Ewell's corps to the north, resembled a fish hook. To the east of Cemetery Hill the extreme right of the line was held by Major General Henry W. Slocum's XII Corps; I Corps, now commanded by Major General John Newton, extended the line westwards to Cemetery Hill where it joined XI Corps. At this point the line turned southwards along Cemetery Ridge, with Major General Winfield S. Hancock's II Corps in the centre and Major General Daniel E. Sickles's III Corps holding the Union left, which at this stage was marked by the Plum Run and did not include the Round Tops. Unfortunately, Sickles did not feel comfortable holding the lower southern end of Cemetery Ridge and advanced his troops to slightly higher ground 1,000 yards to the west, although this created an awkward salient in the Union line and deprived him of the support of other troops on the ridge. To the rear of what should have been Sickles's position on the ridge was Major General George Sykes's V Corps, in reserve. Still on the road but expected to reach the battlefield during the afternoon was VI Corps, commanded by Major General John Sedgwick.

Lee's deployment paralleled that of his opponent. Ewell's II Corps was facing Culp's Hill and Cemetery Hill, while Hill's III Corps was in position on Seminary Ridge and Longstreet's I Corps was coming into line on its right. Longstreet, taking note of the strength of the Union position, suggested to Lee that a march to the south would place the Army of Northern Virginia between Meade and Washington, and that since Meade would have to respond, Lee could defeat him in a battle fought on ground of his own choosing. Lee, however, chose to reject this sound advice, deciding instead that by attacking the enemy's flanks he could inflict severe damage on Meade's army before it had been fully concentrated. His orders required Longstreet to mount a concentrated attack on the Union left, overrunning the Round Tops in the process, and that upon the sound of his guns going into action Hill and Ewell would launch attacks against Cemetery Hill and Culp's Hill on the Union right. However, thanks largely to Longstreet's interference with the details of his corps' approach march to its assembly area, it was late afternoon before it was in a position to begin its attack.

Meanwhile, at a conference with his corps commanders, Meade had made Sykes's V Corps responsible for the security of the Union left and it had begun to move into a position behind Little Round Top. As yet, with the exception of a handful of signallers, no one on either side appreciated the critical importance of this feature. By chance, reflected sound from the skirmishing already taking place between the lines suggested to Meade that something was already happening on the hill itself, and he asked his chief engineer, Major General Gouverneur K. Warren, to investigate. As he reached the summit, the signallers drew Warren's attention to some suspicious movement behind the trees on Seminary Ridge. Warren asked a battery in the Devil's Den to fire a round in that direction. The sound of the shot caused a stir in the extended Confederate ranks which, Warren observed to his horror, far outflanked the position. Realising that if the undefended hill fell into enemy hands the army's position on Cemetery Ridge would become untenable, he despatched two of his staff officers to bring up reinforcements. The result was that Colonel Strong Vincent's brigade of Sykes's First Division was rushed to the summit. The brigade, a mere 1,336 men strong, consisted of the 20th Maine (386), the 16th Michigan (263), the 44th New York (391) and the 83rd Pennsylvania (295). Vincent, discovering a natural terrace following the line of the hill from its south-eastern slopes round towards the saddle joining the Round Tops, deployed his regiments with the 16th Michigan on the right, the 44th New York and 83rd Pennsylvania in the centre and the 20th Maine on the left.

The Confederates had meanwhile emerged from the trees on Seminary Ridge and, full of confidence, were coming on far faster than had been anticipated. The attack on the Round Tops and the Devil's Den was led by Major General John B. Hood's division, one of the best in Lee's army. Hood himself was wounded by shellfire and command passed to Brigadier General Evander M. Law, who attached a higher priority to the capture of the Devil's Den than that of Little Round Top, the significance of which he was far from alone in underestimating. Nevertheless, Vincent's brigade quickly found itself engaged in a series of ferocious firefights as regiments from Alabama and Texas swarmed up the rocky slopes towards them. While these were taking place, the guns and limbers of Captain Charles E. Hazlett's Battery D, 5th US Artillery, were being dragged, with infinite labour, up the reverse slopes of the hill. They went into action as soon as they reached the summit, but their additional fire was not sufficient to beat back the Confederate tide. The little 16th Michigan began to suffer so severely that an alarmed subaltern ordered its Colours to the rear. With them went forty-five men, one-third of the regiment's remaining strength. Vincent rallied the remnant but was mortally wounded shortly after. It was beginning to look as though his brigade could not withstand the pressure for much longer when Warren brought up Brigadier General Stephen H. Weed's brigade, also from V Corps. Weed's leading regiment, the 447-strong 140th New York, went straight into action as it came streaming across the summit. This stabilised the situation on the eastern and north-eastern slopes of the hill, although Hazlett and Weed would be killed before the Confederates sullenly withdrew.

On the hill's southern slopes, however, equally dramatic events were taking place. Two Confederate regiments, the 15th and 47th Alabama, had taken Round Top and, after resting, had been directed to wheel left across the saddle and join the attack on Little Round Top. The 47th, engaged frontally by the 20th Maine and raked by the 83rd Pennsylvania from the left, lost a third of its men and withdrew. The 15th Alabama, on its right, continued to advance and would have turned the left flank of the 20th Maine had not its commander, Colonel Joshua L. Chamberlain, extended his line and bent it back until it presented a right angle.

Chamberlain, who was to be awarded the Medal of Honor for his conduct this day, is still regarded by the US Army as the ideal citizen soldier. By profession, he was a university lecturer, although he was also a graduate from a theological seminary. By the end of the war he had achieved the brevet rank of major general of volunteers and been detailed to accept the surrender of the Army of Northern Virginia at Appomattox. Declining a commission in the regular army, he returned to his native Maine, where he served as governor for three years, then resumed his career as a lecturer at Bowdoin College, of which he became president. Before his death in 1914 he also held several government appointments, made a fortune in business and wrote a number of books.

For the moment, Chamberlain's attention was fully occupied with the climactic struggle that was developing between his regiment and the 15th Alabama. The 20th Maine was stretched so thin that it was reduced to a single rank, frequently with gaps of several paces between men. Both regiments fired into each other until the powder smoke hung so thick between them that only their opponents' legs could be seen beneath it. Slowly, the 20th Maine was forced to give ground until its casualties lay behind the enemy's firing line. It was at this moment that Sergeant Andrew J. Tozier, one of the regiment's Colour bearers, won his Medal of Honor. Disapproving of his comrades' retrograde movement, he planted his Colour in the earth to signify that he would retire no further, defending it with discarded muskets and ammunition lying at his feet. This had the desired steadying effect and the fight raged on. It was too hot to last long, for on both sides men were dropping steadily and ammunition was beginning to run out. Colonel William C. Oates, commanding the 15th Alabama, was also seriously alarmed by a report that a body of Federal troops was positioned along a stone wall running to the left of the saddle, to his right rear. This actually consisted of the 20th Maine's Company B, which Chamberlain had deployed as skirmishers, together with some men of the 2nd US Sharpshooters, who had retired there after being driven in by the Confederate advance. Oates, believing that there could be as many as 200 Federals hovering on his flank, therefore decided to withdraw to Round Top. Simultaneously, Chamberlain reached the conclusion that he must either withdraw or counter-attack with the bayonet. He decided upon the latter. Taken aback, the 15th Alabama gave ground and then dissolved as the men behind the wall fired a volley into their flank. The 20th Maine pursued them as far as the slopes of Round Top, then rallied and returned to its position. Its losses amounted to 135 killed and wounded, over one-third of its strength. Oates reported the 15th Alabama's casualties as being 17 killed, 54 wounded and 90 missing, the last being mainly killed or wounded left on Little Round Top.

Yet if one crisis had been resolved, another, equally dangerous, was developing. The remainder of Longstreet's corps had smashed into the awkward salient created by the forward deployment of Sickles's III. In a bitter, stubborn, confused fight lasting four hours the Federals were driven steadily back towards Cemetery Ridge. Names such as The Peach Orchard, The Wheatfield and The Devil's Den would acquire sinister and bloody connotations because of the killing that took place in and around them. In the end, it required counter-attacks by elements of II, V, XII and the newly arrived VI Corps before the line was stabilised on the ridge.

Sickles, whose rash deployment had resulted in this near-disaster, was, after some influential lobbying on his own behalf, awarded the Medal of Honor for the courage and leadership he displayed during the fighting. He was a colourful character who had read law at university and then become deeply involved in New York politics. In 1859 he had shot dead his wife's lover but been acquitted of murder on the grounds of temporary insanity. Two years later he had raised a brigade for the Union cause in New York. Much of his subsequent meteoric rise in rank was due to his political connections. He had little respect or liking for Meade and resented his being appointed army commander. At Gettysburg, although so seriously wounded that his right leg had to be amputated, he continued to conduct a vigorous defence and encourage his troops until he was taken off the field. He did not hold another active field command after the battle. His subsequent career included a term as minister to Spain, where he developed a close personal relationship with Queen Isabella II, and various political and business enterprises.

The stubbornness of III Corps' retreat is encapsulated in the award of the Medal made to Corporal Nathaniel M. Allen of the 1st Massachusetts Infantry. As the regiment was pressed steadily back, Allen, who was carrying the National Colour, noticed that the Regimental Colour was no longer alongside. Glancing behind, he saw that its bearer had been killed and was now lying on top of it. Running back in the teeth of the enemy's fire, he pulled the Colour from under the man's body and brought both it and his own out of action. Two more soldiers of III Corps also received the Medal of Honor, Sergeant Thomas Horan of the 72nd New York Infantry for the capture of the 8th Florida's Regimental Colour during a local counter-attack, and Sergeant Harvey M. Munsell of the 99th Pennsylvania, for gallant and courageous conduct as a Colour bearer throughout the battle, and also for having performed this extremely dangerous duty in no less than thirteen engagements. Elsewhere, the Medal was won by Second Lieutenant Edward M. Knox of the 15th Battery, New York Light Artillery, who, after other batteries had withdrawn, continued to hold his ground until, the horses having been killed, he hauled his gun out of action by hand, being seriously wounded as he did so; and by Bugler Charles W. Reed of the 9th Independent Battery, Massachusetts Light Artillery, who rescued his wounded captain from between the lines.

Inevitably, after the rebels had overrun III Corps' salient they came up against II Corps' positions on Cemetery Ridge, especially after A. P. Hill began committing brigades from the Confederate III Corps to the fray. Earlier in the day, Meade had made II Corps' commander, Major Winfield S. Hancock, responsible for the entire II and III Corps sector, leaving Brigadier General John Gibbon in temporary command of II Corps, members of which would win more Medals of Honor during the battle than any other in the Army of the Potomac. For example, Corporal Raymond W. Hill of the 108th New York volunteered to cross bullet-swept ground to bring forward a box of ammunition to his hard-pressed comrades in the firing line, and Captain James Parke Postles of the 1st Delaware similarly volunteered to deliver a critical order to an embattled unit. Lieutenant James J. Purman and Sergeant James Pipes, both of Company A, 140th Pennsylvania Infantry, which was retiring before the enemy's rapid advance, carried a wounded and helpless comrade to a place of safety, both being themselves wounded in the process, Purman so severely that his left leg had to be amputated; the following year, Pipes, who had been commissioned and risen to the rank of captain, further distinguished himself while commanding a skirmish line at Reames Station, Virginia, sustaining the loss of an arm.

When the Colour party of 126th New York was struck down by an exploding shell, Sergeant George H. Dore ran forward to retrieve the Colour in face of the rapidly advancing enemy, braving the fire of both sides. As II Corps pressed home a vigorous counter-attack Sergeant Hugh Carey of the same regiment captured the Colour of the 7th Virginia Infantry after being twice wounded in the effort. Near by, when the Colour bearer of the 125th New York was shot, Corporal Harrison Clark seized the flag and led the regiment's charge with it. On his own initiative, Captain John B. Fassett of the 23rd Pennsylvania, serving as an aide, led an infantry regiment to the relief of an artillery battery and recaptured its guns from the enemy. The 1st Minnesota, just 262 men strong, made a desperate charge that halted an entire Confederate brigade, incurring 82 per cent casualties, the greatest regimental loss in a single action in American history. During this, Corporal Henry D. O'Brien of the regiment's Company E snatched up the Colours when they fell and rushed ahead towards the enemy ranks, took part in a fierce struggle in which he was wounded, yet refused to hand over the Colours until he was wounded a second time.

In the units that had been rushed forward to prevent a collapse of the line, Private Charles Stacey of the 55th Ohio (XI Corps) voluntarily took an advanced position in the skirmish line in order to locate Confederate sharpshooters, remaining there under heavy fire until his company retired into the main line; and Captain John Lonergan of the 13th Vermont (I Corps) was responsible for the recapture of four guns plus two additional guns from the enemy, as well as a number of prisoners. During the counter-attack phase on the Devil's Den sector, six members of the 6th Pennsylvania Reserves (V Corps) (Corporal Chester S. Furman, Sergeant John W. Hart, Sergeant Wallace W. Johnson, Sergeant George Mears, Corporal J. Levi Roush and Corporal Thaddeus S. Smith) received the award after volunteering to attack a house that had been occupied by a squad of the enemy's sharpshooters and compelling those within to surrender.

Thus far, Ewell's Confederate II Corps had not attacked Cemetery

Hill and Culp's Hill, as the original plan demanded. Indeed, it was not until Longstreet's and Hill's troops began falling back on Seminary Ridge that it went into action. Its attack was made without adequate reconnaissance, was uncoordinated and badly timed. Consequently, it failed in its object, although it did secure a small lodgement on Culp's Hill.

The second day's fighting had therefore ended without decisive result. It was true that the Army of the Potomac had lost some ground, but it was of no tactical value and, once the Round Tops had been reinforced, it was again in a stronger position than it had been when the day began. It had, however, incurred a shocking 9,000 casualties, a factor which, at the commander's conference held by Meade that night, led to a unanimous decision to remain on the defensive next day. Meade predicted that Lee, having unsuccessfully attacked both his flanks, would next attack the centre of the Union line on the sector held by II Corps, command of which was returned to Hancock. This, encouraged by a groundless belief that Meade's centre was weak, was exactly what was in Lee's mind. Longstreet did his best to talk Lee out of it, pointing out not only that such an attack would have to cross a mile of open ground and be cut to pieces by the enemy's fire long before it could come to grips, but also that better results could be obtained by manoeuvring against the Federal left. Lee, over-confident in his troops' ability, declined to accept his advice. Instead, he decided that the attack would by mounted by 13,000 comparatively fresh troops drawn from Longstreet's and Hill's corps. Simultaneously, Stuart's cavalry, which had ridden in from Carlisle to receive a frosty welcome during the afternoon, was to penetrate the enemy's rear areas and fully exploit the chaos that would ensue when Meade's centre was broken.

The morning of 3 July began badly for the Confederates when, after protracted fighting, they were forced off their lodgement on Culp's Hill. Nevertheless, a grand battery of 140 guns was assembled to prepare the way for the great assault on Cemetery Ridge. In response, the Federals allocated some eighty of the 106 guns on the ridge to the counter-battery role, holding a further 136 in reserve until the attack developed. At 13:00 Lee's grand battery opened fire and Meade's replied. The artillery duel lasted about two hours, during which the infantry of both sides sought whatever cover they could find. Some of the Federal guns were knocked out, several limbers exploded and the infantry sustained casualties, but most of the Confederate fire, aimed a little too high, passed over the ridge to explode beyond. The less intense Federal reply was largely ineffective. At about 14:45 the fire of the latter slackened, suggesting that the Confederate artillery had done its work. In fact, the Federals were simply conserving their ammunition to meet the anticipated assault.

At a little before 15:00 Longstreet reluctantly sanctioned the advance. What followed has become known to history as Pickett's Charge, after one of the participating divisional commanders, Major General George E. Pickett. It was an astonishing demonstration of superhuman courage and determination. Paying particular attention to their dressing, the Confederates emerged from the trees of Seminary Ridge, descended the forward slopes and began marching across the shallow valley as though they were taking part in a review. They immediately became the target of every Federal gun from Cemetery Hill to the Round Tops. The gaps shot in their ranks were immediately closed. Soon they came within killing range of II Corps's infantry, lining stone walls and entrenchments along the crest of Cemetery Ridge. Now more of the rebels were falling or limping their painful way back across the valley, but still they came on. Some 400 yards short of their objective they increased their pace, despite the fact that the Federal artillery had switched to canister and was tearing the ranks apart. The head of the great column, dimly seen through a fog of smoke and dust, was constantly being shot away, although fallen Colours were constantly raised and continued to advance towards the summit. Feelings of sincere admiration, tinged with fellow feeling and pity, stirred among those waiting to receive the assault. A Vermont brigade wheeled out of the Federal line and began raking the attackers from their right flank. Even so, the attackers were now so close that Union gunners began hastily limbering up and heading for the rear, together with some of the fainter-hearted who quailed before the advance of these superb soldiers. Led by Brigadier General Lewis Armistead, a small body of Confederates, numbering not less than 150 and not more than 350, smashed through the Federal line and overran a wrecked battery. Armistead was mortally wounded almost at once and in a brief, savage fight, his men were surrounded and forced to surrender by Federal regiments converging on the penetration. The remainder of the attackers, finally recognising that the position was hopeless, began shredding away to the rear. Harried by elements of II Corps, their retreat was covered by hitherto uncommitted brigades and by the Confederate artillery. Lee, horrified by the enormity of his mistake, rode out to meet the survivors and honestly accepted responsibility for the disaster. About half of those who had taken part in the attack failed to return.

Yet heroism was by no means confined to Lee's troops that day. On Cemetery Ridge, Hancock and Gibbon had recklessly exposed themselves to encourage their troops during the bombardment and the attack, and both had been wounded. Once more, the roll of II Corps's Medal of Honor winners was long and impressive. When five of Battery A 4th US Artillery's six guns were disabled and all the battery's officers had been killed or wounded, command devolved until Sergeant Frederick Fuger, who continued to fight with the remaining gun until orders came for the battery to be withdrawn. Colonel Wheelock G. Veazey, commanding the 16th Vermont Infantry, wheeled his regiment out of line under heavy fire, charging and dispersing an enemy brigade on the right flank of the Confederate attack, a remarkable achievement given that his troops were fighting their first battle. As the rebels closed in on the crest, the Colour bearer of the 14th Tennessee planted his Colour just 50 yards in front of the 14th Connecticut's position. Major Ellis, commanding the latter, called for volunteers to capture the flag, around which the enemy had lain down and opened fire. The call was answered by Sergeant Major William B. Hincks and two more soldiers, one of whom was shot as the trio vaulted the stone wall. Outrunning his remaining companion, Hincks passed through a storm of bullets and seized the Colour, brandishing his sword at the prostrate rebels and overawing them with a flow of senior non-commissioned invective. He then returned to his own lines with the Colour, upon which a dozen battle honours were inscribed. His citation records that his act provided encouragement for his regiment at the crucial moment of the battle. As the rebels broke into Federal lines Major Edmund Rice of the 19th Massachusetts led a counter-charge and in the subsequent hand-to-hand fighting was severely wounded, having penetrated deep into the opposing ranks. During this fight four more members of the same regiment received the award for the capture of enemy Colours – Corporal Joseph H. de Castro for those of the 19th Virginia, Sergeant Benjamin H. Jellison and Private John H. Robinson for that of the 57th Virginia, and Colour Sergeant Benjamin F. Falls for that of an unspecified regiment. In the fighting along the summit and in following up the Confederate withdrawal yet more Colours were captured. Private Elijah W. Bacon and Corporal Christopher Flynn, both of the 14th Connecticut, took those of, respectively, the 16th Carolina and 52nd Carolina; Captain Morris Brown, Jr., and Private Jerry Wall, both of the 126th New York, each took those of an unspecified unit; Private John E. Clopp of the 71st Pennsylvania took those of the 9th Virginia, wresting them from the hands of the Colour bearer; Privates John B. Mayberry and Bernard McCarren, both of the 1st Delaware, each captured the flag of an unspecified unit; Corporal John Miller of the 8th Ohio captured two unspecified flags, and Private James Richmond of the same regiment captured a further unspecified flag; Private Marshall Sherman of the 1st Minnesota took the Colours of the 28th Virginia; Sergeant James H. Thompson of the 1st Pennsylvania Rifles took those of the 15th Georgia; and Sergeant James Wiley of the 59th New York took those of an unspecified Georgia regiment. A further Medal of Honor was awarded to Private Oliver P. Reed of the 20th Indiana, a III Corps unit ordered by Meade to converge on the area of the Confederate attack, for the capture of the Colours of the 21st North Carolina.

The jubilation on Cemetery Ridge was entirely understandable, as was the depressed atmosphere on Seminary Ridge opposite. Lee's cup of sorrow was not quite full, however, for three miles to the east of Meade's main position Stuart's cavalry had not only failed to break into the Federal rear areas, but had also been fought to a standstill. The only bright moment of the Confederate day came during the evening when Federal cavalry rashly charged unshaken infantry on Longstreet's right flank and were shot to pieces.

On 4 July both armies, now very tired, remained in their positions. Lee no longer possessed the strength to mount an attack, and Meade did not wish to mount one – indeed, had he done so, he would almost certainly have received a bloody nose. During the afternoon the hot, humid weather in which the battle had been fought broke in a torrential downpour. Under cover of this, Lee sent off his wounded and then began to withdraw his army into Virginia.

The Battle of Gettysburg cost the Army of the Potomac 3,155 killed, 14,529 wounded and 5,365 missing, a total of 23,049; the Army of Northern Virginia lost 3,903 killed, 18,735 wounded and 5,425 missing, a total of 28,063. This was more than the limited manpower resources of the southern states could afford. As Lee's army continued upon its retreat, the Confederacy received two further crushing blows, for on 4 July the fortress of Vicksburg surrendered and much of Tennessee passed into Federal hands. Nevertheless, it would fight grimly on for two more years in the hope that war-weariness would induce Washington to settle for a negotiated peace.

Mobile Bay
5 AUGUST 1864

By the late summer of 1864 it was appreciated by both sides that the Confederacy was incapable of winning the Civil War, yet such was the determined nature of its resistance that a negotiated peace remained a distinct possibility. There were many in the north who were anxious to end the continued loss of life, or sought to restore the civil liberties that had been be curtailed, or wanted resumption of normal commercial activity. This feeling of war-weariness seriously threatened President Abraham Lincoln's chances of being re-elected in November, as well as providing encouragement for his rival, General George B. McClellan, whose Democratic Party was known to be in favour of bringing the conflict to an end as quickly as possible.

Lincoln had recently appointed General Ulysses S. Grant as the US Army's General-in-Chief. Grant was in favour of fighting the war through to the bitter end. Aware that the Achilles' heel of the Confederacy lay in its limited manpower resources, he decided to impose a policy of remorseless attrition. This would be achieved first by wearing down Lee's Army of Northern Virginia in a series of battles it could not avoid, and simultaneously directing Major General William T. Sherman's western armies to carve a swathe across the main body of the Confederacy by taking Atlanta and marching onwards to the sea. As part of this strategy it was planned to take the port of Mobile, Alabama, as this would not only divert Confederate troops from Sherman's front, but also signal to Napoleon III, who had intervened militarily in Mexican affairs, that despite the rebellion the United States was still a power to be reckoned with in the area. Above all, it was essential that the Lincoln administration should be provided with a tangible success that would demonstrate that victory over the Confederacy was within sight.

Mobile was also chosen as an objective because it was a favourite destination for blockade runners, whose fast ships kept the Confederacy supplied with vital war materials. In Nassau, Bahamas, or in a Cuban port, the blockade runners would exchange southern cotton for these materials and then wait for a dark and preferably moonless night to slip past the US Navy's patrolling warships to a Confederate harbour. Their base at Mobile was guarded by a small squadron of Confederate warships under the command of Admiral Franklin Buchanan. The largest of Buchanan's ships was the *Tennessee*, designed for ramming but too slow for the role, whose great guns, engine and boiler were protected by a stoutly armoured casemate amidships. Also under Buchanan's command were three smaller and less well protected gunboats, the *Morgan*, the *Gaines* and the *Selma*. In addition, the entrance to Mobile Bay was defended by the guns of Fort Morgan to the east and Fort Gaines to the west, between which lay no less than 180 tethered mines, known at the time as torpedoes.

The task of eliminating Buchanan's ships and taking physical possession of Mobile Bay was given to Rear Admiral David Glasgow Farragut's West Gulf Blockading Squadron, which he had successfully led at the capture of New Orleans and in the operations against Vicksburg. The squadron reflected the changing technology of the time in that it included fourteen wooden ships, including his own flagship, the USS *Hartford*, equipped with sail as well as steam propulsion, and four steam-driven ironclad monitors, *Tecumseh*, *Manhattan*, *Winnebago* and *Chickasaw*. The monitors were similar in design to their semi-submersible namesake that had fought an epic duel with the Confederate ironclad *Merrimack (Virginia)* in Hampton Roads two years earlier, although some were fitted with two revolving gun turrets.

At about 08:00 on the morning of 5 August Farragut's squadron, deployed in two lines with the monitors to starboard and the wooden warships to port, began approaching the entrance to Mobile Bay. Fort Morgan promptly opened fire and the Confederate squadron, led by the *Tennessee*, steamed down the bay to meet them, opening fire as soon as they were within range. While the monitor *Tecumseh* was manoeuvring to engage the *Tennessee*, her hull was shaken by an explosion and a fountain of water erupted alongside. She had struck a mine and began to sink immediately. Recognising the cause of the explosion, the steam sloop *Brooklyn*, leading the port column, promptly went astern and came to a standstill. Together, these two events combined to throw both Federal lines into temporary disarray, but Farragut, while conscious of the danger presented by the minefield, was not to be deterred, giving vent to his famous expletive, 'Damn the torpedoes! Full speed ahead!'

The engagement now became general, with shot and shell flying thick and fast. Through this the crew of a boat lowered by the USS *Metacomet* pulled steadily towards the stricken *Tecumseh*, winning the admiration of both sides, and succeeded in saving ten men from the semi-submersible as she went under. Elsewhere, the small Federal gunboat *Philippi* sustained such serious damage that she had to be run aground near Fort Morgan. The last ship in Farragut's line, the USS *Oneida*, had her steering gear shot away and a shell burst her boiler, scalding the engine-room crew with steam. The *Galena*, coming alongside to assist her, also sustained heavy damage, although, after the two ships had been lashed together, she succeeded in towing her out of range. The punishment, however, was far from being one-sided. One of the Confederate gunboats, the CSS *Gaines*, was sunk, and a second, the *Selma*, was so badly damaged that she surrendered. Admiral Buchanan's third gunboat, the CSS *Morgan*, under Commander G. W. Harrison, put several damaging broadsides into Farragut's flagship and other Federal vessels, but the odds against her were too great to sustain. As Farragut's squadron fought its way into the interior of the bay, Harrison headed for the cover provided by the guns of Fort Morgan, grounding briefly but holding off the pursuit of the *Metacomet*. Having reached comparative safety, he later despatched a boat that completed the destruction of the grounded *Philippi*.

The battle was far from over. The mighty Confederate ram *Tennessee*, now isolated and bypassed by her opponents, turned slowly back into the centre of the bay in a desperate lone attempt to sink or at least damage some of her many opponents. The ensuing fight bore some resemblance to a medieval bear-baiting contest in which the huge bear beats off the tormenting dogs one after another. Belching fire and smoke from her guns, the *Tennessee* was surrounded by Farragut's ships. She was rammed several times by the steam sloops *Lackawanna* and *Monongahela*, but in the process they sustained more damage than their target. She was next rammed by the *Hartford*, with similar lack of result, and subjected to the fire of every Federal gun that would bear. The armoured monitors *Manhattan* and *Chickasaw* closed in from ahead and astern, followed by the third monitor, the *Winnebago*. Their fire cut the *Tennessee*'s exposed steering chain so that she became unmanageable, and shot her funnel to tatters, thereby reducing the power reaching her engines. The chains holding up the gun-port shutters were shot away, the result being that as one shutter after another fell into place the Confederate gunners were unable to return fire. Finally, the 15-inch gun mounted by the *Monongahela* punched a hole through the massive armoured casemate, which was further weakened by the fire of *Chickasaw*'s two 13-inch guns from astern. As the *Tennessee* was now unable to steer, steam or fight, the wounded Admiral Buchanan recognised that the ship had been fought to her limits and at about 10:15 authorised her captain, Commander James W. Johnston, to surrender.

The Battle of Mobile Bay resulted in the award of almost one-third of the 322 Medals of Honor earned by the US Navy and Marine Corps for the entire Civil War, perhaps because it was considered essential to emphasise a decisive victory at a moment of great political sensitivity. Many of the awards, particularly those applicable to the USS *Hartford, Brooklyn* and *Richmond,* went to men who had performed their duties in an exemplary manner. This was not the stated purpose of the Medal and in a later era the recipients would have been honoured with a less prestigious award or a commendation. Of these exemplary conduct awards, Coxswain John Cooper's of the *Brooklyn* is notable in that the following year he won a second Medal of Honor rescuing a comrade from certain death in an ammunition fire. Coxswain Edward Price, also of the *Brooklyn*, showed great presence of mind when, after the sponge stave broke in the barrel of his gun, he cleared the blockage by pouring powder in the weapon's vent hole and fired it to blow the sponge head out. Also aboard the *Brooklyn* was Seaman Joseph Irlam, who was stationed at the wheel. When heavy fire struck down several men at their guns, leaving the crews short-handed, Irlam released two men stationed with him to join them, remaining at the wheel throughout the action with only one man to assist him. One award, made to Captain of the Forecastle John Smith of the *Lackawanna*, contains an element of humour, for, finding it impossible to depress his gun sufficiently when his ship was alongside the *Tennessee*, Smith, enraged, flung a holystone at a rebel, shouting abuse at him from one of the latter's gun ports.

Nevertheless, there were many men who did display the supreme courage required for the award, including Seaman James Avery, Quarter Gunner Charles Baker, Ordinary Seaman John Donnelly, Captain of the Forecastle John Harris, Seaman Henry Johnson and Landsman Daniel Noble, who manned the boat sent by the *Metacomet* to the assistance of the stricken *Tecumseh*. Aboard the *Hartford*, Landsman Wilson Brown was blown into the ship's hold by the explosion of a shell that fatally wounded the man on the ladder above him. On recovering consciousness, Brown returned to his station at the shell whip on the berth deck and remained there although four of the six men manning this station were killed or wounded by the enemy's fire. When a shell burst between the *Hartford*'s two forward 9-inch guns, killing or wounding fifteen men, Coxswain Thomas Fitzpatrick was struck in the face by several splinters. Disregarding his injuries, within the space of a few minutes he had his gun in working order again with a new track, breeching and side tackle, and had cleared the area of casualties, serving as an inspiration to the crew. During the same incident, Ordinary Seaman Charles Melville, who had been taken below to have his wound dressed, returned to his gun and continued to serve it, though barely able to stand. Likewise, when the other members of his gun crew were either killed or wounded, Landsman William Pelham assisted the wounded below and then joined the crew of an adjoining gun which was short-handed. A shellburst severed the toe of Coal Heaver James Gardner, who was serving at a shell whip. He bandaged the wound himself and continued to perform his duties until severely wounded by another shellburst. Landsman John Lawson was hit in the leg and flung violently against the side of the ship when an enemy shell killed or wounded the entire six-man crew of the shell whip at which he was working on the berth deck. Coming to, Lawson returned to his station and remained there, refusing to go below for treatment. Shell Man William A. Stanley also received serious wounds but continued to handle ammunition until, weak from loss of blood, he was forced to go below.

Aboard the badly damaged *Oneida*, Quartermaster John E. Jones, stationed at the wheel, was wounded when the steering ropes were shot away but, in the teeth of the enemy's fire, went to the poop to relay signals as the *Calena* came alongside, then set about reeving new wheel ropes. One of the *Oneida*'s landsmen, David Naylor, was serving as a powder boy at the 30-pdr Parrott gun when his passing box was shot from his hands and fell into one of the *Calena*'s boats, which at that time lay under the bow. Undaunted by his narrow escape, Naylor jumped into the boat, retrieved the box and returned to his duties. Another of the ship's landsmen, John Preston, though seriously wounded, remained with his gun crew until ordered to go to the surgeon, to whom he reported himself as being 'only slightly injured'. He assisted with the wounded but made so many requests to return to his gun that the surgeon examined him for a second time, discovering that he had sustained serious damage to both eyes. Quartermaster James Sheridan, captain of one of the *Oneida*'s 11-inch guns, received several wounds but remained at his station until firing had ceased, then took the place of the signals quartermaster, who had been injured by a fall.

Elsewhere, two of the *Lackawanna*'s crew particularly distinguished themselves. When an enemy shell exploded in the ship's magazine,

Armourer George Taylor, already wounded, ran into the compartment and extinguished the resulting fire by hand. On deck, Quarter Gunner James Ward refused to go below when wounded, assisted for a while at one of the guns when most of the crew were struck down, but for most of the action remained in the chains, where, terribly exposed to the enemy's fire, he continued to heave the lead until almost thrown overboard when his ship rammed the *Tennessee*. Coxswain Thomas Taylor of the *Metacomet* received an unusual but deserved award of the Medal by encouraging the crew of the ship's forward pivot gun when the officer in charge displayed cowardice, thereby 'bringing honor to the occasion', as his citation comments.

The Battle of Mobile Bay was an undisputed victory for the Union, although the Confederate Navy took some comfort from the fact that the tonnage lost by each side was approximately equal (two Federal warships sunk in exchange for one of its own lost and two surrendered) and had inflicted by far the heavier casualties (13 killed and 20 wounded as against 145 killed and 170 wounded). Furthermore, under cover of darkness the CSS *Morgan* made good her escape to Mobile, hotly pursued by Federal warships during her voyage up the bay. Mobile itself remained in Confederate hands until April 1865. Fort Gaines was surrendered with undue haste shortly after the battle, but Fort Morgan, bombarded by land and sea, continued an honourable resistance for a further two weeks.

Although the port of Mobile was now closed to blockade runners, the effect of Farragut's victory was primarily psychological, reinforcing as it did the argument of Lincoln's supporters that the war *could* be fought to a finish. After the battle, the Confederacy continued its stubborn resistance for a year, but its fortunes declined steadily until its ability to wage war had been so reduced that surrender became inevitable.

The Sioux War of 1876

In the years following the Civil War the United States began to expand westwards at an unprecedented rate. Some of those who sought new homes for themselves in the apparently limitless lands available were restless former soldiers who had been unsettled by the war. Others were immigrants who had delayed their departure for the New World until the war ended and whose wagon trains crossed the Great Plains in ever increasing numbers. The settlers established farms, ranches, factories, and communities where none had existed before, the process being accelerated as railways and telegraph lines snaked out towards one another from east and west.

Naturally, the process impinged on the territory of the Plains Indians, who had hunted and pursued their nomadic lifestyle across these vast areas without restraint since time immemorial. They now saw their freedom and the things they valued most being taken from them by strangers to the land and they fought back hard to stem the tide of white men that seemed about to overwhelm them. Many found the government's concept of tribal reservations demeaning in that they already regarded the land as their own, while others were angered by the apparent inability of the Great White Father, as they called the President, to enforce among his own citizens the treaties that had been signed in his name. Consequently, savage violence between red and white men was commonplace along what has become known as the Old Frontier, and it fell to the much-reduced US Army to keep the peace to the best of its abilities.

One area which generated considerable trouble was the Montana goldfields, which were difficult to reach save by a route known as the Bozeman Trail which left Fort Laramie, Wyoming, and led north-west-wards through the Powder River country into Montana. Unfortunately, the route passed through the best hunting grounds of the warlike Sioux, Cheyenne and Arapaho, who not only regarded certain areas as sacred but were also under the impression that all the territory between the

Black Hills of Wyoming and South Dakota, the Big Horn Mountains and the Yellowstone River had been recognised as being theirs in perpetuity. However, as the government had expended most of its gold reserves during the Civil War and was anxious to renew them, it required the tribes to open the Bozeman Trail to prospectors, which the Indians declined to do. In response, the army established a series of badly sited forts along the trail in a vain attempt to protect civilian travellers. It was from the garrison of one of these, Fort Phil Kearny, that an insubordinate officer, Captain William Fetterman, led eighty men into an ambush in which all were massacred and mutilated on 21 December 1866. The army was to extract some measure of revenge but it became apparent that protection of the Bozeman Trail was not an economic proposition. In 1868 a treaty was concluded recognising the rights of the Sioux to the land and the forts along the trail were abandoned, after which they were burned by the triumphant Indians.

All might have settled down had not more gold been discovered in the Black Hills some seven years later. The army strove to keep the hordes of prospectors out, but it was an impossible task. In an attempt to keep the peace the government offered to buy the mineral rights from the Indians, who rejected the sum proffered as being inadequate. In the autumn of 1875 the Sioux and Cheyenne broke out of their reservation and began to hunt and raid in territories that had not been ceded to them. They pointedly ignored a proclamation issued on 3 December warning them that they would be treated as hostile unless they returned to the reservation by 31 January 1876. In March of that year an attempt to coerce them was fiercely resisted during an engagement at the Powder River, leaving no one in any doubt that the tribes were spoiling for a fight. The army therefore began moving units into positions from which the rising could be contained and the Indians driven back to their reservation.

The architect of the plan was Major General Alfred J. Terry, commanding the Department of Dakota. Terry had no accurate information regarding the Indians' whereabouts, although they were thought to be somewhere in the wide area between the Yellowstone River and the Big Horn Mountains, and probably camped on one or more of the Yellowstone's tributaries, the Powder, the Tongue, the Rosebud or the Big Horn. His intelligence suggested that he would be faced by perhaps 800 braves, although the truth was that for once the tribes were moving together and were capable of deploying in excess of 1,500 warriors. However, working on the low estimate supplied by the Indian Bureau,

Terry envisaged the converging advance of three columns, each of which would be capable of dealing with any such opposition and shepherding the Indians back to their reservation. The first column, under Colonel John Gibbon, consisting of six companies of the 7th Infantry and four troops of the 2nd Cavalry, a total of 450 men, would march east along the northern bank of the Yellowstone from Fort Ellis. The second, under Terry's personal command, consisted of twelve troops of the 7th Cavalry, two companies of the 17th Infantry and a detachment of 20th Infantry manning three Gatling machine-guns, a total of 950 men; this was to leave Fort Abraham Lincoln on 17 May and march west along the Yellowstone until it effected a junction with Gibbon's force. The third column, under Brigadier General George Crook, comprising five troops of the 2nd and ten of the 3rd Cavalry, plus two companies of the 4th and three of the 9th Infantry, more than 1,000 men, was to leave Fort Fetterman on 29 May and enter the operational area from the south. In theory the Indians would be trapped between Terry's northern and southern elements as they converged and be forced to submit. In fact, because the two elements were separated by several hundred miles, they could neither provide mutual support for the other's operations, nor even communicate directly with each other. Furthermore, the tribes possessed interior lines and were thus able to concentrate against each of Terry's columns in turn, thereby discounting his numerical superiority.

It was Crook's column that got into action first. Crook's experience of fighting Indians was confined mainly to the south-west, where hit-and-run raids, ambushes and pursuits were the norm. Consequently, he was a great believer in mobility, mounting his infantry on mules so that they could keep up with his cavalry on the march. Likewise, he preferred to travel with as few wagons as possible, leaving those that he had in a secure area and using more mules to keep the fighting troops supplied. What he did not expect, and nor did anyone else, was that the Sioux and Cheyenne were eager and prepared to fight a major battle or two against the army.

On the evening of 16 June Crook's column bedded down for the night beside the upper reaches of the Rosebud River, so called because of the plentiful wild roses that grew along its banks. There Crook received a warning from the Sioux leaders, Chiefs Sitting Bull and Crazy Horse, telling him that if he crossed the river he did so at his peril.

His command crossed the following morning, behind a screen of 300 Indian scouts. The crossing was made on a wide frontage, with the cavalry on the left and the mounted infantry on the right. Both were immediately assailed by waves of charging Indians. The cavalry held its own with difficulty, but the infantry were forced to abandon their mules and form a defensive circle on high ground. This was assailed so fiercely that the circle was split first into two portions, then four. However, the infantrymen held their ground and at length their attackers fell back. The battle raged on, with attack followed by counter-attack. By noon, Crook was able to regain some sort of control over the situation. Believing that a hostile village was situated some miles downstream, he despatched Captain Anson Mills with eight troops of cavalry to take it. Some minutes later, he observed from high ground that the hills on either side of the valley closed in on the river at a point known as Dead Canyon. As Mills would have had to pass through this to reach the village, and it seemed an ideal spot for an ambush, Crook changed his mind, sending his aide and an orderly to recall him. No sooner had Mills received his fresh orders than the Indians mounted a new attack on the main body of the column. Instead of retracing his steps directly upstream, therefore, he decided to ride obliquely across the battlefield, behind the attacking Sioux and Cheyenne. This unsettled the enemy, who, after a fight lasting six hours, finally began fading away from the battlefield.

Crook's casualties amounted to 28 killed and 56 wounded. Crazy Horse later admitted that 36 of his braves had been killed, and 63 wounded. The troops and their Crow and Shoshoni Indian scouts had fought well and retained the battlefield, enabling Crook to claim a victory. Three members of the 3rd Cavalry were awarded the Medal of Honor, First Sergeants Michael A. McGann and John H. Shingle for gallantry in action, and First Sergeant Joseph Robinson, for his coolness and courage in command of the skirmish line and for bringing up the lead horses at a critical moment during the fluid fighting. Nevertheless, Crook had been badly shaken by the Indians' ferocity and determination. His losses had been heavier than expected and he had expended a prodigious quantity of ammunition. The following day, therefore, he decided to retreat across the river and fall back on his supply base at Goose Creek, near the modern town of Sheridan, thereby turning a modest tactical victory into a strategic defeat. Cock-a-hoop, the Indians watched him go, then returned to their main encampment on the Little Big Horn River with the news that the army had been beaten, raising the tribes' war frenzy to fever pitch. Nothing was now more certain that when the soldiers came again, they would receive an even warmer welcome.

Meanwhile, unaware of Crook's reverse, which put the whole operational plan in jeopardy, on 21 June General Terry held a commanders' conference aboard the river steamer *Far West*, moored beside the northern bank of the Yellowstone. Those present included Colonel Gibbon, Lieutenant Colonel George Armstrong Custer, commanding the 7th Cavalry, and Major James Brisbin, commanding the four troops of the 2nd Cavalry. Terry's Indian scouts believed that the Sioux were encamped in the valley of the Little Big Horn, an opinion confirmed by a reconnaissance in force carried out by Major Marcus Reno, Custer's second-in-command, which had come across a well-used trail leading in that direction some days earlier. Terry, anxious to trap them there, ordered Custer to lead his regiment up the Rosebud, then cross the watershed and drive down the Little Big Horn valley, specifically avoiding the trail discovered by Reno; simultaneously, Gibbon's command was to be ferried across the Yellowstone to the mouth of the Big Horn, from where he was to march into the valley of the Little Big Horn from the north, so providing an anvil against which the enemy would be driven by Custer's advance down the valley. Custer declined the offer of the Gatling machine-guns, which he believed would slow him down, and also the addition of Brisbin's four troops to his command, undoubtedly because he wished such credit as was to be earned to be his and his regiment's alone.

A library has been written about Custer, and while this is not the place to enter into a discussion of the man, some mention of his career is necessary as his personality was a major factor in what followed. On the outbreak of the Civil War he had graduated from West Point at the bottom of his class. He had served with the 5th Cavalry at the First Battle of Bull Run. His courage was beyond doubt, as was that of his brother Tom, who twice won the Medal of Honor during the war. George Custer was also dashing and had a good eye for the tactical battle. In 1862 he was promoted captain and was breveted a total of five times for gallantry during the war, which he ended commanding the Michigan Cavalry as a major general of volunteers. He displayed an indifference to established tactical doctrine, the fact that he was so often successful being ascribed by himself to 'Custer's Luck'. On the darker side, while averse to discipline himself, he would impose it in no small measure. After the war, he reverted to his substantive rank of lieutenant colonel, although he continued to be addressed as general as a matter of courtesy. He was given command of the 7th Cavalry, which, because its troops served together for most of the time, he was able to turn into a fine regiment with a strong *esprit de corps*. With it he executed ruthless dawn raids on troublesome Indian encampments during the winter months, hanging any brave not killed in the fighting, making prisoners of the women and children, slaughtering the tribe's pony herd and burning its tepees. Understandably, he was cordially hated by his victims, to whom he was known as Yellow Hair. There was, too, another equally unattractive facet to his character. Given to self-projection in an inordinate manner, he designed his own unofficial uniforms and saw to it that the press reported every detail of his numerous successes to an appreciative public. He also sought the admiration of superiors and subordinates alike; those of the latter who failed to provide it in full measure were not only excluded from the charmed inner circle over which he and the beautiful Mrs Custer presided at Fort Abraham Lincoln, but also seriously damaged their promotion prospects. Recently, however, he had come within a hair's breadth of losing command of the 7th when he made unsubstantiated charges of corruption against the administration of President U. S. Grant. Chastened, he had set out on the present campaign determined to perform some spectacular act that would restore his standing, and, as luck would have it, the written orders he received after the conference on the *Far West* contained the following paragraph: 'The Department Commander places too much confidence in your zeal, energy and ability to wish to impose upon you precise orders which might hamper your action when nearly in contact with the enemy.' In other words, Custer could do as he pleased.

On 22 June Custer led the 7th Cavalry into the Rosebud valley. The following day, in intense heat, the regiment covered 35 miles. On the 24th it was in the saddle continuously from 05:00 until noon, having marched a further 45 miles. The weary men and animals were granted a three-hour rest, then the march was resumed until the trail discovered by Reno was reached. Custer's orders, it will be remembered, required him to cross it and proceed to the headwaters of the Rosebud before crossing the watershed into the Little Big Horn valley, and timing of the entire operation depended upon this. They also instructed him in positive terms *not* to use the trail. Custer, however, wanted to be at the Sioux first and, placing the widest possible interpretation upon the discretionary powers he had been granted, decided to do just that. At 20:00 he summoned his officers, telling them that the march would continue throughout the night, and that the regiment would rest the following day and attack on the 26th. During a night march lasting five hours the 7th followed the trail up the Wolf Mountains, the range separating the Rosebud from the Little Big Horn, but covered only 10 miles. Close to the watershed Custer halted while his Indian scouts climbed a high point to look down into the valley below. They reported a huge pony herd and the smoke from many breakfast fires. This, together with the size of the trail, convinced them that the gathering of hostiles was far larger than had been anticipated. Shortly after, it became apparent that the regiment's progress was being watched from high ground by more Indians.

All chance of surprise had now been lost, yet Custer, obsessed with restoring his reputation, decided to attack immediately in the belief that if he did not do so the Sioux and Cheyenne would escape from the trap Terry had prepared for them. Having already disobeyed his orders, he took the decision in the full knowledge that his men and horses alike were deadly tired. Furthermore, these errors were compounded by completely ignoring the tactical manual as, without adequate reconnaissance or any knowledge of the Indians' strength or positions, he decided to divide the regiment in the presence of the enemy. Captain Frederick W. Benteen, the regiment's senior captain, with whom Custer shared a mutual antipathy, was to take three troops and carry out a reconnaissance over the hills to the south. Benteen's deliberately vague orders were to prevent the Indians escaping in that direction, to engage any hostiles he might find, or to return to the regiment, as circumstances dictated. Obviously, as the principal action was to be fought further down the valley, if any credit was to be earned during the day, Benteen would not share in it. Secondly, Major Reno, whom Custer did not care much for either, was to cross the Little Big Horn with another three troops and mount a strong diversionary attack on the southern end of the great village. While this was in progress, Custer, with five troops under his personal command, would launch the main attack on the opposite end of the village from behind the hills to the east. Finally, the pack train, escorted by the remaining troop under Captain Thomas McDougall, was to accompany Benteen.

By midday the 7th had crossed the watershed and was moving down the stream that was to become known as Benteen's Creek, with Custer's and Reno's columns on opposite banks. At about 14:00 a party of some forty Sioux were seen galloping away from an abandoned tepee. Custer sent Reno an order to advance as quickly as he thought prudent and commence his diversionary attack. Shortly after, the two columns went their separate ways, Reno's continuing down the stream to the point where it entered the Little Big Horn, Custer's towards the high ground on the right. Reno forded the river, halted briefly to tighten his girths, then deployed into line and advanced across the flood plain towards the village. At about this time, a figure, believed to have been Custer, was seen waving his hat in encouragement from a bluff across the river. What is certain is that Custer was now aware of the size of the Indian village and decided that he needed Benteen's help after all, for he despatched Sergeant Daniel Kanipe to hurry the pack train forward, followed by Trumpeter John Martin to fetch Benteen and his three troops. Neither Kanipe nor Martin were aware of it at the time, but they were the luckiest men in the regiment.

The Indians spotted near the abandoned tepee had now reached the encampment to give warning of the 7th's approach, so that Reno had barely time to sound the Charge before hundreds of hostiles came swarming out of the village towards him. His open left flank was quickly turned and he ordered a withdrawal to a copse beside the river. He quickly decided that since this was untenable he must reach the high ground across the river if any of his men were to survive. As the Indians were found to be in possession of his original crossing place, he used another. Here, the withdrawal became a disorderly rout, for the horses at first refused to descend the high river bank and the enemy became intermingled with his own men. Somehow, many of the troopers managed to break free of the mêlée, cross the river and drag their mounts up the steep slopes of a flat-topped bluff that would become known as Reno's Hill. Three officers, twenty-nine troopers and scouts were known to have been killed, seven were wounded, and the fate of another fifteen remained unknown, the total accounting for approximately half of Reno's command. The survivors prepared to fight for their lives.

They could hear the sound of heavy firing to the north, but the fate of Custer's column remained unknown. Only two things were certain. Custer had decided not to wait for Benteen, and his Crow Indian scouts, scenting disaster, had simply ridden off. The column, strung out over three-quarters of a mile, continued along the ridge northwards and had reached an area from which an attack on the village could be mounted. At this point, a chief named Gall led a large body of Indians across the river and up a re-entrant to attack the column. Simultaneously, Crazy Horse led an even larger body round the northern end of the ridge to attack from the opposite direction. More Indians, having repulsed Reno, closed in on the column's rear. As to the events of the next hour or so, all we know is the little the Indians chose to relate. One account says that the five troops 'kept in order and fought like brave warriors as long as they had a man left'; another that 'they made five brave stands'. No one escaped, nor was anyone spared. The exact number of men who died with Custer may never be known, although it exceeded two hundred. Among them were his brother Thomas, commanding C Troop, another brother, Boston, who was serving as a civilian guide, a nephew, Henry Reed, who was simply along for the ride, and his brother-in-law, Lieutenant James Calhoun, commanding L Troop. Perhaps some might have cut their way out had sabres been carried, but they seldom were on the frontier because of the noise caused by their rattling. About fifty Sioux and Cheyenne were killed during the fighting, and a larger number are said to have died from their wounds later.

When Benteen reached Reno's position at about 16:15 the situation was far from clear. Reno, badly shaken, stated his intention of remaining on the defensive. However, hearing the continued sound of fighting, some officers, led by Captain Thomas Weir, insubordinately took their men forward along the ridge in the vain hope that they could assist Custer. They reached the point from which Custer had watched Reno's attack develop, but all they could see in the distance were dust clouds and galloping Indians. Almost immediately, they came under fierce attack themselves and were forced to conduct a disorderly retreat to Reno's Hill. Desperately, as the Indians closed in to finish the hated 7th Cavalry once and for all, the defenders beat off one assault after another, piling ration and ammunition boxes from the pack train into makeshift breastworks whenever there was a pause. At sunset, the attacks slackened, but by then another eighteen men had been killed and forty-three wounded.

Most of the Indians retired to the village for a night-long celebration of their victory, but many remained in the vicinity of Reno's Hill, which remained under sporadic fire. The numerous wounded began suffering the agonies of thirst. A successful plan was devised whereby four volunteers deliberately made targets of themselves on the summit for twenty minutes, during which they provided covering fire while a party descended to the river and filled water bottles. The four volunteers – Sergeant George Geiger, Blacksmith Henry Mechlin, Saddler Otto Voit and Private Charles Windolph – all received the Medal of Honor. So, too, did every member of the water party, a multiple award that was criticised in some quarters. Despite this, some members of the party undeniably acquitted themselves beyond the strict call of duty during the battle. Sergeant Rufus Hutchinson, for example, carried wounded men to a place of safety under fire and provided leadership for his troop throughout the battle, while Private Peter Thompson, shot through the head on his first descent to the river, insisted on making two more trips, contrary to his sergeant's orders. Others who received the award for their part in the battle included Sergeant Benjamin C. Criswell, who recovered the body of Lieutenant Hodgson from within the enemy's lines, brought up ammunition and encouraged the men in the most exposed positions; Corporal Charles Cunningham, who refused to leave the firing line when wounded in the neck and fought on throughout the engagement; Sergeant Richard P. Hanley, who single-handedly and without orders, recaptured a stampeded pack mule laden with ammunition; Private Henry Hoden, who distributed ammunition under fire; and Sergeant Thomas Murray, who brought up the pack train under fire and, on the second day, distributed rations while the position was under attack.

During the night, one officer and several men who had remained hidden in the riverside copse since Reno's retreat, managed to reach the summit of the hill safely. On the morning of 26 June the Sioux and Cheyenne resumed their attacks on the hill, two determined assaults on the summit being beaten off. To Reno's relief, during the afternoon, the Indians broke camp and disappeared in the direction of the Big Horn Mountains, setting fire to the grass as they left. Being so heavily encumbered with wounded, he decided to remain where he was.

Terry and Gibbon entered the valley from the north on the morning of 27 June, as intended. The stripped and mutilated bodies of Custer's men provided 'a scene of sickening, ghastly horror'. Reno's wounded were taken downstream by litter and placed aboard the *Far West*. News of the disaster reached Washington as the nation was commemorating its first centennial, casting a dismal shadow over the celebrations and creating a clamour for vengeance. This proved elusive, for although the army fought several successful engagements during the ensuing months, the tribes instinctively understood that the scale of their victory would provoke a massive response and had dispersed, some parties seeking temporary sanctuary in Canada while others returned sullenly to their reservations. Never again would they win such a victory, and never again would they take the warpath in such numbers.

After the battle the 7th drew up a petition requesting that Reno and Benteen should be promoted. Their request was denied, thanks largely to a whispering campaign begun by the surviving pro-Custer faction among the regiment's officers, some of whom had little to be proud of. Embittered, Reno took to the bottle for comfort. After being twice court-martialled for conduct unbecoming an officer and a gentleman, he was dismissed the service in 1880 and died in poverty nine years later. Benteen had to wait until 1882 for his promotion and rose no higher than major. However, in 1890, two years after his retirement, the army honoured him with the brevet rank of brigadier general for his part in the defence of Reno Hill.

Rorke's Drift

The Zulu War of 1879 was engineered by Sir Henry Bartle Frere, the United Kingdom's High Commissioner in South Africa, as a pre-emptive strike against the Zulu nation, which possessed the most efficient and potentially dangerous native army in Africa. Frere believed that, sooner or later, the Zulus would pour across the frontiers of the territories for which he was responsible and indulge in an orgy of killing and destruction, and, that being the case, the best way to deal with the threat was to destroy the Zulu army at the first possible moment. In fact, Cetewayo, king of the Zulus, took the view that his people's interest lay in maintaining the best possible relations with Queen Victoria's ministers. The king's army existed because the entire framework of Zulu society was built around it and, well aware of the resources that the United Kingdom had at its disposal, Cetewayo had no intention of launching an invasion of British colonial territory. Frere, however, could see no further than the strictly disciplined Zulu regiments with their individual titles, distinctive head plumes and strong *esprit de corps*. He may have believed that he was acting from the best possible motives, yet if the Zulu army was as dangerous as he believed it to be, he must have known that a war would involve heavy loss of life on both sides. Disregarding this probability, he used his professional politician's skills to exaggerate the importance of certain incidents and manipulate the finding of a boundary commission to the point that, on 11 December 1878, he felt able to send Cetewayo an ultimatum demanding, *inter alia*, that the king should disband his army within twenty days. No self-respecting ruler could possibly accept such terms, and Frere now had the war that he wanted, despite the disapproval of the London administration, whose instructions to avoid hostilities arrived just too late.

Frere's Commander-in-Chief in South Africa was Lieutenant General Lord Chelmsford, who had seen active service in two campaigns but whose abilities as a field commander are best described as modest.

Chelmsford had available some 6,000 regulars and colonial volunteers, plus 9,000 native levies, twenty field guns and ten rocket launchers. His plan bore a startling resemblance to that of Terry's, which had come to grief on the Little Big Horn three years earlier, in that it involved three columns, none of which could communicate with or support one another, entering Zululand at widely separate points and converging on Ulundi, Cetewayo's capital, where the Zulu army would be destroyed by disciplined firepower.

Chelmsford decided to accompany the Central Column himself. The column consisted of the 1st and 2nd Battalions 24th Regiment (later the South Wales Borderers), a Royal Artillery field battery, mounted infantry and local volunteer units, engineers, two native battalions and a slow-moving train of ox-wagons, giving a total of 4,700 men of whom 1,852 were Europeans. Although sometimes described as a Welsh regiment (which indeed it became two years later), the 24th's official designation was actually the 2nd Warwickshire Regiment and it contained men from all over the United Kingdom, with a strong Welsh representation. What made the regiment unusual was that both its regular battalions were in the field at the same time, for the usual custom with British line regiments was that while one battalion was on active service the other manned the depot, their roles being exchanged from time to time.

By 20 January the column had crossed the Buffalo River at Rorke's Drift, a ford named after a Swedish missionary, and established a camp beneath a high, rocky hill named Isandhlwana. Although it was now in Zululand and there had already been minor skirmishes, there was a general air of complacency. Contrary to the advice of Boers accompanying the column, who had long and bitter experience of fighting the Zulus, the wagons were not circled into a defensive laager, nor were outposts set sufficiently far out to provide adequate warning of the enemy's approach. On the 21st Chelmsford sent out a patrol to reconnoitre the stronghold of a Zulu chief. During the night he received a message from the patrol commander to the effect that the Zulu presence in the area had grown to an estimated 2,000 warriors. On its own the patrol could accomplish nothing, but it did represent a tempting target for the enemy. He therefore decided to form a relief column consisting of the 2/24th, less one company at Rorke's Drift and another on outpost duty, plus four of the artillery battery's six guns. To make up the number of those remaining in the camp he ordered up a force known as No. 2 Column, commanded by Colonel Anthony Durnford, from Rorke's Drift. This consisted of 300 mounted Basutos, several Natal Native Contingent companies and a rocket detachment.

At 04:30 Chelmsford and the relief column marched out of the camp and made contact with the original patrol. With the coming of first light a number of Zulus were chased off a nearby ridge and several of them were killed. By now, Chelmsford was sufficiently satisfied that the situation was under control for him to order a halt for breakfast and send back instructions for the camp at Isandhlwana to be shifted to a new site on the banks of the Mangeni, a tributary of the Buffalo. As yet, he did not know the whereabouts of the main Zulu army. It was certainly not at the head of the plain over which he had just marched, nor was its presence apparent in the open country to the south. A more imaginative commander might have allowed for the possibility that it was approaching under cover of the reverse slopes of the Nqutu plateau, now lying to his left rear, within easy attacking distance of the camp at Isandhlwana.

Back at the camp, the morning had begun without the slightest hint of what was to come. The troops had gone to breakfast at 07:30 but were then stood to in front of the camp when a police trooper reported the presence of Zulus on the Nqutu plateau. As they posed no threat to the camp and eventually moved off in different directions the companies were allowed to stand down but remained in position. At 10:00 Durnford's No. 2 Column arrived from Rorke's Drift. The camp now seemed secure and the men were allowed to finish their breakfast. In response to reports that more Zulu parties had been spotted, several patrols were sent out. At 11:00, learning that one of the enemy groups was apparently heading in the direction of Chelmsford's relief column, Durnford decided to take out his own column to serve as flank protection for the general.

Hardly had he left than events developed at bewildering speed. A member of one of the patrols sent up on to the Nqutu plateau pursued some Zulus driving cattle to the edge of a rocky valley at its northern end. Below lay the entire Zulu army, 20,000 strong, the commanders of which had decided not to attack the camp on the 22nd because, being the day of a new moon, this was not regarded as propitious. Once the army had been discovered, however, such considerations counted for nothing. With a baleful roar, the Zulus surged over the summit of the plateau in a mile-wide tidal wave of tossing plumes. Their attack took its traditional form, which they called the Buffalo. The two outer wings, known as the Horns, swung wide to encircle the camp on both flanks; the centre, which they called the Chest, headed straight for it; and behind the Chest came a strong reserve, known as the Loins. In the camp, buglers sounded the Alarm, the companies ran to take up their positions and the two guns opened fire, their shells bursting among the black horde now streaming down the slopes of the plateau.

Durnford's small column, caught out in the open on the plain, was swamped by the Left Horn. The rocket detachment managed to fire one round before it was overrun. Three men of the 24th serving as its escort, speared and left for dead, later made good their escape. Imposing such checks as they were able, Durnford and his mounted Basutos retired towards the camp, taking position on the right flank of the defenders' line. The defence of the camp was the responsibility of Lieutenant Colonel Henry Pulleine of the 1/24th, who has been criticised for siting the line 1,000 yards from the camp. The left of the line was bent back in a refused flank to meet the Zulus' converging attack, but there were gaps of 200–300 yards between the companies. It goes almost with saying that if Pulleine had chosen to fight closer to the camp the effect would have been to concentrate his firepower into a continuous line, the ammunition supply to the companies could have been maintained more easily, and the frontage on which the enemy could attack would have been greatly restricted.

Despite this, the troops remained perfectly steady, the precise volleys from their Martini-Henry rifles slicing into the twelve-deep enemy ranks. The Zulus dropped in heaps until, between 150 and 300 yards from the thin scarlet firing line, they lay down and would advance no further. Still the dreadful volleys raked the huddled mass until the Zulu chiefs had to use their authority to prevent their men from bolting. At this moment the ammunition supply failed, partly because the ammunition boxes were difficult to open, partly because the company runners had so far to travel, but mainly because bloody-minded quartermasters refused to issue ammunition to any other than their own units. At about 13:00 an eclipse cast its forbidding shadow across the battlefield. On the right, Durnford's troopers, their ammunition expended, mounted their horses and fell back a little way. Encouraged, the Zulus began working their way forward to within assegai throwing distance. The spluttering response told them all they needed to know. With another great roar they charged forward. The native troops broke at once as the Zulus poured through the gaps between the 24th's companies, which became embattled islands in a sea of black. 'Ah, those red soldiers at Isandhlwana!' recalled one Zulu after the war. 'How few they were, and how they fought! They fell like stones – every man in his place.' The fight surged on into the camp, where the Zulus, now possessed of a killing frenzy, spared no one. The two guns, though limbered up and heading for the rear, became stuck in a gully and were overrun.

Covered by Durnford's men, who fought hand-to-hand until overwhelmed, the survivors from the camp fled along the road to Rorke's Drift, only to find it blocked by the Zulus' Right Horn. They swung left and, pursued without mercy, headed for what became known as Fugitives' Drift on the Buffalo, ten miles distant. Recognising that all was lost, Pulleine had handed the Queen's Colour of the 1/24th to Lieutenant Teignmouth Melville, the battalion's adjutant, with orders to save it. Accompanied by Lieutenant Neville Coghill, Melville reached the swollen river but was swept off his exhausted horse and lost his grip on the Colour. Coghill, who had reached the far bank, returned and rescued him, but the two were quickly surrounded and killed, taking a number of their attackers with them. Posthumous awards of the Victoria Cross were made to them both in 1907, following the recognition of such awards during the Second Boer War. The Colour itself floated downstream and was later recovered from a pool. Adorned with a wreath of immortelles placed upon it by Queen Victoria, it hangs today in Brecon Cathedral.

About 350 men managed to escape from Isandhlwana. Six private soldiers of the 24th (two bandsmen, an officer's servant and the three men wounded with the rocket detachment) reached safety. Five British officers also survived, including Lieutenant Horace Smith-Dorrien, who became an army commander during World War I; they attributed their escape to the fact that they were wearing blue patrol jackets, for Cetewayo had told his warriors to concentrate on killing red soldiers, as the others were of no account. One man who not only survived but also won the Victoria Cross was Private Samuel Wassall of the 80th (later The South Staffordshire) Regiment who, as he approached Fugitives' Drift, saw one of his comrades apparently drowning in the river. Dismounting on the Zulu side, he rescued the man, remounted his horse and crossed the river, pursued by a hail of bullets.

During the battle and the pursuit the British and colonial units lost a total of fifty-two officers and 1,277 other ranks killed. The lowest estimate of Zulu dead was 2,000, the highest 3,000, and to this must be added the many seriously wounded who would never recover. Isandhlwana, the Zulus were later to say, may have been a victory, but its effects were like a spear in the belly of the nation. Be that as it may, when Chelmsford's column returned to the camp at 20:00 it found a horrible shambles of stripped, mutilated bodies and such destruction that the role of the Central Column in the invasion of Zululand was clearly at an end. The Zulus had gone, but their camp-fires could be seen burning on the nearby hills. Chelmsford was particularly concerned by the glow of a major blaze in the direction of Rorke's Drift, suggesting that the post had fallen and that his line of retreat into Natal had been cut.

The post at Rorke's Drift consisted of two, single-storey, thatched buildings. One, formerly the missionary's house, was being used as a hospital and contained thirty-five patients. The other had been a church and was now a storehouse containing mealie sacks and boxes of meat and biscuit. The officers present were Major Henry Spalding, the post commander, Lieutenant Gonville Bromhead, commanding B Company 2/24th, Captain George Stephenson, commanding a company of the Natal Native Contingent, Lieutenant John Chard of the Royal Engineers, Surgeon Major James Reynolds of the Army Medical Department, and Acting Assistant Commissary James Dalton of the Commissariat and Transport Department, a former infantry sergeant major who had retired to South Africa but had engaged for the present campaign. Also present were the Revd George Smith, a missionary who had volunteered his service as chaplain, and Mr Otto Witt, the incumbent missionary.

During lunch heavy firing had been heard from the direction of Isandhlwana. This did not cause undue alarm, but at 14:00 Spalding left for the town of Helpmakaar, hoping to find a company of the 1/24th which was to have reinforced the post but was now two days overdue. This left Chard in command, as his seniority predated Bromhead's, and Stephenson, an irregular, was not eligible. Neither Chard nor Bromhead, aged respectively thirty-two and thirty-three, were held in high esteem by their superiors. As an engineer Chard was regarded as slow and pedestrian, while Bromhead suffered from a serious hearing defect that had begun to affect his career. Against this, both were experienced, sensible officers.

At about 15:15 two badly shaken NNC officers crossed the ford on exhausted mounts, bringing with them the news that the camp at Isandhlwana had fallen and that one wing of the Zulu army was advancing rapidly on Rorke's Drift. One of the officers, Lieutenant James Adendorff, volunteered to assist with the defence of the post while the other galloped off to warn the inhabitants of Helpmakaar. Shortly afterwards a third horseman, despatched by a staff officer from Fugitives' Drift, confirmed what had taken place. It seemed that the Zulu Right Horn, disgruntled at not having been involved in the fighting at

Isandhlwana, was determined to save face by washing its spears in the blood of the Rorke's Drift garrison. Bromhead immediately gave orders for the tents to be struck and suggested loading the hospital patients aboard the wagons with a view to retiring on Helpmakaar. However, Dalton pointed out that the fit, athletic Zulus would soon overtake the slow-moving ox-wagons and, that being the case, the only remaining alternative was to stand and fight. Chard agreed and the entire garrison began putting the post into a defensible state.

Loopholes were knocked in the walls of the buildings while a barricade of mealie bags was constructed around the perimeter. This ran from the north-west corner of the hospital to a rocky ledge extending along the front of the post, then back to the north-eastern corner of the store house; on the southern face a shorter barricade, supplemented with two wagons with biscuit boxes between the wheels, connected the storehouse with the hospital; and adjoining the eastern face of the barricade was a small stone cattle kraal that was also included in the defences.

At about 15:30 some mounted Basutos who had been escorting Durnford's wagons to Isandhlwana rode in. Chard asked them to provide vedettes which would report on the Zulus' progress. Simultaneously, the Revd Smith, Mr Witt and Private Wall climbed a hill to the south of the post. Suddenly, the massed ranks of the enemy, some 4,500 strong, became visible, wading across the Buffalo with linked arms. 'Here they come!' shouted Wall as the observers ran back down the slope. 'Black as hell and thick as grass!'

Mr Witt galloped off in the direction of Helpmakaar. After firing a few shots, the Basuto vedettes did likewise. Next to go were Stephenson's NNC company, taking their officer and European sergeant with them. Furious, some of Bromhead's company snatched up their rifles and fired at their running backs. When the unpopular sergeant pitched forward, dead, no one felt like making an issue of the subject.

The time was now 16:20 and in the space of a few minutes Chard's garrison, which had barely been large enough for the task in hand, had been reduced from over 500 to 139, including the sick and wounded. This meant that there were not enough troops to man the entire perimeter and he constructed an additional barricade from the north-west corner of the storehouse to the ledge, dividing the defended area into two halves. It was decided that the hospital would be evacuated and that, under pressure, the garrison would retire into the area surrounding the storehouse.

The first Zulu attack came in at 16:30. Once more, the terrible musketry volleys tore holes in the advancing ranks but the Zulus, eager to get to grips, came on at a run over their own dead. Yet closing with the redcoats was difficult, for the chest-high barricade meant that they had to use at least one hand to scramble over and with their shields down they were vulnerable to the garrison's long bayonets. The attack was beaten off, but was followed by another and another until the sequence of events became blurred in the defenders' minds. Chard and Bromhead formed one reserve after another with soldiers from the least seriously threatened area of the perimeter and rushed with it to reinforce the most dangerous sectors. B Company's senior NCO, Colour Sergeant Frank Bourne, was a tower of strength, carrying out his officers' orders promptly and providing reassurance for the men with his familiar voice and presence. Bourne had joined the army in 1872, when he was aged eighteen, and his rapid promotion testifies to his abilities as a soldier. Commissary Dalton, an excellent shot, was positioned at the corner of the hospital during the first attack and picked off man after man until the attack collapsed in that quarter. He later saved the life of a man of the Army Hospital Corps by shooting dead the Zulu who was attacking him and, though shot through the shoulder himself, continued to lead by example. Despite the carnage that was taking place all round him, the Revd George Smith walked steadily round the perimeter with words of encouragement and fresh ammunition for all.

Between attacks, the Zulus opened a steady rifle fire on the defenders from the high ground around the post. It is sometimes thought that they were using weapons captured at Isandhlwana, but this is not entirely true. There had always been plenty of unscrupulous traders willing to supply them with guns and they possessed an ample supply of firearms. They were poor shots but as their fire was directed into so small an area it was bound to do some damage; in fact, about one-third of the garrison's casualties resulted from this cause. In particular, the space between the hospital and the storehouse became the most bullet-swept area of the defences. Whenever he was not attending to the wounded in the storehouse, which had been converted into a makeshift dressing station, Surgeon Major James Reynolds dashed across this with fresh supplies of ammunition for the hospital's defenders. That communication between the storehouse and the hospital was maintained at all was due to the efforts of Corporal William Allen and Private Frederick Hitch, both of whom sustained serious wounds but, after having these dressed, voluntarily distributed ammunition to their comrades throughout the action.

Chard and Bromhead both appreciated that the hospital was the

weakest point of the defences. It contained several rooms with barricaded doors leading on to a veranda but were not connected internally.
Those patients who could had already left the building and were playing
an active part in the defence. Others assisted the fit men firing through
the loopholes, but a number of helpless patients remained. By 17:00 the
Zulus were swarming round the building. Bromhead led a series of
counter-attacks that drove them off. Despite this, Chard, having reached
the conclusion that his men were now spread too thinly to hold the
entire perimeter, decided to abandon the western defences and ordered
the troops there to withdraw behind the cross-wall. This left those in the
hospital isolated, their only way out being to knock holes in the parti-
tions dividing the rooms, then by means of a window facing the
storehouse. There was a desperate urgency to the task as the Zulus had
set fire to the building's thatch and were battering their way through the
door of the first room. Private Joseph Williams killed several of them,
but was seized and speared to death, as were Private Horrigan and two
patients trapped on the wrong side of the first hole. The remainder of the
defenders, Privates Henry Hook, John Williams, William and Robert
Jones, continued their work amid choking smoke, dragging patients
through the holes they had made and bayoneting any Zulu who
attempted to follow. One of the twelve patients still living, Sergeant
Maxfield, was delirious and refused to leave, being stabbed to death in
his bed, and another was speared as he crossed the 30-yard gap to the
storehouse. The remaining ten reached safety, covered by fire from the
cross-wall.

At about 18:00 Chard abandoned the kraal, enabling him to concentrate the garrison within the storehouse compound. The remaining
mealie bags were piled into a redoubt with a firestep for marksmen. This
was to serve as the rallying point where a last stand could be made and
the more seriously wounded were placed inside. The attacks continued
to roll in, but with the coming of darkness the Zulus realised that they
had made a serious mistake in setting fire to the hospital, for the flames
from the burning building illuminated the entire area. It was during this
period that Acting Storekeeper Alexander Byrne, who had been going
among the men with a dixie of sorely needed water, was shot dead by a
Zulu sniper. The incident was witnessed by Corporal Ferdnand Schiess
of the Natal Native Contingent, a Swiss who had served in the French
Army and was now living in South Africa, and it roused him to a pitch of
fury. Schiess had been wounded in the foot a few days earlier but had
left the hospital to play his part in the defence when the Zulu attack

began. Now, aware that the Zulu responsible for Byrne's death had concealed himself behind the abandoned area of the barricade, he hobbled along the line of mealie bags and killed the man, plus two others who attacked him, before returning to the inner defences.

Although uncertain of the precise time, Chard's own account of the action states that by 22:00 the Zulus had ceased their mass attacks, although they continued to fire into the defences and hurl assegais until midnight. His men, especially those who had been wounded, were tormented by a raging thirst and at about this time he led a sortie which recovered a water cart that was lying outside the barricade. Sniping continued until 02:00, then the Zulus seemed to lose heart. By 04:00 it seemed as though they had gone. Suspecting that they might launch a surprise attack, Chard and Bromhead set their desperately weary soldiers to knocking down the walls of the gutted hospital to prevent their being used as cover, and gathering up the weapons that covered the body-strewn ground around the perimeter. The garrison's ammunition supply would not have lasted much longer, so it was with a great sense of relief that the last of the Zulus were seen disappearing over the hills at about 07:00.

Meanwhile, Chelmsford's column was marching towards the post, expecting to find the same scenes of horror they had left at Isandhlwana. It passed the retiring Zulus within shouting distance but, for the moment, both sides had seen enough of killing and they went their separate ways. At about 08:00 Chelmsford's mounted infantry advance guard saw a man waving a flag from the roof of the storehouse. More men appeared, clambering on to the barricade to cheer and wave their helmets. Chelmsford's immense relief that the post had survived was compounded by astonishment when Chard reported that the garrison's losses amounted to only fifteen killed and twelve seriously wounded, two of them mortally. The bodies of 370 Zulus were found in the immediate vicinity of the post, more had been carried by their comrades as far as the drift, and yet more were found in the surrounding bush and on the high ground. The precise number of Zulu dead and seriously wounded will never be known.

Eleven Victoria Crosses were won by the defenders of Rorke's Drift. They were awarded to Lieutenants Chard and Bromhead; Surgeon Major Reynolds; Acting Assistant Commissary Dalton; Corporals Allen and Schiess; Privates Hitch, Hook, William and Robert Jones and John Williams. Chard and Bromhead, the elderly subalterns considered to be lacking in promise, became brevet majors and were summoned to a personal audience with Queen Victoria. Chard later achieved the rank of colonel. The actor Sir Stanley Baker, who played Chard in the 1964 film *Zulu,* purchased his medals in the belief that the original Cross had been lost and replaced by a copy. On Sir Stanley's death the medal changed hands several times and was eventually subjected to fluoroscopic test which confirmed that it was genuine. It presently remains in private hands and it is impossible to estimate what its value might be at auction. Bromhead later served in India and Burma, dying at Allahabad in 1892. Reynolds achieved the rank of lieutenant colonel and survived until 1932. Dalton was granted a permanent commission but after spending a short time in England he returned to South Africa, where he had interests in gold mining.

The fortunes of the rest varied enormously. On leaving the regular army, Corporal Allen, also referred to as Allan, served as a sergeant instructor of musketry with volunteer and militia battalions in South Wales. Schiess was the first member of the South African armed forces to win the VC while serving under British command, but his story had a tragic ending. Unable to find work, and too proud to trade on the fact that he had won a VC and was one of Rorke's Drift's defenders, he lived in poverty until discovered by members of the Royal Navy, who subscribed to pay for a passage to England, where his prospects might have been brighter. Sadly, it was too late, for his health was broken and he died at sea off Angola. Frederick Hitch's shoulder had been smashed by a Zulu bullet and he was discharged from the army in August 1879. He worked first as a commissionaire at the Imperial Institute in London, then as a cab driver. In 1880 he married the daughter of the manager of the Café Royal, with whom he had a large family. When he died in 1913 so many cabbies attended his funeral that much of London was left cabless. The Fred Hitch award for gallantry by cabbies still exists. Alfred Hook purchased his discharge in 1880. He worked at the British Museum and served as a sergeant in the 1st Volunteer Battalion, The Royal Fusiliers, before retiring to his native Gloucestershire, where he died in 1905. Robert Jones served with his regiment in India until 1882, when he was transferred to the reserve. He became a farm labourer at Peterchurch in Wiltshire, married and had six children. He was much troubled by recurring dreams of the events at Rorke's Drift and in 1898 died as a result of a blast from a shotgun; suicide was suspected, although his family stoutly denied this, pointing out that the gun had a hair trigger. The case of William Jones was equally sad. He was discharged in 1880 but was unable to find regular work, although he toured for a while with

Buffalo Bill's Wild West Show. After this he slid into such poverty that he was forced to pawn his VC. When he died in 1913 he was interred in a common grave in Philips Park Cemetery, Manchester. John Williams became a sergeant and served in India 1880–3, then returned to Monmouthshire, his native country. In 1914, although beyond the age for active military service, he enlisted in the 3rd Volunteer Battalion, The South Wales Borderers, and served at the regimental depot in Brecon until 1920. He was the last of the Rorke's Drift VC holders to die, on 25 November 1932.

Less well known are the men who received the Distinguished Conduct Medal for the action at Rorke's Drift. They included the Revd George Smith, who was also awarded a commission in the Army Chaplains' Department; Colour Sergeant Bourne, Corporal Michael McMahan and Private John Roy, all of the 24th; Corporal Francis Attwood, Army Service Corps; Wheeler John Cantwell, Royal Horse Artillery; Assistant Commissary Walter Dunne and Storekeeper Alexander Byrne (posthumously), both of the Commissariat and Transport Department.

Smith, accorded the nickname 'Ammunition Smith', was present at the Battle of Tel-el-Kebir and took part in the Sudan campaign. Bourne was offered a commission but declined for the moment as he was the youngest of six sons and could not afford the expenditure that life as an officer would entail. He continued to serve with the regiment in India and Burma and was promoted quartermaster sergeant. In 1890 he received a quartermaster's commission and was appointed adjutant of the School of Musketry at Hythe. He then left the army but rejoined on the outbreak of World War I and became adjutant of the School of Musketry at Dublin. At the end of the war he received an OBE and the honorary rank of lieutenant colonel. Whenever possible, he made a point of attending the funerals of the Rorke's Drift garrison. In 1936 he made a radio broadcast describing the defence of the post. Aged ninety-one, he was the last of its defenders to die. The date of his death was almost symbolic, as it took place on 8 May 1945, better known as VE Day. For the many across the world who have an interest in the period, Frank Bourne, OBE, DCM, has become the archetypal senior NCO of Queen Victoria's army.

By no means all of those who received the lesser award had such long and distinguished careers. In 1880 Corporal Michael McMahan's DCM was withdrawn for desertion and theft. Private John Roy, suffering from an attack of malaria, had been one of the patients in the hospital and had regularly been in trouble for bad conduct, drink-related crimes and rendering himself unfit for duty by contracting syphilis. He was promoted corporal in November 1879 and was presented with his medal by the Queen at Windsor Castle the following month. Taking his discharge in 1880, he emigrated to Australia. He did not prosper, began to lose his sight and became so helpless that a charity concert was organised to provide some funds for his keep. Corporal Francis Attwood received immediate promotion to sergeant. John Cantwell, another soldier to whom trouble came naturally, had been stripped of his bombardier's stripes the day before the action. Walter Dunne saw further service during the First Boer War and later in Egypt, where he was present at the Battle of Tel-el-Kebir.

The defence of Rorke's Drift did much to deaden the shock created by the disaster at Isandhlwana. Details of the action quickly became known around the world. The German Kaiser ordered the story to be read at the head of every regiment in his army as an example of inspired junior leadership, expert improvisation and determined courage. The self-confidence of the Zulus was seriously damaged by the two engagements, which left one-fifth of their nation's manhood dead or seriously wounded. In contrast, the rest of the war seemed anti-climactic and on 4 July 1879 Chelmsford won the decisive victory he sought at Ulundi. As for Sir Bartle Frere, who had engineered a war resulting in the needless deaths of many brave men on both sides, he was sharply reprimanded and then humiliated by having his authority restricted to Cape Colony, which seems a modest enough punishment in the circumstances.

The Storming of Nilt Fort

2 DECEMBER 1891

As is evident from the previous chapter, acts of supreme courage are not restricted to major engagements. Heroic deeds, often performed in minor and long-forgotten encounters by British and Indian soldiers, were a regular feature of life on the North-West Frontier of India. The frontier, where barely a year went by without a punitive expedition being mounted against rebellious tribes, became a school for soldiers who learned their business in harsh mountainous terrain against an enemy who regarded war as the only sport fit for men and whose prisoners could expect a long, painful death at the hands of their womenfolk. Generally, punitive expeditions fought their way through tribal territory until they reached the fort of the chief leading the uprising. The fort would then be blown up, after which the tribe would agree to return within the law. Some sort of indemnity was exacted and an agreed number of weapons were surrendered. Peace would return for a while, then the whole process would begin again. These small campaigns were carried out against the backdrop of what became known as the Great Game, which was the equivalent of the twentieth century's Cold War. On the one hand, the Great Game involved Great Britain thwarting Russian ambitions regarding India, and on the other it suited the Russians to create unrest in Afghanistan and along the frontier since this would tie down British resources that might otherwise have been available for a European conflict.

When the kingdom of Kashmir became a British protectorate it was inevitable that some sort of trouble could be expected in Hunza-Nagar. This area lay to the north of Gilgit in a mountainous region bounded in the north by the towering Hindu Kush and Karakoram ranges, close to the point where the British, Russian and Chinese empires met. The most populous part of the region was the Hunza valley, down which the river of that name flowed to Gilgit. Two tribes occupied the valley, the Hunzas on the right bank and the Nagars on the left. Their rulers, known as Thums, were nominally subjects of the Maharajah of Kashmir, to whom they paid a nominal tribute, but in reality they went their own way, which meant raiding, exacting tolls from caravans and selling slaves in Central Asia. They were able to field about 5,000 fighting men and had never been tamed because their valley was almost inaccessible. To reach it from the south involved crossing high passes that were swept by tearing blizzards in winter and only open for four months of the year, marching for days across a wide area of semi-desert, then negotiating a narrow track into the valley that clung to the mountainside. In some places the track consisted of nothing more than a flimsy wooden walkway resting on poles driven into the ground, and in others it was bordered by a sheer drop of several hundred feet to the icy torrent raging below. In such circumstances it was impossible to support a large military force in the valley, and as the future for anything less seemed most uncertain in view of the numbers to which they would be exposed, the tribes understandably felt that they could continue to do just as they liked.

When Kashmir became a protectorate, a treaty was concluded with the Thums, under the terms of which they recognised Great Britain as the sovereign power and promised to behave themselves in return for an annual subsidy. However, in 1890 the Russians claimed they were annexing the adjacent Pamir region. A Captain Gromchevstky and his Cossack escort entered the Hunza valley, distributed arms and generally made light of the British presence in the area. A strongly worded British protest resulted in the Russians withdrawing their claim, but the damage had been done. The tribes declared that they were subject to no one, returned to their old ways and for a time menaced Gilgit itself.

It was decided to mount a punitive expedition into the Hunza valley, commanded by Colonel Algernon Durand, the British Resident in Gilgit. In view of the peculiar difficulties involved, the final stages of the advance would have to be carried out in winter, when the melt-water streams feeding the Hunza had frozen and the level of the river itself had dropped, rendering it fordable in most places and creating verges along which it was possible to travel. The short summer months of 1891 were therefore taken up with bringing supplies forward to Gilgit, but early blizzards closed the passes, leaving Durand's force not only short of many items, but also cut off from the outside world and the prospect of receiving reinforcements. An added worry was the possible intervention of the Shinaka tribe, who were neighbours of the Hunzas and could put no less than 15,000 men in the field.

Colonel Durand's force consisted of three Kashmiri Imperial Service battalions, 188 men of the 5th Gurkha Rifles, thirty men of the 20th Punjab Infantry who provided the Residency guard, two guns of the Hazara Mountain battery and 160 irregulars. The Imperial Service battalions had been made available for general service by the Maharajah of Kashmir and trained by British officers but were as yet untried in action. The total fighting strength of the force amounted to about 2,000 men of whom half were engaged in protecting the expedition's line of communication. In addition, some 200 Pathan labourers, armed with carbines for their own defence, were recruited to work on improving the track sufficiently to permit the passage of the mule battery.

On 1 December the expedition left Chalt, the last fort in Kashmir, and proceeded up the Hunza valley. Durand had already received a message from Safdar Ali, the Thum of Hunza, protesting about the incursion into tribal territory and telling him that after his head had been cut off he would be reported to the Indian government. If the agenda seemed muddled, the sentiments were perfectly clear. The advance was not contested and on the morning of 2 December was within sight of Nilt, considered by the tribesmen to be the impregnable gateway to their country. An officer who accompanied the expedition, E. F. Knight, described the position:

> On the right and left are the great gorges of Nilt and Maiun, which pour their tributary waters into the Hunza river. At the mouth of the Nilt gorge stands the fortress of Nilt, while on the cultivated terraces beyond the two gorges are the large fortresses of Thol and Maiun and several smaller forts. The two gorges descend from the glaciers and snowfields of mighty mountains whose peaks attain a height of 25,000 feet. The cliffs that fronted us on the opposite side of both gorges are inaccessible in most parts and were lined at their summits from the edge of the glaciers high above down to the river bed with sangars (stone breastworks) filled with the enemy's marksmen, ever ready to roll down an avalanche of rocks on any foe that should attempt the scaling. We were confronted, in short, by a line of defences which extended from the glaciers on one side (of the valley) to those on the other, held by some 4,000 determined men.

The Hunzas opened fire from the fort as soon as the expedition's advance guard came into view. The Gurkhas, taking advantage of the stone walls dividing the fields, advanced by section rushes and began engaging the loopholes from a range of 100 yards. Other troops climbed the spur to the right of the advance and began firing down into the interior of the fort, which was also being shelled, without apparent result by the two 7-pdr mountain guns. The stand-off lasted for about an hour, during which casualties began to mount. Durand ordered that the main gate of the fort should be blown in by demolition charges, after which an assault party of 100 Gurkhas would storm the place, covered by fire from the rest of the force. At this point Durand was severely wounded in the groin. Command was assumed by Captain Bradshaw, who decided to proceed with the plan, although carrying it out was no easy matter, as may be gathered from Knight's description of the defences.

> The fort is enclosed by a massive stone wall nearly twenty feet in height and twelve feet in breadth, loopholed for musketry, with towers at intervals. The wall is surrounded by another loopholed wall eight feet in height, some six yards from the first wall. This outer wall, where it does not hang over the precipice, has a deep trench outside it, at the bottom of which the enemy had placed a strong abatis of branches lashed together, and, lastly, another abatis lined the outer edge of the trench.

The Gurkhas, led by Lieutenants Boisragon and Badcock, charged the outer abatis. Their kukris quickly chopped a hole in this, then they jumped into the ditch and dealt similarly with the inner abatis. Captain Fenton Aylmer, Royal Engineers, who was responsible for blowing in the main gate, climbed the inner wall of the ditch, followed by two of his sappers, Hazara Singh and Abdulla Khan, the two Gurkha officers and a handful of men. Running along the outer wall, they came upon a flimsy gate that was quickly demolished. Passing through, they found themselves between the two walls and under fire from loopholes in the main wall. Turning to the right, they followed the wall until they reached a large gate flanked by two towers. Bombarded with large stones flung from above, and under fire from nearby loopholes, Aylmer, Hazara Singh and Abdulla Khan laid the demolition charge. In the process, Aylmer was wounded in the leg from a loophole, a Gurkha was shot dead and another man was seriously wounded. Lighting the fuse, Aylmer and the party retired a safe distance along the wall. They waited, but after the given time had passed without an explosion, Aylmer returned to the charge, cut the fuse and relit it with difficulty in a high wind, then withdrew again. While working beneath the arch, his hand and arm were hit by a heavy rock thrown from above.

This time, his efforts were rewarded. With a mighty roar the gates were blown in, a stone barricade behind it was demolished, and the air was filled with dust, smoke and flying debris. The party rushed the gate, only to find the Hunzas charging down the alley inside it. First into the archway was a Gurkha, who was immediately shot dead. Leaning round the corner, Aylmer twice emptied his revolver into the crowd, killing and wounding several. A fierce and protracted hand-to-hand fight then took place in the archway. None of the three British officers nor any of their few remaining sepoys would have survived if the constricted space had not prevented the enemy bringing his vastly superior numbers to bear. Badcock, with his revolver, shot dead the fort's commander, but sustained a wound in the shoulder shortly after. Two of the sepoys were killed and nearly all the others wounded. Seeing that the fight could only end one way, Boisragon braved the fire from the loopholes to bring up the rest of his Gurkhas. This he soon did, for having lost sight of the demolition party and turned left instead of right when they crossed the ditch, they had discovered their mistake and were on their way back. Boisragon reached the main gate with them in the nick of time, for Aylmer, semi-conscious after being wounded yet again by a bullet in the arm, was being dragged to safety by Abdulla Khan. Faced with fresh and very aggressive assailants, the tribesmen gave way after a stiff fight, to be hunted down in the fort's alleys. About a hundred of them were killed in the fort itself and more were shot down as they tried to escape across the Nilt. The attackers' losses were remarkably low in the circumstances, amounting to only six killed and twenty-seven wounded.

For their part in the capture of the fort Fenton Aylmer and Guy Boisragon were awarded the Victoria Cross. Badcock was also recommended for the award, but this was declined on a technicality and instead he received the Distinguished Service Order, which was itself a notable achievement for a junior officer. Sappers Hazara Singh and Abdulla Khan were awarded the Indian Order of Merit and, in due course, both became viceroy's commissioned officers.

If the Hunza and Nagar were initially dismayed by the loss of the fort, they quickly recovered from the shock and took every possible step to ensure that the expeditionary force would penetrate no further into their valley. The tracks across the Nilt and Maiun gorges were broken, new sangars were constructed on the banks of the Hunza and irrigation channels were diverted over the riverside cliffs so that their lower sections became walls of ice. During the next eighteen days every attempt to break through was foiled by a combination of terrain and the enemy's fire, accompanied by a rain of boulders and great fireballs of resinous wood. Word was received that the Shinakas were about to take the field. In these circumstances the expedition risked either being cut to pieces or forced into an ignominious retreat unless a breakthough could be obtained quickly.

The key to the enemy's position was discovered by a Dogra soldier of one of the Kashmiri battalions, Sepoy Nagdu. A skilled climber, Nagdu volunteered to try to find a way up the 1,200-foot precipice on the opposite side of the Nilt gorge. Night after night he made solitary climbs, sometimes under fire, until he discovered a route from the bottom of the gorge to the clifftop just below the enemy's strongest sangars. Returning, he pointed out that the cliff was so steep that the enemy would have to leave their sangars and lean over the edge to fire at those using the route. As Captain Bradshaw was temporarily absent in Gilgit, the force was now commanded by Captain Colin Mackenzie, a Seaforth Highlander. Mackenzie endorsed everything that Nagdu said and decided to launch a daylight assault.

During the night of 19 December two fifty-strong parties of known climbers from the Kashmiri Bodyguard Regiment, one commanded by Lieutenant Manners Smith and the other by Lieutenant Taylor, silently took up a position in the Nilt ravine. As dawn broke they began to climb, with Smith's party in the lead, covered by the fire of 135 picked marksmen from the spur above Nilt fort. This fire was so effective that after a while not a man in the sangars dared to show himself. It took almost four hours, including a false start, before the climbers were within striking distance of the clifftop. By then they were clearly visible to the tribesmen across the Hunza, who shouted a warning. Some of those in the sangars rushed out to hurl rocks, only to be shot down by the marksmen. Some men, including Taylor, were injured, but by then they had passed the most dangerous part of the climb. Smith reached a ledge only 60 yards from one of the sangars, where he waited for several of his men to catch up, then clambered over the edge of the cliff. He charged round to the rear of the sangar, shooting dead the first man to oppose him. His sepoys came up, bayoneting the rest of the defenders, then the rest of the climbers arrived, clearing sangar after sangar until the entire mountainside was filled with fleeing tribesmen, many of whom were shot down.

Once it was clear that the position had fallen, the tribesmen abandoned their remaining forts and defences and retreated to the higher reaches of the valley. After the sappers had repaired the track across the Nilt gorge the force set off in pursuit, making a 30-mile forced march to the tribal capital without being opposed. The Thums quickly requested terms, agreeing to accept British sovereignty, renounce their lawless ways and avoid contact with the Russians. This time they kept their word. Indeed, many of their young men volunteered for service in the Indian Army and when the entire frontier region was shaken by the great tribal rebellion of 1897–8, the Hunza and Nagar remained loyal.

John Manners Smith received the Victoria Cross for his part in the final assault on the Nilt position. He later achieved the rank of lieutenant colonel. Guy Boisragon subsequently served in Egypt and during World War I, becoming a brigadier. Both these officers belonged to the Indian Staff Corps and 5th Gurkha Rifles. Fenton Aylmer enjoyed a long and distinguished career during which he was knighted and achieved the rank of lieutenant general. This was marked by a series of coincidental associations with the ill-starred Charles Townshend. During the Hunza-Nagar campaign Townshend had commanded the Kashmiri Raja Pertab Regiment, of which Sepoy Nagdu, the courageous climber, was a member. In 1895, Townshend conducted the defence of the remote Chitral Fort and Aylmer was serving with the force that relieved him. When, in 1915, Townshend, now a major general commanding the 6th Indian Division, rashly allowed himself to be besieged by the Turks in Kut-al-Amara, Mesopotamia, it was Aylmer who was given the impossible task of breaking through to him. Aylmer was colonel commandant of the Corps of Royal Engineers 1922–32 and died in 1935.

San Juan Hill/El Caney

1 JULY 1898

Spain's refusal, during the 1890s, to grant her colony of Cuba full independence, coupled with her repressive measures against those who sought it, generated strong anti-Spanish feelings among the American public – feelings raised to fever pitch by certain elements of the popular press which were highly selective in their reporting. Matters reached a head when the second-class battleship *Maine*, on a courtesy visit to Cuba, blew up and sank with heavy loss of life in Havana harbour during the night of 15 February 1898. The cause was almost certainly an accidental coal dust explosion in a fuel bunker that triggered a second explosion in a neighbouring magazine. Subsequent courts of inquiry failed to produce any connection between the loss of the ship and the Spanish authorities, but the most vociferous portion of the American press, led by William Randolph Hearst, were convinced that the latter were somehow responsible. Outraged by this apparent act of treachery, the public clamoured for war. President McKinley's administration, having no alternative other than to bow to their wishes, declared war against Spain on 25 April.

The problem was that the United States was not ready for war, even against the declining power of Spain. An increase in the strength of the regular army from 28,000 to 60,000 was authorised, but even this was considered inadequate for the task and it was necessary to form volunteer units from the thousands of men who swamped the recruiting offices before taking the field could even be considered. Again, the huge expansion in itself created enormous supply problems. In terms of weaponry, the Spanish were actually the better equipped. Their standard rifle was the clip-loaded Mauser, whereas rounds had to be inserted individually into the magazine of the standard American rifle, the Krag-Jorgensen. Furthermore, as there were only sufficient Krag-Jorgensens available to equip regular units, the volunteers were issued with the old single-shot Springfield rifle. Again, while the Spanish used smokeless ammunition for their small arms and artillery, very little of this was available to their opponents, whose positions would be disclosed as soon as they opened fire. The Americans, therefore, would be at a serious disadvantage when it came to a firefight.

The course the war would take was actually determined at sea. Having crossed the Atlantic, Admiral Pascal Cervera reached Santiago de Cuba with four modern cruisers and three destroyers on 19 May. There the Spanish squadron remained, blockaded by Rear Admiral William T. Sampson's Atlantic Fleet. It was decided to eliminate it altogether by landing a force at Daiquiri, some miles to the east of Santiago, and capturing the city.

The landing force, designated V Corps, began assembling at Florida under the command of Major General William R. Shafter. During the Civil War Shafter had served with the 7th Michigan Infantry and been awarded the Medal of Honor for an action at Fair Oaks, Virginia, on 31 May 1862. There, he had led a desperate counter-attack in which eighteen of his twenty-two men became casualties. Later the same day he sustained a severe flesh wound when his horse was killed under him, but concealed the fact for several days to avoid being evacuated with the wounded. After the war he had been granted a regular commission and served on the frontier during the Indian Wars. He had been promoted to brigadier general only as recently as 1897, but seniority and friends in high places saw to it that he received the rank of major general of volunteers and with it his present command. He was now aged sixty-three, which might be considered too old for the kind of expedition that was envisaged. Moreover, he was also far from fit, for years of sedentary garrison duty had resulted in his weight rising to beyond 280lbs. His understandable inability to move quickly was further compounded by gout. As if this was not enough, his gross appearance was matched by a coarse, bullying manner that alienated those with whom he had to work.

The 17,000-strong V Corps consisted of three divisions and one independent brigade. The Cavalry Division, commanded by Major General Joseph P. Wheeler, contained two brigades each of three regiments. The 1st and 2nd Infantry Divisions, commanded respectively by Brigadier Generals J. F. Kent and H. W. Lawton, each contained three brigades of three regiments; the Independent Brigade, under Brigadier General J. C. Bates, contained two infantry regiments. With the exception of the 1st US Volunteer Cavalry and one volunteer regiment in each infantry division, all of Shafter's troops were regulars. The corps' heavy weapons consisted of sixteen 3.2-inch field guns and one dynamite gun, four 7-

inch howitzers, four 5-inch siege guns, eight 3.6-inch mortars, one Hotchkiss and four Gatling machine-guns.

The expedition – the largest mounted by the United States thus far – sailed from Tampa on 14 June and made an unopposed landing at Daiquiri eight days later. From Daiquiri a poor road led westwards to the little port of Siboney. This was occupied without resistance on 23 June by the 2nd Division. The road then turned inland to reach Santiago through close, rolling country. The dismounted Cavalry Division continued along this route, fighting a sharp skirmish against a Spanish covering force that then withdrew to Santiago. Wheeler, who had been a Confederate officer during the Civil War, was so excited by the sight of the Spaniards hastily abandoning their positions that he caused some bewilderment by shouting: 'We've got the damn Yankees on the run!'

Despite this success, V Corps soon found itself in difficulty. Its advance was made in temperatures of 90 degrees and over, as well as sweltering humidity. The surface of the road, never intended to support more than country carts, collapsed under the weight of so much traffic. Heavily burdened infantrymen, sweating into their thick uniforms, were required to heave guns and wagons out of the mud. Men began to drop from heat exhaustion or shed their packs and blanket rolls. It was decided to continue the advance with the field artillery and supporting weapons only, leaving the heavier guns to be brought up later.

The Spanish commander in Santiago, Lieutenant General Arsenio Linares, had some 35,000 troops available locally. He could have made Shafter suffer severely during his difficult approach march, had he chosen to do so. He was, however, defensively minded as well as being unduly influenced by an exaggerated threat posed by Cuban rebels. Many of his units were held west of Santiago to meet this, while a mere 1,700 men were detailed to prepare defensive positions east of the city on San Juan Ridge and in the village of El Caney, despite the fact that it was Shafter's advance from this direction that presented the real danger.

By 30 June, V Corps was in a position to strike at Santiago's outer defences. Shafter climbed a hill named El Pozo and surveyed the battle-field. Immediately below was a belt of jungle that his troops would have to pass through on a single track. In the bottom of the valley ran the little San Juan river, which was easily fordable. Across the valley the Spaniards could be seen working on their defences along San Juan Ridge and a detached feature fronting the northern end of the ridge, to be known as Kettle Hill because of a large sugar-refining plant on the summit. Some miles to the north the Spaniards could also be seen strengthening the defences of El Caney village. Three miles west of San Juan Ridge was Santiago itself, with Admiral Cervera's warships lying at anchor in the harbour.

It was immediately apparent that any attack on San Juan Ridge could be taken in flank from El Caney, and that the village would therefore have to be captured first. This task was given to Lawton's 2nd Division, with one field battery and the dynamite gun in support, two hours being allowed for the operation. While this was under way, the Cavalry Division and Kent's 1st Division would pass through the belt of jungle and deploy along the edge of the trees. Once El Caney had fallen, they would assault San Juan Ridge and Kettle Hill, supported by the second field battery, firing from the summit of El Pozo Hill.

Unfortunately, tropical diseases had already begun to strike the Americans. Overnight, Shafter was confined to his bed by an attack of gout and the onset of malaria. Wheeler, too, went down with fever, as did the commander of the 2nd Cavalry Brigade. The brigade was taken over by Colonel Leonard Wood, commanding the 1st US Volunteer Cavalry, which was in turn taken over by its second-in-command, Lieutenant Colonel Theodore Roosevelt. All of this meant that with the corps commander and his deputy out of action, much of the responsibility for carrying through the plan of attack would rest on the shoulders of junior officers.

Early on 1 July, Lawton's division struck north across country and deployed for its attack on El Caney. This commenced promptly at 07:00, being supported from behind by its artillery battery, firing from high ground. The village itself had been turned into a miniature fortress containing one large and four smaller blockhouses, a stone church and houses loopholed for defence, and a trench system fronted by barbed wire. It was held by 500 men under the command of Major General Vara del Rey, an officer of outstanding ability with the capacity to inspire his men. For the Americans, matters began to go awry at once. The dynamite gun, which relied upon compressed air as a propellant for its dynamite-filled projectiles, sprung its breech after firing one round and remained silent for the rest of the day. After searching the trenches with their fire, the light 3.2-inch field guns turned their attention to the buildings in the village, against which they made no impression. Every time one of Lawton's infantry regiments attempted a rush forward, it was met by a storm of fire from the enemy's clip-loaded Mausers and forced to seek cover. Even then its troubles did not end, for the clouds of powder smoke as it attempted to return fire disclosed its position, rendering individuals vulnerable to the Spanish snipers. The 2nd Massachusetts Volunteer Infantry sustained such heavy losses that it had to be pulled out of the line. In response to a runner sent by Lawton to request reinforcements, the bedridden Shafter despatched his only reserve, Bates's Independent Infantry Brigade. Even when this arrived the Spaniards in the village, never more than a battalion strong, experienced no difficulty in holding off ten American regiments, a total of approximately 6,000 men, plus some 1,500 Cuban rebels who were firing into the position from high ground to the north.

Meanwhile, the Cavalry and 1st Infantry Divisions were entering the track that passed through the belt of jungle to the San Juan river. At 08:00 the supporting artillery opened fire from the top of El Pozo Hill. The American battery's position was immediately disclosed by a cloud of powder smoke. The Spanish gunners knew the range to a foot and their carefully concealed, modern 77mm Krupp field guns made such an effective reply that the battery remained virtually silent for the rest of the battle.

It was also apparent to the troops winding their way along the jungle track that the Spaniards had the range of that, too, for shells began to burst among the trees and Mauser bullets clipped a steady shower of leaves and branches from above. On Shafter's orders, an observation balloon was sent up from beside the track. This simply made matters worse as it provided the enemy with a fine aiming point. The observer, however, did report the existence of a secondary trail that emerged near the southern end of the main Spanish position on San Juan Ridge. General Kent ordered the 71st New York Volunteer Infantry to proceed along it. His choice was unfortunate, for the regiment was so completely green that some of its men had only begun learning how to handle their weapons the previous month. As it began to debouch from the trees it was greeted with bursting shrapnel and heavy Mauser fire that scythed through the leading ranks. Those behind would have bolted had not Kent and his staff blocked the trail and told them to lie down where they were. At about the same time, to everyone's relief, the riddled observation balloon collapsed slowly into the trees.

It was now about noon. The Cavalry Division and the remainder of 1st Infantry Division had emerged from the main track, deploying to the right and left respectively along the tree line under heavy fire. Ahead of them lay 600 yards of open, bullet-swept slope on which it seemed impossible to survive, while to the north the roar of battle confirmed that El Caney still remained in enemy hands. In Kent's division a brigade and two regimental commanders were shot down at the head of their men. With casualties mounting, it seemed insane to keep the troops pinned down in an untenable position, yet the only alternatives were to advance into the teeth of the terrible Mauser fire or to retreat, which was tantamount to an admission of defeat.

These were precisely the thoughts passing through the mind of Lieutenant Colonel Theodore Roosevelt, the fiercely patriotic politician who in pre-war days had been Secretary of the Navy. It was Roosevelt who had been largely responsible for raising the 1st US Volunteer Cavalry, better known as the Rough Riders, from an unlikely combination of cowboys and prospectors and eastern college men. The regiment had always been something of a law unto itself, even to the extent of going to war in sensible khaki drill rather than the thick standard blue uniform which was quite unsuited to campaigning in the tropics. At this precise moment the Rough Riders' designated role was to support the attack of the 1st Cavalry Brigade, consisting of the 3rd, 6th and 9th Cavalry, on Kettle Hill. There was, however, no sign that the brigade was about to commence its advance. Roosevelt, on his horse Little Texas, finally reaching the end of his patience, ordered his trumpeter to sound the Charge. The Rough Riders surged forward, passing the lines of the 9th Cavalry, whose men joined the attack, followed by those of the 3rd and 6th Cavalry. The remaining regiments of the 2nd Cavalry Brigade, the 1st and 10th Cavalry, followed hard on their heels, so that the entire division was now mounting the long slope, with individuals pausing to fire at the Spanish trenches from time to time. It was such a bullet, fired from behind, that, to Roosevelt's fury, shot off his spectacles. The Spanish fire inflicted some loss but was unable to halt the momentum of the attack. By the time Roosevelt had reached the enemy wire, where he turned Little Texas loose, he had received a nick in the elbow and the horse had been grazed twice. Beyond the wire the Spaniards were hastily abandoning their trenches and running back towards their main position on San Juan Ridge. By 13:00 Kettle Hill was firmly in the Cavalry Division's hands.

At about the same time, on 1st Division's sector, Lieutenant Jules Ord had reached the same conclusion as Roosevelt. Running to the front, he set off up the slope of San Juan Ridge, calling for the men to follow him. A few did, and then several groups responded. Just how this forlorn hope might have fared will never be known, because at that moment the entire nature of the battle changed. Manhandling their guns' high-wheeled carriages past the prostrate 71st New York on the secondary jungle track, the Gatling machine-gun detachment, commanded by Lieutenant John Parker, went into action as soon as it emerged from the trees. Parker was a rare machine-gun enthusiast at a time when many people believed that such weapons had little use outside frontier warfare. In Cuba, neither Shafter nor anyone else had given him the slightest encouragement, so that his small unit had had to fend entirely for itself. Parker had brought his guns forward on his own initiative. Now, between them, they were pumping out up to 3,600 rounds a minute, subjecting the enemy breastworks to the sort of fire they had not experienced all day. Some of the defenders could be seen fleeing across the crest. Encouraged, three of Kent's regiments, the 6th, 16th and 24th Infantry, followed Ord's forlorn hope up the ridge. Inspired by the infantrymen's progress, the Rough Riders charged down the reverse slope of Kettle Hill and up the slopes beyond. Those Spanish riflemen who still stuck bravely to their posts continued firing until the last possible minute, then made good their escape to Santiago's inner defences.

Although San Juan Ridge had been overrun, the struggle for El Caney continued until late afternoon. Vara del Rey, who had inspired the defenders, was wounded in both legs and killed as he was being carried off the field. By then, about half his men had become casualties and the rest were beginning to run short of ammunition. As the volume of Spanish fire dropped the Americans closed in until they were close enough to rush the position. White flags appeared in the blockhouses and those of the Spaniards unable to escape raised their arms in surrender. Only about forty of the garrison managed to reach Santiago. What impressed the Americans most about their opponents, both at San Juan Ridge and El Caney, was their extreme youth.

Shafter, who had wildly overestimated the number of Spaniards holding both positions, was shocked by the 1,572 killed and wounded his troops had sustained during the battle, which were almost twice those of the enemy. When Wheeler estimated that a further 3,000 casualties would be incurred in storming Santiago's inner defences, Shafter gave way to despair, proposing a withdrawal to a defensive position near Siboney. The proposal was rejected out of hand by his angry divisional commanders, then vetoed by Washington. Orders were therefore given for the heavy guns to be brought up and a regular siege commenced.

Although the Spaniards had no reason whatever to complain about the performance of their troops, all was far from well with them. Linares, having sustained a wound on San Juan Ridge, handed over command of the Santiago area to Major General Jose Toral. It was Toral's belief that the city would fall, which would also mean the loss of Cervera's warships. On 2 July Cervera received a direct order from the Captain General of Cuba to take his squadron to sea and head for Cienfuegos, which provided a safe anchorage 500 miles to the west. There was never the slightest chance that the squadron could break through Admiral Sampson's blockade. The Spanish cruisers were wrecked, set ablaze or driven ashore by the big guns of the American battleships long before they could come within effective range. With the fleet gone, Toral saw no further point in holding Santiago and considered withdrawing into the interior. Because many of his troops were sick, however, he decided against this, believing that the Cuban rebels would attack his column at every opportunity. Had he but known it, Shafter's troops were being decimated by tropical disease. As it was, he was only aware of the arrival of heavy guns and reinforcements, suggesting that V Corps was growing stronger daily. On 17 July he surrendered unconditionally, thereby ending hostilities on the Cuban mainland. The following month a smaller expeditionary force eliminated the Spanish military presence on the island of Puerto Rico.

Spain, her fleet gone and no longer able to communicate with or support her troops in Cuba, bowed to the inevitable and opened peace negotiations. As a result of these, Cuba gained its independence. Puerto Rico and the island of Guam were ceded to the United States, which also purchased the Philippine Islands for $20 million. The Spanish-American War thus marked the first appearance of the United States as a world power.

For the army it also marked a stricter interpretation on the circumstances in which the Medal of Honor could be awarded. The linked battles for San Juan Ridge (entered as Santiago in the citations) and El Caney resulted in over twenty awards, the greatest number being won by members of the 17th Infantry at El Caney. All the awards save one were made for bringing in wounded comrades from between the lines under fire. The exception was Captain Albert L. Mills, Assistant Adjutant General of Volunteers, who received the award for distinguished gallantry in encouraging those near him by his bravery and coolness after being shot through the head and entirely without sight.

Neither Ord nor Parker received the award, despite the decisive part they had played in the battle, it being considered that they had simply done their duty. Roosevelt ended the war as a brigadier general. Within a year he had become Governor of New York, and two years after that he became President of the United States. As the attack of his Rough Riders

SAN JUAN HILL/EL CANEY

on Kettle Hill had caught the public imagination, it was almost certainly at the urging of his political supporters that he requested the award of the Medal of Honor. The request was denied at the time, although many felt that the award was justified and continued to press the establishment to change its mind for the next century. Finally, on 16 January 2000, President Clinton made a posthumous presentation of the Medal to Roosevelt's grandson, Tweed.

Colenso
15 DECEMBER 1899

Following the removal of the Zulu threat in 1879, the Transvaal Boers demanded independence for their country, which had been annexed by Great Britain two years earlier. When this was refused, they rebelled the following year and in 1881 inflicted a series of sharp defeats on British troops. As a result of these, the independence of the Transvaal Republic was recognised, subject to certain conditions.

In 1886 the discovery of gold in the Witswatersrand brought an influx of foreigners, many of them British, into the Transvaal. It was soon apparent that these Uitlanders, as the new arrivals were known, would outnumber the native Boer population. Alarmed lest they achieve political power, the Transvaal government imposed prohibitive taxes on the Uitlanders, yet denied them the full rights of citizenship. In 1895, the Uitlanders, resenting this unfair treatment, appealed for help and found a sympathetic ear in Cecil Rhodes, the Prime Minister of Cape Colony. Believing that they would rise if offered armed support, Rhodes arranged for a force under Dr Leander Starr Jameson to cross the frontier from Mafeking. At the last minute, having been informed that a rising would not take place, Rhodes withdrew from the venture. Jameson, however, recklessly proceeded with his invasion, only to be defeated and marched off to gaol three days after crossing the frontier.

After the Jameson Raid, relations between Great Britain and the Transvaal deteriorated steadily. In March 1899 a meeting held between the two governments to discuss the Uitlanders' grievances solved nothing. Both sides began to prepare for war and on 8 October of that year President Kruger of the Transvaal, with the backing of President Steyn of the neighbouring Orange Free State, issued an ultimatum that no self-respecting government could possibly accept. The Boer War officially began at 17:00 on 11 October 1899. The following day the Boers crossed into Cape Colony and Natal. After some minor if expensive successes near the frontier, substantial British forces were forced into a humiliating retreat and were soon besieged in Ladysmith, Kimberley and Mafeking.

These reverses were initially put down to the fact that since the Crimean War the British Army had not been engaged in serious hostilities against a European enemy. This was too simplistic and it is doubtful whether any European army could have done any better against the Boers at this stage. The fact was that the Boers did not possess an army in the conventional sense. The only regular units they possessed were two small corps of professional artillerymen, and even they had their own methods, preferring to fight their guns in small groups or even individually from concealed positions with a good field of fire, rather than in wheel-to-wheel batteries in the manner of the major military powers. The basic unit of the Boer armies was the mounted commando, recruited locally from farmers and frontiersmen who provided their own horses and weapons. They were, by nature, fine horsemen and excellent shots, their preferred weapon being the same clip-loading Mauser used by the Spaniards in Cuba. Regarding the concept of standing up to be shot at as ridiculous, they took advantage of every scrap of cover whether in defence or attack. This combination of mobility, firepower and fieldcraft made them very formidable opponents indeed.

After the opening moves of the war, the British priority was to relieve Ladysmith and Kimberley. General Sir Redvers Buller, VC, was appointed Commander-in-Chief South Africa two days after hostilities began. Buller had won his Victoria Cross in the Zulu War, when, during the difficult retreat from a failed attack on the Zulu fortress of Hlobane, he had rescued three men in succession from certain death at the hands of the enemy. He brought a wide experience to his task, having served in India, China, Canada, West Africa, Egypt and the Sudan, but was to claim that his instincts had been blunted by recent years spent in the War Office. A soldier's general, he was very popular with the troops, eating the same rations as they did and scorning his tent to sleep in the open when there was no cover for them. Shy by nature, he compensated for this by adopting an arrogant manner and was sometimes insufferably rude, particularly to his staff. He did not want his present appointment, commenting that he would have been much happier as someone else's second-in-command. Sadly, he was neither a gifted general nor a lucky one. Worse still, he did not regard the Boers as a serious enemy. Altogether, Buller had about 47,000 troops under his command. These were divided into three separate columns. Buller himself would command the one on the eastern sector of the front and advance to the relief of Ladysmith; in the centre Major General William Gatacre would eject the Boers from a position they had occupied at Stormberg Junction in Cape Colony; and in the west Lieutenant General Methuen was to relieve Kimberley, then Mafeking.

On 10 December Gatacre's column failed in the attempt to capture Stormberg Junction. Its retreat was conducted in an orderly enough manner, but the order to withdraw did not reach 696 men who were surrounded and forced to surrender. The following day, Lord Methuen, who had already driven the Boers from their positions at Belmont and the Modder River, was sharply repulsed at Magersfontein, where the commander of the crack Highland Brigade was killed and his men were decimated. On the eastern front, Buller had been planning to approach Ladysmith by working round the right flank of the Boer position at Colenso, on the Tugela river. When news of the disasters at Stormberg and Magersfontein reached him on 12 December he decided to abandon this plan and smash his way through the Boers with a frontal attack.

Colenso was a small town situated at the point where the road and railway line to Ladysmith crossed the winding Tugela. The Boers, commanded by General Louis Botha, had some 6,000 men and eight guns in the area. Some were holding a feature known as Hlanghwane Mountain to the north-west of the town, but the majority were entrenched in carefully concealed positions on high ground across the river. Opposite the town itself were the Colenso Kopjes, several low hills incorporating a post known as Fort Wylie. Some two miles to the west of the kopjes was the higher Red Hill. Between the two was a wide area of comparatively flat ground that Botha believed, correctly, Buller would try to penetrate. On this sector the Boers had also entrenched themselves along the river. In accordance with their usual practice, their guns, including several automatic 1-pdr pom-poms, were dispersed in suitable positions on the high ground.

Buller had 21,000 men available, including five field batteries, a naval brigade manning two 4.7-inch guns and twelve 12-pdr guns, a mounted brigade (Colonel the Earl of Dundonald), the 2nd Infantry Brigade (Major General H. J. T. Hildyard), the 4th Infantry Brigade (Major General the Hon. N. G. Lyttleton), the 5th Infantry Brigade (Major General A. F. Hart), and the 6th Infantry Brigade (Major General G. Barton). The artillery was commanded by Colonel C. J. Long, a courageous officer who had distinguished himself against the dervishes at Omdurman the previous year. Buller's plan required Dundonald's mounted brigade to capture Hlanghwane Mountain on the right;

Barton's brigade, on the right of the main infantry attack, would advance on the right of the railway; Hildyard's brigade would advance on the left of the railway through Colenso, cross the river by one of the two bridges and take the kopjes beyond; Long, with two field batteries and part of the naval brigade, was to support the attack and advance along the same axis as Barton; on the left Hart's brigade was to cross the river to the west of the confluence of a stream called the Doornkop Spruit, then wheel right along the river towards the kopjes; for the moment, Lyttleton's brigade was to remain in reserve. The fatal flaw lay in the fact that Buller not only planned the battle from an inaccurate map that did not show either the true serpentine course of the river or the correct position of the fordable drifts, but also failed to carry out any detailed reconnaissance.

The battle began shortly after dawn on 15 December. For the British, it started badly, then steadily dissolved into chaos. Dundonald failed to make any impression on the defenders of Hlanghwane Mountain. Long, disoriented by the pre-dawn mist, soon left the infantry behind and led the 14th and 66th Batteries, Royal Field Artillery, each with six 15-pdr guns to a position close to the river. The position was closer to the enemy than Long had intended, but it had several distinct advantages, namely that it consisted of a shallow fold in the ground surrounded by scattered thorn trees and scrub. This made it difficult for either the enemy's artillerymen or his marksmen lining the river bank to spot the guns. Supported by the naval guns firing from the rear, the two batteries systematically engaged one Boer earthwork after another and began to silence the enemy's guns.

Meanwhile, to the left, Hart's brigade was in desperate trouble. Hart, while personally courageous, was so old-fashioned in his methods that under any other commander than Buller he would have been regarded as a liability. He did not approve of the new-fangled ideas of fighting in open order and independent firing. In his view, soldiers should advance in quarter-columns, fight shoulder-to-shoulder and fire volleys, just as they had done in the Crimean War, because that was the only way to keep them 'in hand'. As if this was not bad enough, even before his regiments moved off that morning he had subjected them to thirty minutes of parade ground drill 'to sharpen them up'. Consequently, as his brigade approached the Tugela, it presented a splendid appearance, reminiscent of the British approach to the Alma, over forty years earlier. It was magnificent theatre, but hardly compatible with contemporary conditions, for the mass of marching men quickly became the target of every

Boer gun and rifle within range. Unbelievably, the brigade's already unpromising future began to assume the proportions of a major disaster. Searching for the drift which he had been ordered to cross, Hart led his regiments into a loop of the river that symbolically resembled a hangman's noose. Delighted by the *rooineks'* stupidity, the Boers on the far bank began firing into the loop from three sides. Unable to advance or retire, yet taking heavy casualties, Hart's men had no alternative other than to seek what cover they could on their own bank and return fire as best they could. There they remained for the rest of the battle.

Nevertheless, after an hour's firing, during which they expended 1,000 rounds of ammunition, Long's gunners had all but silenced the Boer artillery. In the circumstances, their own casualties had been remarkably light, for of the eighty-four officers and men present only eight had been killed and a dozen wounded. Long, unfortunately, was among the latter, having been shot through the liver while walking along the gun line encouraging his men. However, the two batteries' tasks also included the support of Hildyard's brigade as it crossed the river at Colenso. The problem was that the brigade had not yet appeared and ammunition was down to about six rounds per gun, although Long had already despatched two officers to bring up fresh supplies. Wishing to preserve this to support the attack, Major A. C. Bailward, the senior officer remaining in the gun position, ordered the men to retire to the cover of a donga (dry watercourse) some 50 yards behind the guns, there to await the arrival of either Hildyard's brigade or the ammunition wagons. Across the river, the Boer gunners returned to their weapons and opened fire.

Buller, shaken by the disaster that had befallen Hart's brigade, was brought to the brink of despair when Long's batteries fell silent. He issued orders cancelling the entire operation, although these were actually superfluous as Hildyard had already halted on his own initiative. At this pivotal moment Buller met the two officers Long had sent back. Both were inexperienced and at some stage of their journey to the rear they had looked back towards the line of deserted guns with not a living soul to tend them. The picture they painted was needlessly black, for the guns were in no danger of capture; their escort, four infantry companies lying two to the right and two to the left of the gun line, was perfectly capable of dealing with any such threat. Forgetting this, Buller, horrified by the prospect of losing guns to the enemy, halted nine ammunition wagons on their way up to the gun position, ordering Hildyard to send forward two battalions to cover the withdrawal of the two batteries, 'but on no account to get involved'. Shortly after this ambiguous order was given a shell exploded near by, killing Buller's surgeon and badly bruising the general's ribs.

Now in a state of shock, Buller called for volunteers to bring out the guns. His ADCs, Captains Harry Schofield and Walter Congreve, responded immediately, as did another staff officer, Lieutenant Frederick Roberts, the only son of Field Marshal Lord Roberts, VC. Together, they galloped for the gun position with two teams under Corporal George Nurse of the 66th Battery. Seeing what was afoot, the Boers swept the entire area with shrapnel and intense rifle fire. Congreve and Roberts were wounded, the latter mortally, but with the assistance of Private George Ravenhill of 2nd Royal Scots Fusiliers, who provided two of the escort companies, two of the guns were limbered up and brought out. A second attempt, made by Lieutenants Schreiber and Grylls of the 66th Battery, failed with the loss of both officers. Captain Hamilton Reed of 7th Battery RFA, which had been in action some distance to the west, then brought up three teams in a courageous attempt to rescue more of the guns. After he and half his men had been hit, and thirteen out of twenty-one horses had been killed, he was forced to desist. Buller forbade any further efforts to save the guns. Some, but not all of this was watched with a sense of bewilderment by the original gun detachments, waiting for a fresh ammunition supply in their donga, for as far as they were aware nothing was amiss. Later in the day, Major William Babtie, Royal Army Medical Corps, rode up to the donga under heavy rifle fire and attended to the wounded, going from place to place without heed to the shots directed at anyone who exposed himself. After this, he and Congreve went out to bring in the dying Lieutenant Roberts, again under heavy fire.

Buller sent in Lyttleton to provide covering fire while Hart withdrew his sorely tried brigade. With regard to the guns on Long's position he had three choices. He could wait until nightfall and then recover them under cover of darkness – a course of action that he rejected despite the many who volunteered for the task; he could order the naval brigade to shell the position, thereby destroying the guns and preventing their use by the enemy – an option that he does not seem to have considered; or he could simply abandon the guns. In pain and unable to think clearly, he opted for the last and ordered a general retreat. By 11:00 the Battle of Colenso was over. During the afternoon the Boers crossed the river, took possession of the guns and made prisoners of those in the donga. The wounded they released, allowing them to be carried away to the waiting ambulances. A point of interest is that one of the volunteer stretcher-bearers present was Mohandas (Mahatma) Ghandi, who would one day lead India to independence. The battle had cost Buller 143 killed, 755 wounded, 240 missing and ten guns captured; the Boer losses amounted to six killed and twenty-one wounded.

The fairest verdict upon Colenso was passed by the German Army's official observer, who wrote: 'The general and not his gallant force was defeated.' Buller declined to accept responsibility and blamed Long for deploying his guns too far forward. Long bore the stricture in dignified silence until 1906, when General Botha, the Boer commander at Colenso, shed a different light on the matter. Botha said that his own plan required his men to remain quietly in concealed positions from which they could have inflicted severe losses on the British infantry as they crossed the river, but that Long's unexpected appearance at the forward edge of the battle had forced him to spring his trap too soon. 'That man (Long) saved the British Army that day,' he wrote. 'It was his action that exposed our plan, and forced us to fight, and then the whole battle turned that way and Buller's army never advanced across the road bridge, as it was intended, to where we had planned to crush it, in that little flat across the river under the hills. It was a great disappointment for us.'

No fewer than seven Victoria Crosses and nineteen Distinguished Conduct Medals were awarded for actions relating directly to the attempted recovery of the guns. Those awarded the Victoria Cross were Major William Babtie, Captain Walter Congreve, Corporal George Nurse, Private George Ravenhill, Captain Hamilton Reed, Lieutenant Frederick Roberts and Captain Harry Schofield. Babtie was knighted later in his career, achieved the rank of lieutenant general and became Director of Army Medical Services. Congreve also received a knighthood in due course and became a general. He served in World War I, during which the French honoured him with the Légion d'Honneur and the Russians with the Order of St Anne, 1st Class. He was serving as Governor of Malta when he died on 26 February 1927. His son, Major William Congreve, was awarded a posthumous VC during the Battle of the Somme. Nurse, who had managed to limber up the second gun to be recovered, received a commission as a reward for his initiative. Ravenhill became one of the eight men to forfeit the award when he was convicted on theft in 1908. Reed became a major general and served in World War I, during which he commanded the 15th (Scottish) Division 1917–19 and was honoured with the American Legion of Honour 3rd Class and the French

Croix de Guerre. Schofield became a lieutenant colonel and served during World War I as the British Commandant of Lines of Communication in France 1915–17.

The award made to Roberts marks a particularly important point in the history of the Victoria Cross. Roberts died from his wounds the day after the battle, but in the circumstances the award could not reasonably be refused and was made posthumously, thereby setting a precedent. Six more posthumous awards were made for acts carried out during the war. In 1902 King Edward VII approved the principle and in 1907 six further awards were made in respect of instances between 1857 and 1897 where the men concerned would have received the VC if they had survived. In 1920, the *de facto* position was formally recognised by an appropriate amendment to the Royal Warrant.

Together, the defeats at Stormberg, Magersfontein and Colenso, occurring within days of each other, made up what became known in Britain as Black Week. Yet mortification soon turned to anger and thousands of men enlisted for service in South Africa with volunteer units. The probability that, sooner or later, Buller would have been replaced as Commander-in-Chief, became a certainty when, the day after Colenso, he caused outrage in government circles by sending a signal to General Sir George White, commanding the troops besieged in Ladysmith, advising him to fire off his ammunition and obtain the best terms possible from the Boers. Sensibly, White chose to ignore his advice. Lord Roberts, whose own VC had been won during the Indian Mutiny when he saved the life of a soldier and captured a rebel standard, was appointed Commander-in-Chief shortly after the battle. Buller's authority was restricted to Natal and he was forbidden to undertake major operations without Roberts's approval. After further messy and expensive reverses, notably at Spion Kop, he did manage to break through to Ladysmith in February 1900. Roberts, having relieved Kimberley and Mafeking, defeated a Boer army at Paardeberg and went on to capture both the enemy's capitals. To the end, Buller remained popular with the troops, who tended to blame intermediate commanders for the mistakes that had been made. When he returned home in October he was welcomed as a hero by a public as yet unaware of the whole story.

The character of the war had changed by this time. It took a further eighteen months, and much effort, to defeat a guerrilla campaign waged by Boer commandos. At the end of this a sensible peace was concluded, leading to the creation of the Union of South Africa.

The Boxer Rising

1900–1901

By the end of the nineteenth century the Chinese Empire was in terminal decline. Medieval, inefficient and corrupt, it was ruled with a rod of iron by the Dowager Empress Tzu Hsi, a woman whose response to any argument among her subjects was to order their instant execution. Humiliated by the Opium Wars, and humiliated yet further during her more recent war with Japan, China was at the mercy of the powers of the day, which included Great Britain, France, Germany, Austria-Hungary, Russia, Italy, the United States and Japan, who extracted one concession after another from the Imperial government in furtherance of their respective commercial and political interests. It was impossible for the empire to challenge the powers militarily, for the Chinese regular army was not only as disorganised and inefficient as the rest of the country, but also carefully structured so that it never became a threat to the ruling Manchu dynasty.

Small wonder, then, that a large proportion of the population bitterly resented the influence of the powers in their country, or that an active resistance movement dedicated to their removal should emerge. The surprise is, that when such a movement did emerge, it was not led by members of the ruling classes, but by peasants and former soldiers. The movement, which developed in the manner of a secret society, was called the I Ho Ch'uan, or Fists of Righteous Harmony, better known in the West as the Boxers because of the type of physical exercises they performed. Even to this day, the Boxers' origins and organisation remain obscure. What is clear is their hatred of all foreigners, who were known to them as First Class Devils, Chinese converts to Christianity, who were Second Class Devils, and Chinese in foreign employ, who were Third Class Devils. Believing that their rituals gave them an immunity to their enemies' weapons, they used extreme violence to pursue their aims, one of the favourite activities being the murder of Christian missionaries. It was clear that they possessed links with the imperial court and the army, for by the end of 1899 the Dowager Empress had decided that they could be used, unofficially, to render the presence of foreigners in China as unpleasant and dangerous as possible. In this she had the support of Prince Tuan, father of the heir apparent, but not that of General Jung Lu, Commander-in-Chief of the Northern Armies, who believed that armed intervention by the powers would spell disaster for the dynasty.

By the spring of 1900 the Boxers were in full cry across large areas of China, murdering foreigners, destroying their property and wrecking railways. Naturally, the diplomatic corps in Peking protested to the Tsungli Yamen, the Chinese Foreign Ministry, which issued assurances that these regrettable disturbances were being brought under control. In fact the scale and frequency of outrages grew worse as the Boxers approached the capital. The legation ministers requested permission to summon guards from the warships lying off the mouth of the Pei-ho River. After some wrangling the Yamen agreed to permit the passage of a small number of soldiers for each legation. By the evening of 3 June the troops had arrived. They numbered thirty-seven Austrians, seventy-eight French, fifty-two Germans, eighty-one British, forty-one Italians, twenty-five Japanese, eighty-one Russians and fifty-six Americans, a total of 452, including twenty-two officers. Of these, thirty French and eleven Italians were immediately despatched to defend the Roman Catholic Peit'ang Cathedral, now crowded with Christian refugees, on the other side of the city. As regards heavy weapons, the Royal Marines brought with them an ancient four-barrelled Nordenfeldt machine-gun that jammed during every cycle, the Austrians had a 1-pdr Maxim but only 120 rounds for it, the US Marines had a Colt M1895 light machine-gun with a reputation for running away when it overheated, and the Russians arrived with a consignment of 9-pdr shells but no gun, the latter having been carelessly left behind on the platform of Tientsin railway station. Upon this tiny force depended the defence of an area that was not really defensible. At this period Peking consisted of several walled cities, one inside the other. The outermost was the Tartar City, enclosed by a thick battlemented wall some 40 feet high. Within lay the Imperial City and inside that was the Forbidden City, containing the emperor's palace. The Legation Quarter, approximately 1,500 yards square and bisected by a canal running from north to south, lay between the southern walls of the Imperial and Tartar Cities.

On 10 June contact between the Legation Quarter and the outside world ceased when the telegraph line was cut. The following day the Japanese Chancellor, Mr Sugiyama, was hacked to death by a mob on his way from the quarter to the railway station. On 15 June the Boxers all but destroyed the Chinese City, lying to the south of the Tartar Wall. Every business that had dealings with foreigners was set ablaze until, unchecked, the conflagration raged out of control. The Tsungli Yamen sent the ministers a reassuring note, promising that the hooligans would soon be brought under control and life could return to normal. On 19 June the Yamen sent another note, bitterly complaining of Allied aggression at the Taku Forts (concerning which the ministers knew nothing) and ordering the complete evacuation of the legations by 16:00 the following day, together with the departure of their occupants to Tientsin under escort. In principle, the ministers had no objection to this, but requested a meeting at 09:00 next morning to agree a later departure date. When no reply was received to this the German Minister, Baron von Ketteler, decided to visit the Yamen personally, contrary to the advice of his colleagues. On the way he was shot dead by a Chinese soldier. As it was now apparent that to accept the Yamen's offer of safe conduct would be tantamount to suicide, preparations were made to defend the Legation Quarter. Promptly at 16:00 on 20 June, the Chinese opened fire.

Four legations, those of Austria, Belgium, Holland and Italy, lay outside the defensible perimeter and were abandoned at once. The various national contingents were each allocated a sector of the defences for which they were responsible, erecting makeshift barricades from carts, barrels and sandbags. Their numbers received a welcome increase when 125 of the male refugees, more than half of whom had some previous military experience, volunteered to serve with the troops. The senior officer present was a Captain von Thomann of the Austro-Hungarian Navy, who became *de facto* Commander-in-Chief. Unfortunately, while his abilities as a naval officer were beyond doubt, he was no soldier. Three days after the siege began he made a disastrous decision that almost resulted in the premature abandonment of the outer defences. By common consent among the ministers he was removed. His replacement was Sir Claude Macdonald, the British Minister, partly because of his pre-eminent position in the diplomatic corps and partly because of his previous military experience, which included active service in Egypt and the Sudan. The appointment was not universally popular among the various national contingents, who, at this stage, were as suspicious of each other as were their respective ministers. Macdonald, however, exercised command with a professional diplomat's skill, touring the defences to provide moral support and encouragement for the permanently tired junior officers and NCOs holding the perimeter.

Gradually, he became accepted and generated considerable personal respect for himself. Likewise, shared hardship and danger broke down the barriers between the national contingents until they began to see the good in one another and work as a team. Those civilians who had not volunteered for service in the firing line were formed into committees responsible for rations, fuel, water, sanitation, fire precautions and Chinese labour, the last recruited from among the many Christian refugees present. Those of the legations' womenfolk who were not engaged in nursing set to with their sewing machines and made thousands of sandbags from sacking, blankets, curtains and even dresses.

The Boxer Rising was more a series of interconnected events than a battle in the conventional sense. The common factor was the siege of the Legation Quarter and the international efforts to break it. The events themselves included the siege, the first abortive attempt at relief, the defence of the International Settlement and the capture of the Chinese city of Tientsin, and the second successful relief attempt.

The siege lasted for fifty-five days. It was a matter of attack and counter-attack, brutal close-quarter street fighting in which the bayonet played a major part, incessant sniping and bombardment. Fortunately, much of the Chinese artillery fire was aimed too high. Early in July, much to the consternation of the Boxers and their supporters, the garrison found the means to reply. A small muzzle-loading rifled cannon, a relic of the Second China War, was discovered by Chinese labourers digging a trench. Its calibre was much the same as the Russians' 9-pdr shells, the fillings of which were already being used by two ingenious artificers, Armourer's Mate J. T. Thomas, Royal Navy, and Gunner's Mate Joseph Mitchell, US Navy, to refill the Italians' expended 1-pdr shellcases. The two turned their attention to modifying the 9-pdr shells for use with their new acquisition. This required splitting the composite round so that the propellant could be loaded first and then the projectile itself. The Italians produced a carriage for the weapon, which became known as Old Betsy, The Dowager Empress or the International Gun. Its first round, aimed at a Chinese battery only 300 yards distant, was high. To everyone's glee, it sailed over the wall of the Forbidden City and burst within. The second round fell short, but the third exploded among the enemy guns.

The atmosphere in which the siege was conducted was little short of surrealistic, for throughout the fighting both the Imperial Palace and the Tsungli Yamen maintained a polite discourse with the embattled diplomats. Thus, regrets that the 'disturbances' should have deprived the ladies of the Legation Quarter of their summer break in the cool hills were followed up with mass attacks by suicidal Boxers; the arrival of carts laden with melons and rice, sent in by the Dowager Empress, was followed by more attacks and sniping; and while Macdonald was reading the Imperial Family's official condolences on the death of the then Duke of Edinburgh, his bedroom was wrecked by a shell. For most of the siege the head of Professor Huberty James, an academic from the Imperial Peking University who had been captured and tortured by the Boxers, gazed into the defences from the pole on which it had been mounted by his murderers.

The siege and related operations were the first occasion on which the Victoria Cross and the Medal of Honor were awarded to men fighting in the same actions. The Royal Marine Light Infantry detachment in Peking was awarded one Victoria Cross, five Distinguished Conduct Medals and two Conspicuous Gallantry Medals, one of the last going to Sergeant J. E. Preston, who was also one of those to receive the DCM. The Victoria Cross was awarded to Captain Lewis Halliday for actions on 24 June. On that day a Boxer attack succeeded in reaching the west wall of the British Legation. Halliday led out a seven-strong party to dislodge them. Turning a corner into an alley, the party suddenly came face to face with five Boxers, all of whom, unusually, were armed with rifles. In the close-quarter exchange of fire one Marine was mortally wounded and Halliday was shot through the left shoulder and lung. In return, Halliday shot four of the enemy dead with his revolver, the fifth escaping when the weapon misfired. Later, Halliday led out a larger sortie that captured and demolished a building from which the enemy were firing, and in so doing enlarged the field of fire from the legation wall. By now, in great pain and weak from loss of blood, he was unable to carry on and was taken to the hospital, where he was confined for the rest of the siege. Later in his career, he served during World War I, was knighted and became a lieutenant general. He also served as Hon. Colonel Commandant Royal Marines 1939–40.

The US Marine Corps detachment, together with its attached naval personnel, was awarded a total of twenty Medals of Honor actions during the siege, one of them posthumous. The detachment's principal responsibility was to keep the enemy off that section of the Tartar Wall that overlooked the Legation Quarter, for if that had been lost it would have been impossible for the defence to have continued much longer. Of all the Medals awarded, none was harder earned than that won by Private Daly.

A native of Long Island, Daly had been in the Marine Corps for just a year. He was a born soldier, being disciplined, self-sufficient, aggressive when he needed to be, physically tough and apparently immune to fear. The Americans were generally considered to be the best shots in Peking, but Daly was in a class of his own. On the night 14 August Captain N. T. Hall posted him to an advanced barricade on the wall with the object of picking off Chinese snipers who were troubling parties working on the defences behind and below. Hall said he would send up a few more men to help but left when Daly said that he would rather work alone. During the first hour he picked off eight of the enemy, more than enough to guarantee an attack on his position. In fact he was attacked eight times during the night by small parties of Boxers. He systematically killed each of his attackers with bullet, bayonet and butt-stroke, and between attacks continued to pick off any of the enemy who dared show themselves. When, shortly before dawn, the American working party completed its task, Daly made his way back to the Marines' main barricade, leaving behind a score of bodies on the wall and more elsewhere. He was to become a legend in his own lifetime and will shortly appear again in these pages.

Even before the siege began Macdonald had been so concerned by the growing unrest in Peking that he had telegraphed Vice Admiral Sir Edward Seymour, the senior naval officer with the warships standing off the Pei-ho bar, requesting the urgent despatch of substantial reinforcements for the small legation guards. Seymour had reacted promptly, assembling a 2,000-strong multi-national force of marines and naval ratings with which he left Tientsin in five trains on the morning of 10 June, expecting to reach Peking that evening. Unfortunately, the Boxers had not only damaged the track in numerous places, but also mounted attacks on the stationary trains while repairs were completed. These were beaten off, but the result was that by the evening of 11 June the leading train had only reached Lang Fang, 40 miles short of Peking. Scouts sent forward returned to report stiffening enemy resistance. By now the size of the force had been reduced because of the need to drop off troops to hold stations along the line. As it was also running short of ammunition and food, Seymour decided to remain where he was for the present and sent back a train for fresh supplies. The train returned empty on the 15th with the news that the track had again been broken between Yangts'un and Tientsin. This meant that as far as rail transit was concerned, the force could neither move forwards nor backwards. Reluctantly, Seymour reached the conclusion that the force would have to withdraw to Tientsin on foot. The heavy weapons were abandoned and the wounded were placed aboard commandeered junks. The junks, which grounded regularly on mud banks, slowed the pace of the march to a snail's pace. The country through which the troops passed now swarmed with Boxers, with whom units of the Imperial Army had begun to side openly. It became necessary for the force to fight its way through every village, adding to the growing toll of casualties. At dusk on 21 June the column reached Hsiku, a few miles from Tientsin, and was fired on from a large building across the river. During the night the junks were formed into a pontoon bridge. Early the following morning this was crossed by a force of Royal Marines and seamen under Major J. R. Johnstone. The building was stormed at the point of the bayonet and was found to be part of a huge arsenal, enclosing no less than 40 acres, the presence of which had not been previously suspected. The arsenal contained over 250 field guns, 14,000 rifles of various types and millions of rounds of ammunition, enabling the column to replenish its depleted supplies. Seymour, recognising that his men were worn out, wisely decided to take possession of the arsenal and remain there for the moment, a decision influenced by the sound of heavy fighting from the International Settlement at Tientsin, just three miles distant, which suggested that substantial Chinese forces lay across his path. Indeed, hardly had the weary troops settled in than the arsenal was besieged by elements of two Chinese regular divisions and a large number of Boxers.

The difficult nature of the withdrawal that had been carried out by Seymour's force is illustrated by the citations of two of the Medals of Honor awarded. Of Seaman George Rose the citation records, *inter alia*: 'On the 13th he was one of a few who fought off a large force of the enemy saving the main baggage train from destruction. On the 20th and 21st he was engaged in heavy fighting against the Imperial Army, being always in the first rank. On the 22nd he showed gallantry in the capture of the Siku (sic) Arsenal. He volunteered to go to the nearby village, which was occupied by the enemy, to secure medical supplies urgently required. The party brought back the supplies, carried by newly taken prisoners.' The citation for Ordinary Seaman William Seach reads: 'June 13: Seach and six others were cited for their courage in repulsing an attack by 300 Chinese Imperialist soldiers and Boxer militants with a bayonet charge, thus thwarting a planned massive attack on the entire force. June 20: During a day-long battle, Seach ran across an open clearing, gained cover and cleaned out nests of Chinese snipers. June 21: During a surprise sabre attack by Chinese cavalrymen, Seach was cited for defending (machine) gun emplacements. June 22: Seach and other breached (climbed) the wall of a Chinese fort (i.e. the Hsiku Arsenal), fought their way to the enemy's guns and turned the cannon upon the defenders of the fort.'

A great deal had happened in Tientsin since Seymour's trains steamed out on their abortive mission. On 15 June the Boxers occupied the walled Chinese city. Two days later they were joined by regular troops in a sustained attack on the International Settlement. Here the position was not quite as critical as it was in the Legation Quarter, for most of the civil population had wisely left for Japan. There was a garrison of about 2,500 men, mostly Russians, and defences had been laid out by a young American mining engineer named Herbert Hoover, who would one day become President of the United States. As possession of Tientsin was vital for further progress in the direction of Peking, the commanders of the Allied warships immediately bombarded the Taku Forts at the mouth of the Pei-ho, which were then stormed by landing parties who faced only irresolute opposition. Advancing up the river, these troops relieved the International Settlement on 23 June.

Next day a Chinese named Chao Yin-ho entered the perimeter. He was the servant of a former Grenadier Guards officer, Clive Bigham, who was on his way to take up a position at the Peking Legation and had joined Seymour's expedition. As earlier attempts to get a message through had failed, Seymour had despatched Chao to contact the nearest Allied troops. Chao, a man of great resource, had bluffed his way past the Boxers but had then been pinned down by the fire of Russian sentries. He had, however, served in the Royal Navy and knew semaphore, in which he signalled his message. He was taken before the senior British naval officer present, who accepted the story he told, despite the general belief that Seymour's force had been completely wiped out. On 26 June a 2,000-strong column, mostly Russian but including two companies of recently arrived Royal Welch Fusiliers, broke through to the Hsiku Arsenal, enabling Seymour's men to re-enter Allied lines, bringing with them their 232 wounded. Chao was rewarded with $1,000, an immense sum for a man in his position, and when Bigham returned to England, having decided not to take up his post in Peking, he became a steward aboard the USS *Newark*.

Allied reinforcements were now converging on the Pei-ho from all directions. Among them was HMS *Terrible*, whose 12-pdr guns, mounted on field carriages, had taken part in the Battle of Colenso and would be similarly employed during the forthcoming operations. As the railway had now been thoroughly wrecked, it was decided that the second attempt to relieve the besieged legations in Peking would follow the line of the river. However, it took a considerable time to assemble the carts, pack animals and coolies required to provide the relief force with sufficient transport for its supplies, and before the operation could even begin the enemy would have to be ejected from the walled Chinese city of Tientsin.

The massive walls of Tientsin formed a rectangle with a gate in the centre of each of the four faces, approached by causeway. As the Allies could not afford the time to batter a breach through the stout masonry it was decided to take two of the gates by storm. The Japanese, British, Americans and French would assault the south gate in three columns while the Russians and Germans attacked the east gate. The assault began at 05:30 on 13 July and was met by a storm of fire, not only from the walls but also from Chinese troops in the open country to the west, which caused heavy casualties. There was, too, a degree of confusion among the attackers, resulting not least from language difficulties. By nightfall little progress had been made.

During the day's fighting the US 9th Infantry was particularly hard hit, being pinned down and taking severe casualties, including their commanding officer, Colonel Emerson H. Liscum, who had taken the Colours from their fallen bearer and was encouraging his men to return the fire when he was mortally wounded. Three members of the regiment were awarded the Medal of Honor for their actions during the day. Captain Andre W. Brewster braved the enemy's fire to save two of his men from drowning in one of the many waterways that criss-crossed the area. First Lieutenant Louis B. Lawton, despatched to the rear to bring up reinforcements, did so across a wide area swept by the enemy's fire and was wounded three times in the process. Private Robert von Schlick received a posthumous award. His citation reads: 'Although previously wounded while carrying a wounded comrade to safety, he rejoined his command, which partly occupied an exposed position upon a dike, remaining there after his command had been withdrawn and obliviously presenting himself as a conspicuous target until he was literally shot off his position by the enemy.'

Near by, the British naval brigade had also come under a heavy cross-fire and was sustaining casualties. Seeing an able seaman fall some 50 yards from cover, eighteen-year-old Midshipman Basil Guy went out with the intention of bringing him in. The two men immediately became the focus of the enemy's fire. The seaman was too heavy for Guy to lift, so after bandaging his wound the midshipman returned to cover. When stretcher-bearers arrived he went out with them and was helping to bring in the casualty when the man was hit again and died before he could be got to safety. Guy was awarded the Victoria Cross. He later served in both world wars and retired with the rank of commander, having also been awarded the Distinguished Service Order.

The enemy's resistance had been stubborn but during the night many of the Chinese lost heart and left the city by the north gate. At 03:45 on 14 July the Japanese blew in the outer south gate, the inner gate being opened for them from within by Lieutenant Smedley Butler, US Marine Corps, who had fought his way over the wall to do so. Japanese, British and Americans poured into the city, which was thoroughly looted after the last pockets of opposition had been eliminated.

Butler, then aged nineteen, was a very remarkable man. Contrary to his parents' wishes he had left home to join the Marine Corps at the age of sixteen, receiving a second lieutenant's commission just before his seventeenth birthday. Promotion to first lieutenant came quickly, as did active service against insurgents in the Philippines. During the battle for the walled city he was wounded twice but refused to leave the firing line and ensured that those of his men who had been hit were safely evacuated. It will be recalled that at this stage navy and marine officers were not eligible to receive the Medal of Honor. Had it been otherwise, Butler would have set a national record. As it was, he received the Marine Corps Brevet Medal, a distinction only awarded on twenty-two occasions, as well as brevet promotion to captain.

In Peking, the minds of the Dowager Empress's advisers had suddenly grasped the full implications of the Allied successes at Tientsin, coupled with the sustained military build-up that was taking place there. They seemed, however, to interpret the delay in advancing beyond Tientsin as a reluctance to become involved in major operations within China, when, of course, the real reason was the difficulty in putting together the logistic element of the expedition. Nevertheless, the imperial authorities had begun to lose faith in the Boxers and were inclined to the view that if a more moderate stance was adopted, retribution might be avoided and some form of compromise reached. A truce was therefore arranged with the defenders of the Legation Quarter as a gesture of goodwill. However, the longer the relief force took to complete its preparations, the stronger grew the war party's influence with the Dowager Empress, to the point that the moderate mandarins who had arranged the ceasefire were decapitated.

The relief force, commanded by Lieutenant General Sir Alfred Gaselee and consisting of over 18,000 men (approximately 2,900 British, Indian and Chinese, 2,200 Americans, 9,000 Japanese, 2,900 Russians and 1,200 French) and seventy guns, finally set out from Tientsin on 4 August in intense heat. It broke through one Chinese blocking position at Peits'ang next day and another at Yangts'un the day after. Thereafter, resistance to its advance began to crumble. By 8 August a number of extremely brave Chinese and Japanese couriers had begun to slip through the lines, establishing contact between it and the Legation Quarter. Gaselee was able to predict that his troops would reach Peking on 13 or 14 August and received in return a map from Macdonald showing the defended area and the best points of entry to the city.

Within the Forbidden City the enraged war party ordered the immediate destruction of the Legation Quarter, which was subjected to frenzied attacks. Until now, Macdonald, anxious to preserve ammunition stocks, had discouraged the use of his automatic weapons, but with relief so close he was not inclined to grant the enemy a last-minute victory and permitted them to rattle away unchecked. They silenced the Chinese guns and cut such swathes through the attackers that the latter began to show a marked decline in their enthusiasm.

The last phase of the relief force's advance was marked by rivalry between the national contingents as to who would gain the prestige of being the first to enter the city. Early on 14 August the Americans, French, Japanese and Russians became involved in heavy fighting around the southern and eastern gates of the Tartar Wall. The British, however, had the benefit of Macdonald's map as well as the advice of a returned businessman who guided them through the gutted warren of the Chinese city. From the Tartar Wall a seaman signalled with semaphore flags, 'Come in by the water gate.' This was the opening through which the canal bisecting the Legation Quarter left the city. At about 14:30 some seventy men of the 7th Rajputs crossed the moat under sporadic fire and, helped by the American Marines within, broke through the grating to enter the city amid wild applause. An hour later the Americans and French also overcame the defences, although the Japanese and Russians both incurred a hundred casualties in fighting that lasted until nightfall. The defenders of the Peit'ang Cathedral, whom few had expected to survive, were relieved by the Japanese on 16 August.

The previous day, the Imperial Family left Peking on what was called, for the sake of face, a tour of inspection. When they returned in January

1902 their dynasty had but a few brief years left before a revolution replaced it with a republic. In the meantime, Gaselee's troops, joined by the German East Asia Brigade at the end of September, eliminated the last pockets of Boxer resistance in northern China. The imperial authorities, having no further use for the Boxers, either beheaded them or handed them over for execution. China was forced to make a humiliating apology, grant further concessions and pay an indemnity of £67.5 million.

At a time when nationalism was at its strongest, the Boxer Rising provides a rare and short-lived example of international co-operation against what amounted to a well-organised terrorist organisation, no matter what its motives were. As well as the future President Hoover, a surprising number of those present would achieve high office later in life, notably three officers of the Royal Navy. Captain John Jellicoe and Commander David Beatty would both command the Grand Fleet during World War I, and Lieutenant Roger Keyes would lead the Zeebrugge Raid during the same war and become Chief of Combined Operations in World War II.

At the tactical level the careers of two members of the US Marine Corps also provide an interesting footnote. In 1914 unrest in Mexico led to the United States' occupation of the port of Vera Cruz. The then Major Smedley Butler carried out several reconnaissances ashore in disguise then led his battalion with distinction during two days of house-to-house fighting, winning his first Medal of Honor. The following year he won a second Medal of Honor when law and order broke down in Haiti and the United States was forced to intervene. The citation for this second award reads as follows:

As Commanding Officer of the detachments from the 5th, 13th and 23rd Companies and Marine and Sailor detachments from USS *Connecticut*, Major Butler led an attack on Fort Riviere on 17 November 1915. Following a concentrated drive, several different detachments of Marines closed in on the old French bastion in an effort to cut off all avenues of retreat for the Cacos bandits. Reaching the fort on the southern side where there was a small opening in the wall, Major Butler gave the signal to attack and Marines from the 15th Company poured through the breach, engaged the Cacos in hand-to-hand fighting, took the bastion and crushed Caco resistance. Throughout this perilous action, Major Butler was conspicuous for his bravery and forceful leadership.

By 1929, after further service in China, Butler had become the youngest Marine ever to achieve the rank of major general. He might well have become the corps' commandant had he not made a critical remark about the Italian dictator Mussolini that was not considered to be politically acceptable at the time. He retired from the service in 1931 and died in Philadelphia in 1940.

Dan Daly, now a gunnery sergeant, also saw action at Vera Cruz and in Haiti, where he won his second Medal of Honor. On the evening of 24 October 1915 the thirty-five-man patrol of which he was a member was ambushed by 400 Cacos while fording a river. The patrol managed to reach a defensible position, although the horse carrying its machine-gun was killed in the river. When the Cacos attacked during the night the patrol commander called for the machine-gun. Daly voluntarily made his way through the enemy to the river, cut the gun free from the dead horse, strapped it to his back and returned to the patrol, which remained under fire throughout the night. 'At daybreak,' the citation records, 'The Marines in three squads advanced in three different directions, surprising and scattering the Cacos in all directions. Gunnery Sergeant Daly fought with exceptional gallantry against heavy odds throughout this action.'

Butler and Daly remain the only two members of the US Marine Corps to have been awarded the Medal of Honor twice.

THE FIRST WORLD WAR
1914–18

Mons, Le Cateau and The Aisne
AUGUST–SEPTEMBER 1914

By 1914 it was clearly apparent that the firepower developed by the magazine rifle, the machine-gun and quick-firing artillery had given troops
fighting defensively a clear advantage over those who were attacking, an
advantage that was multiplied many times when the defenders occupied
an entrenched position fronted by barbed-wire entanglements. The
lessons of recent history, however, were perverse, for during the American Civil War, the Franco-Prussian War, the Spanish-American War, the
Boer War and the Russo-Japanese War they revealed that while the army
which attacked certainly sustained the heavier casualties, in the end it
was victorious. Therefore, in 1914, every General Staff in continental
Europe thought in terms of offensive operations.

For the German Army, the first priority was destruction of the French
armies. This was to be achieved by means of the Schlieffen Plan, con-
ceived in 1905 by the then Chief of German General Staff, Count von
Schlieffen. It was predicted that as one flank of the contending armies
would inevitably rest on the frontier of Switzerland, this could be used
as a pivot enabling the disengaged German right wing to be flung
forward in a huge wheel that would pass to the west of Paris and eventually pin the French back against their own frontier defences, where, cut
off from their supplies, they would be forced to surrender. The problem
was the vast amount of space required to develop this enormous
manoeuvre, space that could only be obtained by marching through
Belgium. As Great Britain was bound by treaty to defend Belgian
independence, this violation of neutrality brought her into the war.

In some ways, the German Army of 1914 was the most formidable in
the world. It was superbly equipped, led by a brilliant General Staff and
an officer corps that was professional and efficient, as indeed were its
long-service NCOs. Its mobilisation had been a model of pre-planned
organisation. On the other hand, it was a conscript army whose soldiers
were trained for a war of manoeuvre *en masse* that made few demands on
the individual soldier's initiative, knowledge of fieldcraft or marksman-

ship. The German soldier was simply to advance and attack in dense formations because his generals, recalling their successes in the Franco-Prussian War, believed that weight and mass were the key to successful offensive operations. The outer edge of the great German wheel through Belgium was formed by General Alexander von Kluck's First Army, a huge force that consisted of no less than seven corps because of its critical role. To conform with the General Staff's timetable its heavily laden infantry would have to march hard day after day as well as eliminate whatever opposition lay in its path. Little or no margin had been allowed for such checks, as Kluck had been selected for the task because of his hard-driving and ruthless methods.

The British Expeditionary Force, commanded by Field Marshal Sir John French, was in many respects the antithesis of Kluck's army. Its leaders were, to be sure, unused to handling large formations in the field but the troops possessed many of the qualities the Germans lacked. The BEF consisted entirely of long-service regulars and recalled reservists, many of whom had seen active service in India, South Africa and elsewhere. The lessons of the Boer War had been taken to heart. The infantry were fully aware of the value of concealment and had been trained to fire sixteen *aimed* rounds per minute from their clip-loading Lee-Enfield magazine rifles, a rate of fire that could not be equalled by any of the European powers' huge conscript armies.

The BEF consisted of I Corps, commanded by Lieutenant General Sir Douglas Haig, II Corps under Lieutenant General Sir Horace Smith-Dorrien, a survivor from Isandhlwana, and the Cavalry Division commanded by Major General Edmund Allenby. On entering Belgium it was ordered to come into the line on the left of General Lanrezac's French Fifth Army, which was being pressed back by the German Second Army under General von Bülow, to the east of Kluck's line of advance. On the evening of 22 August II Corps dug in along the line of the Mons–Condé Canal while I Corps presented a refused flank, running south from Mons, so as to maintain contact with the French. West of Mons the canal ran in a straight line, but at Mons it looped around the northern edge of the town before continuing eastwards, forming a salient.

On 23 August II Corps was attacked by Kluck's III, IV and IX Corps. The British infantry, unable to believe their eyes on seeing the dense formations advancing against them, raked the German ranks with their terrible sixteen rounds a minute, their bullets often finding more than one billet, until every assault was shot flat. Prisoners, under the impression that they had been facing massed machine-guns, were reluctant to believe that each infantry battalion only possessed two. Becoming cautious, the Germans began advancing by short rushes, supported by their well-handled artillery, which caused most of the British casualties. Nevertheless, by the end of the day they had failed to secure a crossing of the canal. Smith-Dorrien's men, scorning their opponents as being little better than amateurs, were confident they could hold the position until kingdom come, and were less than pleased when they were ordered to withdraw that night so that the BEF could conform to the withdrawal of the French on their right.

During the fighting, the railway bridge at Nimy, at the northern edge of the Mons salient, was held by one company and the machine-gun section of the 4th Royal Fusiliers. Naturally the enemy made the bridge their special target and such was the volume of fire that casualties among the machine-gun section were heavy, although as soon as one of the gunners was killed another man took his place. When the battalion received orders to pull back, Lieutenant Maurice Dease and Private Sidney Godley were among those who volunteered to remain with the machine-guns and cover its withdrawal. Dease, manning one of the guns, continued to fire although he was repeatedly hit. After he had received his fifth wound he could do no more and was carried to a place of safety, where he died. Godley had to move three bodies aside before he could get to his gun. The nearby explosion of a shell sent a splinter into his back shortly after Dease had been taken away. Despite being in intense pain, as well as being struck by a bullet that lodged in his skull, he single-handedly held the enemy in check for the next two hours. At the end of this superhuman effort, all his ammunition having been fired off, he smashed up his gun and threw the pieces into the canal. He crawled back to the edge of the town where two civilians took him to the hospital and it was there, while having his wounds dressed, that he became a prisoner-of-war when the Germans arrived.

It had soon become clear to the BEF's high command that Mons could not be more than a holding action. II Corps therefore ordered 57 Company Royal Engineers to blow the canal bridges to the west of Mons. This was easier said than done, for the company was required to deal with eight bridges yet possessed only one exploder. In the event only the bridge at Jemappes was blown, although elsewhere Captain Theodore Wright, the company's adjutant, and Lance Corporal Charles Jarvis, earned the sincere admiration of the neighbouring troops as they vainly worked under fire for hours preparing demolition charges at their respective bridges. The survival of the bridges was not a disaster, for the canal was not a major obstacle and the Germans, having plenty of bridging equipment available, would not have been held up for more than a few hours.

Next morning they were across and in contact with elements of the BEF's rearguards. Between Elouges and Quiévrain an attempt to work round the British left flank was foiled by the steady fire of two infantry battalions occupying natural defensive positions. The commander of the 2nd Cavalry Brigade, seeing the enemy advance brought to a standstill, ordered the 9th Lancers to charge. The regiment did so, coming under fire not only from the enemy infantry but also several artillery batteries, and suffered serious casualties. The charge was brought to a standstill by a wire fence surrounding a sugar refinery. Swinging to the right, the lancers rallied near Elouges under the cover of a railway embankment.

Near by, the 119th Battery Royal Field Artillery, commanded by Major Ernest Alexander, was being engaged by three German batteries and a machine-gun. The gunners were beginning to drop fast and it was clearly time to go. The problem for Alexander was that if he called the teams forward most of the horses would be killed and the guns would be lost. He and his gunners therefore began manhandling the guns back towards the point where they could be limbered up in comparative safety. Shorthanded, they made such slow progress that Alexander ran across to the rallied lancers and asked for their help. This was willingly provided by Captain Francis Grenfell, who, although he had already sustained two wounds, led a party of volunteers to assist in hauling the guns out of their exposed position. By the time the battery had been limbered up and was on its way, about a quarter of its personnel had been killed or wounded, one of the latter being rescued by Alexander under heavy fire. Grenfell, badly wounded and his uniform ripped by bullets, would probably have been captured had he not been picked up by a magnificent silver-and-blue Rolls Royce and taken to a hospital. By coincidence, the car was driven by his friend the Duke of Westminster, who was serving as a signals officer with the Cavalry Division and scouring the field for stragglers.

Lieutenant Dease, Private Godley, Lance Corporal Jarvis, Major Alexander and Captain Grenfell all received the Victoria Cross for their part in the fighting at Mons. Dease's and Godley's awards were the first to be made during the war. On learning what had taken place, King George V personally ensured that Godley received the award. Godley's wounds were treated in a German field hospital and he was then taken to a prisoner-of-war camp, where he remained for the rest of the war.

Chivalry still had a place in war and on Christmas Day 1914 the camp's German officers, recognising that the Victoria Cross equated with their own much-coveted Pour le Mérite, invited him to dine with them. After the war Godley became a school caretaker and was active on behalf of service charities, sometimes dressing up as 'Old Bill', the famous cartoon character created by Bruce Bairnsfather, whose wry, often cynical, humour reflected the attitude of troops serving in the trenches of the Western Front. In April 1939 Godley returned to Nimy for the opening of a new bridge which incorporated a plaque commemorating his own heroism and that of Lieutenant Dease. On the same occasion he was presented with a special medal by the people of Mons. He died in 1957 but was not forgotten, for in 1976 a new housing estate at Bexley was named after him, as in 1992 was a new housing block in Tower Hamlets. These commemorative namings were entirely appropriate as the Royal Fusiliers was essentially a London regiment with its headquarters in the Tower.

The citation for the award made to Lance Corporal Jarvis claims, incorrectly, that he blew his bridge. Jarvis himself made no such claim and it was certainly not his fault that the bridge remained unblown. What is true is that he demonstrated so high an order of courage that the award was recommended and granted. After leaving the army he worked as a labourer and was employed at Portsmouth naval dockyard during World War II. Francis Grenfell, son of Lord Grenfell, numbered Winston Churchill and John Buchan among his friends. While recovering from the wounds received at Mons he learned that his twin brother had been killed in action on the Aisne. He returned to the 9th Lancers as a squadron commander in October 1914 but was again seriously wounded a few weeks later. Recovered, he rejoined the regiment in April 1915 but was killed on 25 May leading an attack on the Ypres–Menin road. In addition to the Victoria Cross, Ernest Alexander also received the Belgian Croix de Guerre. He subsequently retired from the army with the rank of major general.

The fighting on 23 August cost Kluck some 3,000 casualties, while the BEF sustained about 1,600. On the 24th both sides lost about 2,000 killed, wounded or captured, a large proportion of the British loss stemming from the failure of a withdrawal order to reach one battalion, which was eventually surrounded and forced to surrender. Some of Kluck's corps had now caught up with the main body of his army, but the fact remained that on the latter date he had only been able to advance a maximum of three-and-a-half miles. As the delays imposed on him during these two days had disrupted his timetable, he went hard after the BEF as it retreated from the area to conform with the French.

Lying across the path of the British withdrawal was a densely wooded area, the Forest of Mormal. To avoid possible confusion, it was decided that the BEF's I and II Corps would withdraw respectively to the east and west of the forest. During the night of 25–26 August the German advance guards unexpectedly caught up with I Corps at Maroilles and Landrecies. At Maroilles they were driven back with comparative ease, but at Landrecies a sharp action took place. The burden of this fell on the 3rd Coldstream Guards, who repulsed several attempts to penetrate their line by the light of burning buildings. A German battery arrived and subjected the guardsmen to artillery fire until, at about midnight, a howitzer of 60th Battery Royal Field Artillery was brought up by hand and silenced the enemy guns with its third shot. After that the attacks ceased. During the fighting Lance Corporal George Wyatt of the Cold-stream won the VC. His citation reads: 'Part of Lance Corporal Wyatt's battalion was hotly engaged close to some farm buildings, when the enemy set alight some straw sacks in the farmyard. The lance corporal twice dashed out under very heavy fire from the enemy, only 25 yards away, and extinguished the burning straw, making it possible to hold the position. Later, although wounded in the head, he continued firing until he could no longer see owing to the blood pouring down his face. The medical officer bound up his wound and ordered him to the rear, but he returned to the firing line and went on fighting.' He survived the war, during which he achieved the rank of lance sergeant and also received the Russian Order of St George, then served as a police officer for many years in Yorkshire.

I Corps managed to disengage cleanly next morning but the unex-pected encounter had shaken its commander, Sir Douglas Haig, and he decided to continue his withdrawal southwards. This was to have an unfortunate effect on Smith-Dorrien's II Corps, which had reached the area of Le Cateau the previous evening and begun taking up positions on the plateau to the south-west of the town. Unfortunately, 26 August dawned misty, enabling the Germans to approach the British lines unde-tected. Suddenly, the 5th, 3rd and 4th Divisions, holding the line, found themselves violently assailed frontally by the German V and IV Corps. Furthermore, the 5th Division, on the right, expecting to see Haig's I Corps arrive to extend its line, suddenly found its flank in danger of being turned by the German III Corps and was forced to swing back its right to meet the threat. On the left the 4th Division, attacked by the enemy's II Cavalry Corps, followed his IV Reserve Corps, adjusted its position so that it lay obliquely to the main line. For six hours the Germans pressed home attacks in their dense formations, sustaining fearful casualties from the fire of the riflemen and a number of artillery batteries that had been deployed on the forward slopes to encourage the infantry. For their part, the exposed British artillery suffered cruelly at the hands of their German counterparts. Some guns were smashed and it became impossible to withdraw others because their horse teams were shot down by shellfire and the enemy infantry. Thanks to the arrival of a French cavalry corps on his left, and the self-sacrificial stand made by the 2nd Suffolk Regiment and the 2nd King's Own Yorkshire Light Infantry, who fought on until overrun in the angle of 5th Division's line, Smith-Dorrien was able to withdraw his corps in good order. His men had sustained 7,812 casualties and he had lost thirty-eight guns, but he had inflicted far higher personnel losses and imposed a further delay on the enemy. Without meaning to do so, Kluck paid Smith-Dorrien and his men a compliment by reporting to his superiors that he been engaged by the entire BEF. Never again during what became known as the Great Retreat did the German First Army dare to tread so closely on II Corps' heels.

Among those who received the Victoria Cross for their actions during the battle was Lance Corporal Frederick Holmes of the King's Own York-shire Light Infantry. Holmes carried a badly wounded comrade, who weighed twelve stone, no less than two miles before handing over his burden to a party of stretcher-bearers. He then returned to his battalion, which by this time had sustained serious losses in killed and wounded. He helped to drive a gun out of action, placing the wounded driver on one of the horses, but shortly after was so seriously wounded himself that his leg was in danger of amputation. Returning to the Western Front in October 1915, he was promoted to sergeant and was then posted to India. In March 1917 he was commissioned and sent to Mesopotamia, where he sustained a fractured skull. No longer fit for active service, he was employed in the Military Record Office in London. He finally left the army with the rank of captain and emigrated to Australia.

Major Charles Yate of the same regiment received the posthumous award of the VC. He commanded one of the two companies that remained in the trenches to the bitter end so that their comrades could withdraw. When all his officers had been killed or wounded and the remaining ammunition had been expended, he led his nineteen survivors against the enemy in a desperate bayonet charge in which he was severely wounded. He was picked up by the Germans and died as a prisoner-of-war the following month.

Near by, numerous acts of heroism were performed by artillerymen striving to limber up their guns in a hail of fire from the enemy infantry, who were now within 200 yards of the muzzles. Four out of six of 37 Battery RFA's 4.5-inch howitzers were got away, but to recover the remaining two was a task that seemed suicidal. Nevertheless, when Captain Douglas Reynolds asked for volunteers there was no shortage of men willing to take the risk. Two teams galloped forward to what seemed like certain death. One was quickly shot down, but the other got to the gun position, wheeled round, limbered up and brought one of the howitzers out of action, one of the drivers being hit in the process. Reynolds and Drivers Frederick Luke and Job Drain all received the Victoria Cross. Reynolds, promoted to major, was killed in action on the Western Front on 23 February 1916. Luke and Drain both became sergeants and survived the war. During World War II, Luke saw further service with the RAF Regiment. In addition to these awards, 37 Battery as a whole was granted the honour title of Le Cateau.

The retreat that followed lasted for ten days and was carried out in intense heat under a blazing sun. For the mounted troops it was bearable, but for the infantry it was an ordeal that was never forgotten. As yet, they had little respect for the methods of their opponents and sang lustily, one of the favourite impromptu songs being

> *Oh, we don't give a **** for old von Kluck*
> *And all his ***ing army,*

sung to the tune of 'The Girl I Left Behind Me'. However, as hour after hour became day after day of solid marching, thirst and weariness put an end to the singing. In a daze, they continued to put one foot in front of another like automata always hoping vainly that the morrow would bring rest. Some men had hallucinations, others fell asleep while marching, fell and could not be roused. Sometimes, when a halt was called in a town or village, they belligerently announced that they would rather stand and fight than march another step, and it took all their officers' powers of persuasion to get them moving again. For the Germans, their advance was as much, if not more, of an ordeal. Some of them had been marching up to 35 miles a day since they crossed the German frontier with Belgium. One of their officers commented that it would have been a remarkable achievement for the toughest of farm boys, but many of those in the ranks had come straight from factories, shops and offices.

They were kept going by promises that they were on the point of winning the greatest victory in the history of the German Army, and by consuming large quantities of alcohol that deadened the pain of aching legs and feet worn raw.

During the retreat there occurred an incident that was to have an important bearing on subsequent events. The morning of 1 September found Brigadier General C. J. Briggs's 1st Cavalry Brigade (The Queen's Bays, 5th Dragoon Guards, 11th Hussars and L Battery Royal Horse Artillery) bivouacked in and around the village of Néry, some 50 miles to the north-east of Paris. Briggs had intended moving off at 04:30 but because of a heavy ground mist the move was postponed for an hour. L Battery used the delay to feed and water its teams, which were then hooked into their vehicles, leaving the poles resting on the ground to ease the weight on the wheelers' shoulders while they were standing.

Shortly after 05:00 the mist began to lift. The battery commander, Major Sclater-Booth, was summoned to brigade headquarters in the village. Hardly had he arrived than a shell burst overhead and an 11th Hussar patrol galloped in to report the presence of German cavalry. Soon the village and the surrounding bivouacs were being swept by artillery, machine-gun and rifle fire from a plateau to the east, separated from the village by a deep ravine. Running back to his battery, Sclater-Booth caught a glimpse of three of his six 13-pdr guns going into action, then lost consciousness when a shell burst in front of him.

The enemy were the German 4th Cavalry Division, screening the right flank of Kluck's advance. It possessed three four-gun horse batteries, one of which immediately concentrated on L Battery, lined up in close order and ready to move off. Within minutes the battery had become a shambles of dead gunners, dismembered horses, overturned limbers and apparently abandoned guns. Screaming with terror, the horses tried to bolt but could not because the dropped limber poles were driven into the ground by the forward movement, holding them fast. Shouting, 'Come on! Who's for the guns?' Captain Edward Bradbury ran forward. His call was answered by the battery's three subalterns and those gunners still on their feet. Together, they managed to unlimber three of the guns, swing them round and bring them into action. Bradbury and Sergeant David Nelson manned one, Lieutenants Campbell and Mundy the second and Lieutenant Gifford and some gunners the third. Over 20 yards of shell and bullet-swept ground separated the guns from the ammunition wagons, and although every round had to be brought across this, there was never a shortage of volunteers.

Campbell's gun was wrecked by a direct hit almost immediately. Campbell and Mundy ran to assist Bradbury, the former being killed seconds later. After firing several rounds Gifford and some of his detachment were killed and the rest were seriously wounded. Nevertheless, their fire must have been hurting, for the German batteries now turned their attention to Bradbury's gun. For an hour it fought alone against odds of twelve to one. It became the focus of a hurricane of bursting high-explosive shells, yet incredibly it survived. By 07:15, however, Mundy was seriously wounded, all the ammunition carriers had been hit and only Bradbury and Sergeant Nelson, who had also been wounded, remained at the gun. Seeing their predicament, Battery Sergeant Major George Dorrell ran forward to join them. Bradbury left them to fetch ammunition. His leg was torn off by a bursting shell but he continued to direct their fire until he died. Together, Dorrell and Nelson fired off their last few rounds, then the 13-pdr fell silent.

It looked as though L Battery was finished. In a trice, however, the whole situation was transformed. The British cavalry was as thoroughly trained in the use of the Lee-Enfield rifle as was the infantry. Consequently, the German attack on the village, deprived as it was of artillery support, made no headway. Briggs, the brigade commander, had already begun to regain the initiative by sending two squadrons of the 5th Dragoon Guards to make a dismounted attack on the enemy's right flank. He had also despatched an urgent request for reinforcements, which at this moment began entering the battle. They consisted of the 4th Cavalry Brigade, including I Battery RHA and several infantry battalions from the 4th Division. Hardly had L Battery fired its last round than the enemy guns were blanketed by fire from I Battery. The German divisional commander, seeing his troops trapped between the hammer and the anvil, ordered a hasty retreat. This quickly produced a disgraceful panic that ended in headlong flight. Eight of the enemy guns were simply left where they stood; the remaining four were found abandoned in a wood. Setting off in pursuit, the 11th Hussars returned with seventy-eight prisoners. The catch would have been greater had not the enemy galloped so hard, for by the end of the day the German 4th Cavalry Division was dispersed across many miles of wooded country and had ceased to exist as a fighting formation. It did not reassemble until 4 September and even then was not considered to be fit for duty.

British casualties at Néry amounted to 135 officers and men, of whom five officers and forty-nine men belonged to L Battery. The Victoria Cross was awarded to Captain Bradbury, Battery Sergeant Major Dorrell and Sergeant Nelson. Dorrell was subsequently commissioned, rose to the rank of lieutenant colonel and served in the Home Guard during World War II. Nelson was also commissioned and had achieved the rank of major when he was killed on the Western Front in April 1918. L Battery as a whole was granted the honour title of Néry. One of its 13-pdr guns that took part in the engagement is on display at the Imperial War Museum.

The effects of this comparatively minor engagement soon made themselves felt. Despite battlefield evidence to the contrary, Kluck had formed a stubborn opinion that the BEF had been roundly beaten and was retreating out of harm's way, when the truth was that it was simply conforming to the movements of its French allies. At this point his First Army was ordered to begin wheeling eastwards to the north of Paris, a significant departure from the original Schlieffen Plan, and proceed in echelon to the right-rear of Bülow's Second Army. To make matters worse, on 2 September French troops ambushed a staff car containing maps showing the routes along which the corps of Kluck's army were marching, these details being confirmed by air reconnaissance the following day. Furthermore, if his 4th Cavalry Division, which provided the eyes and ears of his right wing, had not been destroyed at Néry, Kluck would have been aware that the French were forming a new army, the Sixth under General Joseph Manoury, to the west of Paris, and that this presented a grave threat to his flank and rear. In other ways, too, the odds against him were mounting, for the BEF had been reinforced to the strength of three corps, and its right-hand neighbour, the French Fifth Army, now had a new and more aggressive commander in the person of General Franchet d'Esperey, whom the British promptly nicknamed Desperate Frankie.

All was therefore in place for the Allied counter-stroke, subsequently known as the First Battle of the Marne. On 7 September Manoury struck into Kluck's right rear. Once more, Kluck underestimated the threat and sent back a single corps to contain the French, but as the pressure grew he was forced to commit most of his army. This opened a wide gap between his own and Bülow's army, into which the BEF advanced against slight opposition. It was immediately apparent to the German General Headquarters that their right wing was in serious danger of entrapment. Kluck and Bülow were therefore ordered to withdraw northwards behind the River Aisne – orders which in themselves acknowledged the failure of the great Schlieffen Plan that had promised a quick, decisive victory. Deprived of this, many of the exhausted German infantry simply gave up and surrendered.

On 14 September the BEF crossed the Aisne under fire and assaulted the enemy dug-in on the high ground some distance beyond. During the day's hard fighting several more VCs were won. Near Vailly, Captain Theodore Wright of 57th Field Company Royal Engineers, engaged in directing cavalry across a pontoon bridge, was mortally wounded while helping another wounded man to safety, the award being made for this and his earlier act at Mons. Some miles to the west, near Missy, Captain William Johnston and Lieutenant R. B. Flint of 59th Field Company were operating two rafts that ferried troops and ammunition. As all the other crossings near by had been destroyed, this remained the only link between the south and north banks and it was vital to 5th Division's operations that it should be maintained. Appreciating this, the Germans kept up an intense fire on the crossing site all day, during which the two officers continued operating their rafts without pause. Johnston, who was to be killed by a sniper in the Ypres salient the following year, was awarded the VC and Flint received the DSO.

Three VCs were also won by infantrymen on 14 September. Near Chivy-sur-Aisne Lance Corporal William Fuller of the 2nd Welch Regiment advanced under very heavy machine-gun fire to pick up Captain Mark Haggard, who had been seriously wounded. He succeeded in carrying him to a dressing station, but Haggard, a nephew of the writer H. Rider Haggard, died from his wounds the following day. Fuller later became a sergeant and in 1938 received the Royal Humane Society's Medal for Life-saving when he rescued two boys from drowning.

At Verneuil Private George Wilson of the 2nd Highland Light Infantry began the day by shooting two Germans dead and capturing eight more, releasing two prisoners from the Middlesex Regiment in the process. He went forward with a rifleman from the King's Royal Rifle Corps to locate a machine-gun that was holding up the advance and had already caused heavy casualties. The rifleman was killed but Wilson went on until he reached the area from which the machine-gun was firing. Now in a berserk state, he shot the six men manning the weapon, then bayoneted their officer, who had emptied his pistol at him but missed with every shot. He then returned to his own lines where he was knocked unconscious by a bursting shell. When he came to he was disgusted that no one had thought to bring in the machine-gun he had captured. He went out three times to bring in the gun and its ammunition, then once more to retrieve the body of the rifleman who had accompanied him. His act was surely one of the most remarkable and courageous of the war, yet his life was not a happy one. A small man, his health was broken by the war. He was found work by the Edinburgh Corporation but took to drink and at one stage pawned his VC for £5 in an attempt to solve his financial problems. He died aged thirty-nine, seven years after the war ended and was buried with full military honours.

Near the village of Chivy an attack by the 1st Queen's Own Cameron Highlanders was halted with severe loss by flanking fire from enemy machine-guns. Private Ross Tollerton, a recalled reservist, saw that his platoon commander, Lieutenant J. S. M. Matheson, had been hit and went to his assistance. Matheson, shot through the spine, was unable to move and as he was lying face-down he was in danger of suffocating in the mud. With the assistance of a sergeant who was immediately shot dead, Tollerton lifted the officer on to his back and carried him to a place of comparative safety. He then went back to the firing line, where he was wounded in the hand and head. When the battalion received orders to pull back, Tollerton returned to Matheson with the intention of carrying him to the British lines. Soon, however, the enemy was all round them and it became impossible to move. For three nights the two were forced to remain where they were, surviving on water. During this time Tollerton received a wound in his back from a shrapnel shell bursting overhead. When the Germans pulled back he managed to attract the attention of British troops digging a trench. They sent out a stretcher party and while Tollerton was directed to a dressing station, Matheson was transported to hospital. Incredibly, the officer recovered and rose to the rank of major. After the war Tollerton was employed as a school janitor and joined a Territorial battalion of the Royal Scots Fusiliers, becoming a company sergeant major. He died in 1932, his name being commemorated by a road named after him in his home town of Irvine, Ayrshire.

The following day, 113th Battery Royal Field Artillery was in action at Vendresse. It came under heavy counter-battery fire and casualties began to mount. Bombardier Ernest Horlock was wounded twice and on each occasion returned to the guns after his wounds had been dressed, disobeying two direct orders from the medical officer to proceed to the field hospital. He was promoted to sergeant two days later and became a sergeant major in February 1916. He went on to serve at Salonika and in Egypt. On 30 December 1917, while returning to the Middle East from leave, during which he was married, his ship was torpedoed off Alexandria. He did not survive.

A Victoria Cross was awarded to Captain Harry Ranken, the Medical Officer of the 1st King's Royal Rifle Corps, for his acts on 19 and 20 September. While attending to casualties under rifle and shrapnel fire he was severely wounded by a shell that all but tore off one of his legs. After staunching the bleeding and binding the wound, he continued to crawl among the other casualties and dress their wounds, thereby sacrificing his own chance of survival. Finally, too weak to continue, he allowed himself to be carried to the rear, but by then his case had become desperate and he died shortly after. Like Ross Tollerton, he was a native of Irvine and a road was also named after him.

At dawn on 28 September, near Chavanne, the 2nd Coldstream Guards sent out a three-man reconnaissance patrol towards the German lines. Unfortunately, the autumn mist that the patrol had been using for cover suddenly lifted and it came under fire. Only one man, slightly wounded, managed to make his way back. Private Frederick Dobson, another recalled reservist, immediately volunteered to go out to find the two missing men. The ground was open and in full view of the enemy, who opened fire on him, forcing him to crawl all the way. He found that one of the men had been killed and that the other had been hit in three places. After dressing his wounds he crawled back and returned with Corporal A. Brown and a stretcher. Fortunately, the mist had returned again, enabling them to drag the injured man to safety. Dobson's recommendation for the VC was met with a mean-spirited response by Sir Douglas Haig, who commented: 'I am not in favour of this coveted award being created for bringing in wounded officers or men in European warfare.' He recommended Dobson for the DCM but was personally overruled by the King. Dobson was therefore awarded the VC and Brown the DCM. Dobson became a lance corporal but sustained several wounds and was discharged in July 1917 as being no longer fit for war service. He worked as a miner for a while and was then employed as a commissionaire at a Leeds cinema.

By the end of the month the Battle of the Aisne was over. Attack had been followed by counter-attack, with little ground being gained or lost. Both sides entrenched their positions and began stringing wire entanglements. In an effort to restore mobility the Allies and Germans made a series of attempts to outflank each other to the west, so that the lines became longer and longer until they eventually reached the sea. During this period the BEF was relieved and transported to Flanders, where its principal task was to halt the German drive on the Channel ports. Earlier optimistic thoughts that the war would be over by Christmas were set aside. The British Empire mobilised for a long war, the first imperial troops to reach France being an Indian corps that went into the line beside the BEF. On 31 October Sepoy Khudadad Khan of the 129th Duke of Connaught's Own Baluchis became the first native-born Indian soldier to be awarded the VC. His regiment took part in an attack at Hollebeke, about five miles to the south-east of Ypres in Belgium. The attack succeeded but was immediately followed by a counter-attack in overwhelming strength. Khudadad Khan was serving with the battalion's machine-gun section, one gun of which was blown apart by a shell. The detachment's British officer was badly wounded and had to be taken to the rear, but the remaining gun did considerable execution among the attackers. One by one the crew were killed until only Khudadad Khan, who was wounded, remained. He continued to fire into the advancing ranks until the position was overrun. The Germans left him for dead, but after they had gone he managed to render his gun useless and crawl back to his battalion. He later received a viceroy's commission as a subadar.

The German Kaiser denied that he had once called the BEF 'a contemptible little army', yet during the First Battle of Ypres, lasting from 18 October until 30 November, he gave vent to an hysterical outburst prompted by his generals' failure to capture the town, describing its members as 'trash and feeble adversaries, unworthy of the steel of the German soldier'. These same 'feeble adversaries' inflicted such losses on newly arrived German reserve corps, recruited from young idealistic volunteers, including a high proportion of university students, that the Germans themselves referred to the battle as 'The Massacre of the Innocents'. Yet when several regiments of the Prussian Guard, the elite of the Imperial German Army, attacked on 11 November, they received similar treatment, an event which in itself proved the quality of the BEF.

Yet by the end of the battle the BEF had, in modern parlance, been 'used up'. Most of its units had been reduced to a fraction of their original strength. Many of its members, including wounded men returning to duty, were posted as instructors to the new armies that were taking the field. Having repeatedly shot the Kaiser's grey-clad hordes to tatters, those who served with the original BEF took a perverse pride in his reported jibe, choosing to call themselves the Old Contemptibles throughout their lives and being honoured as such by their nation.

Gallipoli
1915

By the end of 1914 it was fully appreciated that many courageous deeds were being performed that did not quite merit the award of the VC or the DCM yet were worthy of greater recognition than a mere Mention in Despatches. It was decided, therefore, to award the DSO more frequently to officers of field rank, i.e. majors and above, as well as to captains and subalterns in exceptional circumstances, and to institute a new award, the Military Cross, for junior officers and warrant officers. In March 1916 the Military Medal was introduced for other ranks, over 120,000 MMs being awarded during World War I alone.

By the end of 1914, too, it was apparent that the powers of defence so outweighed those of attack that, on the Western Front at least, it would be almost impossible to restore mobile warfare with the resources at the generals' disposal. Together, massed artillery, machine-guns and entrenched positions fronted by barbed-wire aprons virtually guaranteed the failure of any attack, save at a prohibitive cost in life. Heavier and heavier preparatory bombardments merely added to the problem as if any ground was gained it became impossible to exploit the breach because the enemy could seal off any penetration by rushing in reinforcements across clean ground before the attacker could bring forward his horse-drawn artillery over the shell-torn wastes of no man's land. Yet the politicians demanded victory and the generals, knowing that only mobility could achieve this, could merely plan offensives that they hoped would secure the decisive breakthrough into the open country beyond the trench lines.

At the highest levels, the British War Cabinet was divided on the aims of its grand strategy. The Westerners, as they were called, believed that victory could only be achieved by defeating the main mass of the German Army on the Western Front. The Easterners, on the other hand, believed in a more indirect approach involving an attack on Turkey, which had allied herself with Germany and Austria-Hungary during the autumn of 1914. Turkey, it was argued, was the weakest link in this alliance. If she could be knocked out of the war, the ramshackle Austro-Hungarian Empire, having already sustained horrific losses in the fighting against Russia on the Eastern Front, would soon follow. That would leave Germany isolated and, fighting on two fronts as she was, she would probably ask for terms.

Superficially, Turkey did not seem to be a formidable opponent. In recent years she had lost two Balkan wars and a war with Italy. Since, then, however, her army had been restructured and trained by German officers. Furthermore, Allied calculations seemed to take no account of the fact that the Turks would fight far harder in defence of their heartland than they would elsewhere.

British interest centred upon the Dardanelles, the straits connecting the Aegean with the Sea of Marmora. If the Dardanelles could be forced, Constantinople could be bombarded into submission. The ease with which this might be accomplished was demonstrated by a successful naval bombardment of the southern Dardanelles forts on 31 October 1914 and the incredible feat of the tiny fifteen-man submarine *B11* which, on 13 December, broke through the Turkish minefields to penetrate The Narrows, where she torpedoed and sank the old battleship *Messudieh* in Sari Sighlar Bay, then returned safely despite the considerable navigational risks involved. Her commander, Lieutenant Norman Holbrook, was awarded the Victoria Cross, the first submariner to be so honoured. He subsequently rose to the rank of commander and served at the Admiralty during World War II.

Early in 1915 it was decided that a further naval bombardment would take place and that troops would be landed on the Gallipoli peninsula to take possession of the silenced forts on the western shore of the Straits. During late February and early March the outer forts were silenced and the guns within destroyed by Royal Marine landing parties. Turkish resistance, however, was stiffening and the use of mobile howitzer batteries, which were difficult to locate, made the task of sweeping the minefields on the approach to the inner forts both difficult and dangerous. Added to this, the minesweepers were simply North Sea trawlers that had been conscripted along with their crews, and were totally unsuited to the work not only because they drew too much water, rendering them terribly vulnerable to the very mines they were intended to sweep, but also because they lacked the power to make much headway against the strong currents running through the Straits from the Sea of Marmora.

In the light of this the decision was taken to batter the Turkish inner defences with the strongest force yet employed, thereby creating the conditions that would allow the minesweepers to continue their work. On the morning of 18 March 1915 no less than eighteen British and French battleships, accompanied by cruisers and destroyers, sailed into the Straits. They were met by a heavy and destructive fire but by 16:00 had all but silenced the inner forts. However, as they turned away to allow the minesweepers to resume their task, three battleships (HMS *Irresistible, Ocean* and the French *Bouvet*) ran over an uncharted mine-field and sustained damage from which they sank, the last with heavy loss of life. When the minesweepers came forward they were driven off by the elusive howitzer batteries. At the end of the day the Allied losses amounted to three battleships sunk, three seriously damaged and almost 700 men killed, for no tangible gain. Turkish losses came to eight guns hit out of a total of 176, forty men killed and seventy wounded.

It was now apparent that if there was to be any chance of reaching Constantinople, it would be necessary to mount a major military opera-tion to secure the Gallipoli peninsula, thus gaining control of the western shore of the Straits. A further strategic advantage of such a course would be to draw off Turkish troops from southern Palestine, where they posed a threat to the Suez Canal. Against this, there were numerous disadvantages. Any doubts the Turks might have had regard-ing Allied interest in the Dardanelles were dispelled by the events of 18 March. They immediately began moving strong reinforcements into the peninsula and constructing defences to cover probable landing sites. The peninsula itself was eminently suitable for defence, consisting as it did of a central spine to which steep ridges separated by gullies rose sharply to the crest from either shore. In such terrain it was almost inevitable that even if the Allies should succeed in getting ashore, fight-ing would quickly resolve itself into the same sort of stalemate that existed on the Western Front. For their part, the Allies had virtually no experience of mounting large-scale amphibious operations. The essen-tial command, control and communications network existed only in the sketchiest form. No specialised landing craft were available, so that most of the troops would have to come ashore in unprotected ships' boats or unarmoured lighters. Worse still, although detailed knowledge of the terrain did exist, it was not made available to those who would carry out the operation, the consequence being that objectives were set without any appreciation of the difficulties involved. Worst of all, perhaps, was a serious underestimation of the Turks' will to fight.

The landings were scheduled to take place on the morning of 25

April, under the overall command of General Sir Ian Hamilton. On the right, Major General Sir Aylmer Hunter-Weston's 29th Division would come in at S Beach in Morto Bay and V Beach, both at the southern tip of Cape Helles, near Sedd-el-Bahr; on W and X Beaches, some 3,000 yards to the north-west at Tekke Burnu; and on Y Beach, 4,000 yards north again. On the left, Lieutenant General Sir William Birdwood's Australian and New Zealand Army Corps (ANZAC) would go ashore between Gaba Tepe and Ari Burnu.

First to land were the leading elements of the ANZACs. Unfortunately, as a result of currents that were stronger than had been anticipated, imprecisely communicated changes of plan and navigational error, the troops were landed all of a heap around Ari Burnu instead of on a 2,000-yard broad frontage to the south of this feature. Local opposition was quickly dealt with but it took time for regiments to sort themselves out and discover where they were. At length, driving small parties of Turks before them, they began to move inland towards their objectives, which in itself was no easy matter because of the rugged terrain and the inaccurate maps that had been issued. Nevertheless, by 07:00 a small party of men had reached the summit of the highest ridge and were able to look down at the Dardanelles below.

At about the same time the Turks, who had never expected a landing to be made in this desolate area, recovered from their surprise. It was the ANZACs' grave misfortune that their reaction was led by Colonel Mustapha Kemal, commanding the Turkish 19th Division. Kemal was one of the original Young Turk officers who sought to modernise his archaic country and in due course would become the new Turkey's first president. For the present he was regarded as being no more than able, but he was about to reveal himself as being one of the Ottoman Empire's most outstanding soldiers. First he rallied the stragglers retiring from the beach defences, then counter-attacked with one regiment and brought forward the rest of his division from Boghali, on the Dardanelles side of the peninsula. By 10:00 the Australians and New Zealanders were engaged in a full-scale battle. Their advance parties were either overrun or driven in. The Turks were mown down as they charged, but came on over their own dead and wounded to close with the bayonet, for which they had a natural affinity. They were met by bigger, stronger men than themselves who were every bit as aggressive. Deadly personal struggles raged over tactical features that were taken, lost and retaken many times under the leadership of junior officers, NCOs and private soldiers. At the end of a day's fighting that many remembered as being the most savage of the entire war, the ANZAC lines had been stabilised and, with minor changes, were to remain as they were for the rest of the campaign.

To the south the 29th Division, an all-regular formation save for one Territorial battalion, endured an equally grim day. On the left, at Y Beach, the 1st King's Own Scottish Borderers, one company of the 2nd South Wales Borderers and the Plymouth Battalion Royal Marines made an unopposed landing. By 06:30 they had established themselves and their patrols were probing inland. Likewise, at X Beach the 2nd Royal Fusiliers sustained no casualties and scaled the cliffs while the boats returned to the ships to embark the second assault wave.

At W Beach, however, the story was very different. The naval bombardment had touched neither the enemy trenches nor the wire strung along the beach and in the shallows. Although they numbered just three platoons, the Turkish defenders were full of fight and had been ordered to hold their fire until the oncoming ships' boats, jammed with the 1st Lancashire Fusiliers sitting shoulder to shoulder, were within 100 yards. The result was devastating. As each boat was raked continuously, the dead and wounded hindered those trying to scramble out into the shallows. Many of those in the water were shot down as they waded towards the beach, some of the wounded being drowned as the weight of their equipment pulled them to the bottom. The water became stained to the colour of claret. The Lancashire Fusiliers, however, like the King's Own Scottish Borderers, were one of the 'Unsurpassable Six' infantry regiments that, at Minden in 1759, had routed three French cavalry charges in succession, then driven the enemy infantry off the field. Now, there was no way to go but forward and the Fusiliers knew it. Responding to their officers' shouts of 'Remember Minden!' they rushed the wire and struggled to tear their way through it, although too few men with wire cutters remained alive. In some places gaps were cut or stakes were ripped out or the wire was flattened by the weight of bodies hanging in it. Singly and in small groups, men charged to almost certain death in a desperate attempt to close with the defenders.

Meanwhile, Brigadier General Steuart Hare, the officer responsible for the first-wave landings, observed what was taking place and ordered the last of the Fusiliers' boats to make for a small beach to the left, under the cliffs of Tekke Burnu, which provided cover from the Turkish fire. Scrambling to the summit, the Fusiliers opened fire into the enemy's flank. Faced with this new onslaught, the defenders began to falter. Finally, as more and more troops came ashore, the position was taken. Few regiments in history have suffered as did the Lancashire Fusiliers

Balaklava – 'The Charge of the Light Brigade', a watercolor sketch by William Simpson. The Brigade is shown as it was deployed at the start of the charge. By the time it reached this point its leading regiments had been decimated. The Heavy Brigade and the horse artillery battery are not shown but were halted near the extreme right of the picture. Beyond the Light Brigade is Causeway Heights, on which two of the redoubts can be seen. *National Army Museum*

Inkerman – an imaginative view of the Guards beating off one of the numerous Russian attacks, with French troops coming into action in the background. In fact, the Russians were wearing flat 'muffin' forage caps rather than their spiked helmets, and the mist was denser than shown, preventing the generals on both sides from exercising control. For this reason Inkerman became known as 'the soldiers' battle'. It was also the last battle fought by the British Army in full dress. *National Army Museum*

The Indian Mutiny – The storming of the Kashmir Gate, Delhi, as depicted in *The Illustrated London News* of 28 November 1857, two months after the actual event.

China

right: Ensign John Chaplin and Private Thomas Lane planting the Queen's Colour of the 67th (South Hampshire) Regiment on the central tower of the Small North Fort at Taku, 1860. Both were awarded the Victoria Cross for their part in the action. *Royal Hampshire Regiment Museum*

opposite above: The Small North Fort at Taku after capture, the British and French flags flying from the central tower. A wide belt of sharpened bamboo stakes surrounds the fort, and the bodies in the foreground are those of the garrison who tried to escape over the walls. *Royal Hampshire Regiment Museum*

opposite below: The interior of the North Fort after capture, scaling ladders still in position. Among the numerous casualties are guns of various types, including on the right a 'jingal', an enormous musket fired from a wall mounting and much favoured by the Chinese. *Royal Hampshire Regiment Museum*

The Great Locomotive Chase – As the pursuit closes in, *The General* runs out of steam and Andrews' Raiders attempt to escape. *US Army Military History Institute*

Gettysburg – The repulse of the Confederate attack on the Union centre, 2 July 1863. The figure on the grey horse right centre is Major General George C. Meade, the Union Commander. *Anne S. K. Brown Military Collection, Brown University Library*

right: Colonel Joshua L. Chamberlain, theological graduate and university lecturer, was awarded the Medal of Honor for his leadership in the field at Gettysburg. *Corbis*

Mobile Bay – Union warships surround the stricken Confederate ram CSS *Tennessee* during the closing stages of the battle, which resulted in the award of nearly one hundred Medals of Honor to the US Navy and Marine Corps. *Bridgeman Art Library*

Little Big Horn – *right:* Under heavy fire, Sergeant Richard Hanley prevents an ammunition mule stampeding into the Indian lines. *US Army Military History Institute*

above: Sergeant George Geiger, Blacksmith Henry Mechling, Private Charles Windolph and Saddler Otto Voit deliberately chose an exposed position to give covering fire for Reno's water parties. All received the Medal of Honor. *US Army Military History Institute*

Isandhlwana – *left:* Lieutenants Teignmouth Melville and Neville Coghill saving the Queen's Colour of the 1st/24th Regiment at Isandhlwana. *National Army Museum*

below: 'The Defence of Rorke's Drift', painted by A. de Neuville the year after the event. On the left Surgeon Major James Reynolds assists in the rescue of patients from the burning hospital; Lieutenant John Chard, Royal Engineers, the commander of the post, directs operations from the centre of the picture; to his right the bearded Revd George Smith distributes ammunition; Lieutenant Gonville Bromhead is bareheaded on the far right, fighting with rifle and bayonet. *National Army Museum*

left: Lieutenant Neville Coghill, VC. *Corbis*

right: Lieutenant John Rouse Merriott Chard, a modest and unassuming VC. *Popperfoto*

Colenso – The 66th Battery, Royal Field Artillery, fires its last shot at Colenso. The fallen figure in the foreground is Lieutenant the Hon. Frederick Roberts, son of Field Marshal Lord Roberts VC. Lieutenant Roberts was mortally wounded while assisting in an attempt to withdraw the guns. His posthumous award of the Victoria Cross established a long overdue precedent. *National Army Museum*

The Boxer Rising – US Marines beside the fortified ramp leading to the top of the Tartar Wall behind the American Legation. There was much bitter fighting on this sector of the defences and at one stage the Chinese held the ramp on the right of the photograph. *Royal Marines Museum*

Néry – Fortunino Matania's painting of the last gun of L Battery, Royal Horse Artillery, in action against twelve-fold odds on 1 September 1914. The action ended with the capture of all twelve German guns. *National Army Museum*

Battery Sergeant Major George Dorrell, who won his VC at Néry 1 September 1914, eventually rising to the rank of Lieutenant Colonel. *Imperial War Museum Q 79792*

Gallipoli – The converted collier *River Clyde* at V Beach, showing the ports cut in her side through which the 1st Royal Munster Fusiliers and the 2nd Hampshire Regiment left the ship. In the foreground are the lighters and the steam hopper *Argyll*. A painting by Charles Dixon. *Royal Hampshire Regiment Museum*

The Somme – Private W. F. McFadzean won his posthumous VC for an astonishing act of bravery to save his comrades from certain death, knowing he could not survive himself. *Imperial War Museum Q 79785*

Jutland – A German shell explodes on Q (midships) turret of the battlecruiser HMS *Lion*. Only prompt action by the mortally wounded Major Francis Harvey, Royal Marine Light Infantry, prevented the ship from being blown apart. Major Harvey was awarded a posthumous Victoria Cross. *Imperial War Museum SP 1704*

Boy First Class Jack Cornwell won his posthumous VC aboard HMS *Chester*. At sixteen, he was the youngest recipient of the Victoria Cross in the twentieth century. His VC is on display at the Imperial War Museum in London. *Imperial War Museum Q 20883*

Zeebrugge – The cruiser HMS *Vindictive* comes alongside the Mole at Zeebrugge, nudged into position by the Mersey ferry *Daffodil*, in this painting by Charles J. De Lacy. *Imperial War Museum PIC 1084*

Captain Alfred Carpenter VC (right) with the mascots of HMS *Vindictive*. On his right is Commander E. Osborne. *Imperial War Museum Q 20831*

The Argonne – Corporal Alvin C. York, all-American hero, won his Medal of Honor by single-handedly killing 25 of the enemy, taking 132 prisoners and causing 35 enemy machine-guns to be abandoned. This dramatic painting of the event is by F. E. Schoonover. *Anne S. K. Brown Military Collection, Brown University Library*

The Battle of Britain – Flight Lieutenant E. J. B. Nicolson, 249 Fighter Squadron, RAF, recipient of the only VC to be awarded for action during the Battle of Britain. *Imperial War Museum CH 1700*

Tobruk – Captain James Jackman VC, 1st Battalion Royal Northumberland Fusiliers, posthumous winner of the last of five VCs awarded during the battle. *Imperial War Museum HU 2041*

Dieppe – A German officer interrogates wounded prisoners. Most of the Canadians were pinned down on the beach by crossfire and only a handful of the Calgary Regiment's Churchill tanks managed to reach the esplanade, many of the rest getting stuck in the sliding shingle beach. *Imperial War Museum HU 1903*

Lieutenant Colonel Charles Merritt, South Saskatchewan Regiment, was awarded his VC while a prisoner of the Germans, who eventually shipped him off to Colditz Castle. *Imperial War Museum MH 4207*

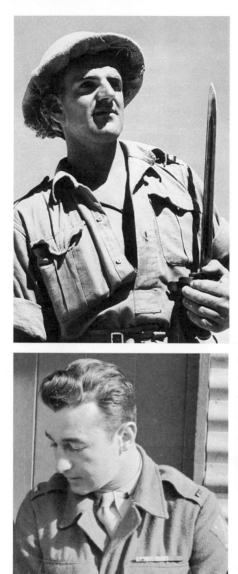

Alamein – *left:* New Zealander Sergeant Keith Elliott led his nineteen men to a notable victory 15 July 1942, capturing five machine-guns, one anti-tank gun, killing 'a great number of the enemy' and taking 130 prisoners. He was presented with his VC by General Montgomery. *Imperial War Museum E 4120E*

below: Another New Zealander, Captain Charles Upham, won his second VC in the same action, one of only three men to hold a VC and Bar. He returned to sheep farming in New Zealand after the war. *Imperial War Museum HU 43225*

Guadalcanal – *left:* Marine Platoon Sergeant Mitchell Paige won his Medal of Honor at Bloody Ridge on the night of 25 October 1942 for close machine-gun and bayonet action against the Japanese. *Corbis*

Ploesti – An impression by Stanley Dersh of the low-level raid on the Ploesti refineries. *Anne S. K. Brown Military Collection, Brown University Library*

Imphal – The two Japanese Type 97 medium tanks knocked out by Gurkha Rifleman Ganju Lama at Ninthoukhong, an action for which he was awarded the Victoria Cross. *Imperial War Museum IWD 3904*

Iwo Jima – Old Glory flies from the summit of Mount Suribachi, below which can be seen the original landing beaches. Some of the most severe fighting took place in the tangled, rocky terrain of the plateau in the distance. *US National Archives*

and still retained the will to win. Of the 950 officers and men who had embarked into their boats from HMS *Euryalus* that morning, six officers and 183 men were killed, four officers and 279 men were wounded, and sixty-one men were missing, presumably drowned, a total of 533 casualties. Hunter-Weston, the divisional commander, personally witnessed the landing, which he described as 'a deed of heroism that has seldom been equalled'. Recognising that it would be difficult to discriminate, he recommended the award of six Victoria Crosses to the 1st Lancashire Fusiliers, two to officers and four to NCOs and men who had particularly distinguished themselves by their outstanding leadership and courage, the recipients to be elected by the regiment. The recipients were Major Cuthbert Bromley, Corporal John Grimshaw, Private William Keneally, Sergeant Alfred Richards, Sergeant Frank Stubbs and Captain Richard Willis. Two DSOs, two MCs and one DCM were also awarded.

Bromley, who had displayed inspired leadership throughout the landing, was wounded later in the campaign and evacuated to Egypt. Having made a full recovery, he was drowned when the troopship on which he was returning to Gallipoli was torpedoed and sunk. Grimshaw's pack and water bottle were riddled and his cap badge was smashed by a bullet, but he continued with his task of company signaller despite intense, close-range fire. He later served on the Western Front, where he was commissioned in the field. After the war he became a recruiting officer and finally retired from the army in 1953, having completed forty-one years' service. He was the last survivor of the Lancashire Fusiliers' 'Six VCs Before Breakfast', dying on 20 July 1980. Keneally, who had distinguished himself as a runner on the bullet-swept beach and by his attempts to cut the enemy wire under intense fire, became a sergeant but was mortally wounded at Gully Ravine later in the campaign. Richards's right leg was almost severed by the enemy's fire but, realising that unless the wire was penetrated his men would continue to be shot down, he ignored his agony and crawled forward, leading them through it. His leg was subsequently amputated above the knee and he was discharged from the army later in the year. His disability did not prevent him joining the Home Guard during World War II, in which he served as provost sergeant of the 28th County of London Battalion. Stubbs also led his men through the wire and up the cliff but was killed later that morning as the remnants of his company were advancing on the final objective, a feature designated Hill 114. Willis had commanded his company for fifteen years when he led its rush ashore, waving it on with his walking stick. He displayed exemplary leadership during the nightmare action that followed, at one stage shooting dead a Turkish sniper who had been responsible for many casualties. In June he sustained a serious wound and was evacuated to England. He saw further active service on the Somme and in the Ypres salient, rising to the rank of acting lieutenant colonel. On leaving the army in 1920 he took up teaching as a career. He died on 9 February 1966, the last twenty years of his life being marked by failing eyesight, poor health and such serious financial problems that the Fusiliers' Compassionate Fund provided assistance on several occasions.

Meanwhile, at V Beach an ordeal of a different kind was taking place. The beach was a natural amphitheatre lying between Sedd-el-Bahr Castle on the right and Cape Helles to the left. It was, therefore, an ideal killing ground. Initially, it was defended by some sixty men under a sergeant, but reinforcements continued to reach the area throughout the day and the following night, bringing with them a number of machine-guns. Its capture, nevertheless, was vital to the success of the whole operation. On the left the 1st Royal Dublin Fusiliers, crammed together in their boats, approached a completely silent and apparently deserted shoreline at 06:20. The Turks waited until the leading boats had touched down before they opened fire. A scene of carnage similar to that at W Beach ensued, save that those who did reach the shore found cover behind a four-feet-high ridge of sand at the water's edge.

To the Dubliners' right a converted collier and mule carrier, the *River Clyde*, commanded by Commander Edward Unwin, a fifty-one-year-old former Merchant Navy officer who had transferred to the Royal Navy and been recalled from the Reserve, grounded smoothly on the shelving sand. She had been specially adapted for the operation in that four sally ports had been cut in her sides with the intention that the 2,000 troops aboard would leave through these and run along gangways down to a flat-bottomed steam hopper, the *Argyll*, which would serve as a bridge to the shore. Just in case the bridge was too short, the *River Clyde* was also towing three decked lighters that could be used to close the gap. The idea was Unwin's and it was intended to solve two problems simultaneously, namely that of the shortage of ships' boats and the need to get troops ashore rapidly to reinforce the assault wave.

Unwin had been forced to manoeuvre a little to avoid reaching the shore ahead of the Dubliners' boats. This may have influenced the course of the *Argyll*, commanded by Unwin's first lieutenant, Midshipman George Drewry, which grounded on a sandbank and swung broadside-on to the beach, to port of the *River Clyde*. This meant that the hopper could no longer be used as a bridge. Drewry and a member of his crew, Able Seaman George Samson, began hauling the towed lighters forward towards the collier's bow. Unwin, seeing what had happened, decided to link the lighters to a spit of rock to starboard of the *River Clyde*. Accompanied by Leading Seaman William Williams, who had begged to join the steamer's crew, he ran down the gangway and jumped into the water. He managed to position the lighters with some assistance from a steam pinnace, but realised that they would drift away unless he and Williams hauled on the bow rope. Satisfied that he had done the best job possible, he signalled for the landing to begin.

Two companies of the 1st Munster Fusiliers began streaming through the sally ports, which immediately became the Turkish riflemen's point of aim. Men were shot down as they emerged, as they ran along the gangways and as they clambered across the lighters. Those few that reached the shore were pinned down alongside the Dubliners behind the ridge of sand. By now, Unwin and Williams had been working waist-deep in the water for an hour while bullets kicked up spouts of water around them or clanged off the lighters. Williams, described by Unwin as the bravest man he ever met, received a mortal wound and the bridge of lighters swung away, severing the link with the beach. For the moment, the landing ceased. Unwin, suffering severely from cold, was taken aboard the *River Clyde* and rubbed down.

Drewry, assisted by Samson, as well as Lieutenant Tony Morse, Midshipman Wilfrid Malleson and other men from HMS *Cornwallis's* boats, strove to reconstruct the bridge, this time to the hopper, and by 09:00 had done so, sustaining a shrapnel wound to the head in the process. He tried to swim from lighter to lighter with a securing line but such was his exhaustion that he nearly drowned and Malleson completed the task. A third company of Munsters attempted to reach the shore but was decimated. Meanwhile, Unwin, somewhat recovered, disregarded the doctor's advice and returned to busy himself about the hopper and the lighters, all of which were now littered with dead and wounded. At 09:30, under direct orders from the divisional commander, a third attempt was made to land troops. One company of the 2nd Hampshires dashed through the *River Clyde's* sally ports but had no better luck than the Munsters. Shortly after 10:00 the landing ceased altogether when the brigade commander, Brigadier General H. E. Napier, was shot while trying to cross the lighters, as was his brigade major.

Unwin, despite being close to exhaustion and having been hit in the face by bullet fragments, now devoted his attention to saving wounded men from the rocks. His gallantry under what was described as a murderous fire inspired Sub-Lieutenant Arthur Tisdall, of the Royal Naval Division's Anson Battalion, to help him. More men joined them. Altogether, Tisdall made four or five trips to and from the rock spit, pushing or pulling a boat filled with wounded. Samson, when he was not helping to secure the lighters, tended wounded aboard the *Argyll* and brought several wounded men out from the shore. The following day, having been thirty hours continuously in action, he was giving covering fire from the *River Clyde* when he was hit by bursting shrapnel. When he was taken below he was found to have sustained seventeen separate wounds and for a while his life hung in the balance.

Notwithstanding further naval gunfire support, those on V Beach remained pinned down throughout the rest of the day, their situation being described by one witness as 'heartbreaking and infuriating'. The coming of darkness brought some relief, enabling the thousand or so Munster Fusiliers and Hampshires still aboard the *River Clyde* to disembark. Then the moon rose and the Turks opened fire again.

For their part in the events of 25 April Drewry, Malleson, Samson, Tisdall, Unwin and Williams all received the Victoria Cross. Drewry, aged twenty, became the first Royal Naval Reserve officer to receive the award. Prior to the war he had enjoyed an adventurous career in the Merchant Navy and was presented with a Sword of Honour by the Imperial Merchant Service Guild in recognition of his actions at V Beach. Promoted lieutenant, he assumed command of a decoy trawler, HMT *William Jackson*, during the summer of 1918 but on 2 August of that year he sustained fatal injuries when struck by a block falling from a derrick. Malleson was the only one of the V Beach VCs to survive unscathed. He later entered the submarine service, then commanded the cruiser HMS *Berwick* and was brought out of retirement during World War II, in which he served as captain of the Malta dockyard. Samson survived his terrible wounds but was discharged because of them in June 1916. A former merchant seaman, he returned to the sea after the war. On 23 February 1923 he died from pneumonia and was buried with full military honours in Bermuda. Tisdall was killed in action only ten days after the V Beach landing. Unwin, as we shall see, was to play a further part in the campaign. He subsequently commanded HMS *Amethyst*, a light cruiser, and was then engaged in administrative duties in Egypt before finally retiring in 1920 with the rank of captain.

The early hours of 26 April found the troops still sheltering behind the bank of sand. They were tired, shocked by the previous day's slaughter, their units were hopelessly mixed up, their brigade commander and his brigade major were dead and there was no apparent plan as to what to do next. General Hunter-Weston had arrived aboard the *River Clyde* at about midnight and given orders for the attack to be renewed. It was left to two staff officers, Lieutenant Colonel Charles Doughty-Wylie, a member of Sir Ian Hamilton's staff who had served in Turkey prior to the war and actually been honoured by the Sultan, and Major Garth Walford, the brigade major of 29th Division's artillery, to restore some sort of order and carry out these instructions. A three-pronged attack was planned. On the right the Hampshires were to storm Sedd-el-Bahr Castle and village; in the centre the major part of the Munsters were to break through the dense wire apron on the beach and take Hill 141; and on the left a mixed force of Dubliners and Munsters was to try and establish a link with W Beach. Released at last from their torment, the troops attacked with the bayonet, supported by machine-gun fire from the *River Clyde*. The castle was cleared without too much difficulty, but in the village ferocious hand-to-hand fighting took place, with quarter being neither asked nor given by either side, and it was not until 15:00 that the Turkish survivors fled to the north. Hill 141 was also taken in an attack that the Turks found impossible to stop. Walford and Doughty-Wylie, displaying complete disregard for death, were in the forefront of the breakout from the beach, the former being killed not far from the castle and the latter, who had largely been responsible for snatching victory from the jaws of defeat, also being killed as he reached the summit of Hill 141. Both received the posthumous award of the Victoria Cross.

The attack of the Royal Munster Fusiliers took place during the afternoon. The enemy's wire apron began some 25 yards from the bank behind which they had been sheltering, at the top of a slight rise. Many of them did not reach it, but among those who did was Corporal William Cosgrove, a sixteen-stone, six-foot-six giant of a man from County Cork. For all that, his account of the action reveals a gentle man with every consideration for his comrades and even a word of praise for the Turks. Finding that the wire cutters were useless, he began uprooting the posts by main force despite being under fire not only from the trenches in front but also from the uncleared houses in the village. Others assisted with the work until a gap had been made, through which the Munsters surged 'like devils'. During the final charge on the trenches Cosgrove did not realise that he had been hit by several machine-gun bullets and it was not until after the savage fight in the enemy position was over that he collapsed. Without Cosgrove it is doubtful whether the attack would have succeeded and in recognition of the fact he was awarded the Victoria Cross. On his recovery he was promoted to sergeant. He remained with the Munsters until the regiment was disbanded on the creation of the Irish Free State in 1922, then transferred to the Royal Northumberland Fusiliers. He retired with the rank of staff sergeant in 1934, being further honoured with the award of the Meritorious Service Medal and the King George V Jubilee Medal. By now, his health had begun to deteriorate rapidly and on 14 July 1936 he died. The ship carrying his body to Cork was met by three hundred old comrades of the Royal Munster Fusiliers who acted as his bearers and guard of honour at his funeral, at which the Last Post was sounded.

Elsewhere, W and X Beaches had been joined but at the isolated Y Beach the Turks had counter-attacked in strength. Ammunition began to run low and amid confusion and misunderstanding the troops were actually taken off. Nevertheless, the fighting at Cape Helles had cost the Turks the better part of two regiments, each of which was only slightly smaller than a British brigade, and for the moment they had no more reserves to commit to the fight. During the next few days, as the 29th Division linked its beachheads and consolidated its hold on the southern end of the peninsula, it was confronted only by several scattered detachments of desperately weary Turks. Yet somehow the terrible events of 25–26 April seem to have stunned commanders and their staffs into a sense of inertia, and no advantage was taken of the enemy at the very time he was at his most vulnerable. When the 29th Division finally attempted to advance during the last days of the month it was met by strongly entrenched Turkish reinforcements and sharply repulsed.

The rest of the campaign took the form of a stalemate similar to that which existed on the Western Front, as each side committed more and more formations to the struggle. On the Cape Helles sector several unsuccessful attempts were made to capture the village of Krithia, which two British officers had entered and found deserted on the day of the landings. On the ANZAC sector attempts by the Australians and New Zealanders to improve their positions amid the tangle of gullies and ravines were fiercely resisted by Kemal's troops, who bitterly contested every yard of ground. On both sectors the Turks counter-attacked with suicidal courage, being mown down in droves. High summer came, bringing with it the torments of heat, flies, dysentery and the stink of the unburied dead. On 7 August an attempt was made to outflank the Turkish defences with a landing at Suvla Bay, to the north of ANZAC. It failed, for although the troops reached the shore safely, thanks to the provision of armoured lighters and the control exercised by Unwin, their commanders were again gripped by inertia and the Turks quickly contained the now-useless beachhead.

This, coupled with the loss of more capital ships from various causes, proved to be the last straw for the War Cabinet. Early in July, General Sir Ian Hamilton had written to Kitchener describing the nature of the killing machine that the campaign had become:

> The old battle tactics have vanished ... The only thing is by cunning or surprise, or skill, or tremendous expenditure of high explosive, or great expenditure of good troops, to win some small tactical position which the enemy may be bound, perhaps for military or perhaps for political reasons, to attack. Then you can begin to kill *them* pretty fast.

At sea, submarines continued to take incredible risks in passing through the Dardanelles minefields to penetrate the Sea of Marmora. During a patrol lasting from 27 April until 18 May, Lieutenant Commander Edward Boyle's *E14* sank a torpedo gunboat, a minelayer and, on 10 May, the large transport *Guj Djemal*, carrying 6,000 troops and a field battery. This was followed, between 19 May and 7 June, by a patrol carried out by Lieutenant Commander Martin Nasmith's *E11*, which resulted in the sinking of eleven Turkish vessels, including a large gunboat and two transports, some of his victims being destroyed *inside* Constantinople harbour. This caused a panic in the city itself and for a while paralysed Turkish shipping in the area. Boyle and Nasmith were both awarded the Victoria Cross as well as appropriate Allied decorations. Both carried out further patrols in the Sea of Marmora, during one of which, on 8 August, Nasmith torpedoed and sank the Turkish battleship *Hairredin Barbarosse*. Boyle rose to the rank of rear admiral and during World War II served as Flag-Officer-in-Charge, London 1939–42. Nasmith, later Admiral Sir Martin Dunbar-Nasmith, served as Commander-in-Chief Plymouth and Western Approaches 1938–41, then as Flag-Officer-in-Charge, London 1942–46.

Altogether, thirty-nine Victoria Crosses were awarded for the Dardanelles campaign and considerations of space alone prevents their all being mentioned here. Some, however, are of special significance or importance. That awarded to eighteen-year-old Second Lieutenant Dallas Moor of the 2nd Hampshires is, perhaps, one of the saddest commentaries on war. On 4 June, during the Third Battle of Krithia, the

Hampshires did well, taking their objectives at very heavy cost, losing most of their officers. However, on either flank less progress was made and the battalion was forced to withdraw some distance. Lieutenant Colonel Williams, the commanding officer, gave Moor specific orders to hold the line and shortly afterwards became a casualty himself. This effectively placed the young subaltern in command of the battalion, a fearful responsibility.

Shortly after dawn on 6 June the Turks, having been reinforced, mounted a counter-attack. The troops holding the first line of trenches, who belonged to another regiment, broke and began streaming to the rear in a panic rout. Without hesitation Moor and a few of his men rushed into the open to rally them. Some of the fugitives were so beyond reason that Moor had to shoot four of them to bring the rest to their senses. If this seems ruthless today, it must be remembered that many more lives would have been lost had the Turks been able to follow up the panic and break the British line. Having rallied and reorganised the leaderless men, Moor led them in a counter-attack that recovered the lost trenches, from which a second Turkish attack was beaten off that evening. The recommendation for Moor's VC came not from his own battalion – as acting CO there was no one to recommend him – but from officers of the neighbouring 2nd Royal Fusiliers, who witnessed the action.

In September Moor was evacuated to England, suffering from dysentery. In October 1917 he joined his regiment's 1st Battalion on the Western Front, serving with it until evacuated with a severe arm wound in December 1917. On his return, he served on the staff of the 30th Division. During his time on the Western Front further acts of gallantry resulted in his being awarded the Military Cross and Bar, but tragically he did not live to receive either award, having, during the last days of the war, fallen victim to the influenza epidemic that was sweeping across Europe.

For Australia and New Zealand, Gallipoli represents a defining moment in their rise to nationhood. The first Australian VC of the war was awarded to Lance Corporal Albert Jacka of the 14th (Victoria) Battalion, Australian Imperial Force, for an action on 19 May. Jacka came to be regarded as the ideal Australian citizen soldier. He was tough, aggressive, blunt, outspoken and used his initiative. As an NCO he appreciated the need for discipline but was reluctant to administer it in the formal British manner, preferring to bloody the noses of errant soldiers rather than charge them with minor offences.

On 19 May the Turks mounted a general assault against the ANZAC perimeter. They were cut down in their thousands and the offensive was called off. However, in one position known as Courtney's Post they secured a lodgement in a fire bay. Jacka was largely responsible for halting their further advance, but attempts to eject them failed with loss of life. Jacka then asked his comrades to create a diversion while he approached the fire bay from no man's land. Before the Turks were aware of what was happening, Jacka had jumped in among them, bayoneting two, one of whom was an officer, shooting five, then two more as they tried to escape over the parapet. When his VC was published in the *London Gazette*, Jacka was presented with £500 and a gold watch by a Melbourne businessman and his face appeared all over Australia on magazine covers and recruiting posters.

Thereafter, he received rapid promotion. By November 1915 he had risen to the rank of company sergeant major and on 29 April 1916 he was commissioned as second lieutenant, becoming a captain on 15 March 1917. He fought with his battalion on the Western Front and, on 7 August 1916, during the Battle of the Somme, he led seven men in an astounding local counter-attack that rescued forty prisoners belonging to a neighbouring Australian unit, killing a score or so of the enemy and capturing forty-two more, being hit no less than seven times in the action. For this he received an MC; many thought that a Bar to his VC would have been more appropriate and put the lesser award down to the bluntness, verging on insubordination, with which he addressed his superiors. He received a Bar to his MC the following year when he single-handedly captured a two-man enemy patrol in no man's land. He distinguished himself at Messines Ridge and again at Polygon Wood, but was not awarded the DSO for which he had been recommended. After being wounded and badly gassed in 1918 he saw no further active service. Charles Bean, the Australian official war historian, commented that Jacka had earned the VC not once, but three times, an opinion shared by many.

Jacka received a hero's welcome on his return to Australia, founded a business and became mayor of his local community, St Kilda. The war, however, had taken its toll. His health and finances declined and he died after a short illness on 17 January 1932, aged only thirty-nine. It was estimated that 6,000 people filed past his coffin as it lay in state at ANZAC House.

Between 7 and 9 August no fewer than seven Australians won the Victoria Cross during the fighting for possession of a prominent feature known as Lone Pine, which was a battle in itself. The Turks believed the position was impregnable, but during the afternoon the 2nd, 3rd and 4th Battalions of the Australian 1st (New South Wales) Brigade stormed it in surprise attack. Casualties had nevertheless been heavy and the brigade's 1st Battalion was ordered up from reserve to meet the anticipated Turkish counter-attack. Much of the subsequent fighting took the form of deadly bombing duels. In this context it must be mentioned that the grenades of the day were primitive in comparison with the fragmentation grenades issued later. The Turks used steel spheres about the size of a cricket ball, and the Australians were often forced to resort to jam tins packed with scrap metal. Both types of missile were exploded by an external fuse that had to be lit, and were almost as dangerous to their users as to their recipients.

In one exposed post that was subjected to a continuous rain of bombs, Lance Corporal Leonard Keysor of the 1st Battalion, a Londoner by birth, proved to be the soul of the defence, being awarded a hard-earned VC. He smothered Turkish bombs with sandbags to deaden the effects of their explosion, or, if the burning fuse was long enough, hurled them back. To the astonishment of his comrades, he caught several bombs in flight and returned them to their owners. Whenever a supply of Australian bombs became available, Keysor, scorning cover, went on the offensive. By the time his battalion was relieved by the 7th (Victoria) Battalion he had been throwing bombs for fifty hours and sustained two wounds.

Commanding the 7th Battalion's D Company was Second Lieutenant William Symons. The citation for his Victoria Cross graphically describes the desperate nature of the fighting in which he was involved:

He was in command of the right section of the newly-captured trenches held by his battalion and repelled several counter-attacks with great coolness. At about 5 a.m. on the 9th August a series of determined attacks were made by the enemy on an isolated sap, and six officers were in succession killed or severely wounded, and a portion of the sap was lost. Lieutenant Symons then led a charge and retook the lost sap, shooting two Turks with his revolver. The sap was under hostile fire from three sides, and Lieutenant Symons withdrew some 15 yards to a spot where some overhead cover could be obtained and in the face of heavy fire built up a sandbag barricade. The enemy succeeded in setting fire to the fascines and woodwork of the head cover, but Lieutenant Symons extinguished the fire and rebuilt the barricade. His coolness and determination finally compelled the enemy to discontinue their attacks.

In a letter to his mother, written two days later, Symons commented that the bottom of the trench was filled with dead or wounded Turks and Australians, lying four or five deep in places.

Near by, Lieutenant Frederick Tubb, commanding the battalion's B Company, was engaged in an equally desperate struggle for a stretch of captured trench that was separated from the Turkish-held portion by a sandbag barricade. During the first counter-attack a number of the enemy swarmed over the barricade but were shot or bayoneted. Tubb continued to fire over the parapet at those beyond as well as others attempting to approach the position above ground. His party was then subjected to continuous bombing. Gradually their numbers were whittled down until only Tubb, wounded in the scalp and arm by bomb fragments, Corporal Alexander Burton, Corporal William Dunstan and a few men remained fit to fight. At this juncture all but one foot of the barricade was blown down, almost certainly as a result of a charge laid or thrown by the Turks. While Tubb and the others repelled the attack that followed, Burton and Dunstan rebuilt the barricade under a hail of bombs and bullets. This happened twice more, Burton being killed by bomb fragments as he worked on the barrier. Having failed in three determined attempts to recapture the trench, the Turks did not try to rush the position again, contenting themselves with bomb-throwing and sniping. For their action in preventing what could have been a serious breakthrough Tubb, Burton and Dunstan were all awarded the Victoria Cross, making four won by their battalion during the battle.

Elsewhere, the Turks had penetrated a trench called Sasse's Sap, leading directly to the 3rd Battalion's headquarters and that of the 1st Australian Brigade. Among those who foiled this attack and won the Victoria Cross was nineteen-year-old Private John Hamilton of the 3rd Battalion. Earlier in the action Hamilton, like Keysor, had returned enemy bombs to their throwers. Now, he climbed on to the parapet of his trench and for the next six hours, protected only by a few sandbags, he sniped at Turks trying to bomb their way forward along the sap, as well as directing his comrades where to throw their own bombs. As a direct result of this the enemy attack collapsed.

On the morning of 9 August the 1st Battalion returned to the line, relieving the 3rd Battalion. Shortly after, the Turks mounted another attack and captured a stretch of Sasse's Sap. The counter-attack was led by the recently promoted Captain Alfred Shout, a Boer War veteran who had already won the MC during the present campaign. Accompanied by Captain Cecil Sasse and several men carrying sandbags with which to build a trench barricade, he advanced on the Turks crowding the sap. The two officers led the way along the trench side by side, with Sasse firing his rifle at those in front and Shout hurling bombs at those beyond. In this way Sasse accounted for a dozen of the enemy and Shout a further eight, putting the rest to flight. Some 20 yards of the trench had been recovered and a barricade was built. During the afternoon they successfully repeated the action. They had almost completed their task when Shout decided to treat the Turks to a final volley of bombs. He lit the fuses of three and had thrown one when another exploded as it was leaving his hand, inflicting such severe injuries that he died three days later. He was awarded a posthumous VC and Sasse was awarded the DSO.

As might be expected, the fortunes of the surviving Lone Pine VCs were as varied as the men themselves. Keysor continued to serve with the 1st Battalion when it moved to the Western Front, then transferred to the 42nd Battalion, in which he received a commission, being wounded twice in 1918. After the war he returned to London and joined his father's clock-importing business, remaining reticent about his exploit for the rest of his life. As a captain Symons served on the Western Front with the 37th Battalion AIF. He adopted the surname Penn-Symons and pursued a successful business career, settling in England. During World War II he commanded the 12th Battalion, Leicestershire Home Guard. Tubb recovered from his wounds and became a major. He was killed in action at Polygon Wood, Ypres, on 20 September 1917. Dunstan was invalided back to Australia and discharged on medical grounds in 1916. He immediately enlisted in the citizen forces and was granted a commission. After the war he worked for a newspaper group of which he became general manager. Hamilton continued to serve with the 3rd Battalion on the Western Front, becoming a sergeant. He was commissioned shortly after the war ended. Between the wars he worked as a docker, storeman, packer and shipping clerk on the Sydney waterfront. He enlisted again during World War II, becoming a captain in the Army Labour Service, serving in New Guinea and Bougainville.

While the Australians were fighting at Lone Pine the Wellington Battalion of the New Zealand Brigade had temporarily captured the dominant feature of Chunuk Bair, from which the Dardanelles were visible. During this action Corporal Cyril Bassett of the Divisional Signal Company won the New Zealand Army's first VC of the war. The brigade commander, Brigadier General F. E. Johnston, lost contact with the Wellingtons and ordered a telephone line to be run up to them. This was no easy matter as the line, lying on the ground or strung over scrub, was as vulnerable to shellfire as the passage of troops. Bassett was given responsibility for establishing the link, which was completed on 7 August. Throughout the next two days he worked on under shell and rifle fire, sometimes within 100 yards of a Turkish counter-attack, locating breaks in the line and repairing them, as well as bringing in a badly wounded man. When, later, he was told that he had been awarded the Victoria Cross, he insisted that a mistake had been made. He saw further active service on the Western Front, where he was commissioned in 1917. On his return to New Zealand he resumed his career in banking and eventually became a branch manager. During World War II he served with the Corps of Signals in the National Military Reserve, rising to the rank of lieutenant colonel.

On 10 August the Turks recaptured Chunuk Bair in a mass attack that cost them dear. The loss of the feature convinced Hamilton that the campaign was going nowhere, despite the exemplary courage and fortitude displayed by the troops. He was unaware that since it began there were three occasions on which the Turks, brought to the brink of despair, had believed their line was about to be broken. The British War Cabinet was convinced that what had once seemed to offer a shortcut to victory had now become an expensive blind alley. It was decided, therefore, to bring the campaign to an end. Suvla Bay and ANZAC were evacuated on the night 19–20 December and Cape Helles on the night of 8–9 January 1916. In each case the deception and embarkation plans were so thorough that the Turks did not discover what had taken place until the following morning, and not a single casualty had been incurred.

The British and Dominion armies sustained the loss of 200,000 men killed, wounded or missing during the campaign, to which must be added approximately 40,000 French casualties. Of the total, 46,000 were killed in action or died from disease. No accurate record of Turkish losses exists, but 300,000 is considered to be a probable estimate, of whom one-third were killed.

The future Field Marshals Birdwood, Slim, Harding and Blamey all took part in the Gallipoli campaign as junior officers. Clement Attlee, who would one day become the United Kingdom's Prime Minister, and the novelist Compton Mackenzie were among the many famous names who served on the peninsula. The troops involved were subsequently employed on the Western Front, or in Egypt and Palestine. For some in high places the result of the campaign spelled disaster. Among them was Winston Churchill, one of its most powerful advocates, who was forced to resign his position as First Lord of the Admiralty and entered the political wilderness for a while. Yet some, like Captain Unwin of the *River Clyde*, believed to their dying day that a stroke against Constantinople was the correct strategy. However, for such an attempt to have succeeded, it would have to have been made months earlier than was the case.

Jutland
31 May – 1 June 1916

The principal role of the Royal Navy's Grand Fleet during World War I was to defend the United Kingdom against invasion and, if possible, bring to battle and destroy the German High Seas Fleet. The latter, numerically the smaller, did not seek a general fleet engagement but sought to entrap and destroy a portion of the Grand Fleet and thereby significantly weaken its opponent. If it succeeded, the results could be far-reaching, for the British, conscious of the increased possibility of invasion, would probably withdraw some of their troops from France. This, in turn, would mean that the French Army, currently under immense pressure at Verdun, would have to take over a much larger sector of the Western Front at a time when its Russian ally was showing the first signs of collapse. If, on the other hand, the High Seas Fleet sustained a defeat, it would have little immediate effect upon the Central Powers' ability to wage war in continental Europe. An immense burden therefore rested upon the shoulders of Admiral Sir John Jellicoe, the Grand Fleet's commander, of whom it was said, with some justice, that he was the only man who could lose the war in an afternoon.

As well as numbers, however, the Royal Navy had another advantage, namely possession of the German naval codes. During 30 May radio intercepts revealed that the High Seas Fleet was leaving harbour with a major naval operation of some sort in mind. Jellicoe estimated correctly that this would take place in the general area of the Skaggerak and led his battle fleet out of its anchorage at Scapa Flow in the hope of intercepting and destroying the enemy in the general engagement that had been eagerly sought since the war began. Simultaneously, the battle cruiser fleet, commanded by Vice Admiral Sir David Beatty, left its base at Rosyth on the east coast of Scotland to scout ahead. Altogether, the Grand Fleet consisted of 28 dreadnought battleships, 9 battle cruisers, 8 armoured cruisers, 26 light cruisers, 78 destroyers, 1 minelayer and 1 seaplane carrier.

If Vice Admiral Reinhard Scheer, commanding the High Seas Fleet, had been aware that the British were at sea it is probable that the encounter would never have taken place as he was not prepared to commit his 16 dreadnoughts, 6 pre-dreadnoughts, 5 battle cruisers, 11 light cruisers and 61 destroyers to a general engagement with the massed might of the Grand Fleet. His plans involved his being kept informed of British naval movements by the Zeppelin airships and a U-boat screen, but bad flying weather inhibited the former and the information provided by the latter was so incomplete that no conclusions could be drawn from it. Yet in some respects the Germans were better prepared for the coming battle than their opponents. They had, for example, taken special precautions to prevent the flash from an explosion inside a gun turret reaching the magazine below, while, as yet, the British had not. Their modern capital ships were compartmentalised to a greater degree than the British, which meant that they could absorb far greater punishment without the risk of sinking. Their ammunition, too, was reliable, whereas it was found that some of the British armour-piercing shells, instead of penetrating to explode inside a ship, broke up on impact. All of these things would become apparent during the early stages of the engagement.

It was shortly after 15:00 that Beatty, with six battle cruisers, supported by four slower dreadnoughts plus cruiser and destroyer units, came into contact with the German scouting force, commanded by Vice Admiral Franz Hipper and consisting of five battle cruisers, plus cruisers and destroyers. Hipper promptly turned south, believing that he could lead Beatty to destruction by luring him under the guns of the High Seas Fleet. Beatty swung on to a parallel course and at 15:48 both sides opened fire, closing the range steadily from 18,000 to 12,000 yards. The Germans' gunnery was the better and they quickly began to obtain the greater number of hits. On Beatty's flagship, the battle cruiser *Lion*, Q (midships) turret was penetrated. Most of the turret crew were killed by the explosion. A fire began to rage in the cordite charges ready for loading. Realising that this would soon reach the magazine, Major Francis Harvey of the Royal Marine Light Infantry, mortally wounded and with both legs smashed, used his dying breath to order the closing of the magazine doors and the flooding of the compartment. In so doing he undoubtedly saved the ship from total destruction and was awarded a posthumous Victoria Cross.

At 16:05 the battle cruiser *Indefatigable* was hit by at least two shells, one of which penetrated A turret. The flash travelled down the trunk to the magazine and the ship exploded in a huge column of flame and smoke. Only two of her crew survived. By now, Beatty's four supporting dreadnoughts, commanded by Rear Admiral Hugh Evan-Thomas, had caught up. Their gunnery was much superior to that of the battle cruisers and they began to punish the Germans severely. Indeed, Hipper was to comment after the battle that only the poor quality of the British ammunition saved him from complete disaster. At 16:26, however, the battle cruiser *Queen Mary*, under fire from two ships, blew up from precisely the same cause as the *Indefatigable*. Shortly after, Hipper, concerned by the amount of damage his ships were sustaining, turned away, but at 17:00 sighted the main body of the High Seas Fleet. He felt that he had succeeded in leading a sizeable portion of the Grand Fleet into a trap, but it was by no means as simple as that. The destroyer flotillas of both sides surged forward to launch torpedo attacks and became embroiled in a savage mêlée during which the German destroyers *V27* and *V29* were sunk. Of all the torpedoes launched only one, fired by HMS *Petard*, found its mark, blowing a huge hole in the side of the German battle cruiser *Seydlitz*.

Emerging from the mêlée, HMS *Nestor* and *Nicator*, the former commanded by Commander The Hon. Edward Bingham, pressed home an attack on the leading ships of Scheer's line, displaying suicidal courage in the teeth of intense fire from the enemy battleships. During this *Nestor* sustained such serious damage that she was immobilised. Bingham refused an offer of assistance from *Nicator* and his ship went down with colours flying when she was battered to scrap by the advancing enemy, as was another crippled British destroyer, *Nomad*. Incredibly, Bingham and seventy-four out of his crew of eighty-three were chivalrously picked up by a German destroyer and, with very mixed feelings, spent the rest of the battle under guard below decks. For his determined leadership and courage, Bingham was awarded the Victoria Cross. The only one of the Jutland VCs to survive the battle, he subsequently achieved the rank of rear admiral.

Meanwhile, the light cruiser *Southampton*, pressing on to the south, had reported the position, strength and course of the High Seas Fleet to Jellicoe. This information was confirmed by Beatty, who reversed course and headed north at 17:26. His retirement was covered by Evan-Thomas's battleships, the good shooting of which obtained hits on the *Konig, Grosser Kurfurst* and *Markgraf*, the leading dreadnoughts of Scheer's line, as well as on Hipper's battle cruisers. The tables had now been turned, for now it was the unsuspecting High Seas Fleet that was being led into a trap. Scheer was also handicapped by the fact that his pursuit of Beatty was restricted to a speed of 15 knots, the maximum his elderly pre-dreadnoughts could produce.

All of this gave Jellicoe time to deploy the Grand Fleet in line of battle across Scheer's known course. Shortly after 18:00 Beatty sighted this and, reinforced by three battle cruisers that had led Jellicoe's approach, swung eastwards to remain at the head of the British line. The evening's poor visibility was further reduced by the drifting funnel smoke of hundreds of ships, so that when Hipper and Scheer emerged from the murk at about 18:15 they found, to their horror, that they were confronted by the entire Grand Fleet. Two minutes later the British opened fire. Hipper's flagship, *Lützow*, was reduced to a battered, sinking wreck, forcing Hipper to transfer his flag to a destroyer, so that for the next two hours the German battle cruisers were commanded by Captain Hartog of the *Derfflinger*, which herself had sustained twenty hits, was down by the bows and had lost the ability to use her radio. The rest of Hipper's battle cruisers were left in little better state. All of *Von der Tann*'s turrets were put out of action, *Seydlitz* was awash from the bows to her middle deck, and only *Moltke*, which Hipper was eventually able to board, retained the full capacity to fight. In Scheer's battle line, *König*, hit time and again, took on a serious list, and *Markgraf*, hit in the engine room, was forced to reduce speed.

For Scheer, this was the worst-case scenario, but he had allowed for its happening and exercised his ships in a manoeuvre known as the Battle Turn-Away. This involved each ship reversing course individually rather all turning in succession about one point. At 18:35 he gave the signal and the High Seas Fleet faded into the mist. A final salvo from *Derfflinger* struck the recently arrived battle cruiser *Invincible*, which blew up from precisely the same cause as the earlier losses.

While the capital ships exchanged salvoes, other equally deadly duels were being fought between the cruisers and destroyers of both fleets. The light cruiser *Chester* suddenly found herself confronted by an entire German light cruiser squadron consisting of the *Frankfurt*, *Wiesbaden*, *Pillau* and *Elbing*. Hit repeatedly and sustaining serious casualties, she succeeded in leading her opponents within range of the British battle cruisers, which reduced the *Wiesbaden* to a burning wreck, put a 12-inch shell into the *Pillau*'s engine room, putting four boilers out of action and starting fires, and seriously damaged the *Frankfurt*.

Serving aboard *Chester* was sixteen-year-old Boy First Class John Cornwell, who was employed as sight-setter and communications number at one of the cruiser's 6-inch guns. One by one the gun crew were killed or seriously wounded, but Cornwell remained at his post, relaying orders and resetting the gun sight, despite having himself sustained a wound that he must have suspected was mortal. When the last of the crew were hit and the gun could no longer be worked, John Cornwell remained standing at his post with his headphones on, quietly awaiting orders. In the lull that followed the escape of the German cruisers that was how he was found, but there was no hope of saving his life. He was granted a posthumous Victoria Cross and to this day remains one of the best-known winners of the award. A housing association for naval and Royal Marine personnel and their widows was named after him, as were several roads in British naval shore establishments.

Courage, however, was not a British monopoly. Whatever chance the *Wiesbaden* might have had of putting herself to rights was destroyed by the guns of the destroyer *Onslow* and the armoured cruisers *Defence* and *Warrior* when they came upon her. Now a hopeless case, she continued to fight on as best she could until a torpedo finally sent her to the bottom. In return, *Defence* was blown apart by the fire of *Derfflinger* and four German battleships and *Warrior* was badly damaged.

Elsewhere, Commander William Loftus Jones, commanding the destroyer *Shark,* led a torpedo attack against the German battle cruisers. Under fire from the enemy cruisers as well as destroyers, *Shark* managed to get off one torpedo before she was smothered by shellfire, set ablaze and brought to a standstill. Refusing an offer of assistance from the destroyer *Acasta*, Loftus Jones continued to fight his ship. One by one her guns were knocked out until only the midships gun, crewed by three men, remained in action. Loftus Jones, already wounded in the thigh and face, directed their fire until his right leg was shot off above the knee. Propped up, he ordered a White Ensign to be hoisted in place of that which had been shot away. By now, *Shark* was sinking by the bows and he gave the crew permission to abandon ship. Shortly after, two torpedoes gave her the *coup de grâce*. Six of her crew survived and were awarded the Distinguished Service Medal. Loftus Jones received the posthumous award of the Victoria Cross in recognition of his gallantry and that of his men.

At this stage Jellicoe could have embarked on a direct pursuit of Scheer, in which case he would undoubtedly have been able to sink some of the High Seas Fleet's damaged stragglers. On the other hand, this would not give him the decisive victory he sought and, guessing correctly that Scheer's next move would be to head for home, he set a course that would interpose the Grand Fleet between the Germans and their base. Scheer, in fact, had been badly shaken by the encounter and acted exactly as Jellicoe predicted, his change of heading being reported by *Southampton*. At 19:10 the High Seas Fleet again ran head-on into Jellicoe's line of battle and sustained a pounding of which the battle cruisers received the major share. *Lützow*, crippled and sinking, was later torpedoed by her own escorting destroyers. *Von der Tann*, her control tower smashed and with only one gun in action, gallantly remained in the line in the hope of drawing fire away from her consorts. *Seydlitz* and *Derfflinger* both had fires raging aboard. Among the German dreadnoughts, *Markgraf*, *Grosser Kurfurst* and *König* all received further punishment, the last two shipping hundreds of tons of water through their riven hulls. After five minutes of this, Scheer gave the order for another Battle Turn-Away. Close to hysteria, he instructed the four remaining battle cruisers to 'close the enemy and ram' in the hope of distracting Jellicoe's attention but, recovering himself shortly afterwards, countermanded this. This second withdrawal was, in fact, ably covered by two German destroyer flotillas which laid a smokescreen and mounted a torpedo attack. None of the thirty-one torpedoes launched found a target, for the British battleships turned away, allowing the torpedoes to pass between them. Engaged by the British destroyers and cruisers as well as the battleships' secondary armament, six of the German destroyers sustained damage and a seventh, *S35*, was blown apart.

Both fleets, now out of visual contact, adopted a parallel southerly course. At 20:20 the battle cruisers again engaged briefly, the Germans having the worst of the encounter as they were silhouetted against what remained of the light while the British were almost invisible against the darker eastern horizon. Scheer's pre-dreadnought squadron, leading the line since the Battle Turn-Away, was sent to assist but turned away after hits had been scored on *Schleswig-Holstein*, *Pommern* and the cruiser *Stettin*. Anxious to avoid a renewal of the battle at first light, which was expected at about 03:30, Scheer knew that he could not delay turning south-eastwards for much longer. In this he was assisted by the fact that the Grand Fleet's speed was several knots faster than his own, so that when he did give the order to change course at 21:30 he broke through the light units covering the rear of Jellicoe's line. There followed a series of confused actions involving close-range gunfire, torpedo attacks and collisions. The British lost several destroyers, the armoured cruiser *Black Prince* and the light cruiser *Tipperary* as well as the cruisers *Southampton* and *Dublin* seriously damaged. The German cruisers *Frauenlob* and *Rostock* were torpedoed and sunk. The cruiser *Elbing*, also torpedoed, was rammed by one of her own dreadnoughts, the *Posen*, then abandoned. The pre-dreadnought *Pommern*, torpedoed by the destroyer *Oberient*, blew up and sank. Off the Horns Reef, which marked the beginning of the 120-mile swept channel to the High Seas Fleet's anchorage at the Jade, the battle cruiser *Seydlitz*, so badly damaged that she was drawing 42 feet of water forward, ran aground and had to be towed into harbour stern-first the following day. Finally, at 05:20, the dreadnought *Ostfriesland* struck a British mine. Beatty remained off the Horns Reef until 11:00 on 1 June then turned for home in rising seas that claimed the *Warrior*, damaged and under tow.

The Battle of Jutland, unique in the history of naval warfare, was over. The Grand Fleet lost three battle cruisers, three armoured cruisers and eight destroyers, a total of fourteen ships. The High Seas Fleet lost one pre-dreadnought battleship, one battle cruiser, four light cruisers and five destroyers, a total of eleven ships. British casualties amounted to 6,097 killed, half of whom were lost in the three battle cruisers, and 510 wounded; the Germans lost 2,551 killed and 507 wounded. On the basis of these figures, plus the fact that he had saved his fleet from destruction, Scheer claimed a victory. In the United Kingdom, the public was deeply disappointed that the battle had not been a second Trafalgar. All of this ignored a number of important factors. It was, after all, Scheer who had run for cover. Only ten of his capital ships remained undamaged and he could only promise the Kaiser that the High Seas Fleet would be ready for action again in six or seven weeks. In fact, of his four remaining battle cruisers, repairs on *Seydlitz* and *Derfflinger* were not completed until, respectively, 16 September and 15 October. In sharp contrast, on the day following the Grand Fleet's return to harbour, Jellicoe could report that he had twenty-four undamaged battle cruisers and dreadnoughts available for action at four hours' notice, while of his eight capital ships undergoing repair the last left the dockyard on 2 August.

The real results of Jutland were psychological. After the battle the High Seas Fleet rarely left harbour and it never again sought such an encounter. Its best officers and men transferred to the U-boat branch, which inflicted far greater damage on British shipping than the High Seas Fleet could ever hope to do. Its morale declined steadily until, on being ordered to sea in the last days of the war, it mutinied, initiating the collapse of Imperial Germany.

The Somme
1 JULY 1916

Of all the battles that took place along the deadlocked Western Front between the latter days of 1914 and the spring of 1918, that of the Somme is the most deeply ingrained in the British subconscious, as is the date 1 July 1916, the day upon which the British Army sustained the greatest number of casualties in its long history.

The object of the Somme offensive was to provide some relief for the French, whose armies were being bled white in the fearful battle of attrition raging at Verdun, as well as ejecting the Germans from the Thiepval–Pozières ridge, along which they had dug in during the autumn of 1914. In places, their positions occupied the reverse slopes and were carefully concealed, although air reconnaissance revealed that their first and second defence lines extended to a total depth of 5,000 yards. This was, in fact, one of the best defended sectors of the entire Western Front, incorporating barbed-wire aprons 50 yards deep, shaped to channel attacks into killing grounds swept by machine-guns within fortified posts or concrete blockhouses, and large dugouts some 30 feet below the surface, equipped with electric lighting, running water, ventilation and emergency rations.

The offensive was originally planned to commence on 29 June and consist of a general assault along 21 miles of front. On the right the attack would be delivered by General Fayolle's French Sixth Army, although the main blow was to be delivered by General Sir Henry Rawlinson's Fourth Army, the left flank of which was to be protected by the Third Army under General Sir Edmund Allenby. On 3 July a breakout force, known as the Reserve Army and consisting of the Cavalry Corps and two of Rawlinson's infantry divisions was to be formed under Lieutenant General Hubert Gough with the intention of exploiting the gains made and breaking through into 'clean' open country. In preparation for this, the greatest offensive yet undertaken by the British Army, 2,000 guns were to fire a preparatory bombardment lasting for five days.

By this stage of the war the British Expeditionary Force, now commanded by General Sir Douglas Haig, had become a citizen army. The regular and territorial divisions had been thinned not only by the battles of 1914 and 1915 but also by the need to provide a stiffening of experienced personnel for Kitchener's New Army divisions. In the main, these consisted of enthusiastic volunteers, many of whom had enlisted in 'Pals' battalions recruited from friends and neighbours or men from similar backgrounds who wished to fight together. Some regular commanders and their staffs mistakenly lacked confidence in the ability of these formations to carry out elementary tactical movements such as disciplined rushes over fire-swept ground and insisted that they carried out their attacks in straight lines at a walking pace. In reaching this decision they grossly underestimated the intelligence and initiative that was present in abundance in the New Army. In addition to the British divisions, ten Commonwealth divisions would also take part in the offensive – five Australian, four Canadian and one New Zealand, plus a South African brigade.

The bombardment commenced on 24 June. It wrecked large sections of the German front-line trenches, caused casualties and extensive damage and cut gaps in the wire, albeit unevenly. Unfortunately, bad flying weather made it difficult for the Royal Flying Corps to adjust fire on to the German artillery positions, which thus escaped a great deal of the punishment intended for them. On the ground, patrols reported that large stretches of wire remained uncut, so the assault was postponed until 1 July. What no one knew was that the bombardment was barely touching the enemy's deep dugouts, although it did stretch the nerves of those within to the point that they longed for the attack to begin so that they could, for a while, escape from the crowded, stale, claustrophobic conditions, described in a letter by one German soldier as his 'grave in the earth', into fresh air and daylight.

At 07:30 on Sunday 1 July officers' whistles shrilled all along the line as the British and French scrambled out of their trenches to form the first assault wave. Simultaneously, the weight of the bombardment lifted on to the German rear trenches. On the right, the French broke through the enemy front line in a series of controlled rushes. By 16:00 their neighbours, the British XIII Corps, had also taken their objective, Montauban ridge, at the cost of 6,000 casualties. Ironically this, the only British success of the day, was achieved by two New Army divisions that chose to ignore the crass directive requiring them to walk across no man's land in rigid ranks. Only 200 yards separated the 18th Division from the enemy trenches, which were taken at a run before a coherent defence could be organised. The 30th Division had twice as far to go but was able to press home its attack because the artillery preparation had cut sufficient gaps in the German wire.

Everywhere else, the story was one of supreme courage and self-sacrifice ending in tragic and total failure. The steadily advancing lines were flayed by concealed machine-guns. The men where cut down in ranks or strove to penetrate the walls of blast and flying steel erected by the German artillery's defensive barrages. In places, brave but inexperienced groups broke through the wire and pushed on past the enemy's forward trenches. In so doing they neglected to clear the deep dugouts and were either surrounded and forced to surrender or shot down from behind. Most of the few lodgements secured were soon lost to local counter-attacks. By 10:00 it was all over. Khaki bodies lay thick everywhere in no man's land and in the German wire. In shellholes the wounded waited stoically for nightfall before trying to limp or crawl back to their own lines. So horrific had been the sight, and such was the Germans' admiration for their opponents' contempt for death, that in places pity and fellow feeling led them to leave their trenches and render such help as they could. By the evening, as the British reserve brigades came forward to occupy their own forward trenches, everyone knew that there had been a major disaster. When all the casualty returns were in, it was possible to calculate that in a mere three hours' fighting the British Army had lost 19,240 killed, 35,493 wounded, 2,152 missing and 585 known captured, a total of 57,470.

Of the fifty Victoria Crosses won during the long Battle of the Somme, eight were awarded for acts performed on 1 July, more than on any other day of the battle.

Captain Eric Bell of the 9th Royal Inniskilling Fusiliers (36th (Ulster) Division) received the award posthumously. On 1 July he was commanding a trench mortar battery that advanced with the infantry. When the advance was halted by a machine-gun firing from a flank he stalked the weapon and shot the gunner. Later, during the trench-clearing phase, he went forward alone on three occasions and threw grenades among the enemy. When the supply of grenades was exhausted, he stood on the trench parapet under intense fire, using a rifle with some effect to break up a counter-attack. He was killed while rallying troops who had lost their own officers. He was aged only twenty.

Near by, the 9th Royal Irish Fusiliers, also belonging to the 36th Division, were mown down by another concealed machine-gun as they tried vainly to take positions south-east of Beaumont Hamel. A battalion roll call at nightfall revealed that only a handful of officers and eighty men remained alive and unhurt. During the night the battalion's adjutant, Lieutenant Geoffrey St George Cather, went out into no man's land, across which the Germans had now resumed firing. By midnight he had carried three wounded men to safety, given water to others and arranged their rescue. He went out again at 08:30 next morning and brought in a fourth man. Finally, at 10:30, while taking water to another of the many wounded, he was killed by machine-gun fire.

Another posthumous award was made to Captain John Green, Royal Army Medical Corps, the medical officer of the 1/5th Sherwood Foresters (46th Division). On 1 July the Foresters took part in a divisional attack intended to capture Gommecourt Wood, on the northern edge of the village of the same name. The battalion was among those which, having proceeded beyond the first line of enemy trenches, was fired into from the rear when the Germans emerged from their dugouts, as well as frontally from the second line of trenches. Green, following up the advance, came across Captain Frank Robinson, lying seriously wounded and entangled in the enemy wire. Robinson was the battalion's machine-gun officer, but when all his men were shot down within 150 yards of leaving their own trenches he had decided to continue alone. Under fire, Green disentangled him and carried him to a shellhole where he dressed his wounds. He then carried Robinson back towards the first line of British trenches. At this point Robinson was hit again and, while pausing to dress this fresh wound Green was shot through the head and killed. Robinson was brought in and although he died from his wounds two days later he was able to provide the principal witness statement resulting in Green's award.

Opposite the village of Fricourt the 10th Green Howards (21st Division) were effectively pinned in their own trenches by very heavy and accurate fire from German machine-gunners who had emerged from their dugouts the minute the barrage had lifted to their second line. Realising that something would have to be done very quickly, Major Stewart Loudoun-Shand jumped on to the parapet and by his example encouraged his company to leave the trench and commence their attack. Inevitably, he was hit and fell mortally wounded but insisted upon being propped up and continued to encourage his men until he died. Of his company, only twenty-eight men survived the attack. This act of suicidal courage was witnessed with awe and gratitude by the 12th Northumberland Fusiliers from their own trench 400 yards to the rear, for had the Green Howards continued to falter they would have had to have made the attack themselves. Loudoun-Shand's VC was the first of four to be won by his regiment during the Battle of the Somme.

Shortly before 07:00 Private William McFadzean of the 14th Royal Irish Rifles (36th Division) was distributing grenades to those about to attack. Somehow, a box of grenades was mishandled, fell to the bottom of the trench and burst open. To his horror, Billy McFadzean saw that the pins retaining the safety clamps on two of the grenades had been worked free by the impact. Knowing that in only a few seconds many of his comrades would be killed by the explosion, he flung himself without hesitation on top of the grenades and was killed instantly. On 18 December 1916 King George V presented the Victoria Cross to Billy's father at Buckingham Palace, commenting, 'Nothing finer has been done in this war for which I have yet given the Victoria Cross than the act performed by your son in giving his life so heroically to save the lives of his comrades.'

On 1 July Private Robert Quigg of the 12th Royal Irish Rifles (also 36th Division) took part in three attacks north of Beaumont Hamel. Early next morning, on learning that his platoon commander, Lieutenant Sir Henry Macnaghton, who also happened to be his squire, was lying wounded somewhere in no man's land, Quigg braved shell and machine-gun fire to go out and look for him. Altogether, he went out seven times and on each occasion brought in a wounded man, the seventh being dragged to safety from within a few yards of the German wire. After seven hours of this work he was so exhausted that he could do no more. Seldom has a VC been harder earned. In further recognition of his deed, Quigg also received the Russian Medal of the Order of St George and the French Croix de Guerre. On his return home Lady Macnaghton presented him with a gold watch as a mark of appreciation for his vain search for her son, whose body was never found. Quigg later served in Mesopotamia and Egypt, reaching the rank of sergeant. In 1926 he was severely injured in an accident and left the army, spending the rest of his life in a cottage on the Macnaghton estate. In 1953 he was presented to Queen Elizabeth II. At his funeral two years later he was accorded full military honours.

Some way to the north the 4th Division had attacked a sector of the enemy line close to Beaumont Hamel. The first wave was cut down before it reached its objective and officer casualties were so high in the second wave that the men, left virtually leaderless, began to drift back towards their own lines. At this point Drummer Walter Ritchie of the

2nd Seaforth Highlanders, a regular battalion, intervened. He had already acted as runner, repeatedly carrying messages across the fire-swept ground and now, seeing the drift to the rear, decided to halt it on his own initiative. Ignoring the enemy's fire, he climbed on to the parapet of a captured trench and blew the Charge on his bugle, which, contrary to orders, he had taken into action. Drawn to the sound, men who had lost their officers or become separated from their units, rallied, enabling the position to be held against counter-attack. Even so, the cost was high, for when the 2nd Seaforths were relieved the following after-noon their strength amounted to just four officers, two of whom were wounded, and some eighty other ranks.

Throughout his life, Ritchie refused to discuss the exploit that led to his being awarded the VC. Before the war ended he sustained four wounds and was gassed twice. In 1921 he joined his regiment's 1st Bat-talion, in which he was promoted to sergeant, and later became the battalion's drum major. After leaving the army in 1929 he served as a recruiting officer in Glasgow.

On the Thiepval sector, to the north of the River Ancre, the 49th Divi-sion was to provide immediate support for the 32nd Division's attack. One of the units sent forward by the former was the 1st/7th West York-shire Regiment, which incurred heavy casualties, particularly among the officers. By nightfall a confused situation existed and two West York-shire companies withdrew. However, a thirty-strong platoon, now commanded by Corporal George Sanders, did not. Sanders, who pos-sessed natural powers of leadership, decided to hang on to the gains they had made. During the next thirty-six hours the platoon, lacking food and water, not only beat off three counter-attacks but also rescued several prisoners who had fallen into enemy hands. By the time it was relieved its strength had been reduced to nineteen men. Like Ritchie, Sanders avoided discussing the circumstances that led to his being awarded the VC, preferring to comment on the fact that five of his men had won the Military Medal during the action, and that spoke for itself.

In June 1917 Sanders was commissioned, being posted to his regi-ment's 1st/6th Battalion, and in December that year was appointed acting captain. During the great German offensive of spring 1918 he was wounded in the right arm and leg but continued to fire his pistol with his left hand until he was surrounded and captured. As a prisoner-of-war he remained unaware that he had been awarded the MC for the tenacity with which he had held his position until it was overrun. After the war he worked for Leeds Corporation and the North-Eastern Gas

Board. During World War II he served in the Home Guard. When he died after a long illness on 4 April 1950 no less than four holders of the VC attended his funeral, at which he was accorded full military honours.

Serving with the 17th Highland Light Infantry (32nd Division) was Sergeant James Turnbull, a towering figure of fine physique and above-average stamina. His battalion's objective was a prominent feature named the Leipzig Redoubt, near the village of Authuille. On this sector the enemy wire remained largely uncut and the few gaps that existed were covered by machine-guns. Despite this, the battalion stormed the first line of trenches but was unable to take the second because of a crossfire that cut down the leading companies, and consolidated the gains that had been made. On the way through the first line, Turnbull, whose ability as a cricketer and great height enabled him to throw a grenade further than anyone else in the battalion, had mentally noted the position of a large enemy grenade store. The Germans clearly regarded the penetration of the Leipzig Redoubt as an extremely serious matter for they mounted fierce counter-attacks throughout the day. Turnbull, holding an advance post, was largely responsible for breaking these up, sending parties of men to bring up fresh supplies of grenades from the German store and hurling the bombs great distances to burst among the advancing enemy. Whenever the supply of grenades ran out he seized a machine-gun and kept the Germans pinned down. In this way, for sixteen long hours, he foiled every attempt to encircle his battalion. Ironically, it was after the counter-attacks had ceased and he was going about his normal duties as a platoon sergeant that he was picked off and killed by a sniper. His VC citation records that he displayed 'the highest degree of valour and skill in the performance of his duties'. Had it not been for his presence, the 17th Highland Light Infantry might well have ceased to exist. As it was, when the battalion was relieved its casualties amounted to twenty-two officers and 447 other ranks.

In the light of a catastrophe such as that which had occurred on 1 July it might be wondered why Haig allowed the offensive to continue, especially as he had promised Rawlinson that if excessive losses were incurred it would be halted. In fact, it took some time before the full extent of the carnage became known, and as gains on the right had been made it was apparent that the German defences were not impregnable. Furthermore, he was committed to supporting the French and could not go back on his word without the risk of creating serious, and possibly fatal, strains within the Entente.

During the next two weeks Rawlinson restricted his attacks to local objectives, eroding the German defences piece by piece. It was now the Germans' turn to suffer, for their doctrine on positional warfare demanded the recapture of lost ground by immediate counter-attacks. This exposed them to the same ordeal by fire that the British had been forced to endure on 1 July. In this context the British Army, recognising the difficulty involved in carrying the Vickers-Maxim medium machine-gun across no man's land, had developed the Lewis light machine-gun which, though heavy by today's standards, provided assaulting troops with the means to break up counter-attacks with immediate automatic fire. The effect of the heavy German losses became evident on 11 July when General Erich von Falkenhayn, the German Army's Chief of General Staff, called off his offensive at Verdun.

On 14 July Rawlinson changed his tactics, delivering a night attack behind a creeping barrage that punched a 6,000-yard gap through the enemy's second line. Unfortunately, the cavalry arrived too late to exploit this and the front congealed again. Despite the alarm created at home by the mounting lists of killed, wounded and missing, the policy of wearing down the enemy with local attacks was maintained throughout July and August. Having lost the protection of their deep dugouts, the Germans took to holding the front with a chain of linked outposts supported by a counter-attack force to their rear. The result was that they sustained even higher casualties. At the end of August Falkenhayn was replaced by the team of Field Marshal Paul von Hindenburg and General Erich Ludendorff, fresh from their successes on the Eastern Front.

On 15 September the British used tanks for the first time in battle. They were too few in number to have more than a local effect on the fighting, although Haig was able to report that despite their mechanical shortcomings, the fact was that when they were present the attack had succeeded, and when they were not it had failed. The Germans, having examined several examples that had been knocked out, saw only their mechanical faults and their vulnerability to the 'K' ammunition already in use against armoured bunker slits, and decided that for the moment they would not start a tank-production programme of their own. This short-sighted view failed to allow for the British correcting known faults in later production models, and, when the moment came, deprived the German Army of priceless time when it finally decided to produce tracked armoured vehicles.

The battlefield, already a cratered charnel house shared by the living with the dead, was turned into a quagmire by the autumn rains. During

October the Germans were finally driven off the Thiepval–Pozières ridge. During the third week of November, Gough's Fifth Army, as the Reserve Army had become, finally took Beaumont Hamel. It snowed on the night of 17–18 November. When the snow thawed the entire shattered area became a swamp in which further operations became impossible.

As to what had been achieved by these months of murderous fighting, the Allies had gained a strip of land 20 miles long and 7 miles deep. They had inflicted about 650,000 casualties, including a high proportion of the professional junior officers and NCOs who formed the hardcore of the conscript German Army. Hindenburg and Ludendorff expressed doubts as to whether the morale of their troops could withstand many more intense artillery bombardments and sustained infantry attacks without breaking altogether. The following February they voluntarily surrendered several more miles of territory, pulling back their line to a shorter and even stronger defensive position.

British casualties amounted to 418,000 and French to 194,000. For the former, however, statistics do not reveal the unseen consequences of the battle. The New Army was composed mainly of volunteers, many of them the best of their generation who, in the normal course of events, would have later become leaders in their respective spheres of national life. The loss of so many such men, who could not be quickly or easily replaced, was to be sorely felt in the years to come. Prior to the Somme, the British outlook on the war had been one of innocent idealism tinged, perhaps, with disappointment at the failure of the Gallipoli enterprise and the superficially inconclusive nature of Jutland. After the Somme it was replaced by cynicism, for rarely since have the British trusted their political and military leaders in the way they had done formerly, an attitude that was reinforced by the horrible nature of the Battle of Passchendaele, otherwise known as Third Ypres, fought the following year. As yet, perspective did not allow men to see that the Somme provided the groundwork for the final defeat of the German Army. Unwilling to risk their lives in vile conditions to no visible purpose, they simply ceased to volunteer, so that in 1917 conscription had to be introduced simply to maintain manpower levels.

Zeebrugge and Ostend

22–23 APRIL AND 9–10 MAY 1918

The year 1917 had been a bad one for the Allies. Russia had finally collapsed and, wracked by revolution as she was, would play no further part in the war, in consequence of which large German forces could be transferred from the Eastern to the Western Front. Italy had sustained a major defeat at Caporetto. The French Army had been shaken by mutinies following the failure of the Nivelle offensive, while between July and November the British had incurred heavy casualties for little gain at Passchendaele, where a battle of attrition similar to the Somme had been fought out in endless rain and deep mud. Even the euphoria caused by the infant Tank Corps' great breakthrough on the Cambrai sector of the front in November turned sour when most of the gains made were lost to German counter-attacks shortly after. It was true that the United States had declared war on Germany in April, but it would be many months before American armies could be raised and shipped across the Atlantic to take the field.

Simultaneously, the United Kingdom had faced an even more serious crisis. By the spring of 1917 the German campaign of unrestricted submarine warfare was sinking more British and Allied ships than the shipyards could replace. With the lost ships went their cargoes of food and the raw materials necessary to produce weapons of war; indeed, at one stage it was calculated that the country's food supply would last only a few weeks. Admiral Jellicoe himself forecast that if matters continued as they were, it would be impossible to maintain the struggle beyond 1918. The principal cause of the U-boats' success was the Admiralty's refusal, for reasons that it felt were good and sufficient, to introduce a system of escorted convoys, with the result that the U-boats found easy targets among the many ships sailing individually and without protection. In the prevailing circumstances the Admiralty had no alternative but to change its mind. By November 1917 escorted convoys had become the norm, losses of merchant ships declined dramatically, and the number of U-boats sunk began to rise.

The danger, while contained, still existed. A high proportion of U-boat victims were sunk in the English Channel or in the Western Approaches to the British Isles. Many of the U-boats responsible were based at Bruges in Belgium, which, although it lay eight miles inland from the Belgian coast, was still a port from which access could be obtained to the North Sea by means of a direct canal to Zeebrugge or a system of smaller canals leading to Ostend. When the Germans had overrun Belgium in 1914 they recognised the strategic significance of Bruges at once, since it lay some 300 miles closer to the Straits of Dover than the naval bases in Germany, from which U-boats had to make the long trip round the north of Scotland to get at their prey. Altogether, some thirty U-boats were based at Bruges, together with up to thirty-five destroyers or torpedo boats that made damaging sorties into the Straits. For the U-boats the passage into the English Channel was made the more difficult because of mine and deep net barrages as well as continuous patrolling by the Royal Navy, but on average two a day managed to slip through by travelling surfaced during the hours of darkness. Appreciating that the British would probably attempt to block this bolt-hole, the Germans had fortified the Belgian coast between Nieuport and Knokke with minefields, barbed wire and no less than twenty-six coast defence batteries mounting 229 guns with calibres varying between 15 inches and 3.5 inches.

Since 1914 several plans for an attack on Zeebrugge and Ostend had been considered by the Admiralty, but none had been acted upon. More recently, the hope that the Passchendaele offensive would result in a breakthrough, making the German presence on the Belgian coast untenable, had never come close to being realised. Early in 1918, however, Vice Admiral Sir Roger Keyes, commanding the Dover Patrol, put forward a plan to curtail the activities of the German naval forces based at Bruges, and this was accepted. In essence, what he proposed was sealing off the seaward ends of the Zeebrugge and Ostend Canals with sunken block-ships, using obsolete cruisers for the purpose.

Although this sounded simple enough, much detailed planning had to be undertaken before the raid could be mounted. The Zeebrugge Canal entered the sea between two piers, some 200 yards apart. Approximately 2,000 yards to the west of the piers was a mole, one-and-a-half miles long, that curved north-eastwards and so created an artificial harbour. The mole, which carried a road and railway for most of its length, had been constructed in four sections. The first consisted of a 300-yard causeway, the second of a 300-yard steel viaduct through the supports of which the tide flowed to keep the harbour free of silt, the third, over a mile in length, of solid masonry, and the fourth, of a narrow pier 360 yards long and terminating in a lighthouse. A battery of 5.9-inch guns was located at the end of the third section, sited so as to fire across the harbour entrance, and another battery, containing 3.5- and 4.1-inch guns, was located on the pier itself, pointing out to sea. The third section also contained machine-gun posts and a number of sheds used for military or naval purposes. Inside the harbour the approach to the canal entrance was covered by an opening net boom. At Ostend the defences were less complex although navigational hazards such as sand-banks made identification of the entrance channel more difficult.

Keyes's plan for dealing with the Zeebrugge defences involved several phases. First, the heavy coast defence batteries along the shore would be engaged by 15-inch monitors for several nights before the raid itself, until the Germans began to believe that their bombardments were a matter of routine. Second, a dense smoke screen would conceal the approach of the raiding force. Third, the guns on the mole would be neu-tralised by a landing force streaming over its outer parapet into the heart of the defences from a specially adapted assault ship. Fourth, enemy reinforcements would be prevented from reaching the mole by blowing up the steel viaduct. Fifth, the blockships would enter the harbour and scuttle themselves inside the canal.

The first element of the plan required no special preparation other than the issue of orders. The second problem was solved with the assis-tance of Wing Commander F. A. Brock, RAF, the son of the head of the famous fireworks manufacturer, who was able to produce a screen of the required density that was to be laid by motor launches and coastal motor boats. The third phase required considerable thought. The old cruiser *Vindictive* was selected as the assault ship and suitably converted. The intention was that her port side should be brought against the outer side of the mole; and to enable the troops to swarm over the wall, which was considerably higher than her deck, a false upper deck was constructed from which twenty-seven hinged gangways could be dropped on to the wall's parapet. To secure the vessel to the parapet derricks with grap-pling irons were fitted fore and aft. To deal with the enemy batteries on the mole an 11-inch howitzer was mounted on the quarterdeck, plus one 7.5-inch gun on the foredeck and another on the false deck. Fire support for the infantry assault would be provided by three pom-poms, six Lewis guns mounted in the enlarged fighting top on the foremast, ten Lewis guns mounted on the false deck, Stokes mortars installed fore and aft, and two flamethrowers. Additional protection for the bridge, fighting top and flamethrower bays was provided by draping them with splinter mats. It was thought that because of her draught, *Vindictive* might be unable to carry out her part in the raid if she sustained damage while passing over a suspected shallow minefield on her run in towards the mole, so it was decided that as back-up she would be accompanied by two double-hulled, shallow-draught Mersey ferries, the *Daffodil* and *Iris*, which would land troops by means of ladders to reinforce the infantry attack. In addition, *Daffodil* was tasked with pushing *Vindictive* hard against the mole with her bows and keeping her there for as long as was necessary. Apart from the addition of steel plating and splinter mats, the two ferries required no further work. The troops who would carry out the attack on the mole consisted of the newly formed 4th Battalion Royal Marines, 200 seamen who received instruction in handling infantry weapons, and a further fifty seamen who received training in demolition techniques. Training for the attack itself took place on a replica of the relevant section of the mole constructed on King's Down near Dover.

The destruction of the steel viaduct was the responsibility of two obsolete submarines, *C1* and *C3*, the bows of which were packed with five tons of high explosive. It was decided that *C3* would carry out the task, with *C1* standing by to complete it in case she was unsuccessful, and that she would ram herself hard and fast into the steel web of the viaduct's supports and stanchions. A fuse would then be activated, giving her small volunteer crew time to escape in a motor skiff, after which they would be picked up by a launch.

Five obsolete light cruisers were to be used as blockships, *Thetis*, *Intrepid* and *Iphigenia* at Zeebrugge and *Brilliant* and *Sirius* at Ostend. Fitted with scuttling charges, they were packed with rubble and concrete to make them more difficult to clear once they had settled on the bottom. The weight and positioning of this extra ballast had to be carefully calculated so that the blockships could still manoeuvre in the restricted waters of the canals without grounding before they had reached their intended positions, yet still be capable of riding up the silt banks. Each of the cruisers still retained three of her guns, fitted with half-inch steel shields. Duplicate steering and control positions were added and given the protection of splinter mats and, to make the ships less conspicuous, their masts were removed. Finally, smoke generators were fitted to assist the escape of the crews manning the blockships, who were to be picked up by motor launches.

The raiding force sailed at 17:00 on the evening of 22 April, joining its escort some 7 miles east of Ramsgate. At first, the voyage was lit by a brilliant moon, but as the hours passed cloud obscured this, a mist descended and it began to drizzle. This was ideal from the point of view of concealment, although it meant that a supporting attack by Handley-Page heavy bombers had to be cancelled and the two monitors *Erebus* and *Terror* were a little behind schedule in starting their nightly bombardment. As the force approached Zeebrugge the motor launches and coastal motor boats surged ahead, laying a dense fog with their smoke generators. A gentle northerly wind drove this towards the shore at the same speed as the ships. The Germans, alerted by the phenomenon, ran to their guns and began firing blindly into the mist. Then, at 23:56, the wind backed, revealing a sea covered with small craft and *Vindictive* emerging from the murk, exactly on course and 300 yards short of the mole. The old cruiser, illuminated by star-shells and searchlights, immediately became the focus of every German gun that would bear, including rifles and machine-guns. Captain Alfred Carpenter, her commander, appreciating that he must gain the shelter of the mole as quickly as possible, swung the ship to starboard and completed the run-in at speed, grinding to a standstill alongside the outer wall at one minute past midnight. Coming up from astern, *Daffodil*, which had sustained a hit on her bridge that wounded her captain, nudged *Vindictive* hard against the wall while *Iris* also came alongside the mole a little ahead of the cruiser.

Vindictive's speed had carried her over 300 yards past the intended landing area, so that instead of being put ashore directly into the interior of the defended zone at the end of the mole, the troops were now outside it. Again, so heavy had been the point-blank fire of the German guns that only two of the eighteen gangways had survived in usable condition. Nevertheless, although they had already sustained serious casualties, the bluejackets and Marines began swarming over these, led by Lieutenant Commander Bryan Adams, and began to advance on the enemy batteries in the teeth of machine-gun and rifle fire not only from the defended zone but also from a German destroyer moored alongside the mole's inner wall. Three platoons under Captain Edward Bamford, Royal Marine Light Infantry, established a defensive front to ward off counter-attacks from the town. Adams, many of whose men had fallen as they approached the batteries in a series of rushes, returned and asked Bamford to reinforce him, which he did with two platoons, displaying total disregard for his own safety as he led by example.

Another of the landing detachments' leaders, Lieutenant Commander Arthur Leyland, had his jaw smashed by a fragment of shell just as *Vindictive* came alongside. Regaining consciousness, he went ashore and, despite being in great pain, led his men in their attack until he was killed. In his party was nineteen-year-old Able Seaman Albert McKenzie, a Lewis gunner, who in a letter to his brother has left a vivid account of the confused and fierce fighting on the mole. Even before *Vindictive* had reached the mole two of his crew were killed, leaving only himself and two others. After running across the gangway he ran 50 yards towards the enemy batteries, then lay down to give covering fire. As he did so he noticed Wing Commander Brock firing his pistol down a spiral staircase that evidently led to the shore quarters of the enemy destroyer's crew. Brock followed this up with a grenade, at which a door flew open and a crowd of Germans rushed across the mole to their ship. McKenzie shot down a dozen of them before his ammunition drum was empty. At this point the barrel of his Lewis gun was shot off, leaving him with only the stock and the pistol grip, which he used to good effect against a German who attacked him. 'I kindly took a bloke's photo (i.e. knocked the man flat) with it,' he recounts. 'He looked too business-like for me, with a rifle and bayonet. It half stunned him and gave me time to get my pistol out and finish him off.' McKenzie then snatched up a rifle and bayonet and joined in the attack, of which he remembered little save 'pushing, kicking and kneeing every German who got in the way'. Obviously, the fight was a great deal bloodier than he cared to tell, and at the end of it he had to be helped back aboard *Vindictive*, having being wounded in the right foot and back.

Meanwhile, those in the cruiser's foretop had been providing covering fire for the attackers with their automatic weapons. The source of this was obvious and the top was struck by two heavy shells in quick succession, killing or disabling everyone within it. Coming to, Sergeant Norman Finch, Royal Marine Light Infantry, discovered that he had been severely wounded but, searching among the bodies and wreckage, he discovered a Lewis gun in working order with which he continued to harass the enemy until the top was finally put out of action by a third direct hit.

Elsewhere, *Iris* was in trouble. She was rising and falling abruptly with the heavy swell and was unable to secure her grappling hook to the mole's parapet. As the need for her troops had become desperate, Lieutenant Commander George Bradford climbed the port derrick with the grappling hook. This in itself was no mean feat as the ship's violent motion was smashing the derrick against the wall at regular intervals. When his purpose became clear, Bradford came under heavy fire. Disregarding this, he chose his moment and jumped on to the mole from the swaying derrick. No sooner had he attached the grappling hook than he was shot dead. Sadly, this act of supreme courage did not earn the rewards it deserved for it was next discovered that the scaling ladders would not reach the top of the wall. There was, therefore, no alternative other than to bring *Iris* in alongside *Daffodil*, where she might be able to land her troops across *Vindictive*'s decks.

At this point the defenders of the mole received a most unpleasant surprise. The old submarine *C3*, commanded by Lieutenant Richard Sandford, had been towed during the passage but had now cast off and was approaching the viaduct. Four shells burst near her when her presence was disclosed by a star-shell but, incredibly, no further gunfire was directed at her, even when she was brilliantly illuminated by two searchlights. One hundred yards short of the viaduct Sandford ordered his skeleton crew up on to the bridge. At this point he could have abandoned the submarine and relied on her gyro compass to take her in to the target. He chose instead to control her approach himself, steering her at speed among the stanchions until, with a scream of tearing metal, she came to a standstill with her explosive charge directly under the viaduct. While his crew launched the motor skiff he carefully set the fuse. As the skiff made its escape the water round it was flayed by rifle and machine-gun fire from the viaduct. At this terrifying moment the crew of the boat had to resort to rowing as the propeller had been damaged during the launch. Although darkness and drifting smoke made it difficult for the Germans to aim accurately, most of the skiff's occupants were hit, Sandford twice. Twelve minutes after they had abandoned *C3*, and exactly on time, the charge detonated, blowing the submarine and a large section of the viaduct skywards in an enormous explosion. No reinforcements could now reach the defenders of the mole. Relieved of their tormentors, the crew of the skiff rowed on until they were picked up by a picket boat which, by coincidence, was commanded by Sandford's elder brother, Francis.

It was at this point, approximately twenty minutes after *Vindictive* had come alongside the mole, that the efforts of the landing parties began to pay dividends. With *Thetis* leading under Commander F. Sneyd, the three blockships were now approaching the harbour entrance. *Thetis* took a battering from the guns on the pier, but diverted the attention of the gunners from *Intrepid* and *Iphigenia* following close behind, as well as those of the enemy manning the 5.9-inch battery on the mole, sited to fire across the harbour, who were too busy defending themselves against the marines' and bluejackets' attacks to notice. Unfortunately, the beating taken by *Thetis*, aggravated by the tide's strong easterly set, caused her to miss the gap in the net boom. She ploughed into the mesh, which wrapped itself round her propellers. Trailing net, she was pulled steadily to port. With her engines out of action and making water fast, she grounded 300 yards short of the canal mouth. Her passage, however, had widened the gap in the net boom and her starboard navigating light enabled Lieutenant S. S. Bonham-Carter, commanding *Intrepid*, to bypass the obstacle and steer an accurate course into the canal, where she was positioned exactly according to plan before her scuttling charges were blown. Bonham-Carter then ordered the crew into the boats and activated his smoke generators. Smoke tends to be a double-edged weapon, for it restricted the vision of Lieutenant E. W. Billyard-Leake, commanding *Iphigenia,* already troubled by clouds of steam from a severed pipe. Only a sharp turn to port prevented the cruiser from striking the western pier of the canal, after which she went on and nudged *Intrepid* slightly out of position. Going astern, Billyard-Leake manoeuvred *Iphigenia* across the water- way, scuttled her and abandoned ship under the fog created by his smoke generators. Both blockships and their boats now came under heavy fire from the thoroughly alarmed defenders of the canal entrance.

Into this maelstrom of smoke, flame and sinking ships came Motor Launch 282, commanded by Lieutenant Percy Dean, a Royal Naval Vol- unteer Reserve officer who at forty might be regarded as being too old for operations of this type. Dean, however, remained perfectly cool and in full control of the situation, taking aboard over 100 men from the blockships' boats, some of whom were hit on the launch's crowded deck by the enemy's intense fire. As he gave the order to turn for home, 282's steering gear failed, but by using his engines he managed to turn the craft and was heading for the canal entrance when he was told that there was a man in the water. He immediately went astern and rescued an officer. Two hours later he was able to transfer his passengers to the destroyer *Warwick*, aboard which Keyes was controlling the operation.

The raid had now achieved its objective. At 00:50 Captain Carpenter decided to recall the landing parties. The signal for this was to have been a series of blasts on *Vindictive*'s siren, but this had been shot away and it was sounded by *Daffodil* and *Iris*. During the next fifteen minutes marines and bluejackets tumbled aboard over the gangways, bringing with them as many of the dead and wounded as possible. Then, assisted by *Daffodil*, *Vindictive* swung away from the mole and headed for the open sea accompanied by the two ferries. All three ships made smoke, concealing their whereabouts from the German gunners, most of whose shells fell astern. By the worst possible luck, a random shell exploded aboard *Iris*, which had hitherto sustained comparatively light damage, killing seventy-five of the men packed aboard her. Total casualties incurred during the raid amounted to 160 killed, twenty-eight mortally wounded, 383 wounded, sixteen missing and thirteen captured. Material losses included the destroyer *North Star*, sunk by the German shore batteries, and Motor Launches *110* and *424*. The German casualties were almost certainly lighter.

At Ostend the results of the raid were less satisfactory. Here the Germans seem to have anticipated a raid and had moved two buoys that the raiders were relying on as navigational markers. Commander A. E. Godsal, commanding *Brilliant*, the leading blockship, therefore had to rely on dead reckoning. Emerging from the smoke screen, he found himself blinded by the concentrated glare of searchlights. *Brilliant* ran aground some little distance to the east of the canal entrance and as she was going astern *Sirius*, the second blockship, heavily damaged and in a sinking condition, collided heavily with her port quarter, forcing her further on to the sandbank. As there was nothing more that could be done, the scuttling charges were blown and the crews of both ships were picked up by motor launches.

Keyes was not a man who liked loose ends and obtained permission for a second raid on Ostend. *Vindictive* was hurriedly converted to the blockship role, as was another obsolete cruiser, *Sappho*. The raid was mounted on the night of 9 May, following the usual preliminary bombardment by monitors, an attack by heavy bombers and the laying of dense smoke. During the crossing *Sappho*'s ancient engines, dating from 1891, gave such trouble that she was forced to turn back. *Vindictive*, now under the command of Commander Godsal, continued alone. Godsal's task was not made easier by a natural fog, but his navigating skills enabled him to bring in the old cruiser exactly opposite the canal entrance. The Germans, however, had made plans to deal with a second attempt to block the canal and, despite the smoke and mist their artillery was concentrating its fire on the approach to it. *Vindictive* absorbed numerous hits despite which Godsal managed to nose her into the canal mouth and was about to swing her across the main channel when he was killed by a shell striking the bridge. Lieutenant Victor Crutchley, wounded by the explosion, tried to complete the manoeuvre but by then it was too late for *Vindictive* had run aground beside the channel.

Following closely behind the cruiser was Motor Launch *254*, commanded by Lieutenant Geoffrey Drummond of the Royal Naval Volunteer Reserve. The launch also came in for some severe punishment, including one shell that killed the only other officer aboard and a seaman as well as seriously wounding Drummond and his coxswain. Disregarding his wounds, Drummond brought the launch alongside *Vindictive*, taking off Crutchley, one other officer and thirty-eight men, some of whom were killed or wounded as they scrambled aboard. He retained consciousness long enough to back his craft into open water, then collapsed. Crutchley took over immediately only to discover that the launch was in a sinking condition, but managed to keep her afloat long enough for the crew to be taken on board the destroyer *Warwick*.

Aboard Motor Launch *216*, Lieutenant Roland Bourke, a Canadian RNVR officer from British Columbia, had an uneasy feeling that not all of *Vindictive*'s crew had been picked up. He entered the canal mouth under heavy fire and, seeing nothing, was about to leave when he heard shouts. Turning back, he found an officer and two ratings clinging to an upturned boat. Although the launch was now being hit frequently, he rescued them and managed to guide his battered craft out to sea, where she was taken in tow. Subsequent examination revealed that she had been hit fifty-five times, once by a 6-inch shell that killed two seamen and caused considerable damage.

Keyes was all for making a third attempt to block the Ostend Canal but the idea was not approved, it being generally agreed that now the enemy had been thoroughly alerted the potential gain outweighed the risks involved. Ostend, anyway, had merely been a secondary objective because the canal could only handle shallow draught vessels. At Zeebrugge, however, the results had been more satisfactory. For a while the Germans could not even make a start on reopening the canal as the local dredger had been sunk beside the mole by a coastal motor boat during the raid. This, of course, meant that those of the Bruges U-boats already at sea would have to return to more distant bases in Germany. In the end the Germans were forced to widen the canal opposite the sunken blockships and by dredging a channel through the silt under their sterns it became possible for a coastal U-boat to be warped past the obstruction, but only at high tide. Those ocean-going U-boats and destroyers caught in Bruges at the time of the raid remained there for the rest of the war. Even after hostilities had ended it took the Liverpool Salvage Company a year to restore the canal to working order. The Zeebrugge raid provided a much-needed tonic for Allied morale and, taking place as it did on St George's Day, recalled to Englishmen such events as Drake's singeing the King of Spain's beard at Cadiz over 300 years previously and many other raids carried out from the sea. If it had not quite succeeded in cutting off the Kaiser's distinctive moustache, then it had removed half of it, leaving the rest looking slightly foolish.

The Victoria Cross was earned many times during these operations but the Admiralty considered that Keyes's recommendations were over-generous and reduced the number to be awarded. As a result of a ballot among their peers, Captain Edward Bamford, Captain Alfred Carpenter, Sergeant Norman Finch and Able Seaman Albert McKenzie all received the VC. Bamford was further honoured with French, Russian and Japanese decorations and later became a major. Carpenter, upon whose skill as a navigator the whole enterprise had depended, also received the Légion d'Honneur. On his return home he addressed huge audiences on the subject of the raid. He retired from the navy with the rank of vice admiral and during World War II commanded the 17th Gloucestershire Battalion of the Home Guard before becoming Director of Shipping at the Admiralty in 1945. Finch later received a commission as lieutenant and quartermaster. In 1961 he was appointed sergeant major in the Queen's Bodyguard of the Yeoman of the Guard, dying five years later. McKenzie recovered from his wounds and received his award from King George V, only to die later in the year as a result of the influenza pandemic sweeping Europe.

The Admiralty accepted Keyes's recommendation for the award of the VC to Lieutenants Percy Dean and Richard Sandford. Dean was promoted to lieutenant commander and sat as Member of Parliament for Blackburn 1918–22. Sandford was also awarded the Belgian Légion d'Honneur but in November 1918 became another victim of the influenza pandemic. Posthumous awards of the Cross were made to Lieutenant Commander George Bradford and Lieutenant Commander Arthur Harrison. Bradford's brother, Brigadier General Roland Bradford, killed at Cambrai six months prior to the Zeebrugge raid, had won the VC during the Battle of the Somme.

Three Victoria Crosses were awarded for the second raid on Ostend, going to Lieutenants Victor Crutchley, Geoffrey Drummond and Roland Bourke. Crutchley enjoyed a long and distinguished naval career during which he was knighted and achieved the rank of admiral. During World War II he commanded the Australian Naval Squadron in the Pacific.

Drummond saw further service with the River Thames Patrol in World War II. Bourke achieved the rank of lieutenant commander and returned to Canada after the war, serving with RCNVR during World War II.

Keyes himself received a knighthood and was granted £10,000 by Parliament, a not inconsiderable sum at the time. He rose to become an admiral of the fleet and during World War II served as head of the British military mission to Belgium until the latter's surrender, then as Chief of Combined Operations until January 1942. His son, Lieutenant Colonel Geoffrey Keyes, won a posthumous Victoria Cross while leading a commando raid against Rommel's headquarters on 18 November 1941.

The two little ferries, *Iris* and *Daffodil*, which had played such a prominent part in the Zeebrugge raid, returned to the Mersey having been awarded the proud distinction of adding *Royal* to their names. Their successors, *Royal Iris II* and *Royal Daffodil II*, continued to operate throughout World War II and for many years beyond.

Over There – Belleau Wood and The Argonne

JUNE–NOVEMBER 1918

On the Western Front the year 1918 opened with no apparent end to the war in sight. For the Allies, manpower resources had become a problem. In the British Army, for example, brigades had been reduced from four battalions to three and most companies within infantry battalions were below strength, despite the introduction of conscription the previous year. Across the lines, the Germans were being reinforced steadily with troops drawn from the near-defunct Eastern Front following Russia's descent into revolution and civil war. The scales were therefore beginning to tilt against the Allies and the question uppermost in the minds of most senior commanders was whether the increased threat could be contained until American troops reached Europe in sufficient numbers to redress the balance. The Germans, too, were aware that the window of opportunity for a speedy victory would close steadily as the year progressed and knew that they must take immediate advantage of it.

The major battles of 1918 were unlike those of previous years. Both sides had by now discovered a means of breaking the deadlock of trench warfare. For the Allies it was the tank, which was to play a major role in their offensive plans. For the Germans it was saturation bombardment of the break-in sector with high explosive and gas, followed by an exploitation with storm troops, specially trained to bypass areas of opposition (which would be dealt with by follow-up units) and to press on into the enemy's artillery and command zones, creating chaos and causing a withdrawal. These tactics had worked the previous year against the Russians at Riga, against the Italians at Caporetto, and during the counter-attack that followed the British breakthrough with tanks at Cambrai. Now, General Erich Ludendorff, effectively commander of the German Army, planned a series of massive offensives on these lines, designed to smash the Allied front before the Americans could take the field. To this end the best soldiers were creamed off into storm troop battalions that were given intensive training in their role. In Ludendorff's eyes it mattered not that this would reduce the overall quality of the army, for he believed that success lay within his grasp and, unwisely, told the troops that they would be taking part in the final, victorious offensives of the war.

The first of these, codenamed *Michael*, took place between 21 March and 5 April. It recovered all the ground that had been lost during the Battle of the Somme and achieved a spectacular advance of 40 miles. It failed, however, in its primary object of creating a gap between the British and French armies and, thanks to the self-sacrificial stands made by units in its path, incurred far heavier casualties than had been anticipated. It also led to the appointment of Marshal Ferdinand Foch as Allied Supreme Commander. The second offensive, codenamed *Georgette*, took place in Flanders between 9 and 30 April. Mounted on the assumption that if the British sustained a major defeat the French would seek an armistice, it recaptured Messines Ridge and the ground lost at Passchendaele. Once more, however, due to the dogged resistance offered by units that brought every man into the line, including cooks, clerks and mess staff, it achieved little more and incurred heavy loss. The third offensive, *Blücher*, lasted from 27 May until 6 June. It was directed against the French on the Chemin des Dames sector and was intended to force them to withdraw their reserves from Flanders so that a final blow could be delivered against the British. While it succeeded in crossing the Aisne and driving on to the Marne, it was counter-productive in that Ludendorff now found himself too short of troops to man the extended line formed by the newly created salient.

Meanwhile, growing numbers of the American Expeditionary Force had been landing in France. Commanded by General John Pershing, the AEF was woefully short of *matériel* because the tiny peacetime US Army had been expanded so rapidly that manufacturers simply could not keep pace with the sudden demand. It was, nevertheless, supplied by the Allies with artillery, tanks, steel helmets and many other necessary items. What startled the British and French, whose own armies now consisted mainly of conscripted youths or men grown old in experience if not in years, resigned and cynical, was the Americans themselves. 'The impression made by this seemingly inexhaustible flood of gleaming youth in its first maturity of health and vigour was prodigious,' wrote Winston Churchill. 'None were under twenty, and few were over thirty. Crammed in their lorries they clattered along the roads, singing the songs of the New World at the tops of their voices, burning to reach the bloody field.' Such idealism, innocence and hope had not been seen since the first clashes of 1914.

Pershing was determined that his troops would fight together as an American army and not be absorbed as reinforcements for hard-pressed British and French commanders, although he did permit small numbers to obtain front-line experience on quieter sectors of the line. As each of the Ludendorff offensives broke he was forced to resist intense pressure to commit his divisions. Finally, when *Georgette* began to show signs of menacing Paris itself, he was forced to give way.

The first American unit to meet the Germans head-on was the 7th Machine-gun Battalion, which dug in its forty-eight guns in support of a French colonial division on the south bank of the Marne, near the town of Château-Thierry. When the German storm troopers appeared on the north bank they attempted to rush the bridges but were stopped in their tracks by the battalion's concentrated fire. They tried again, with similar result, and were finally foiled when the bridges were blown by French engineers. No casualties were sustained by the Americans.

To the west of Château-Thierry, where the Allied line still ran north of the Marne, Major General Omar Bundy's US 2nd Division was taking up positions opposite Belleau Wood under the command of the French XXI Corps. The division was an all-regular formation of the 4th Brigade which contained the 5th and 6th Marine Regiments, commanded by Brigadier General James Harbord. A healthy rivalry existed between the marines and the army, each of whom considered themselves to be a cut above the other. The marines, for example, had not welcomed the order to change into army uniform, to which they pointedly transferred their own badges and insignia.

Hardly had the 4th Brigade moved into the line than the French troops in front of them, who had been fighting to slow down the German advance, began retiring through them. A French officer, talking to Captain Lloyd Williams, suggested that the marines would be well advised to conform to the general retreat. 'Retreat, hell!' retorted Williams in amazement. 'We just got here!' It was a remark that would go down in history.

With the French rearguard gone, nothing now separated the 4th Brigade from Belleau Wood, which was soon occupied by the enemy. On 2 June the Germans attacked. The marines, who spent more time on the practice ranges with their Springfield rifles than any other branch of the service, met them with a storm of accurate musketry such as they had not encountered since their first battles with the BEF in 1914. Time and again throughout the day the grey lines of the storm troopers rose and advanced in a vain attempt to close with the invisible Americans, only to be shot flat by riflemen and machine-gunners, then punished by artillery fire as they lay pinned to the ground. With the coming of night they retired into the wood and, having shot their bolt as far as offensive operations were concerned, they began to consolidate their positions among the trees.

This defensive success emboldened the French to return to the attack. As part of this the 4th Marine Brigade, with the 23rd US Infantry on their right and a French regiment on their left, were to capture Belleau Wood, including Hill 142, overlooking the village of Torcy, and the village of Bouresches, on the south-eastern corner of the wood. The wood itself occupied 600 acres of rising ground strewn with boulders and intersected with deep, steep-sided ravines, the trees themselves being so closely planted that visibility was restricted to little more than 10 yards. In this tangle, the Germans had constructed numerous machine-gun posts with interlocking fields of fire, as they had on the approaches to Bouresches, the stone cottages of which had also been prepared for defence. Between the German and American lines, some 200–400 yards apart, lay fields of wheat, standing waist-height. The pastoral landscape, smiling under the summer sun, had barely been touched by war since 1914.

At 16:00 on 6 June the French and American artillery began firing a preparatory bombardment, most of which was wasted as the shells burst in the fields beyond the target area. An hour later the marines climbed out of their trenches and began advancing through the wheat fields in textbook formation. After they had covered about 100 yards the German machine-guns opened up, scything through the ranks as they had done with the British on the first day of the Somme. Many went to ground and in places the attack seemed to have stalled.

It was a moment when inspired junior leadership was required. It showed itself in the form of the apparently immortal First Sergeant Dan Daly, already twice a Medal of Honor winner. Furious at being pinned to the ground, he decided that the textbook did not apply in the present circumstances. Scrambling to his feet, he shouted, 'For Christ's sake, men – come on! D'you want to live forever?' The result was a headlong charge that took the marines into the enemy's outer defences, at the cost of half their number. It was for this, as much as anything else, that Daly is best remembered, although he was to win yet more decorations during the campaign, on one occasion wiping out a machine-gun post with grenades and his pistol in a solo effort, and on another taking thirteen prisoners. Married to the Corps, he remained single his entire life, retiring in 1929 with the rank of sergeant major. He died in 1937.

Once in the wood, the marines discovered that they were under-equipped to deal with the enemy's concealed log wood, boulder and earth machine-gun posts. Other armies had learned through hard experience the value of the grenade, sawn-off shotgun, knife and club in trench fighting, and that of the flamethrower and explosive charge when dealing with bunkers such as these. In the final analysis, the fault lay with General 'Black Jack' Pershing himself, who had fought against Apache Indians, Spaniards in Cuba, rebels in the Philippines and bandits in Mexico. In such encounters, the rifle and bayonet were the only tools the infantry had required and, although he would learn the lesson quickly, he had not thought far beyond that point. For the present, apart from these and their courage and aggression, the marines had little else to deal with their unseen enemy whose interlocking arcs of fire covered every approach to the hidden machine-guns. They paid with their lives for the omission, but retained their grip on the edge of the wood and took Hill 142.

It was on this feature that both the army and the navy CMH were awarded to the same individual, the former because he was serving under 2nd Division's command and the latter because he belonged to the Marine Corps and therefore fell within the jurisdiction of the Department of the Navy. The man was a 40-year-old gunnery sergeant whose name was Ernest August Janson and who, for personal reasons, was serving in the 5th Marines under the name of Charles F. Hoffman. His citation reads:

> Immediately after the company to which he belonged had reached its objective on Hill 142, several hostile counter-attacks were launched against the line before the new position had been consolidated. Gunnery Sergeant Hoffman was attempting to organise a position on the north slope of the hill when he saw twelve of the enemy, armed with five light machine-guns, crawling towards his group. Giving the alarm, he rushed the hostile detachment, bayoneted the two leaders and forced the others to flee, abandoning their guns. His quick action, initiative and courage drove the enemy from a position from which they could have swept the hill with machine-gun fire and forced the withdrawal of our troops.

At Bouresches savage house-to-house fighting continued well into the night. By the early hours of 7 June the leading battalion of the 6th

Marines was reduced to a handful of men who were running short of ammunition. Fortunately, reinforcements and fresh supplies arrived in time for them to retain their gains in the face of determined counter-attacks. During the advance on the village and for much of the fighting Lieutenant (Junior Grade) Weedon E. Osborne, US Navy, a dental specialist serving as a medical officer, followed closely in the path of the leading companies. Without considering his own safety he moved among the wounded, treating them and carrying them out of the line of fire. At length, while carrying a wounded officer to a place of safety, he was killed. For his devotion to duty and courageous performance of his task he was awarded a posthumous Medal of Honor.

The day's fighting had cost the marines 1,087 casualties, more than in the Corps' entire history. Nevertheless, the struggle for the wood continued for the next two days, with little progress being made. On 9 June the 4th Brigade was pulled out of the wood, which was treated to a sustained bombardment by 200 guns. This no doubt eliminated some of the machine-gun posts but the overall result was counter-productive since it felled many trees, creating an impenetrable tangle whereas formerly the enemy had merely enjoyed the protection of close cover. When they renewed the attack the marines had acquired a supply of grenades and many of the men had equipped themselves with cudgels. Even so, progress through the choked, splintered woodland had to be made at a crawl. Whatever plans might have been made, the battle now consisted of hundreds of minor tactical situations that had to be resolved in the face of even stiffer enemy resistance.

Just behind the original American front line was the village of Lucy-le-Bocage. Here Lieutenant Orlando H. Petty, a forty-four-year-old native of Ohio who was a medical officer belonging to the US Naval Reserve Force, won the Medal of Honor. On 11 June the enemy shelled the village continuously with a mixture of high-explosive and gas shells. Despite these trying conditions, Petty continued to run the 5th Marines' dressing station in a calm and professional manner, treating the wounded and arranging for their evacuation. At one stage an exploding gas shell flung him to the ground, ripping his gas mask. Discarding the now useless mask, he continued with his work until the dressing station was demolished by a direct hit, after which he helped to carry the wounded Captain Williams to safety.

On 12 June the wood was subjected to an even heavier bombardment. The attack was resumed and made some small gains, although the Americans sustained heavy casualties not only from the enemy's machine-gunners but also from his artillery. For his actions during this phase of the battle a posthumous Medal of Honor was awarded to Gunnery Sergeant Fred W. Stockham of the 6th Marines' 2nd Battalion:

> During an intense enemy bombardment with high explosive and gas shells which wounded or killed many members of his company, Gunnery Sergeant Stockham, upon noticing that the gas mask of a wounded comrade was shot away, without hesitation removed his own gas mask and insisted upon giving it to the wounded man, well knowing that the effects of the gas would be fatal to himself. He continued with undaunted courage and valour to assist in the evacuation of the wounded until he himself collapsed from the effects of gas, dying as a result thereof a few days later. His courageous conduct undoubtedly saved the lives of many of his wounded comrades and his conspicuous gallantry and spirit of self-sacrifice were a source of inspiration to all.

As the days passed, small gains continued to be made at heavy cost without any end to the battle being in sight. By now the marines were using a full range of trench warfare weapons, including light mortars and French Chauchat light machine-guns. For a while they were relieved by the 7th Infantry from the 3rd US Division so that they could rest and reorganise. On 25 June they returned to the line and, following a fourteen-hour bombardment, launched a co-ordinated two-battalion attack behind a rolling barrage that finally cleared the last of the tenacious defenders from among the trees.

The battle for Belleau Wood had cost the 4th Brigade alone over 4,700 casualties, including over one thousand killed. The Germans, unused to such displays of aggression at this stage of the war, described the marines as *Teufelhunden* (devil dogs) in their reports. Today the wood has returned to the peace of nature although it is no longer called Belleau Wood, for in honour of the battle the French have renamed it Le Bois de la Brigade de Marine.

Although the successes at Château-Thierry and Belleau Wood helped blunt the third of Ludendorff's offensives, a fourth offensive, code-named *Gneisenau*, was actually taking place while the marines of the 4th Brigade were engaged in their epic struggle. Lasting from 9 until 13 June, it was intended to shorten the line between the salients created by *Blücher* and *Michael*. By now, however, the Allies were familiar with the new German methods of attack and little was achieved, some of the ground gained during its early hours being lost to French counter-attacks. On 15 July Ludendorff mounted a fifth offensive, codenamed *Marneschutz-Rheims*, known to the Allies as the Second Battle of the Marne. His intention was to cross the Marne and isolate Rheims by converging thrusts from east and west. Once again, it failed. The Germans were halted and forced to retreat when the French, with British, American and Italian support, counter-attacked into the flank of the Marne salient. The battle, ending on 7 August, marked the point of balance in the 1918 fighting on the Western Front. Total German losses in the five offensives exceeded half a million men, with huge quantities of equipment. Allied losses were comparable, but despite their Herculean efforts the victory the Germans had been promised had simply not materialised. The inevitable result of this was that morale slumped, for the best soldiers had died with the elite storm-troop battalions and the rest of the army was not of the same quality. In this, the last phase of the war, the troops were fighting to keep the Allies out of their homeland, but many were so war-weary that desertions and surrenders began to increase.

This became apparent on 8 August, described by Ludendorff as the Black Day of the German Army, when the British mounted a mass tank attack at Amiens, smashing through the German front to a depth of seven-and-a-half miles. By the time the attack had run down the Germans had sustained over 75,000 casualties, including 29,873 prisoners, many of whom had surrendered in large numbers. The battle initiated a slow but sustained Allied advance that would last for the remainder of the war. The American contribution to this has become known as the Meuse-Argonne offensive. It took place along a 35-mile stretch of front west of Verdun, extending northwards from the Argonne forest to Sedan, and lasted from 26 September until 11 November. Pershing personally commanded the US First Army until 12 October, when he handed over to Major General Hunter Liggett. On this day, too, the US Second Army was formed under Major General Robert Bullard. Altogether, a total of twenty-two American divisions were involved in the offensive, plus six French divisions belonging to General H. J. E. Gouraud's French Fourth Army.

The Argonne forest was every bit as difficult to fight in as Belleau Wood had been. It consisted of close, rolling, boulder-strewn country, intersected by ravines, in which the Americans' tank support was unable to operate far beyond the few roads available. Furthermore, the Germans had also learned lessons from Belleau Wood, for in addition to the natural defensive advantages posed by the terrain, they strung wire and nets between the trees, intended to channel the advancing Americans on to killing grounds covered by interlocked machine-gun posts and artillery fire. Of the numerous Medals of Honor won during this period, two are of particular interest.

Alvin C. York was born on 13 December 1887 in Pall Mall, Fentress County, Tennessee, the third of his parents' eleven children. When his father died he helped to support the family by shooting game in the backwoods. In particular, he became adept at snap or first-time shooting, where the target only remained within his sights for seconds. As a teenager he drank, gambled and was generally wild until he came under the influence of his girl friend, Gracie Williams, who even made him a devout member of the church she attended. When he was drafted into the army in 1917 he impressed his officers with the accuracy of his shooting at ranges of up to 500 yards. However, when required to shoot at figure targets he suddenly realised that he would be involved in killing, and that ran contrary to his now firmly held religious convictions. It took considerable effort on the part of his commanding officer and the regimental chaplain to convince him that he would be fighting in a just cause. His doubts dispelled, he settled down to become a first-class soldier and was promoted corporal.

On 8 October 1918 the regiment to which York belonged, the 328th Infantry (82nd Division), was engaged in an advance through the forest. Suddenly, York's platoon was pinned down by the fire of several machine-guns. York was detailed to take sixteen men and work round the enemy flank. Crawling for much of the time, the squad worked its way through the Germans' forward positions and suddenly came upon a battalion headquarters, the personnel of which surrendered. However, the battalion commander, a major, shouted a warning, as a result of which the enemy in the forward machine-gun posts repositioned their weapons and opened fire. Six of the Americans were killed and another three wounded. Telling the survivors to guard the prisoners, York decided to deal with the situation himself. Using his native fieldcraft, he worked his way into a position from which the rear of the enemy trenches was visible. Whenever a German head appeared, he put a bullet through it. At length, goaded by the mounting loss, a lieutenant and six men tried to charge him. Coolly, York dropped each of them in turn with his pistol, then got on with his work. This was too much for the German major, who offered to surrender the rest of his command. With York's pistol in his back he was led round the various posts, telling his men to give themselves up. Not all were keen to do so and York sometimes found it necessary to fire a shot to convince them. At length he collected 132 prisoners, members of a Prussian Guard regiment, and led them back to his own lines, where he apologised to his officer for not having had the time to count them properly. He had killed twenty-five men and in the abandoned position no less than thirty-five machine-guns were found.

York was promoted to sergeant. He received not only the Medal of Honor, but also the French Croix de Guerre and the Italian Croce de Guerra. In making the presentation to him, Marshal Foch commented, 'What you did was the greatest thing accomplished by any private soldier of all the armies of Europe.' For his part, York declined to talk about the incident, saying, 'It's over – let's forget about it.' He resisted every attempt to lionise him, turning down a lecture tour that would have made him a great deal of money, and refusing to allow his name to be used as an endorsement for commercial products with the curt remark, 'This uniform ain't for sale.' He also declined to take part in a film about his exploit; a film was made anyway, in which York was played by the actor Gary Cooper. He remained a simple man, married Gracie Williams and returned to farming. In 1926, recognising the value of education, he was responsible for opening the college in Fentress County that bears his name. York died in Nashville, Tennessee, in 1964.

In some ways, Samuel Woodfill was very similar to Alvin York. He was born in Jefferson County, Indiana, in 1883. As a boy he frequently absented himself from school to go hunting and by the age of ten had become a notably good shot. His father had served in the United States' war against Mexico and again with an Indiana regiment during the Civil War, so it was natural that he should choose a military career. Enlisting in the army in 1901, he saw service in the Philippines, Alaska and on the Mexican border. Prior to America's entry into World War I he was stationed at Fort Thomas, Kentucky, where he married. In 1917 he received a temporary commission as lieutenant. Posted to France, he served with the 60th Infantry (5th Division).

On the foggy morning of 12 October Woodfill was leading the advance of his company near Cunel. At one point the company became pinned down by artillery and machine-gun fire and began to suffer from the effects of mustard gas. Woodfill and two of his men crawled forward for some 25 yards until they were able to locate the position of one of the enemy machine-guns. Then, leaving the two men where they were, Woodfill worked his way on to the flank of the gun pit. The gun crew were firing ahead and had not noticed him. From a range of 10 yards he shot three of them. An officer then charged him but he managed to kill him with his pistol in the ensuing hand-to-hand struggle.

Calling up his men, Woodfill resumed the advance. When a second machine-gun post was encountered, he immediately ordered the men to charge, shooting three of the crew and capturing another three. A few minutes later, the company ran into a third machine-gun post. Woodfill personally killed five of the enemy with rifle fire then, drawing his pistol, rushed the gun pit, which contained two more men. In the fight that followed he was forced to resort to a pick lying near by, using it to finish off both his adversaries. He was now exhausted and suffering severely from the effects of gas, but only when his company had taken their objective did he seek medical assistance.

Woodfill, described by General Pershing as the outstanding American soldier of the war, received promotion to captain and the Medal of Honor. The French also honoured him with the Croix de Guerre Avec Palmes and made him a Chevalier of the Légion d'Honneur, the Italians with the Meriot de Guerra and the Montenegrins with the Cross of Prince Danilo, 1st Class. Despite all this, he was only permitted to remain in the army until 1923, when he became eligible for a full pension, provided he relinquished his temporary commission and reverted to the rank of sergeant. Back at Fort Thomas, he found it difficult to pay off his mortgage on a sergeant's pay and was forced to supplement his income with temporary jobs. Hearing of his difficulty, a New York theatre company raised sufficient money to pay off the mortgage. In 1922 a new school in Fort Thomas was named after him. On finally leaving the army the following year he took up farming, without much success. Like York, he shunned publicity, commenting, 'I'm tired of being a circus pony – every time there is something doing they trot me out to perform.' His fame returned briefly on the outbreak of World War II, when he was given the rank of major and, with other heroes of the earlier war, was engaged in raising the national morale.

World War I ended less than a month after Woodfill's exploit. Germany suddenly found herself fighting alone against mounting odds when her allies, Bulgaria, Turkey and Austria-Hungary, suddenly collapsed one after the other like a house of cards, and was granted an armistice that came into effect on 11 November. Unfortunately, the victorious Allies imposed such humiliating terms on her that the rise to power of Adolf Hitler's Nazi Party was inevitable, with the result that a second world war became unavoidable twenty years later. In the meantime, nations left scarred by the dreadful slaughter were only too glad that the fighting had ended. In recognition of the sacrifices that had been made, as well as countless unrecorded examples of supreme courage, a Victoria Cross was awarded to the American Unknown Warrior, who was buried at Arlington National Cemetery, Washington, DC, and a Congressional Medal of Honor was awarded to Great Britain's Unknown Warrior, who was laid to rest in Westminster Abbey.

THE SECOND WORLD WAR
1939-45

Tobruk – Operation Crusader

18 November – 7 December 1941

A total of 626 Victoria Crosses were awarded during World War I, but only 181 during World War II, despite the fact that it was the longer of the two conflicts. One reason for this was the so-called Phoney War in which, save at sea, no major operations were undertaken by the British armed services between the outbreak of war in September 1939 and May 1940. Then, apart from the short campaign in France and the easy victory over the Italian Tenth Army in Egypt, the British Army did not become involved in protracted fighting against its principal enemy until 1941. Again, even when it was fully committed on all fronts, the regulations governing the award were more strictly interpreted than had previously been the case. Of course, during this period a number of well-deserved Victoria Crosses were awarded, but many, especially those won at sea or in the air, related to isolated incidents. In one of these, on 12 May 1940, five Fairey Battle light bombers of No. 12 Squadron RAF were ordered to attack the bridge over the Albert Canal at Vroenhoven, Belgium, across which German troops were streaming. The Battles were poorly armed to deal with the swarms of modern German fighters prowling over the enemy bridgehead, which was also protected by numerous anti-aircraft guns. Only one survived to return to its base, but the raid was successful thanks to the determined leadership of Flying Officer Donald Garland and the skill of his navigator, Sergeant Thomas Gray, both of whom received the award posthumously – a remarkable instance of two men in the same aircraft being so honoured. As mentioned in the Introduction, only one VC was awarded during the Battle of Britain, a pivotal event in the war and in world history.

When the Italian Tenth Army surrendered at Beda Fomm on 7 February 1941 it seemed that the threat to the Suez Canal, Great Britain's imperial lifeline, had been removed. At Churchill's insistence, many of the troops responsible for the victory in North Africa were sent to aid the hard-pressed Greeks, who were resisting the Axis invasion of their country with some success, and only a small covering force was left at El

Agheila to watch the remnant of the Italian troops in Tripolitania. Unfortunately, the Italians were shipping reinforcements into Tripoli as fast as they could, and with them came the leading elements of the German Afrika Korps, commanded by Lieutenant General Erwin Rommel. Observing the weakness of the British position at El Agheila, Rommel launched an attack on 24 March, broke through to an unexpected depth and, exploiting his success, drove his opponents back to the Egyptian frontier. By the second week of April the only British presence remaining in Cyrenaica was the fortified port of Tobruk, in which the 9th Australian Division remained besieged.

Tobruk stubbornly resisted Rommel's attacks, remaining a thorn in his side. In May and June he thwarted attempts to relieve the fortress and for the next five months relative calm descended on the desert. This situation did not suit Prime Minister Winston Churchill, who urged General Sir Claude Auchinleck, the Commander-in-Chief Middle East, to take the offensive. Auchinleck, however, refused to be hurried and it was not until November that he was ready to mount Operation Crusader, the intention of which was not simply the relief of Tobruk, but the destruction of the Axis army in North Africa.

The British forces in the Western Desert had now been designated the Eighth Army, commanded by General Sir Alan Cunningham. It consisted of two corps, XIII and XXX, commanded respectively by Lieutenant General A. R. Godwin-Austen and Major General Willoughby Norrie. The plan for Crusader was that XIII Corps (2nd New Zealand and 4th Indian Divisions and 1st Army Tank Brigade, equipped with stoutly armoured Matildas) would bypass the Axis frontier defences to the south then strike along the Via Balbia towards Tobruk. To the south, XXX Corps (7th Armoured and 1st South African Divisions and 22nd Guards Brigade) was to strike north-westwards across the desert, destroy the enemy's armour in the area of Sidi Rezegh airfield and effect a junction with the Tobruk garrison, which would simultaneously effect a breakout in the Belhamed–Ed Duda area. The 7th Armoured Division contained no less than three armoured brigades: the 4th, equipped with newly arrived American M3 Stuarts, the 7th, equipped with cruiser tanks, and the 22nd, also equipped with cruisers. By now, the 9th Australian Division having been relieved, the Tobruk garrison consisted of the 70th Division, the Polish Carpathian Brigade and the 32nd Army Tank Brigade, which included four Matilda squadrons and a regiment of cruiser and light tanks.

The operation got off to good start on 18 November. Torrential rain had made the Luftwaffe's airfields unusable and at first Rommel refused to believe that the British movement across the frontier was anything more than a reconnaissance in force. It was not until the following afternoon that he began to react to the threat posed by the Eighth Army's continued advance. After this, matters began to go seriously awry for XXX Corps. Part of the reason for this was that, as a defence against air attack, the British practised dispersion to an exaggerated degree, not only within formations but also within regiments. Thus, within 7th Armoured Division, the 4th Armoured Brigade, on the right, was separated by a gap of 35 miles from the 7th Armoured Brigade in the centre, which was separated by a gap of 20 miles from the 22nd Armoured Brigade on the left. The result was that the armoured brigades were not in a position to support each other when battle was joined. The Germans, on the other hand, did not practise dispersion to anything like the same degree yet did not suffer unduly from air attack. This enabled their panzer divisions to fight as integrated formations and therefore as a corps when the situation demanded it. The consequence was that when the British armoured brigades came into action piecemeal they were seriously mauled.

During the period 21–23 November the battlefield became an inextricable tangle of friend and foe in which formations of both sides found themselves simultaneously attacking in one direction and maintaining a desperate defence in another. In the north the Tobruk garrison had begun to break out against opposition from the German Afrika (later renamed 90th Light) Division, which was also trying to defend the Sidi Rezegh airfield against 7th Armoured Brigade and the 7th Armoured Division's Support Group, containing the division's infantry and artillery elements. The latter were in turn under attack from the 15th and 21st Panzer Divisions, whose anti-tank gunners were doing their best to hold off the 4th and 22nd Armoured Brigades. To those involved it was a formless nightmare of bitterly fought tactical battles that induced terror and utter fatigue, set in desert landscape littered with smashed guns and burning vehicles of every sort.

In this cauldron of death one man seemed to be in his element. He was Brigadier John Campbell, commander of the 7th Support Group. A Scot by birth, Jock Campbell was an artilleryman who had already been awarded the DSO twice as well as the MC. He was the originator of the so-called 'Jock Columns', small mobile battle groups consisting of artillery, lorried infantry and armoured cars, that scoured the desert looking for trouble. These battle groups had proved their worth against the

Italians during the early days of the desert war, although from the ortho-dox viewpoint they tended to dilute divisional assets, and achieved fewer successes against the Germans. Possessed of a forceful personality and natural powers of leadership, he was capable of inspiring his troops to perform the apparently impossible. As Brigadier C. E. Lucas Phillips relates in his book *Victoria Cross Battles of the Second World War*, Campbell would brook no hesitancy about engaging the enemy. On one occasion he drove up to the commander of a squadron of tanks that had already sustained serious losses and ordered him to attack a much larger column of enemy armour that had come into view some distance away. 'My God, sir, we shall simply all get killed!' exclaimed the squadron leader, having examined the odds against him through his binoculars. 'That is what soldiers are for – get on!' replied Campbell tartly.

One can really do no better than quote the citation for the Victoria Cross that Campbell was awarded for his actions at Sidi Rezegh:

> On 21 November 1941 at Sidi Rezegh, Libya, Brigadier Campbell's small force holding important ground was repeatedly attacked and wherever the fighting was hottest he was seen either on foot or in his open car. Next day, under intensified enemy attacks, he was again in the fore-front, encouraging his troops and personally controlling the fire of his batteries – he twice manned a gun himself to replace casualties. During the final attack, although wounded, he refused to be evacuated. His brilliant leadership was the direct cause of the very heavy casualties inflicted on the enemy, and did much to maintain the fighting spirit of his men.

Later, the 15th Panzer Division recorded that 'again and again strong enemy battle groups with tanks, anti-tank guns and artillery, came out of the desert', foiling its attacks. This was something of an exaggeration, for the groups scrambled together by Campbell could never have been described as strong, although they served their purpose. Campbell sur-vived the battle and was promoted major general, only to die in a traffic accident the following February.

During the morning of 21 November one of the Support Group's infantry battalions, the 1st King's Royal Rifle Corps, mounted an attack on Sidi Rezegh ridge, on the northern edge of the airfield. Advancing by rushes across open, fire-swept ground, the battalion took three-and-a-half hours to reach a point from which an assault could be mounted. By then, two-thirds of the centre company's men had been killed or

wounded and all its officers were down, save for the company commander, Captain Hugh Hope. Pinned down by heavy fire from two
directions, it seemed that it would go no further. This situation rapidly
underwent a dramatic change.

Manning one of the company's Bren light machine-guns was Rifleman
John Beeley, a good if undistinguished soldier of normally cheerful dis-
position. On this particular morning, however, he was anything but
happy. A married man, he had recently received news from home that
his domestic life was in ruins. It may be that he cared not whether he
lived or died, but we shall never know. Reaching a decision, he scrambled to his feet and, firing bursts from the hip with his Bren, charged
towards the summit of the craggy ridge, where he had spotted a strongpoint containing an anti-tank gun and two machine-guns, manned by
seven Germans. Although hit repeatedly himself, he halted 20 yards
from the objective and opened a deliberate fire that killed the entire
enemy detachment, before falling dead across his gun. As his company
swarmed forward on to the ridge, resistance collapsed. Some 800 prisoners were taken as well as large quantities of weapons. Rifleman Beeley's
self-sacrificial attack won him a posthumous VC.

Later that day, both of Rommel's panzer divisions attacked with the
clear intention of recapturing the airfield and wiping out the Support
Group, which was already under shellfire and being dive-bombed. They
were stopped by the 25-pdrs of the 60th Field Regiment, RA, and part of
the 4th Royal Horse Artillery, firing over open sights, and the 2-pdr
portees of 3rd Royal Horse Artillery. The portee was simply a device by
which the little 2-pdr anti-tank gun was carried on the back of a lorry to
avoid its being damaged under tow across the rocky desert surface. The
idea was that it should be unloaded and emplaced before going into
action, but, as on this occasion, it was sometimes impossible to do so
because of the urgency of the situation. When the crews were fighting
their guns mounted, their only protection was a gunshield, which was
no protection at all in the present circumstances.

Commanding A Troop in Major Bernard Pinney's J Battery 3 RHA was
Second Lieutenant Ward Gunn. Like Campbell, Gunn had been educated at Sedbergh and, like him on this day, was described afterwards as
'a man possessed with the joy of battle'. At the height of the action he
edged his vehicles out to bring them within killing range of the German
tanks, directing their fire on foot amid the smother of dust and smoke
thrown up by the enemy's artillery and mortars. Two of the portees were
quickly wrecked by direct hits, followed by a third some minutes later.

The fourth continued firing until only one of its crew was left alive, and he began to drive it out of action. Pinney told Gunn to halt the vehicle, which he did, then manned the gun himself after removing the dead crew. Pinney joined him but was immediately forced to deal with a fire in an ammunition bin. Gunn continued firing until he was killed. Pinney took over until further hits rendered the gun unusable, then joined another of his troops which was concentrating its fire on a group of tanks trying to work round the battery's flank. When this move was defeated the remainder of the enemy armour withdrew. Pinney was killed by a stray shell the following morning. Both he and Gunn were recommended for the posthumous award of the Victoria Cross, which they had certainly earned. With a perversity that is difficult to understand, it was granted only to Gunn. Pinney's J Battery, however, received the Royal Artillery's rarest distinction, an Honour Title, Sidi Rezegh, one of only five awarded during World War II.

Meanwhile, the Tobruk garrison had started its breakout and was making steady progress towards Ed Duda. On 23 November Captain Philip Gardner, serving with the 4th Royal Tank Regiment, was watching the progress of a troop of armoured cars belonging to the King's Dragoon Guards as they probed forward. Two of the cars were observed to be stopped about 200 yards apart and under heavy fire close to the enemy's reported position. Gardner was ordered to go to their assistance. It was decided that he would head for one of the cars while Lieutenant Paul Gearing went to the rescue of the other. The two Matildas passed through the forward infantry position and began descending a long, shallow forward slope. They immediately came under a hail of fire to which the Matilda's stout armour was impervious. As they drew closer they could see that the armoured cars were being steadily shot to pieces. Ordering his own gunner and Gearing to give covering fire, Gardner manoeuvred his tank close to the foremost car, which was lying close to the enemy's wire. He then dismounted and attached a tow-rope to the car, into which he placed its commander, Lieutenant Peter Beames, who was lying near by with both legs blown off and covered in blood. Clambering aboard, he gave the order for his driver to commence towing. Only a few yards had been covered before the tow-rope was severed by the enemy's fire. Dismounting again, Gardner walked to the car and had just reached the conclusion that it was not worth saving when a shell burst near by, sending splinters into his left side. Nevertheless, he lifted Beames on to his shoulders and began to walk back to the Matilda. At this point the tank's cupola was shot off and its 2-pdr gun was split in two by anti-tank rounds, killing the vehicle's operator/loader. Gardner lifted Beames on to the engine deck, where he remained himself to steady the wounded officer after giving his driver the order to reverse. Gearing had meanwhile picked up the crew of the second armoured car and both tanks reached their own lines, pursued by fire of every description. Sadly, Beames did not survive his terrible wounds. Gardner, who already held the MC, was awarded the Victoria Cross. The following year he was captured while trying to escape after the surrender of Tobruk. He escaped again from his prison camp in Germany but was recaptured almost within sight of safety.

By 24 November, Campbell's Support Group, worn down and seriously reduced in numbers by counter-attacks, had been forced to abandon Sidi Rezegh airfield and retire some miles to the south. Rommel now made a decision that was to cost him the battle. Satisfied that he had defeated XXX Corps, he decided upon a dash to the Egyptian frontier with both his panzer divisions and the Italian Ariete Armoured Division, believing that by virtue of the threat posed to the Eighth Army's communications, General Cunningham would abandon Operation Crusader. Such a decision was more akin to gambling than to opportunism, since it took no account of XIII Corps, which was making such excellent progress that the responsibility for effecting a junction with the Tobruk garrison had been transferred to it. In the event, Rommel's foray cost him priceless fuel and tanks without producing any positive results, although the Tobruk garrison temporarily suspended its breakout operations because of the situation at Sidi Rezegh. Cunningham did indeed have doubts about the wisdom of continuing, but as soon as he was aware of these Auchinleck replaced him as Army Commander with his own Deputy Chief of Staff, Major General Neil Ritchie.

On 25 November the breakout was resumed, bringing the Ed Duda escarpment within striking distance. As 4 RTR's Matildas approached the crest they came under extremely heavy artillery fire from Belhamed. They halted, hull down, and began to engage the enemy guns, which included 8-inch howitzers, with their co-axial machine-guns, as at that period the 2-pdr did not fire a high-explosive shell. While this fight was in progress the tanks were joined by Z Company of 1st Royal Northumberland Fusiliers, a machine-gun battalion. Z Company consisted of three platoons, each with three Vickers medium machine-guns carried on small Morris trucks. The company was commanded by Captain James Jackman, an Irishman by birth, who was a very popular and capable officer. Jackman led the company forward in line ahead through the storm of bursting shells and, at a given signal, the platoons deployed to positions that he had previously allocated, on either flank of the tanks. The guns were quickly dismounted and brought into action. Completely ignoring the tempest of explosions around him, Jackman drove round each of the platoons, directing their fire to the best possible advantage. The long-range, sustained fire of so many medium machine-guns not only made life very difficult for the enemy's artillery but also made it impossible for him to mount a counter-attack, enabling the 1st Essex Regiment to come forward and take possession of the feature. Jackman's courage, daring and decisive tactical sense earned him the battle's fifth and last Victoria Cross; sadly, the award was made posthumously, for as he was kneeling beside a gun both he and the gun commander were killed by a mortar bomb that burst just in front of it.

Only a narrow corridor now separated the Tobruk garrison from XIII Corps. The task of closing the gap was given to Major General Bernard Freyberg's 2nd New Zealand Division, which had already overrun the Afrika Korps' field headquarters and reached the eastern edge of the Sidi Rezegh battlefield, pushing the Axis infantry back against the Tobruk perimeter. The task was given to the New Zealand 19th Battalion and 44th RTR, another Matilda regiment. Contrary to contemporary wisdom, which held that tanks could not be used at night, the attack which went in on the night of 26 November was led by one squadron at walking pace, followed ten minutes later by a second squadron, accompanied by the infantry. The Axis defenders of the corridor, already painfully aware that they lay between the hammer and the anvil, were completely taken aback by the sudden appearance of fire-spitting Matildas grinding through their positions and simply melted away into the darkness. Just forty-five minutes after crossing their start line, the New Zealanders were shaking hands with the 1st Essex at Ed Duda.

The news that Tobruk had been relieved struck Rommel like a blow between the eyes. Hastening back from the frontier on the 27th, he discovered that XXX Corps had rallied and that during his absence the 7th Armoured Division, having collected its stragglers and repaired its breakdowns, had again become a force to be reckoned with. By frantic efforts he was able to hold off XXX Corps and prise XIII Corps away from Tobruk for a week, but he was unable to replace the losses sustained by his already weakened army and, recognising that it would be completely destroyed if he remained in the area, he began a well-ordered retreat to El Agheila on 7 December, abandoning his garrisons at Bardia, Halfaya Pass and Sollum on the Egyptian frontier to their fate. Once these had been mopped up, it became possible to count the cost of Operation Crusader. Axis casualties amounted to 38,000 killed, wounded and missing as against 18,000 British and Commonwealth. Some 300 German and Italian tanks had been destroyed compared with 278 British, although a high proportion of the latter could be recovered and repaired. The operation had succeeded in relieving Tobruk as well as mauling the enemy's army and forcing it to evacuate Cyrenaica, but it had been a far tougher struggle than anyone had anticipated.

On the same day that Rommel commenced his withdrawal, the Japanese treacherously attacked Pearl Harbor and immediately followed this up with invasions of Malaya, Hong Kong and the Philippines. Auchinleck, forced to strip his command in order to send substantial reinforcements to the Far East, was therefore unable to consolidate his victory. As a result of this and Rommel's resilience, the desert war still had another eighteen months to run.

The St Nazaire Raid

The early months of 1942 marked the lowest point of the war for the fortunes of the Western Allies. In North Africa, Rommel recovered much of the ground he had lost during Operation Crusader; in the Far East, Malaya, Singapore, Hong Kong and the Philippines all fell to the Japanese, who had also launched invasions of Burma and the Dutch East Indies; and, closer to home, three major units of the German Navy, the *Scharnhorst, Gneisenau* and *Prinz Eugen,* had broken out of Brest on 11 February and, despite the best efforts of the Royal Navy and the RAF, had escaped to home ports. In these circumstances, Allied morale was sorely in need of an uplift.

On October 1941 Captain Lord Louis Mountbatten replaced Admiral Sir Roger Keyes of Zeebrugge fame as Chief of Combined Operations. His task, as described by Winston Churchill, was 'to be offensive – train for the offensive, work out the craft, the equipment, the tactics, the administration and everything else needed to initiate and sustain the offensive'. Keyes was already working along these lines and had carried out several successful raids. Among the targets he had considered was the port of St Nazaire, which was becoming increasingly important to the enemy as a U-boat base. There was, too, another reason why St Nazaire offered an ideal target for a raid. The harbour contained a huge dry dock officially known as the Forme Ecluse, but more commonly known as the Normandie Dry Dock, in which the French liner *Normandie*, only a few feet shorter than the *Queen Elizabeth,* then the largest passenger liner in the world, had been constructed. Since the collapse of France in 1940, the *Normandie* had lain alongside Pier 88 in New York harbour. When America entered the war she was taken over by the US Navy and renamed *Lafayette*. She was in the process of conversion to a troopship that could carry the better part of an American division to Europe when, on 9 February, she was gutted by fire and rolled on to her side in the murky waters of the Hudson River. The inquiry suggested that the cause of the disaster was carelessness on the part of workmen, but most Americans believed that it was the work of Nazi agents, many of whom were active in the United States at the time. Coming as it did amid a season of defeats, the loss of such a prestigious vessel was yet another depressing blow to Allied spirits.

The size of the Normandie Dock made it unique. It was, in fact, the only dry dock on the Atlantic coast of Europe large enough to accommodate Hitler's Bismarck Class battleships. The previous year the *Bismarck* herself had been making for St Nazaire to repair her battle damage when, with considerable effort on the part of the Royal Navy, she had been sunk. More recently, her sister ship, the *Tirpitz*, had been commissioned and sent to Norway in January 1942. The threat of the *Tirpitz* breaking out to play havoc among the Allied convoys when, in that very month, one-third of a million tons of shipping had been sunk by U-boats, mainly off the American coast, was one that simply could not be ignored. However, in January 1942 the Admiralty's Deputy Director of Plans requested Mountbatten to re-examine and bring up to date Keyes's proposal for a raid on St Nazaire on the basis that a considerable reduction in the threat could be obtained if the Normandie Dock was destroyed, as this provided the only bolt-hole for the *Tirpitz* if she sustained damage in action.

The problem was that St Nazaire lay six miles from the sea within the heavily defended estuary of the Loire and was some 250 miles from the United Kingdom. Sustained bombing could not be relied on to achieve success and in any event posed too great a risk to the French civilian population. A major amphibious operation would quickly be detected long before it came within striking distance of the objective, and the defences thoroughly alerted. Nevertheless, an apparently insignificant force might just get through and, if it pressed home its attack with determination, achieve the desired results. As to the method, an obsolete warship would be rammed into the enormous caisson of the Normandie Dock. Her bows would be packed with sufficient high explosive to blow the caisson apart, timed to explode after the crew had got clear. Simultaneously, a commando force would destroy the caisson's pumping station and winding gear as well as other objectives in the dock area. The raiders would then be picked up by coastal craft and return to England. So was born Operation Chariot, which contained echoes of Zeebrugge and would become known as the Greatest Raid of All.

The vessel chosen to play the major role in the raid had been launched as the USS *Buchanan* in January 1919. She was one of the four-funnelled destroyers traded by the United States for bases in the West Indies in

1940 and in British service was given the name *Campbelltown*. For the purposes of the raid she underwent a transformation. Her funnels were reduced to two, which were sharply raked so that superficially she resembled a German destroyer of the Mowe Class. For reasons that will become apparent, her draught was reduced by stripping out her 4-inch guns, torpedo tubes, depth-charge throwers and their ammunition, leaving her armed with one 12-pdr gun on the foredeck and eight 20mm Oerlikon cannon. Thin armour plate was added to the bridge and wheel-house, and armoured screens, intended to protect the commandos during the final run-in, were constructed along her decks. Over four-and-a-half tons of high explosive in oil drums were placed behind the steel pillar that had formerly supported the destroyer's A gun, then encased in concrete to convince any German who came aboard that the *Campbelltown* was simply a blockship. The charges were to be exploded by eight-hour delay fuses rigged for simultaneous detonation, the technical aspects of the work being carried out by Lieutenant Nigel Tibbits, RN, and Captain William Pritchard, Royal Engineers, of whom more anon. Once the ship had rammed the caisson she was to be scuttled to prevent her being towed clear.

As not all the commandos required for the raid could be accommodated aboard *Campbelltown*, the rest of those taking part in the landing phase of the operation would travel aboard 14 Fairmile B Class motor launches, which had been built for a variety of inshore tasks rather than long-distance raiding. Handsome vessels, they resembled a rich man's pleasure craft but, being wooden-hulled, offered no protection at all for those aboard. Those taking part in the raid were fitted with additional fuel tanks and armed with two 20mm Oerlikons in place of their normal 3-pdr gun.

Two more vessels completed those that would actually participate in the raid. Motor gun boat *MGB 314*, armed with a Vickers 2-pdr pom-pom forward, a Rolls semi-automatic 2-pdr aft and two twin .50-inch machine-guns amidships, was to serve as command ship and be responsible for navigation. Motor torpedo boat *MTB 74*, adapted by repositioning her two torpedo tubes on the foredeck, had the task of firing two delayed action torpedoes into the Normandie Dock caisson if *Campbelltown* failed to ram successfully. Finally, two Hunt Class destroyers, *Tynedale* and *Atherstone*, were to escort the raiders until nightfall immediately before the attack, and the submarine *Sturgeon* was to position herself off the Loire estuary and provide a navigation check-point with light signals.

In overall command of the naval aspects of the raid was Commander R. E. D. Ryder, who had enjoyed an adventurous career, including command of a Q ship. During the raid itself he would travel aboard *MGB 314*, commanded by Lieutenant Dunstan Curtis. Also aboard the gunboat were Lieutenant A. R. Green, an expert in navigation, and Leading Signalman F. C. Pike, who was capable of sending and receiving signals in German. In command of *Campbelltown* was Lieutenant Commander Stephen Beattie. Commanding *MTB 74* was Sub Lieutenant R. C. M. V. Wynn, whose craft had originally been modified for a planned attack on the *Scharnhorst* during the time that she lay at Brest. The motor launches were commanded by Royal Naval Volunteer Reserve officers or their Australian, Canadian or New Zealand equivalents.

Today it is the Royal Marines who carry out the commando role, but at the time the commandos were members of the army. Even while the Battle of France was being lost, a suggestion for raiders who could hit the enemy hard whenever and wherever he least expected it was enthusiastically endorsed by Winston Churchill. Volunteers immediately came forward from every regiment and corps. They included regulars, territorials and those who had enlisted on the outbreak of war, and they came from every walk of life. What they all had in common was a determination to hurt the enemy, accompanied by a strong desire for dangerous adventure. They underwent unbelievably tough training in Scotland, where those who could not measure up to the required standard of physical and mental fitness were weeded out and returned to their units. They were formed first into independent companies and then into commandos, which took their name from the Boers' hard-hitting mobile units that had kept so many British troops tied down during the South African War. Since their formation they had raided from the Arctic Circle to the Eastern Mediterranean and proved themselves to be very formidable soldiers indeed.

Chosen to lead the commando element of the raid was Lieutenant Colonel A. C. Newman, a civil engineering contractor by profession who had previously served with a territorial battalion of the Essex Regiment and was now commanding No. 2 Commando. Newman's commando would provide the bulk of the force employed and, because of his overall responsibility, would be commanded by Major William Copland during the raid. Copland, manager of a nail factory in civil life, had originally served as a territorial in the South Lancashire Regiment and had already seen active service during World War I and in Norway. He had played a major part in planning commando training and, at forty-four years of age, had surprised many people by his ability to stand up to it himself. Because of the need for demolition experts, No. 2 Commando was re-inforced with men from Nos 1, 3, 4, 5, 9 and 12 Commandos. Among the new arrivals were two Royal Engineer officers, Captains William Pritchard and Robert Montgomery. Pritchard, as mentioned above, had already worked on the problems presented by *Campbelltown's* explosive cargo. A dock engineer from Cardiff, he had originally joined a Royal Engineer territorial unit with which he had won an MC while carrying out demolitions during the Dunkirk evacuation. Montgomery already had some personal knowledge of the St Nazaire docks and, after he and Pritchard had studied detailed plans of the area, the two were able to advise on the problems likely to be encountered, the vulnerable points at which charges could best be exploded, the most suitable type of explosive and the number of men required. Once ashore, the comman-dos would either form one of the demolition teams and its covering party, or neutralise specific targets such as gun emplacements, or create a defensive screen behind which the others could continue their work and then retire to the embarkation point. Intensive training for all of these tasks took place in great secrecy without the troops being advised as to their destination until the last minute.

The third, and least satisfactory, element of Operation Chariot was a diversionary raid to be carried out by RAF bombers while the amphibi-ous force was approaching its objective. To avoid casualties among the French population, the raid was strictly confined to the harbour area and each aircraft was to release only one bomb at a time during its repeated runs across the target area, the theory being that the protracted raid would keep the defenders' heads below ground at the critical moment. It was unfortunate that, due to the secrecy surrounding the project, the planners did not take the RAF into their confidence. The result was that the aircrew simply carried out their somewhat unusual orders without understanding the overall situation below.

Few had any illusions about the odds they were facing. The coast defence batteries lining both banks of the Loire estuary mounted no less than twenty-eight guns of calibres between 70mm and 170mm. An anti-aircraft brigade stationed at St Nazaire possessed forty-three guns of 20mm, 37mm and 40mm calibre, carefully sited around the docks on jetties, the submarine pens, the Old Mole, and on both sides of the Nor-mandie Dock's southern caisson. These weapons, many of which were emplaced on top of concrete block-houses and therefore difficult to attack, were all capable of firing in the ground as well as the anti-aircraft role. Then there were the German warships moored in the docks themselves, including a flotilla of minesweepers and four harbour defence boats, all of which could be relied upon to use their weapons in the event of an attack. In the river the German Navy had at least one *Sperrbrecher* (boom-breaker), used as a flak ship and mounting several anti-aircraft weapons, including an 88mm. In terms of troops, about 1,000 were manning the coast defence batteries along the estuary and another 5,000 were present in and around the dock area. As if this was not enough, the evening before the raiders were due to leave, air reconnaissance revealed the arrival of five German destroyers, berthed in the Bassin de St Nazaire, which also housed the U-boat pens. Against all this were deployed one obsolete destroyer, less than a score of light motor vessels and 611 men, including 257 commandos. The scene was set for what looked dangerously like a naval version of the Charge of the Light Brigade.

The raiders, hitherto known as the 10th Anti-Submarine Striking Force for the sake of security, sailed from Falmouth at 14:00 on 26 March, taking a south-westerly heading into the Atlantic. To conserve fuel, *MGB 314* and *MTB 74* were towed respectively by *Atherstone* and *Campbelltown*. At 19:11 Ryder ordered an alteration of course to south-by-west, followed at 23:00 to south-by-east. At 07:00 on 27 March the force had just adopted a south-easterly course when a surfaced U-boat was spotted some seven-and-a-half miles ahead. *Tynedale* surged towards her and had got within a mile when she was spotted. The destroyer opened fire and the U-boat dived. After depth charges had been dropped the submarine surfaced again, but dived promptly as soon as she was engaged with gunfire. Nothing further was seen of her and when *Tynedale*'s asdic failed the hunt was called off.

Ryder was worried that if the U-boat had survived she would report the presence of the force. In fact, the encounter produced beneficial results, for although she lay beneath the surface for another five-and-a-half hours, she did finally send a signal to the German Group Commander West to the effect that at 06:20 (German time) she had encountered three destroyers and ten MTBs at a given point, steering west. This was almost the opposite course to that which the raiders were now taking. Puzzled, Group West suspected a minelaying operation and ordered the German destroyers at St Nazaire to put to sea and investigate.

At 12:04 the raiders came across a group of French trawlers. Ryder, aware that German naval personnel with radio equipment sometimes put to sea with French fishermen, decided that rather than risk disclosure of the force's presence he would have to sink them. After the crews of two had been taken aboard the escorting destroyers, their ships were sunk or set on fire, but upon receiving assurances that no Germans were present with the rest of group, Ryder left them in peace. Far from bearing ill will at the loss of their trawlers, the fishermen seemed glad of the opportunity to escape from German-occupied France. On reaching England several joined the Free French forces.

As the afternoon wore on the sky became overcast. Ryder received a signal from the Commander-in-Chief Portsmouth to the effect that the German destroyers had been seen leaving St Nazaire and that two more Hunt Class destroyers, *Cleveland* and *Brocklesby*, were being despatched from Falmouth to strengthen the escort during the withdrawal. At 18:30 one of the motor launches developed such serious engine trouble that its commandos were transferred to another. By 20:00 it was fully dark and the force took up its attack formation. Ryder and Newman, who had been travelling aboard *Atherstone,* transferred to *MGB 314*, which took the lead, followed by *Campbelltown*, then two parallel columns of motor launches, with *MTB 74* bringing up the rear. Leaving *Atherstone* and *Tynedale* to patrol the morrow's rendezvous area, the little force headed north-east towards the Loire estuary with German naval ensigns flying. At 22:00, dead ahead, a series of flashed double dashes indicated the position of the submarine *Sturgeon*. Lieutenant Green's navigation had been a triumph of precision.

Meanwhile, the RAF's diversionary raid had commenced. The area of the Normandie Dock was to be bombed from 23:30 until 00:30, and the northern end of the Penhouet basin, to the north of the dry dock and the Bassin de St Nazaire, until 04:00. The bombers were not to fly below 6,000 feet and their attack was subject to the strict controls described earlier. A few bombs were dropped in the midst of heavy flak, then clouds obscured the target area. In obedience to their orders, the bombers remained above St Nazaire, waiting for a break in the clouds and suspecting little of what was taking place below. Understandably, to the commander of the German naval flak brigade, Captain C. C. Mecke, the continuous droning of invisible aircraft overhead suggested something unusual was afoot. Suspecting a parachute landing, but not ruling out the possibility of an amphibious operation, he alerted all Wehrmacht command posts in the area and told his own gunners to pay particular attention to the port's seaward approaches.

At 00:30 on 28 March the raiding force entered the Loire estuary. It now became apparent why it had been necessary to reduce *Campbell-town*'s draught, for the force entered not by the deep Charpentier's Channel that ran close to the northern shore under the guns of the enemy's coast defence batteries, but across the shoal water that covered most of its width. The tide was high but even so *Campbelltown* grounded twice on mud banks that reduced her speed to 5 knots before her churning screws drove her on into deeper water. Aboard her, Lieutenant Tibbits activated the chemical time fuses, setting them to detonate the demolition charge between 05:00 and 09:00.

At 01:20, with the raiders now in the main channel and less than two miles from their objective, Mecke was informed that seventeen vessels were proceeding upriver. When the harbour master confirmed that no arrivals were expected that night he issued an immediate alert. Search-lights flashed out, illuminating the entire force, and two signal stations ashore flashed a challenge. Aboard *MGB 314*, ahead of *Campbelltown*, Leading Signalman Pike was equipped with a captured German code-book containing the codenames of several enemy torpedo boats known to operate in the area. With Teutonic efficiency, he peremptorily flashed 'Wait!' to one of the signal stations. He then dealt with the second station, making first a torpedo boat's codename, followed by 'Am proceeding into harbour in accordance with orders.' The signal was acknowledged and a searchlight turned off. Pike then dealt similarly with the other station. The force continued upstream unmolested until someone ashore opened fire. Pike signalled: 'Am being fired on by friendly forces!' The firing stopped, but German suspicions were confirmed when, instead of heaving to, as any of their own ships would have done, those in the river actually increased their speed.

Suddenly the night was illuminated not only by searchlights but by tracers of every colour as the force came under concentrated fire. Down came the German colours and up went the White Ensigns. The glare of the searchlights was blinding but Lieutenant Curtis, commanding *MGB 314*, continued on course, leading *Campbelltown* steadily past jetties of the outer harbour towards the Normandie Dock's caisson. To starboard, the *Sperrbrecher* opened fire. Able Seaman William Savage, manning the gunboat's pom-pom, hammered it from end to end until he had silenced every weapon aboard, including the big 88mm. Having passed the Old Mole and satisfied himself that *Campbelltown* was on course for her target, Curtis swung away to starboard.

Every gun in the raiding force was now replying to the enemy with some effect, shooting out searchlights and achieving a temporary reduction in the volume of incoming fire. Aboard *Campbelltown*, as Lieu-tenant Commander Stephen Beattie worked the destroyer up to her ramming speed of 20 knots, the Oerlikons were rattling away, accompa-nied by banging from the 12-pdr forward, the cough of the commandos' 3-inch mortars and the measured thumping of their Brens. Naturally enough, the ship became the enemy's principal target. Shells were burst-ing all over her, taking a toll of the crew and the commandos huddled on deck. The crews of the 12-pdr and a 3-inch mortar were wiped out by a heavy shell. Two of the Oerlikon crews went down but were instantly replaced. In the wheelhouse, the coxswain was shot dead, as was his replacement. With the target now coming into sight, Tibbits took over the wheel. 'Stand by to ram!' ordered Beattie, then instructed Tibbits to make a light adjustment to port so that the ship would strike the caisson squarely. Everyone aboard braced themselves for the impact. *Campbell-town* had now become a 1,000-ton missile travelling at 20 knots. She ploughed through a torpedo net which reduced her speed slightly, then smashed into the caisson with a crash followed by the scream of tearing metal as she punched her way through the huge gate. She came to rest with 36 feet of her bows crumpled back and her forecastle deck protrud-ing beyond and above the caisson's inner face. As soon as the movement ceased Major Copland, described by one of his men as 'walking the deck as calmly as though it was an exercise', began despatching the com-mando assault, covering and demolition parties ashore in the correct order, then followed himself to establish his command post.

Meanwhile, Curtis's *MGB 314* had continued her turn to starboard to come round in three-quarters of a circle. She now headed into the Old Entrance to the Bassin de St Nazaire, where Newman and his staff went ashore to control the land battle. Some of *Campbelltown*'s crew came aboard, bringing their wounded with them. Ryder, accompanied by Pike as a self-appointed bodyguard, also went ashore to satisfy himself that the ramming operation had gone according to plan. He need not have worried, for as they reached the destroyer her scuttling charges went off and she settled immovably on the river bed with her bows still held fast in the caisson. They returned to the Old Entrance to find that Wynn's *MTB 74* had come in alongside the gunboat. Ryder ordered Wynn to launch his two delayed action torpedoes against the lock gates. They struck with a thump and sank. Wynn's task was now complete and Ryder told him to take some of the *Campbelltown*'s crew aboard and head for home.

Back aboard *MGB 314*, Ryder returned to mid-river where he watched the final stages of the naval part in the raid, then turned for home himself. Able Seaman Savage, manning the gunboat's pom-pom without even the protection of a gunshield, and continuing to shoot up targets with uncanny accuracy, was killed. He received a posthumous Victoria Cross, awarded not only for his own gallantry but for that shown by the many unnamed men aboard the unprotected small craft who had fought back at murderously short range.

Some of the defenders ashore, having fallen victim to Dr Goebbels's own propaganda, which portrayed the commandos as demon figures, fled when Copland's men came streaming off the *Campbelltown*. Others, however, did not, and as they were being constantly reinforced from inland, the assault and protection parties had a severe fight on their hands. As the battle became so kaleidoscopic as to require far more space than is available to describe it in detail, it is intended to concentrate on the work of Captain Bob Montgomery's demolition teams, which was essential to the overall success of the operation. The objective of Lieutenant Stuart Chant's team was the Normandie Dock's pump-house. Chant had been wounded in the leg, arms and hand while aboard *Campbelltown* but, supported by his men, had insisted on supervising the task personally. So effective were the charges attached to the huge pumps that when they exploded the entire pump-house went up. A further result of the explosion was that the floor of the motor room collapsed, taking the motors with it. Near by, Lieutenant Christopher Smalley's men went to work on the winding-house, which contained the machinery for hauling the caisson into its recess in the dockside. After two attempts the winding-house was blown apart. Smalley then embarked his party on a motor launch at the Old Entrance but was shot dead as he was about to board. Simultaneously, two more demolition teams had run up the western side of the Normandie Dock. That under Lieutenant Corran Purdon was to destroy the winding-house of the dock's northern caisson, while that under Lieutenant Gerald Brett was to attack the caisson itself. Purdon's team broke into the winding-house and, having laid their charges, delayed firing them until the second team had finished working on the caisson. Brett was hit in the legs while running beside the dock, but had fortunately been reinforced by Montgomery with a second team under Lieutenant Robert Burtenshaw, whose original task had been to tackle the southern caisson if *Campbelltown* had failed to ram it. While fixing charges to the external wall of the northern caisson, both teams came under fire from ships in the Penhouet basin, from one of two tankers undergoing repair in the Normandie Dock, and from German reinforcements reaching the area. Burtenshaw was killed leading an attack on the tanker, which was neutralised by one of the protection squads. Having now lost both his officers, Sergeant Frank Carr took over the work on the caisson. Satisfied with the underwater charges laid against its outer wall, he tried to lay further explosives inside the structure but was prevented from doing so by an access hatch that stubbornly refused to open. On his own initiative, therefore, he decided to fire those charges already in place. The explosion reverberated the steel structure with a sound that could be heard all over the dock area, but did not destroy it. It did, however, damage it sufficiently for water to begin pouring into the dry dock from the Penhouet basin. Purdon now blew the charges at the winding-house, which seemed to leap into the air in one piece, then collapse like a house of cards.

Unfortunately, very few reinforcements were reaching *Campbelltown*'s commandos. Of the port column of motor launches, which were to have landed their commandos at the Old Mole, only one managed to do so, a situation that was repeated when the starboard column attempted to land its troops at the Old Entrance to the St Nazaire Basin. Subjected to heavy, close-quarter fire from every direction, the unprotected launches came close to being massacred. Some were set ablaze, their survivors swimming in a sea of burning petrol from their ruptured fuel tanks. Others, having sustained serious casualties and damage, or unable to reach their objective through the raging flames, turned for home. It was soon obvious to those fighting ashore that very few of them stood any chance of being picked up.

Captain Pritchard and a few men did, however, manage to land at the Old Mole. Pritchard was responsible for demolitions in the southern area of the docks, particularly the bridges adjacent to the locks of the St Nazaire basin. Pritchard managed to reach the southern lock but, lacking the resources to complete the destruction of the bridge, decided to board two tugs moored side by side. Charges placed below the waterline were exploded and the tugs sank. While returning through the Old Town in search of reinforcements, Pritchard was killed.

The raid was now effectively over. Evacuation being impossible, Newman and Copland decided to make as big a nuisance of themselves to the Germans as possible. They ordered their men to break out then, in small parties, to make their way south to the Spanish frontier and on to Gibraltar. Most were picked up within twenty-four hours although, remarkably, five did get all the way through. The Germans, nervous of their captives, were hostile but correct in their treatment of them. With the coming of light, their photographers arrived to take pictures of the British dead, wounded and prisoners, as well as the *Campbelltown,* wedged firmly in the caisson.

In the estuary, fighting continued. *MTB 74,* capable of 40 knots, was an impossible target for the German gunners and would have got clear had not Wynn decided to stop and pick up survivors from one of the launches. The torpedo boat, now a sitting duck, was smashed to pieces and set ablaze. Wynn, insensible, was rescued by his chief motor mechanic, W. H. Lovegrove, who got him over the side into a rubber raft. The incident had an interesting sequel for Wynn, having lost an eye in the engagement, was subsequently repatriated. In 1945, knowing in which prison camp Lovegrove was being held, he somehow managed to get himself attached to the Guards Armoured Division, which liberated the camp, and so repaid the debt.

At sea, the five German destroyers had been ordered back into the estuary to cut off the raiders' retreat. At about 05:30, the third ship in the German line, Kapitanleutnant F. K. Paul's *Jaguar,* noticed a dark shape to port and turned to investigate. It was *ML 306,* commanded by Lieutenant Ian Henderson, which, having failed to land her troops at the Old Entrance, was, much to their disgust, heading for home and, hoping to avoid detection, had stopped when the German destroyers appeared. The *Jaguar* illuminated the launch with one of her searchlights, which was promptly shot out. Henderson got his craft moving again and a fierce but one-sided fire-fight ensued with the destroyer using her heavy automatic weapons and the launch firing back with her after Oerlikon and twin Lewis guns as well as the commandos' Brens and even pistols. Casualties aboard the launch were heavy and Henderson was killed. Sergeant Thomas Durrant of the Royal Engineers, serving with No. 1 Commando, had already been wounded during the approach to the Old Entrance, took over the twin Lewis guns when the seaman manning them was shot dead, and was wounded again. Paul, essentially a humane, chivalrous man, hauled off and invited the launch's survivors to surrender. Durrant replied with a burst that raked the destroyer's bridge. The fight was resumed until it was obvious that the British were running out of ammunition, when Paul again asked them to surrender. He received the same answer as before but by now Durrant, already hit in a dozen places, was hit yet again and collapsed. At this point, with the launch's deck covered with dead and dying men, the commandos' officer, Lieutenant Swayne, called out apologetically that it was impossible to continue. The dead and wounded were taken aboard the *Jaguar*, the decks of which were liberally bloodied. This incident, too, had an interesting sequel, for although Durrant died of his multiple wounds shortly after, a few days later a German naval officer, possibly Kapitanleutnant Paul himself, sought out Colonel Newman in his prison camp at Rennes, and described Durrant's outstanding bravery, respectfully submitting that this merited a high award. Because of Newman's incarceration, Tom Durrant's posthumous Victoria Cross was not gazetted until 19 June 1945. It was an unusual award, not only because it was made to a soldier taking part in a naval engagement, but also because the principal witness happened to be one of the enemy.

Hardly had *ML 306*'s survivors been taken aboard the *Jaguar* than the destroyer again went to Action Stations. At 06:29 her four consorts had sighted *Tynedale* and *Atherstone* cruising off the mouth of the estuary. A running fight lasting nine minutes ensued, during which *Tynedale* was hit twice but scored hits on one of the enemy in return. The two British destroyers had deliberately adopted a southerly course to lead the Germans away from the motor launches' escape route. Finally, *Tynedale* made smoke and the enemy, possibly suspecting a trap, broke off the engagement and returned to the river.

The British destroyers also reversed course and shortly after daybreak met *MGB 314* and three launches at the rendezvous point. After the wounded were transferred to the larger vessels, it was decided to abandon one launch that was in a sinking condition, and at 07:50 the little force got under way. Shortly after, it was joined by the two additional escort destroyers, *Cleveland* and *Brocklesby*, under Commander G. B. Sayer, who was now the senior officer present. Several minor air attacks were made during the morning, in one of which a Junkers 88 was shot down. However, such was the damage already sustained by the smaller craft that they were limping along at about 10 knots. Sayer considered that this prejudiced the safety of the entire force and at 13:50 they were reluctantly scuttled after their personnel had been transferred to the destroyers. The decision proved to be providential because the Wehrmacht's senior commanders, driven to apoplectic rage by events in St Nazaire that very morning, had vengefully despatched a force of bombers from Holland to annihilate the raid's survivors. Unfortunately for the bombers, all they had to go on was the course and speed of the ships reported during the earlier air attacks, and as the destroyers were now proceeding at a steady 25 knots, the pilots found nothing but empty sea at the planned interception point. That evening, the first survivors of Operation Chariot reached Plymouth without further molestation. Three more launches which missed the rendezvous sailed home in company, reaching Falmouth with barely a drop of fuel left in their tanks, having shot down a Heinkel III on the way. Apart from the launch that had broken down during the outward voyage, they were the only little ships to return from the raid.

Back at St Nazaire, as the day had advanced, a large crowd of German service personnel, including senior officers, their wives and girl friends, had converged on the Normandie Dock. They swarmed over *Campbelltown*, the caisson and the approaches to the dry dock. The general opinion was that the British had been brave but also very stupid if they thought the mighty caisson could be destroyed by ramming it with an old destroyer, and no one seemed to think any further than that. Among those British prisoners aware of *Campbelltown*'s secret, anxiety began to grow. The tons of explosives packed aboard her should have gone off between 05:00 and 09:00, but nothing had happened and it began to seem as though all their effort had been for nothing. Complacent in the belief that all was well, their German captors became relaxed and even friendly. Shortly after 10:30 there was an explosion of earthquake proportions, shaking buildings and shattering windows across a wide area. Riven steel, fragments of shattered concrete and masonry, heads, limbs, torsos, torn flesh and blood rained down on the docks and the river for what seemed to be an interminable period. The caisson had been blown off its rollers and now lay resting against the dock wall, while the *Campbelltown*'s bow section had simply vanished. Driven by a torrent of water from the river, the wreck of the destroyer was swept into the dry dock to collide with one of the tankers within. The lowest estimate of those killed was 100, the highest 380. To the delight of the cheering prisoners, a complete panic seemed to grip the shaken enemy and, for no apparent reason, firing broke out in various parts of the town.

Two days later some semblance of normality seemed to have returned, but at 16:00 the first of Wynn's delayed action torpedoes exploded, wrecking the lock gates at the Old Entrance. Suspecting sabotage by the French, the Germans became jumpy and carried out a thorough search of the area, imposing a curfew at 21:00. When Wynn's second torpedo exploded an hour later they again gave way to uncontrolled panic. They shot at anyone running for cover, including civilians of all ages and both sexes, and they shot at one another. In their khaki uniforms, members of the German Todt organisation, responsible for constructing the U-boat pens, became popular targets.

The entire leadership of the Third Reich, from Hitler downwards, was boundless in its fury at what had occurred. Anxious to save face, the German propaganda apparatus went into top gear, claiming that the raiders had been decisively repulsed with heavy loss, but it could hardly deny that the second most heavily defended harbour in France had been penetrated by a tiny British force, or that the great Normandie Dock had been wrecked. The dock remained out of commission for the rest of the war and as a direct result of this the *Tirpitz* was unable to make a foray into the Atlantic shipping lanes. Instead, she remained in the Norwegian fjords, making little contribution to the German war effort save as a perpetual threat to the Russian convoys and only once fired her guns in anger, against shore installations at Spitzbergen. Damaged by midget submarines and strikes from carrier aircraft, she was finally sent to the bottom in November 1944 by RAF Lancasters dropping 12,000lb bombs.

Of the St Nazaire raiders, only 215 reached home. Naval and army losses amounted to 169 killed, plus the capture of those left behind. Of the 611 men participating in the raid, this was a high proportion, but it has to be balanced against the possibility of thousands of lives being lost if the *Tirpitz* had been granted her freedom, and in these terms was an unqualified success. Ryder received the Victoria Cross, plus the French Légion d'Honneur Avec Palmes and Croix de Guerre. He took part in the Dieppe raid later that year and subsequently retired from the navy with the rank of captain, sitting as Member of Parliament for Merton and Morden 1950–55. Newman also received the Victoria Cross, the Légion d'Honneur and the Croix de Guerre. After the war he returned to the civil engineering contractors which he had originally joined in 1922. Beattie, too, received the Victoria Cross, the Légion d'Honneur and the Croix de Guerre, although his VC was awarded not only in recognition of his own valour, but also that of *Campbelltown*'s ship's company, many of whom did not survive. He later achieved the rank of captain and was Senior Naval Officer Persian Gulf 1956–8. Among the numerous lesser decorations awarded for the raid, Copland received the DSO. After the war he returned to manufacturing and later became a director of British Steel.

Dieppe – Operation Jubilee

19 AUGUST 1942

As 1942 wore on, Prime Minister Winston Churchill came under increasing pressure from Joseph Stalin to open what was then known as the Second Front, which would involve nothing less than a full-scale invasion of France. If this did not happen, Stalin hinted, the hard-pressed Soviet Union might conclude a separate peace with Hitler's Germany, leaving Great Britain and the United States, whose full strength had yet to be deployed, to carry on with the war in Europe alone. Washington, too, was eager to carry the war on to the continent. Churchill, however, was convinced that any such attempt was premature and would result in so serious a failure that the war would be prolonged for years. Against this, he had to provide his Allies with proof that his opinion was correct. It was decided, therefore, to examine whether it would be possible to secure a port intact on the heavily defended French coast.

The choice fell on Dieppe. This sector of the French coastline runs from east to west and consists of high chalk cliffs, broken by deep gullies, the estuary of the River d'Arques, and the town and port of Dieppe. The shingle beach in front of the town was overlooked by the East and West Headlands and separated from the sea-front houses and hotels by a sea wall and a broad open space that had once been ornamental gardens. The houses had been prepared for defence and the entire area bristled with machine- and anti-tank guns. It was, in fact, a natural killing ground. The immediate defences were manned by the German 302nd Infantry Division, while inland were the 10th Panzer Division and the 1st SS Panzergrenadier Division *Leibstandarte Adolf Hitler.*

The idea was that the operation, codenamed Jubilee, was to be a large-scale raid. If the port could be captured, well and good; if it could not, the lessons learned could be put to advantageous use later. In either event, the raiders were to be withdrawn within the space of a single tide. The troops selected for the operation were six infantry battalions and an armoured regiment of Major General H. F. Roberts's 2nd Canadian Division, which had reached the United Kingdom during the post-Dunkirk invasion crisis. Since then it had grown bored and restless and wanted to play a more active role in the war than garrison duty. The Prime Minister of Canada, Mr Mackenzie King, was averse to its being deployed to the Middle East, but was prepared to sanction its use in Europe. The Canadians' task would be to capture the town, harbour and East and West Headlands. Armoured support would be provided by the Calgary Regiment, equipped with Churchill tanks. It was envisaged that once the tanks had completed their infantry support tasks they would advance inland and beat up the airfield at St Aubin and the château of Arques-les-Batailles, which was suspected of being a divisional headquarters. Prior to the main landing, the Hess coast defence battery at Vesterival, to the west, and the Goebbels coast defence battery at Berneval, to the east, were to be neutralised, respectively, by Lieutenant Colonel Lord Lovat's No. 4 Commando and Lieutenant Colonel John Durnford-Slater's No. 3 Commando. Serving with the two Commandos were twenty Frenchmen of No. 10 (Inter-Allied) Commando and fifty men of the 1st US Ranger Battalion, a new American unit modelled on the Commandos which had also undergone its basic training at Achnacarry in Scotland. No less than sixty fighter squadrons were to provide close support and air cover. The date and time for the raid, the largest yet mounted, was determined by conditions of tide and darkness and set for dawn on 19 August. The previous night the ships carrying the various elements of the force slipped out of four ports on the south coast of England and assembled in mid-Channel.

No. 4 Commando touched down shortly after 04:30. The plan was that it should approach the Hess battery from different directions in two parties and storm the position after an air strike timed for 06:30. Liaison between the two parties was the responsibility of Captain Patrick Porteous, who had been born into the army on New Year's Day 1918, at Abbottabad on the North-West Frontier of India. He had entered the Royal Artillery in 1937 and, after serving in the 1940 campaign in France, had joined the Commandos later that year.

The battery was defended by approximately 250 Germans, who put up a most determined resistance. Porteous, with Lord Lovat's headquarters group, saw that in penetrating the perimeter the smaller of the two commando detachments had lost both its officers and ran across the bullet-swept ground to take command. Hardly had he done so than a German appeared, shooting him in the wrist. The German was about to kill one of the detachment's sergeants when Porteous used his uninjured hand to shoot him dead.

At 06:30 Spitfires struck the gun positions and, as they droned away, Lovat sent up white Verey lights to signal the assault. While the rest of the commandos cleared the battery buildings, Porteous's detachment stormed one gun position after another in a series of bayonet charges. Porteous received a serious wound in the thigh during the first charge, but continued to lead each attack until the gun position was secured, then collapsed from loss of blood. The demolition parties then went to work, wrecking the guns.

No. 4 Commando sustained the loss of twelve killed, twenty wounded and four missing. It was estimated that not less than 150 of the enemy had been killed. As the commandos withdrew they waved cheekily at a Messerschmidt squadron that roared over the position. The squadron commander, assuming them to be Germans, waved back.

Porteous received the Victoria Cross. Recovering from his wounds, he rejoined No. 4 Commando, serving as its second-in-command when it landed at Oustreham on D Day, 6 June 1944. He retired with the rank of colonel in 1970.

On the opposite flank of the raid things had not gone quite so well. At 03:47 the landing craft carrying No. 3 Commando had run into an escorted German convoy. As a result of the subsequent action the wooden-hulled craft had become scattered, many with numerous casualties aboard. Consequently, the landing was confused and made with far fewer men than had been anticipated. Nevertheless, the commandos so harassed the gunners in the Goebbels battery at Berneval that, although their guns remained in action against the approaching main force of the raid, it is believed that no hits were scored.

In the centre, the 2nd Canadian Division's landing was such a disaster that for a time it was believed that the enemy had received prior warning of the attack. That was not so, for not only was the memory of the St Nazaire raid fresh in everyone's mind, the German 302nd Division was also an efficient, tightly run formation and, by the worst possible luck, the battalion commander responsible for the security of the beach area east of the town had simply ordered a practice alert to sharpen his men up. Thus, when the Royal Regiment of Canada came ashore somewhat late owing to a mistake in marshalling the landing craft, all the defenders had to do was squeeze their triggers. The regiment was all but annihilated by the terrible crossfire that swept the beach and the shallows. Its objective, the Rommel and Bismarck batteries on the vital East Headland, remained untaken.

Elsewhere, the Germans had also reacted with speed and efficiency.

To the west of Dieppe, the South Saskatchewan Regiment made a better landing and some progress inland, but was eventually pinned down despite being reinforced by the Queen's Own Cameron Highlanders of Canada and unable to capture either the West Headland or the Hindenburg battery. With neither headland taken, the beach area in front of the town was swept by a crossfire from both, as well as frontally. Into this inferno came the Essex Scottish and the Royal Hamilton Light Infantry, many of whom died in their landing craft while those who did get ashore were forced to scrape cover for themselves in the shingle.

The last hope of the raid succeeding rested with the Churchill tanks of the Calgary Regiment. Some were knocked out crossing the beach, others, tracks unable to grip on the loose stones, bellied in the shingle. More broke through the wire entanglement to reach the sea wall, which for much of its length was too high for them to surmount. Nevertheless, points were discovered where the shingle was naturally banked against the wall and a number of tanks used these successfully to cross the wall. Beyond, they inflicted casualties and damage but were unable to break into the town because of heavy concrete road-blocks. The problem had been foreseen and was to have been dealt with by engineers with explosive charges. Unfortunately, the engineers, lacking any form of protection, were either dead or pinned down among the infantry. At about this time, the reserve infantry battalion, the Fusiliers Mont Royal, were committed to the landing but fared no better than the rest.

At about 09:00 the force commanders, Major General Roberts and Captain J. Hughes-Hallett, RN, deciding that nothing further would be gained by continuing the operation, gave the signal to withdraw. Those that could do so embarked aboard the landing craft and sailed for home while, overhead, fighters and bombers of the RAF, US Army Air Force and the Luftwaffe engaged in the most concentrated single day's air battle of the entire war.

Yet within this dark picture of apparently futile massacre there were flashes of inspirational courage. When the South Saskatchewan Regiment landed, its orders required it to cross a bridge at Pourville. Four attempts were made to cross under heavy machine-gun, mortar and artillery fire. All failed, leaving the bridge strewn with casualties. At this point the regiment's commanding officer, Lieutenant Colonel Charles Merritt, reached the survivors of the failed attempts. Assessing the situation, he led them in a successful charge across the bridge, waving his helmet and shouting, 'Come on over! There's nothing to worry about here!' Beyond the bridge the regiment was again held up by the fire of several pillboxes. Merritt again led a series of rushes that succeeded in clearing them, personally accounting for the occupants of one by tossing grenades through the fire slits. As a result of the enemy's heavy and continuous fire, several of his runners became casualties, so he personally maintained contact with his companies. At one point, armed with a Bren gun, he stalked and dealt with a sniper who was causing trouble. By now he had been wounded twice, but when the order to withdraw came he calmly issued the appropriate orders and announced his intention of holding off and getting even with the enemy while his men returned to their landing craft. When last seen he was collecting Bren and Tommy guns in a defensive position from which he successfully covered their withdrawal.

At the time Merritt's Victoria Cross was gazetted he was, correctly, reported to be a prisoner-of-war. In due course, the Germans, believing him to be an extremely dangerous man, imprisoned him in Colditz Castle, which was reserved for their most troublesome prisoners. After the war he served as member for Vancouver-Burrard in the Federal Parliament until 1948, then returned to his law practice in Vancouver.

Perhaps the highest form of courage is not generated by the heat of battle but stems from a deep faith demanding ministration to the needs of others, irrespective of the danger. Such was the circumstance leading to the award of the Victoria Cross to Hon. Captain John Foote of the Canadian Chaplain Services. Foote, a native of Ontario Province, was a Presbyterian minister serving as chaplain to the Royal Hamilton Light Infantry. His citation reads:

> Upon landing on the beach under heavy fire he attached himself to the regimental aid post, which had been set up in a slight depression on the beach, but which was only sufficient to give cover to men lying down. While the action continued, this officer not only assisted the regimental medical officer in ministering to the wounded in the regimental aid post, but time and again left this shelter to inject morphine, give first aid and carry wounded personnel from the open beach to the regimental aid post. On these occasions, with utter disregard for his personal safety, Hon. Captain Foote exposed himself to an inferno of fire and saved many lives by his gallant efforts, during the action. As the tide went out, the regimental aid post was moved to the shelter of a stranded landing craft. Captain Foote continued tirelessly and courageously to carry wounded men from the exposed beach to the cover of the landing craft. He also removed wounded from inside the landing craft when ammunition had been set on fire by enemy shells.

At the end of this gruelling time he climbed from the landing craft that was to have taken him to safety and deliberately walked into the German position in order to be taken prisoner so that he could be a help to those men who would be in captivity until the end of the war.

When the war ended he remained with the Chaplain Services until 1948, achieving the rank of major. He then entered politics, representing Durham County in the Ontario Provincial Legislature, occupying the post of Minister of Reform Institutions for a time.

The balance sheet for Operation Jubilee made dismal reading. Including all three services, the Allies sustained over 4,000 personnel casualties, of whom in excess of 1,900 were prisoners, plus material losses including one destroyer, thirty-three landing craft, twenty-eight tanks and 114 aircraft. German losses included 345 killed and 268 wounded, a coast defence battery destroyed, forty-eight aircraft shot down and a further twenty-four damaged. In unseen ways, however, the raid had served its purpose. It convinced Stalin that opening a Second Front was an impossibility for the present. It also confirmed that when the Western Allies did invade France they could not rely upon capturing a heavily defended harbour. They therefore decided that they would land across open beaches, bringing their own prefabricated harbour with them. Every aspect of the tactical battle at Dieppe was carefully analysed and special-purpose armoured vehicles were developed to deal with the various assault engineering problems that had been encountered. Working within the overall framework of Major General P. C. S. Hobart's 79th Armoured Division, on D Day they operated in teams on the British and Canadian sectors of the Normandy landing beaches. Thanks to their presence, British and Canadian casualties amounted to only 4,200 killed, wounded and missing, a fraction of those which had been anticipated. As an investment, therefore, the cost of Operation Jubilee had been tragically high, yet the dividend it paid was the saving of many more lives.

First and Second Alamein

It is said that victory in battle goes to the side that makes fewer mistakes. During the Battle of Gazala/Knightsbridge, lasting from 26 May to 21 June 1942, Rommel certainly made mistakes, but those of his opponents were more frequent and of greater consequence. The result was that the British Eighth Army sustained the greatest defeat in its history, being forced to abandon Cyrenaica and retreat pell-mell deep into Egypt. Almost in passing, it seemed, Rommel stormed Tobruk on 20–21 June and was rewarded with his field marshal's baton. Believing that the British were well and truly broken, he then maintained a deliberately close pursuit, thereby hoping to deny them time in which to recover.

On 25 June General Sir Claude Auchinleck, Commander-in-Chief Middle East, assumed personal command of the Eighth Army. Jumbled together, British, Italian and German units straggled eastwards. The British retreat ended at the little town of El Alamein, about 60 miles west of Alexandria, where the negotiable desert narrowed to a 35-mile-wide strip bounded on the north by the sea and on the south by the impassable shifting sands and salt marshes of the Quattara Depression, lying below sea level. Within this strip ran three ridges, running more or less from east to west, Meteiriya in the north, Ruweisat some miles to the south, and Alam Halfa to the south-east. None were more than a swelling in the stony, grey-brown desert, but the overview they offered made their possession extremely important.

The series of engagements collectively known as the First Battle of Alamein began on 1 July and lasted for twenty-seven days. Auchinleck's object was first to halt the Axis advance, then break through to the west; Rommel's was to break through to Alexandria, Cairo and the Suez Canal. Auchinleck was assisted by the fact that the Eighth Army was now fighting much closer to its supply bases, while Rommel was hindered by a tenuous supply line that stretched as far back as Tripoli. Both sides mounted local attacks that were met by counter-attacks and although each received reinforcements during the battle neither was strong enough to impose a decision on the other.

Ruweisat Ridge was the scene of particularly heavy fighting. On the night of 14 July the 2nd New Zealand and 4th Indian Divisions mounted attacks from the south-east against, respectively, Points 63 and 64 on the ridge, which was held by the Italian Brescia and Pavia Divisions. Both objectives were taken, together with a large number of prisoners. Unfortunately, several pockets of resistance had been bypassed, including the night leaguer of the 8th Panzer Regiment.

First light on 15 July found the 4th New Zealand Brigade holding the western end of Ruweisat Ridge with the 5th New Zealand Brigade approximately one mile to the east. The rest of their division was still in the area of the previous night's start line, six miles to the south-east, and too far away to give immediate support. To make matters worse, the hard, rocky surface of the ridge made digging in very difficult. Worse still was the absence of 22nd Armoured Brigade, which was to have protected the New Zealanders against counter-attack. It was typical of the free and easy unorthodoxy that had affected the Eighth Army's operations for some months that 1st Armoured Division, to which the brigade belonged, placed a broad interpretation on the orders it had received and had sent it off on a fruitless errand to the south during the night.

Shortly after dawn the 8th Panzer Regiment attacked the 5th New Zealand Brigade, overrunning the 22nd Battalion before making off to the south-west with 350 prisoners before 22nd Armoured Brigade could intervene. Rommel, seriously alarmed by the British thrust into his centre, quickly formed a battle group which attacked the 4th New Zealand Brigade at 17:00 and came close to overwhelming it before 22nd Armoured Brigade went into action at 18:15, halting further German progress eastwards. Point 63 was therefore lost, although when the German attack was resumed next day it was broken up with the loss of twenty-four tanks by the combined efforts of 5th Indian and 1st Armoured Divisions, supported by the corps artillery.

Two New Zealanders were awarded the Victoria Cross as a result of this series of actions. The first was won by Sergeant Keith Elliott of the 22nd Battalion, who had already served in Greece and Crete, where he was wounded, as well as being captured and escaping during Operation Crusader. At Ruweisat, Elliott's battalion was not only under attack from three sides by the 8th Panzer Regiment, but also by Italian infantry. The *London Gazette* of 24 September 1942 describes his part in the action:

Under heavy tank, machine-gun and shell fire, Sergeant Elliott led the platoon he was commanding to the cover of a ridge 300 yards away, during which he sustained a chest wound. Here he re-formed his men and led them to a dominating ridge a further 500 yards away, where they came under heavy machine-gun and mortar fire. He located enemy machine-gun posts to his front and left flank and while one section attacked on the right flank, Sergeant Elliott led seven men in a bayonet charge across 500 yards of open ground in the face of heavy fire.

They captured four enemy machine-gun posts and an anti-tank gun, killing a number of the enemy and taking 50 prisoners. His section then came under fire from a machine-gun post on the left flank. He immediately charged this post single-handed and succeeded in capturing it, killing several of the enemy and taking 15 prisoners. During these two assaults he sustained three more wounds in the back and legs. Sergeant Elliott refused to leave his men until he had re-formed them, handed over his prisoners – now increased to 130 – and had arranged for his men to rejoin their battalion.

Owing to Sergeant Elliott's quick grasp of the situation, great personal courage and leadership, 19 men, who were the only survivors of B Company of his battalion, captured and destroyed five machine-guns, one anti-tank gun, killed a great number of the enemy and captured 130 prisoners. Sergeant Elliott sustained only one casualty among his men and brought him back to the nearest advanced dressing station.

On his release from hospital, Elliott was presented with his VC by Lieutenant General Bernard Montgomery, the new army commander, and was commissioned second lieutenant by Major General Bernard Freyberg, commanding the 2nd New Zealand Division. Such were his injuries, however, that he returned to New Zealand in October 1942 and was invalided out of the army in December the following year. On his discharge he became a priest in the Church of England.

The second VC of this action was awarded to Captain Charles Upham of the 20th Battalion, and since he was only one of three men to have received the award twice, some slight digression is worth while. Upham was born in Christchurch, New Zealand, in 1908. He worked in the high sheep country and, having graduated from agricultural college, became in turn a farm manager then a farm valuer. He joined the New Zealand Army in October 1939 and was commissioned as second lieutenant in November 1940. While essentially a quiet, modest man, his qualities have been described as outstanding powers of leadership, tactical skill, indifference to danger and quick-thinking resourcefulness. His physical and mental tenacity was remarkable even in a notably tough division and he fought with a profound belief in his cause. Taken together, these characteristics made him one of the war's most outstanding infantry officers.

Upham served with his battalion in Greece and later in Crete, where, during the German airborne invasion of the island, he was awarded his first Victoria Cross for a series of actions between 22 and 30 May 1941. The story of these is based upon the citation contained in the *London Gazette* of 10 October 1941.

Upham commanded a forward platoon in the attack on the German paratroops holding Maleme and its adjacent airfield on 22 May and fought his way forward for over 300 yards, unsupported by any other arms and against a defence strongly organised and in depth. During this operation his platoon destroyed numerous enemy posts, but on three occasions were temporarily held up. In the first case, under heavy fire from a machine-gun nest, he advanced to close quarters with pistol and grenades, so demoralising the occupants that one of his section was able to mop up the post with ease. Another of his sections was then held up by two machine-guns in a house. He placed a grenade through the window, killing the crew of one machine-gun and several more of the enemy, the other machine-gun being silenced by the fire of his sections. In the third case he crawled to within 15 yards of a machine-gun post and killed the gunners with a grenade.

When his company withdrew from Maleme he helped to carry a wounded man out under fire and, together with another officer, rallied more men to carry the wounded out. He was then sent to bring in another company which had become isolated. With a corporal he went over 600 yards through enemy-held territory, killing two Germans on the way, found the company and brought it back to the battalion's new position. But for this action it would have been completely cut off.

During the following two days his platoon occupied an exposed position on forward slopes and was continuously under fire. Second Lieutenant Upham was blown over by one mortar shell and painfully wounded by a piece of shrapnel behind his left shoulder by another. He disregarded this wound and remained on duty. He also received a bullet in the foot. The bullet was later removed in Egypt.

At Galatas on 25 May his platoon was heavily engaged and came under severe mortar and machine-gun fire. While the platoon remained under cover of a ridge, Second Lieutenant Upham went forward, observed the enemy, and brought the platoon forward when the Germans advanced. The platoon killed over forty of the enemy with its fire and grenades, forcing the remainder to fall back.

When his platoon was ordered to retire he sent it back under the platoon sergeant, setting himself the task of warning other troops that they were in danger of being cut off. As he left to rejoin his own platoon he was fired on by two Germans. He fell and shammed death, then crawled into a position where, having the use of only one arm, he could use his rifle by resting it on a tree. As the Germans came forward he killed one, then, reloading with one hand, killed the second at such close range that the man actually hit the muzzle of his rifle as he fell.

On 30 May, at Sphakia, his platoon was ordered to deal with a party of the enemy that had advanced down a ravine to a point near the New Zealanders' headquarters. Although in an exhausted condition, he climbed a steep hill, placed his men in positions overlooking the ravine, and reached the summit with a Bren and two riflemen. When the enemy appeared, twenty-two of them were killed or wounded at a range of 500 yards and the rest dispersed in panic.

During these operations Upham was suffering from dysentery and able to eat very little. As the citation in the *Gazette* concludes: 'He showed superb coolness, great skill and dash, and complete disregard of danger. His conduct and leadership inspired his whole platoon to fight magnificently throughout, and in fact was an inspiration to the battalion.'

Having recovered from his wounds, Upham rejoined the 20th Battalion and by the time of the Ruweisat operation had reached the rank of captain and was commanding a company. The citation for the Bar to his Victoria Cross did not appear in the *London Gazette* until 26 September 1945, three weeks after the war had ended. In fact, so rare was the award of a second VC to the same individual that when King George VI received the recommendation that Upham should receive it, he was so startled that he asked Major General Howard Kippenberger, a veteran of the 2nd New Zealand Division's battles, whether it was deserved. Kippenberger's reply was unequivocal: 'In my respectful opinion, sir, Upham has won the VC several times over.' The citation describes the action resulting in the award:

> During the opening stages of the attack on the ridge, Captain Upham's company formed part of the reserve battalion, but when communications with the forward troops broke down and he was instructed to send up an officer to report the progress of the attack, he went out himself, armed with a Spandau machine-gun and, after several sharp encounters

with enemy machine-gun posts, succeeded in bringing back the required information. Just before dawn the reserve battalion was ordered forward, but when it had almost reached its objective very heavy fire was encountered in front of a strongly defended enemy locality containing four machine-gun posts and a number of tanks.

Captain Upham, without hesitation, at once led his company in a determined attack on the two nearest strongpoints on the left flank. His voice could be heard above the din of battle, cheering on his men and, with heavy casualties on both sides, the objective was captured. During this engagement, Captain Upham himself destroyed a German tank and several guns and vehicles with grenades and, although he was shot through the elbow and had his arm broken, he went on again to a forward section and brought back some of his men who had become isolated. He continued to dominate the situation until his men had beaten off a violent enemy counter-attack and consolidated the vital position which they had won under his inspiring leadership.

Exhausted by pain and weak from loss of blood, Captain Upham was then removed to the regimental aid post, but immediately his wound had been dressed he returned to his men, remaining with them all day long under heavy artillery and mortar fire until he was again severely wounded. Being now unable to move, he fell into the hands of the enemy when, his gallant company having been reduced to only six survivors, his position was finally overrun by superior enemy forces, in spite of the outstanding gallantry and magnificent leadership shown by Captain Upham.

After treatment in an Italian hospital Upham became a prisoner of the Germans. He decided to cause them as much trouble as possible and escaped on three occasions. Finally, he was classified as being dangerous and was sent to Colditz Castle. There he met another VC recipient, Lieutenant Colonel Charles Merritt of the South Saskatchewan Regiment. Together with others, the two decided that if the Third Reich lost the war, the fate of the prisoners within the castle would be uncertain. Steps were therefore taken for the prisoners to fight as an organised unit, should the need arise.

On his return to New Zealand in September 1945, Upham was embarrassed by the acclaim he received and strove to avoid publicity. In recognition of his achievements the people of Canterbury collected £10,000 to purchase a farm for him but he would have none of it, insisting that the money be used to fund an educational scholarship for the children of returned soldiers. He resumed sheep farming in an isolated area to the north of Christchurch, where he died on 22 November 1994. His war experiences had left him with so deep-seated a dislike of his old enemies that he would not allow a German-made car on his property, let alone German machinery.

Both sides had now consolidated their positions at El Alamein with extensive minefields. Nevertheless, the first attack on Ruweisat Ridge had come so close to success that it was decided to make a further attempt. On the night of 21–22 July the New Zealanders and the Indians attacked again and secured positions on the ridge. At first light the 6th New Zealand Brigade was counter-attacked by German armour and overrun. Once more, the 22nd Armoured Brigade should have been present to fend off the counter-attack but, for various reasons, it was not. The failure was compounded by the virtual destruction of two regiments of the recently arrived 23rd Armoured Brigade, who, it was cynically believed, would be less aware of the risks involved than more experienced formations. The attack of the two regiments, the 40th and 46th Royal Tank Regiments, was to have been made after the ridge had been secured, and should therefore have been cancelled. It was not and on the morning of 22 July it went in along an axis parallel to and south of the ridge in the hope that it would break through the German line and exploit beyond. In the event, eighty-six of the ninety-seven tanks employed were lost either in crossing an uncleared minefield or to the enemy's tanks and anti-tank gun screens.

Simultaneously, to the north, the 9th Australian Division had launched an attack in the area of Tel el Eisa (Jesus Hill), taking part of the tel and gaining ground elsewhere. During this action Private Arthur Gurney of the 2/48th Battalion won a posthumous Victoria Cross. At one point his company was pinned down by the fire of several machine-gun posts, less than 100 yards ahead. All the company's officers were either killed or wounded and heavy casualties were being sustained. On his own initiative Gurney charged one post, bayoneting the three occupants, then the next post, where he bayoneted two men and sent the third back as a prisoner. At this point he was blown to the ground by the explosion of a stick grenade. Getting to his feet, he charged a third post and was last seen using the bayonet vigorously. When his company resumed its attack, inflicting heavy losses on the enemy, Gurney's body was found inside the post.

During the evening, the Australian 2/48th Battalion was ordered to renew the attack with Meteiriya Ridge as its objective, supported by the third regiment of 23rd Armoured Brigade, 50th RTR. The tanks, untrained in infantry/tank co-operation, reached the objective alone, while 2/48th mistakenly dug in 2,500 yards to the rear. At dusk 50 RTR, which had come under intense anti-tank fire, was able to disengage, having lost twenty-three tanks.

By now, the relationship between the Commonwealth infantry divisions and the British armour had become one of mutual distrust, although, as we have seen, there were faults on both sides and bad staff work had been responsible for some of the misunderstandings. By 27 July both sides were exhausted and the battle tailed off. British losses amounted to about 13,000 men and 193 tanks, while those of the Axis were 22,000 (including 7,000 prisoners) and about 100 tanks.

Early in August, Auchinleck was replaced as Commander-in-Chief Middle East by General Sir Harold Alexander and Lieutenant General Bernard Montgomery assumed command of the Eighth Army. Montgomery ruthlessly set about reimposing operational orthodoxy, simultaneously convincing his troops that Rommel could and would be beaten, and building up his strength until he could be certain of mounting a decisive offensive.

While the British had been guilty of mistakes at the operative and tactical levels, it was now apparent to Rommel that he had committed a major strategic blunder by advancing so far into Egypt. His seaborne lifeline from Italy was coming under increasing pressure from the RAF and the Royal Navy's submarines, and such fuel as did reach Tripoli was largely consumed on the long haul to the front. The amount of fuel actually reaching the Axis army amounted to little more than its daily administrative requirements. By the end of August, however, a sufficient reserve had been accumulated for Rommel to make one last desperate attempt to break through. His attack began during the night of 30–31 August. Its course had been accurately predicted and, although the Afrika Korps managed to break through the minebelts on the southern sector of the front, when it swung north it encountered a rock-solid defence at Alam Halfa Ridge and was forced to retire into its own lines having sustained the loss of 49 tanks and other fighting vehicles, 60 guns, 400 transport vehicles and 2,800 casualties.

Following this reverse, Rommel found himself in a strategic straitjacket. Starved of fuel, he lacked the means either to mount another offensive or retreat into Libya, since the latter would involve a return to mobile warfare. Montgomery, fully aware of his opponent's dilemma, planned what he called a 'crumbling' battle, in which, by attacking first in one sector and then another, he would force Rommel to burn priceless fuel as he committed his armour to counter-attacks. Once that fuel had gone, the Axis army could not survive in the desert and would be destroyed. Resisting political pressure to launch his attack at the earliest possible moment, Montgomery concentrated upon building up the Eighth Army's strength and refining its battle drills.

By the third week of October all was ready. On the northern sector of the line was XXX Corps, commanded by Lieutenant General Sir Oliver Leese. This consisted of the 9th Australian, 51st (Highland), 2nd New Zealand, 1st South African and 4th Indian Divisions. Armoured support would be provided by the 23rd Armoured Brigade, now four regiments strong and equipped with Valentine infantry tanks, which had established a close working relationship with each of the infantry divisions and thereby restored the latter's confidence that tanks would be present when they were needed. Behind and overlaying XXX Corps' rear areas was Lieutenant General H. Lumsden's X Corps, containing the 1st and 10th Armoured Divisions. On the southern sector of the front was XIII Corps, commanded by Lieutenant General B. G. Horrocks. This consisted of the 7th Armoured, 50th and 44th Divisions, plus one Greek and two Free French brigade groups. A many-faceted and successful deception plan was mounted to convince the enemy that the principal blow would be delivered on the southern rather than the northern sector of the front.

The Second Battle of Alamein began at 21:40 on 23 October with a heavy bombardment fired by 592 guns. Under its flickering light the shadowy figures of the mineclearing parties and infantry rose from their slit trenches and moved forward, followed slowly by their supporting Valentines. The enemy's defence of his minefields was stubborn in the extreme. Progress was slower than had been anticipated and although gains were mainly piece by piece the British armour was at first unable to debouch from the lanes that had been cleared for it in the Meteiriya and Kidney Ridge areas.

On the night of 25–26 October, Private Percival Gratwick of the Australian 2/48th Battalion won the first Victoria Cross of the battle. The background to his action is described in the British official history:

The objectives – Point 29 and the 'high' ground to the right of it – lay north and north-east at about one mile's distance. Point 29 was in itself an inconsiderable feature, but one which in the almost featureless surroundings had value as an observation post. The task was given to the 26th Australian Infantry Brigade (Brigadier D. A. Whitehead) supported by 40 RTR with about thirty fit Valentines, and two medium and five field regiments of artillery. One thousand rounds of medium shell and fourteen thousand of 25-pdr were allotted for the artillery's programme. The Australian plan was simple: at midnight 2/48th Battalion was to advance north and capture Point 29, and forty minutes later 2/24th was to advance north-east to its own objective. The artillery, besides firing a counter-battery programme, was to put down timed concentrations for each battalion in turn, and the tanks were to stand by to meet a counter-attack at first light. This neat plan came off exactly, and both battalions took their objectives after short fights, and with them about 240 prisoners.

Execution of the plan was not quite as simple as the official historian suggests. The company of 2/48th to which Gratwick belonged ran into determined opposition, and his own platoon was met with intense, short-range fire that killed the platoon commander, his sergeant and many others. The remnant of the platoon, amounting to seven men, was pinned down. Gratwick observed that the fire was coming from two posts. On his own initiative he charged the nearer of the two, hurling grenades that killed its occupants, including a complete mortar crew. He then charged the second and larger post, inflicting further casualties, but was killed by a burst of machine-gun fire as he was about to tackle the occupants with his rifle and bayonet. His company immediately resumed its attack, cleaning out the objective.

By 26 October, Major General R. Briggs's 1st Armoured Division had reached Kidney Ridge. Two miles west of the ridge lay the Rahman Track, which ran from north to south and provided the Axis army with its principal means of lateral communication. Briggs was determined to sever this but the ground between the ridge and the track was dangerously open. During the night of 26–27 October he sent out the 2nd Rifle Brigade, commanded by Lieutenant Colonel Victor Turner, to secure an intervening locality codenamed Snipe, the intention being that this would serve as a firm base for a renewed divisional thrust westwards.

2nd Rifle Brigade was a motor battalion, which meant that while it was much smaller than a standard infantry battalion, it possessed more anti-tank and machine-guns and tracked carriers. The battalion's personnel were old desert hands with a highly developed *esprit de corps*. For this operation, Turner's thirteen available 6-pdr anti-tank guns were reinforced with six more manned by 239 Battery of 76th Anti-tank Regiment, Royal Artillery. The battalion moved off at 23:00, but thanks to a combination of darkness and navigational errors it reached a position half a mile south of that intended. This proved to be providential, for the position consisted of a hollow measuring 900 yards by 400 yards. Turner deployed his anti-tank guns around the perimeter and had them camouflaged with scrub while the battalion's carrier carried out a reconnaissance. It was soon apparent that the outpost had been established in dangerously close proximity to the tank leaguers of the 15th Panzer Division and the Italian Littorio Armoured Division.

At about 03:45 the tank leaguers began to break up. Shortly after, Outpost Snipe scored its first kill, at 30 yards range, against the leading tank of a column that was heading in all innocence for the hollow. Simultaneously, a tracked tank destroyer was knocked out and the rest of the column scattered to await the coming of first light. When it did, Outpost Snipe's real work began. Under constant fire, including that of its own side on two occasions, the outpost killed tanks and other fighting vehicles throughout the day and on into last light, fighting off repeated attacks by tanks and infantry until the hollow became a shambles of smashed guns, carriers and jeeps, dead and dying.

A particularly serious attack was launched against the south-western sector of the defences by eight Italian tanks and an assault gun at 13:00. The only gun that would bear was that of Sergeant Charles Calistan. Turner, acting as his loader, told Calistan to wait until the enemy had closed to within 600 yards. In quick succession, six of the tanks were hit and began to burn. Calistan was now down to his last two rounds with the surviving three enemy vehicles bearing down on him. His platoon commander, Lieutenant J. E. B. Toms, ran across 100 yards of bullet-swept ground to fetch his jeep, which had four boxes of ammunition aboard. Heedless of the fact that the jeep was hit and on fire, Toms somehow survived and delivered his precious load. At this point, Turner's helmet was penetrated by a shell splinter and he was placed in some cover, where he remained conscious and demanded to know what was happening. Calistan and Toms had meanwhile returned to business, knocking out the last three Italian vehicles with three shots, the last within 200 yards of the perimeter. 'Good show!' shouted Turner when he was told. 'A hat trick!' Calistan, a very cool individual indeed, placed a can of water on the burning jeep to make tea for the three of them.

During the afternoon, 21st Panzer Division reached the area. The Axis armour, however, had been ordered to attack Briggs's armoured brigades back on the ridge. In doing so, it exposed its vulnerable side armour to fire from Outpost Snipe; conversely, when it turned to attack the outpost, it exposed its flanks to the fire of the armoured brigades, and thus piled up casualties to no purpose. At one point, when it seemed as though a very determined attack by fifteen tanks would overrun the only three guns in their path and break into the hollow, Turner gave orders for the maps and codes to be burned. Four were knocked out at 200 yards, and then two more, the last just 100 yards from the muzzles. The remainder reversed into a depression some 800 yards distant, from which they continued to fire until dusk. Had they but known it, their opponents were down to three rounds per gun.

Towards evening, Turner began to hallucinate and command was assumed by his adjutant, Captain F. W. Marten, who was now the battalion's senior surviving officer. With the coming of last light comparative calm descended upon the battlefield. At 23:00 Marten was given permission to abandon Snipe. The more seriously wounded were placed aboard three jeeps and six carriers, all that remained of the battalion's transport, and the walking wounded were supported by their comrades in a small column, 200 strong, that trudged back towards their own lines. Only one 6-pdr, belonging to 239 Battery, could be brought out, the rest being rendered unusable by the removal of their breech-blocks and sights. Altogether, the riflemen and gunners had sustained a total of seventy-two casualties.

The story of the defence of Outpost Snipe was greeted with awe and even disbelief throughout the Eighth Army, so much so that a special commission of inquiry visited the hollow a month after the battle to examine the wreckage that surrounded it. Its conclusions were that 21 German and 11 Italian tanks, plus 5 assault guns or tank destroyers, had been destroyed outright, and that a further 15, possibly 20, tanks had been knocked out and recovered, although it doubted whether many of these could have been repaired by the time the battle ended.

Turner received the Victoria Cross. His brother had received the award for an action in France in 1915, but died shortly afterwards of the wounds received. There was also a family connection with General Sir Redvers Buller, VC. After the war, Turner served with the Yeomen of the Guard 1950–67 and was Lieutenant of Her Majesty's Body Guard 1967–70. Sergeant Calistan, already a holder of the Military Medal, was recommended for the Victoria Cross, and in an earlier era would certainly have received it, but by now the stricter regulations governing the award were such that it was denied. In its place he received the Distinguished Conduct Medal and, subsequently, a commission. He was killed during the Italian campaign. More decorations were awarded to those selected from the many who had earned them at Outpost Snipe.

In accordance with his 'crumbling' strategy, Montgomery decided to switch the emphasis of the battle back to the north. On the night of 28–29 October the 9th Australian Division attacked the base of an enemy salient at the northern end of the line, destroying one battalion of the 125th Panzergrenadier Regiment and all but isolating another, together with a Bersaglieri battalion, in a heavily defended locality known as Thompson's Post. The fighting had been extremely bitter, resulting in heavy casualties, but despite this the assault was renewed on the night of 30–31 October, cutting the railway and coast road. This had the desired result, provoking a counter-attack by the 21st Panzer and 90th Light Divisions. In an extremely gallant action lasting most of the day, this was stood off by 40 RTR and the 6-pdrs of 289 Anti-tank Battery, Royal Artillery, supported by field artillery concentrations and bombing. During the night the trapped Panzergrenadiers and Bersaglieri escaped along the shore.

At one stage during the fighting the commanding officer of the Australian 2/48th Battalion, Lieutenant Colonel H. H. Hammar, doubted whether more than sixty fit men remained to him. However, one member of the battalion, Sergeant William Kibby, had added another Victoria Cross to its hard-fighting record, although, sadly, this award was also posthumous. It was made, not for one single act, but for continuous gallantry throughout the battle. Kibby was the platoon sergeant of No. 17 Platoon and when its commander was killed during the early hours of the first attack on 23 October, he took over. When the platoon found itself pinned down by fire from an enemy post, he charged with his tommy-gun, killing three of the occupants and capturing twelve more. During the counter-attacks that followed the capture of Point 29 on 26 October, Kibby not only toured his sections regularly to encourage the men and direct their fire, but also went out on several occasions, under heavy fire, to repair the telephone line to the mortar position, enabling accurate concentrations to be fired on the enemy attacking his company's front. On the night of 30–31 October the platoon was cut to pieces by point-blank machine-gun fire as it stormed its way forward. At length, only one pocket of resistance separated its survivors from their objective. Kibby went forward alone, hurling grenades into the enemy post, but was killed by a burst of machine-gun fire. It was entirely due to his outstanding courage and tenacity that his company was able to take the position.

Having concentrated Rommel's attention firmly on the coastal sector,

Montgomery mounted a fresh attack, codenamed Supercharge, in the area of Kidney Ridge. During the early hours of 2 November the 2nd New Zealand Division, supported by 23rd Armoured Brigade, broke through the last of the minefields. The second phase, commencing shortly before first light, saw the 9th Armoured Brigade destroying the enemy's anti-tank gun screen and sacrificing eighty-seven of its ninety-four tanks in the process. The third phase resulted in a day-long tank battle between the 1st Armoured Division and the Axis armour, which had rushed to contain the penetration. The British lost the greater number of tanks, but the Italian armour was completely destroyed and the Afrika Korps had been reduced to twenty-four tanks.

Ignoring Hitler's unrealistic orders to stand fast, Rommel began disengaging the rump of his army on the night of 3–4 November and commenced the retreat that would take him across North Africa to Tunisia, hurried on his way by the news that the Anglo-American First Army had landed in Morocco and Algeria on 8 November. His losses at Second Alamein amounted to 450 tanks, 1,000 guns and 84 aircraft, plus 55,000 personnel casualties, including 30,000 prisoners, of whom nearly 11,000 were German. The Eighth Army sustained 13,500 casualties, including approximately 4,500 killed, the majority being incurred by the infantry divisions. About 500 of its tanks had been knocked out, of which all but 150 were repairable, and 110 guns destroyed, the majority of which were anti-tank guns. In the air, 77 British and 20 American aircraft were lost.

Guadalcanal

7 AUGUST 1942 – 7 FEBRUARY 1943

In the Pacific, where distances were immense, air power was of paramount importance and therefore any piece of land upon which an airstrip could be constructed was of immense strategic significance. At the Battle of Midway, 4–6 June 1942, the efficient Japanese naval air arm, which had rampaged triumphant across the Pacific and Indian Oceans for six months in the aftermath of Pearl Harbor, was dealt a crippling blow when four of its powerful fleet carriers were sent to the bottom in exchange for only one American carrier. With Japan now placed firmly on the defensive, it was important to her that airstrips should be built wherever possible to harry the anticipated American drive across the Pacific.

When the threat of Japanese occupation became apparent, most Western civilians in the islands of the South Pacific were evacuated. Some courageous individuals, however, chose to remain behind and report by radio on enemy activity. Known as coastwatchers, they were fortunate in having the support of the indigenous population, for had it been otherwise they would quickly have fallen into Japanese hands and, at best, received a quick decapitation. In June 1942 one of these men, Captain Marcus Clemens, reported that the Japanese were constructing an airstrip near Lunga Point on the fetid, jungle-clad island of Guadalcanal, one of the British Solomon Islands group. Bombers stationed there could prey upon the supply route between the United States and Australia, as well as attack American bases in the New Hebrides. As the American Joint Chiefs of Staff were already planning to go over to the offensive in this area, it was decided that the airfield and the nearby island of Tulagi would be captured by Major General Alexander A. Vandergrift's 1st Marine Division, suitably reinforced.

The scene was now set for the first decisive battle that would involve the land, sea and air forces of both sides. On 7 August the Marines landed on Guadalcanal without difficulty and drove the enemy's construction troops off the partially finished airfield. The airfield itself, named Henderson Field in honour of Major Loftus Henderson, a marine officer who had been killed during the Battle of Midway, was completed on 20 July. The first elements of what became known as the Cactus Air Force began flying in immediately. In due course it would be used by fighter, bomber, torpedo and scout squadrons, although it was soon apparent that with the demands made upon it the site would quickly become congested, so a second airstrip, designated Fighter One, was constructed 2,000 yards to the east and opened for business on 9 September.

This was not a challenge that the Japanese could afford to ignore. Using fast destroyer transports, they landed troops at Taivu Point, east of Henderson Field, and at Kokumbona, to the west. By the middle of October the 20,000 troops they had put ashore had been designated the Seventeenth Army and placed under the command of Major General Haruyoshi Hyakutake. In overall terms, the Japanese strategy was to recapture the airfield and in the meantime to neutralise it by bombing from the air or bombardment from the sea. For the Americans, the object was to defend the airfield and then drive the Japanese off the island, which would serve as a stepping-stone for further advance. Neither side could afford to lose this battle, and both made every effort to win.

At sea, no less than seven major engagements were fought, so many ships being sunk off the northern coast of the island that the area became known as Ironbottom Sound. Usually it was the Japanese, more adept in night-fighting techniques and possessing the formidable Long Lance torpedo, who emerged the victors, although they were unable to retain control of the sea. On the night of 13–14 October, the battleships *Kongo* and *Haruna* managed to break through, landing 918 14-inch shells, plus many more of lesser calibre, on or around the two airstrips, although by dint of hard work the Americans quickly had them back in commission. In total, the United States and Royal Australian Navies lost twenty-four major warships, including two fleet carriers, while the Japanese Imperial Navy lost eighteen, including two battleships and a light carrier. However, while the Allied losses could be absorbed by the huge American shipbuilding programme, those of the Japanese were irreplaceable. This was also true of the large number of Japanese transport vessels destroyed by air attacks or American PT (Patrol-Torpedo) boats.

In the air, activity was almost continuous, with the fighters from Henderson Field taking a heavy toll of the enemy's bombers. What puzzled the Japanese bomber crews most was the fact that the American fighters were always waiting for them up-sun and ready to pounce as they approached the target area. Had they but known it, their progress down the Solomon chain was being reported by coastwatchers on other islands, so that the fighter squadrons were scrambled in plenty of time to intercept.

The first Medal of Honor to be awarded during the battle for Guadalcanal went to Captain John Lucian Smith, the commander of Marine Fighting Squadron 223 (VMF-223). Smith had originally joined the Marine Corps as an artilleryman, but after completing his flight training he became a dive-bomber pilot. After transferring to fighters he suddenly found himself commanding a squadron manned by young and recently qualified pilots with no combat experience. It was thanks to his thorough training that the squadron's Grumman 4F4-4s accounted for no less than eighty-three enemy aircraft between 21 August and 15 September, no less than sixteen of the enemy being accounted for by Smith personally. He left Guadalcanal on 11 October and was subsequently awarded the navy's Legion of Merit.

Another of the Cactus Air Force's squadron commanders to receive the Medal of Honor was Major Robert E. Galer of Marine Fighting Squadron 224 (VMF-224). Like Smith, Galer had to instil a sense of aggression into his young pilots. Yet, tough and demanding as he was, he understood that their initial nervousness in flying high-altitude combat missions was compounded by the tensions of being under virtual siege on the ground, where bombing and naval bombardment of the airfield, to say nothing of the continuous enemy threat beyond the perimeter, produced a state of constant fatigue, and recommended their regular rotation. He was himself shot down twice, on the first occasion landing his plane on the water, and on the second parachuting into the sea, to await rescue. His squadron accounted for twenty-seven enemy fighters and bombers in a period of twenty-nine days, of which he was personally responsible for eleven. Galer, who was also a recipient of Navy Cross and the Distinguished Flying Cross, finally retired from the Marine Corps with the rank of colonel.

Before proceeding further it is, perhaps, advisable to examine briefly the Japanese soldier's motivation and method, which differed radically from those of soldiers in other armies. The Japanese soldier believed that his life belonged to the Emperor, whom he regarded as a divine presence. He was hardy, long-suffering, ferociously disciplined, suicidally brave when attacking and he would fight to the death in defence. Since he regarded being taken alive by the enemy as the ultimate disgrace, he looked upon those who were unfortunate enough to fall into his hands as men without honour and treated them with sadistic contempt. He was expert at constructing and concealing defensive positions with local materials. His officers sometimes lacked imagination and would commit him to repeat attacks that had previously failed. He was at his best when he possessed air superiority; lacking this, his operations often went awry. His logistic system bordered on the medieval, concentrating on the delivery of ammunition at the expense of rations. Consequently, when he was winning he could feed on captured rations, but if he was not he went hungry. Likewise, his medical services were primitive.

On 19 August the Marines ambushed a Japanese patrol to the east of their perimeter. Among the captured documents was a marked map showing that part of the enemy's 28th Regiment, which had landed at Taivu under Colonel Kiyanao Ichiki, was about to attack the airfield. General Vandergrift was therefore able to reinforce the threatened sector in ample time. At 02:40 on 21 August, Ichiki, heedless of the lost patrol and unwilling to wait for the rest of his regiment to arrive, launched his attack with 500 men across the sandbar at the mouth of the Ilu River. The Japanese were cut to pieces but tried again, this time along the shore, at 05:00, with similar results. They then retired to a coconut plantation, where they were shelled and strafed from the air. At 15:00 Vandergrift counter-attacked against their flank and rear with the I/1st Marines, supported by five Stuart light tanks of the 1st Marine Tank Battalion. Only Ichiki, one other officer and a hundful of survivors made their way back to Taivu, where Ichiki, having burned the regimental colours, took his own life. The Marines lost thirty-five men killed and fifty wounded.

The arrival of the 28th's second echelon, together with most of the 124th Regiment, prompted the Japanese to try again, this time under the command of Major General Kiyotake Kawaguchi and against the Marines' southern perimeter. The assault force left Taivu in drenching rain on 6 September, its three-mile-long column making slow progress through the jungle. Unfortunately for them, history was about to repeat itself, for on 8 September Colonel Merritt Edson's 1st Marine Raider Battalion, the US Navy's equivalent of the British Commandos, mounted an amphibious raid on the village of Tasimboko, capturing documents that revealed details of the entire operation. Once again, Vandergrift was able to reinforce the threatened sector, subsequently known as Bloody Ridge, using the combined 1st Raider and 1st Parachute Battalions, plus additional artillery.

Instead of waiting for all his troops to arrive, or even permit those that had to rest after their long, tiring march, Kawaguchi fed them into a series of piecemeal attacks as they came up. These were easily contained, but on the night of 12–13 September he mounted a concentrated attack, supported by naval gunfire. Although great holes were torn in their ranks by the American artillery and riflemen, the Japanese pressed home their attack, forcing the defenders to pull back. Some of them even broke through to Vandergrift's command post, where they were killed by the general's escort, staff and clerks. By dawn, however, they had disappeared back into the jungle, leaving the bodies of 700 of their comrades behind. Recognising that his attack had failed, Kawaguchi embarked on a painful, eight-day withdrawal to the west, abandoning his heavy weapons and burdened by over 500 wounded. American losses amounted to fifty-nine killed and 204 wounded.

Two Medals of Honor were awarded for this action. The first went to Colonel Edson, who skilfully withdrew his troops to their reserve line with minimum casualties, then personally conducted its defence amid attacks that often ended in desperate hand-to-hand fighting. Edson had originally served with the 1st Vermont Infantry, a National Guard unit, on the Mexican frontier in 1916, then joined the Marines in 1917, where he quickly established his reputation as a crack shot and earned his pilot's wings. He won the Navy Cross while fighting against guerrillas in Nicaragua, the beard he grew in the jungle earning him his nickname of 'Red Mike'. In 1937 he served in China, where he was able to observe Japanese methods at first hand. During later stages of the fighting on Guadalcanal he commanded the 5th Marines. He went on to become the 2nd Marine Division's Chief of Staff at Tarawa, served as assistant divisional commander at Saipan and Tinian, spent nine months as the Fleet Marine Force Pacific's Chief of Staff, and ended the war as a major general in charge of Service Command. His last battle was political, as part of the successful campaign opposing President Harry S. Truman's proposal to wind up the Marine Corps. He retired to his native Vermont, where he served as Commissioner of Public Safety and was active in the National Rifle Association. His decorations included the British Distinguished Service Order.

The second of the Bloody Ridge Medals of Honor went to Major Kenneth D. Bailey, who was already a holder of the Silver Star. Bailey commanded the Raiders' C Company, which was originally placed in reserve. When those Japanese who broke through the main line surged past the right flank of his company, he used his entire weapon strength not only to close the gap but also to cover the withdrawal of the Raiders and paratroopers to the fall-back position, where he assisted Edson in halting the retreat and reorganising the troops, then extended the line to the left to prevent further infiltration. During this period he sustained a head wound, but continued to lead his men in the fierce hand-to-hand fighting that followed.

For the rest of September and into early October, Vandergrift tried to extend his western perimeter beyond the Matanikau River. These operations met with mixed success, depending as they did on separate units being able to co-ordinate their movements in the broken, jungle-clad terrain, and resulted in serious casualties. One such operation, under the overall control of Colonel Edson, involving the 1st Raider Battalion, now commanded by Lieutenant Colonel Samuel B. Griffith, and I/7th Marines under Lieutenant Colonel Lewis B. Puller, came close to disaster. On 27 September the Raiders, hoping to ford the Matanikau some distance upstream from its mouth, found their path blocked by a Japanese position. When they attempted to fight their way through this, Colonel Griffith was wounded and Major Bailey, now the battalion's executive officer, was killed. A badly phrased situation report reached Edson, who took it that the Raiders were encountering opposition in Matanikau village, beyond the river, and replanned the battle. While II/5th Marines were to hold the attention of the Japanese at the river mouth, the I/7th was to embark aboard Higgins boats and, after landing west of Point Cruz, attack the village from the rear.

The I/7th landed successfully, covered by fire from the destroyer *Ballard*, and had advanced to a ridge some 250 yards inland when, without warning, they were counter-attacked in strength from both flanks and cut off from the beach. Aboard the *Ballard*, Puller received details of the enemy's positions by means of signal flags and while the destroyer bombarded these he ordered his battalion to fight its way back to the beach, regardless of the cost. This it succeeded in doing while the Higgins boats, directed to return by Edson, closed in to the shore.

The petty officer in charge of a section of five boats, Signalman 1st Class Douglas A. Munro of the US Coastguard, was to be awarded a posthumous Medal of Honor for his action. Seeing the water whipped up by constant Japanese machine-gun fire, he reached the conclusion that a bloodbath would ensue unless he did something about it. Signalling the other boats to close up to the shore, he placed his craft between them and the identified source of the enemy fire, which he engaged with his two small guns. He was killed shortly before the evacuation was completed, but his crew, two of whom were wounded, continued to return the Japanese fire until the last boat had been loaded and left the beach.

The I/7th had brought their wounded out with them, but there could be no denying that the operation had failed, the total cost to the Marines being sixty killed and a hundred wounded. On the other hand, it had disrupted Japanese preparations for an attack across the Matanikau and inflicted considerable casualties, as did further operations in early October.

Shortly after, a third Medal of Honor was awarded to a member of the Cactus Air Force. It went to Lieutenant Colonel Harold W. Bauer, commanding Marine Fighting Squadron 212 (VMF-212). On 28 September, while on a preliminary visit to Guadalcanal, Bauer volunteered to fly a fighter during a heavy enemy air attack on the field, shooting down a bomber. On 3 October he did likewise, shooting down four enemy fighters while a fifth made off, trailing smoke. On 16 October he led his squadron's fly-in from Espiritu Santo, a 600-mile passage over water that left fuel tanks all but empty. As the squadron circled preparatory to landing on Fighter One, he observed that a formation of Japanese aircraft was attacking the destroyer *McFarland* and had already set a barge of aviation fuel ablaze. Without hesitation he dived in among them, shooting down four before he was forced to land through lack of fuel. He continued to provide vigorous leadership for his squadron, to whom he was known as The Coach. He was shot down over the sea on 14 November. He was last seen swimming amid the wreckage of his F4F, indicating to his pilots that they should return to base rather than linger above. His fate is unknown.

Both sides were now pouring reinforcements into the island, the Americans by day and the Japanese by night, the latter using nightly convoys of fast transports and destroyers that the Americans named the Tokyo Express. There were now some 30,000 Japanese on Guadalcanal, although this figure was not an indication of their potential as many were either suffering from wounds or the effect of tropical diseases. Nevertheless, a major offensive was planned. Using a trail cut through the jungle by engineers, Lieutenant General Masao Maruyama's 2nd Division would proceed from Kokumbona to a point south of the American perimeter. Operationally, the division was divided into two wings, the right commanded by Major General Kawaguchi and the left by Major General Yumio Nasu. Under cover of a diversionary attack across the mouth of the Matanikau River mounted by Major General Tadashi Sumoyoshi with 3,000 men and a tank company, the 2nd Division was to break through the Marines' perimeter, capture the airfields and drive the Americans into the sea.

Unfortunately, it took far longer than expected to cut the trail, the best that the troops could manage being six miles per day, even after the heavier guns had been left behind. Consequently, the date of the assault was repeatedly put back until 23 October was finally agreed upon. Kawaguchi then said he would not be in position until 24 October. Furious, Maruyama accepted the fact, but dismissed the unfortunate general, appointing Colonel Toshinaro Shoji in his place. In matters of face where high emotion was involved, Japanese senior officers sometimes lost sight of the overall picture. In this case, no one bothered to tell Sumoyoshi of the latest postponement and, as originally planned, he launched his diversionary attack on the evening of 23 October. The Americans, alerted by a probing attack and increased artillery fire, were ready for him. Eight of Japanese Type 97 medium and Type 95 light tanks, arguably the worst in the world, fell easy prey to the Marines' 37mm anti-tank guns as they crossed the sandbar. One survivor penetrated the American wire but sheered off in panic when it was engaged by an M3 half-track 75mm tank destroyer and drove into the sea, where it stalled and was destroyed. Deprived of their tank support, the Japanese infantry were mown down, 650 of them being killed. Three more tanks were later discovered across the river, apparently destroyed by artillery fire before they could get into action. Marine losses came to twenty-five men killed and fourteen wounded.

By now, the approach of Maruyama's division had been detected. On the night of 24–25 October the Japanese 29th Regiment assaulted Bloody Ridge, the scene of Kawaguchi's earlier defeat. As usual, the attack was pressed home with suicidal bravery, regardless of loss, its weight falling on Puller's I/7th Marines. As the pressure mounted, the III/164th Infantry, a recently arrived army regiment, moved up to reinforce the Marines and the line held. At first light the Japanese withdrew, leaving the slopes strewn with bodies.

During the fighting Sergeant John Basilone, an Italian-American from Raritan, New Jersey, won the Medal of Honor. As commander of two sections of the I/7th's machine-gun platoon, his fire was a critical factor in breaking up the enemy assaults. Having identified his position, the Japanese mortared it and made it a special target for their grenade throwers until one section's guns were put out of action and all but two of those manning them were either killed or wounded. Basilone brought up a reserve gun and emplaced it. He seemed to be everywhere, directing fire, repositioning guns to best advantage, clearing stoppages and replacing parts while bullets cracked past his ears. At length he was reinforced, but by now his ammunition supply had run dangerously low. Knowing that some of the enemy had infiltrated past his position, he ignored the risks and brought up fresh supplies with which to meet renewed attacks.

Before joining the Marines, Basilone had served with the army in the Philippines and because of this was known as Manila John. In 1943 he returned to Raritan to receive a hero's welcome and a $5,000 bond from the townspeople. He declined a commission and also the chance to remain in the United States, commenting that it wouldn't seem right if there was to be a landing on the Manila waterfront and Manila John wasn't present. Sergeant Basilone was killed by mortar fire on 19 February 1945 during the landing on Iwo Jima.

Throughout 25 October, Bloody Ridge was shelled at long range and sustained several air attacks. That night the Japanese attacked again, using their 16th and 29th Regiments, but were beaten off during heavy fighting that lasted until dawn. At one point, when an enemy break-through seemed likely, Marine Platoon Sergeant Mitchell Paige, commanding a machine-gun section, continued to direct the fire of his gunners until all his men were either killed or wounded. Alone and under constant fire, he fought his gun until it was destroyed, then moved from gun to gun, maintaining a steady fire on the advancing enemy. When reinforcements arrived, he led them in a bayonet charge that finally broke up the Japanese attack. He received the Medal of Honor for his actions throughout the engagement.

American casualties during the two nights' fighting came to 200 killed and a similar number wounded. Maruyama's losses, however, exceeded 2,000 in killed alone. Some of the survivors marched east to Koli Point under Shoji while Maruyama withdrew to Kokumbona with the rest. Vandergrift, anxious to expand the perimeter westwards and thereby force the enemy to withdraw his heavy artillery beyond the range of Henderson Field, mounted a successful offensive across the Matanikau on 1 November, trapping a considerable number of the enemy in a pocket at the base of Point Cruz, where they fought to the death. The hardest fighting fell to 1/5th Marines, who advanced along the beach against stiff opposition and were forced to beat off counter-attacks. The Medal of Honor was awarded to Corporal Anthony Casamento of the battalion's D Company, commanding a machine-gun section. When all the members of his section had been killed or wounded and he himself had sustained multiple wounds, he continued to provide fire support for the attack, destroying one enemy machine-gun emplacement to his front and suppressing the fire of another on his flank, as well as breaking up counter-attacks.

This operation was suspended when it was learned that reinforcements for Shoji were being landed at Koli Point. It was believed that a new Japanese offensive was about to begin, although the truth was that his strength was merely being augmented to the point that he would be able to march round the American perimeter and rejoin the main body of the Seventeenth Army. Nevertheless, on 3 November the II/7th Marines operating east of the perimeter, suddenly found themselves cut off and surrounded near Gavaga Creek. Vandergrift despatched the I/7th Marines, III/164th Infantry and supporting troops to relieve them. By 9 November the Japanese were themselves trapped between the II/7th and the relief force. By 12 November 350 of them had been killed although, led by Shoji, a larger number managed to slip through a gap in the American lines and escape inland, having abandoned their artillery and food supply. Vandergrift sent Lieutenant Colonel Evans F. Carlson's recently arrived 2nd Marine Raider Battalion, accompanied by native guides and porters, in pursuit. Carlson had much in common with Edson in that he also came from Vermont and had served in Nicaragua and China. In August his battalion had raided Makin Island, destroying stores and killing most of the garrison. Now, during a thirty-day period, it marched parallel to Shoji's column, picking off officers and NCOs and staging no less than twelve major ambushes before returning to its own lines, having killed approximately 500 of the enemy for the loss of only seventeen of its own men.

In the meantime, a fierce naval engagement, which would become known as the first phase of the Battle of Guadalcanal, had taken place during the night 12–13 November. The US Navy's cryptanalysts had already cracked the Japanese naval code and were able to predict that a heavy bombardment of Henderson Field would take place that night. It would be delivered by a force under Vice Admiral Hiroake Abe consisting of the battleships *Hiei* and *Kirishima*, the light cruiser *Nagara* and nine destroyers. To intercept it Rear Admiral Daniel J. Callaghan was directed westwards along the Guadalcanal coast with the heavy cruisers *San Francisco* and *Portland*, the light cruisers *Atlanta, Helena* and *Juneau* and eight destroyers. Callaghan flew his flag in *San Francisco*, which, during an air attack that afternoon, had lost twenty-four men killed and forty-five wounded when a crippled Japanese torpedo bomber had deliberately crashed on her stern, yet caused only minor damage. Also present was Rear Admiral Norman Scott, who had beaten the Japanese at the Battle of Cape Esperance a month earlier and was now flying his flag aboard *Atlanta*.

Callaghan has attracted criticism on a number of counts. Instead of deploying some of his destroyers to scout ahead, he deployed them fore and aft of the cruisers in his battle line. Again, while some of his ships possessed the most advanced surface radar sets, he attached little importance to the fact. Neither did he impose discipline on the TBS (Talk Between Ships) radio channel, which became choked with chatter at the expense of critical situation reports and orders.

At 01:24 on 13 October *Helena*'s radar picked up the approaching enemy. They were coming down from the north-west, intending to turn eastwards towards Henderson Field once they were south of Savo Island. Callaghan intended turning north to cross Abe's T but, because of cluttered communications, could not give the order to do so, as well as increasing speed to 20 knots, until 01:37. Furthermore, the execution of the manoeuvre was untidy and the American line became disorganised. It was also too late, for instead of crossing Abe's T, Callaghan found himself in the middle of the Japanese force. The result was a brutal, close-range mêlée in which gunfire and the enemy's powerful Long Lance torpedoes took a fearful toll.

At 01:50 *Atlanta*, leading the American cruisers, was illuminated by the searchlight of a Japanese destroyer. She immediately engaged the destroyer but was in turn engaged both by enemy battleships and more destroyers. She was quickly reduced to a shattered wreck with Admiral Scott and all but one of the officers on the bridge dead. Struck by two torpedoes, she became a disabled hulk. At this point Callaghan gave the order for the odd ships in his line to fire to starboard and even ships to port. This caused confusion in the already disordered American line as *Atlanta*, although an odd ship, had already opened fire to port. *San Francisco*'s first seven salvoes were directed at the enemy destroyers, but when a dark shape showed up ahead, she put two salvoes into it, setting it ablaze, then engaged the battleship *Hiei* to good effect, as did the cruisers behind, causing Abe to pull his battered flagship out of line. At this point Callaghan made the horrifying discovery that the dark shape his flagship had engaged was the hapless *Atlanta*. Shaken, he shouted: 'Cease fire! Own ships!' It was a meaningless order that was obeyed only by a few, and then briefly.

Suddenly, *San Francisco* was illuminated by a searchlight and became the target of accurate fire from the battleship *Kirishima*. The cruiser's steering was damaged and her speed was reduced as shells slammed into her. One salvo smashed into the navigating and signal bridges, killing or wounding everyone. Callaghan was not among the survivors. As the battle raged around her, three of her crew, Lieutenant Commander Bruce McCandless, Lieutenant Commander Herbert E. Schonland and Boatswain's Mate 1st Class Reinhardt J. Keppler, were to win the Medal of Honor.

In the aftermath of the explosions that had devastated the bridge, McCandless, the ship's communications officer, discovered that he alone was capable of standing. Although shaken and seriously wounded himself, he took over the wheel until replacement quartermasters arrived, and continued to fight the ship in such a manner that the rest of the American vessels, unaware that the admiral had been killed, continued to follow. After the action, through dint of good seamanship, he succeeded in bringing the badly damaged cruiser into harbour. Later, he commanded the destroyer *Gregory* during the Okinawa campaign and was awarded the Silver Star for conspicuous gallantry. He retired from the navy as an admiral in 1952.

Schonland was *San Francisco*'s damage control officer. He was working to reduce the quantity of water flooding into the hull through numerous shellholes when he was mistakenly told that he was the senior surviving officer. After making his way to the bridge, where he found that McCandless had assumed command, he returned to his task, working waist-deep in water by the light of hand-held lanterns while enemy shells continued to strike the ship. Once satisfied that the flooded compartments had all been drained or pumped out, restoring the cruiser's stability, he attended to further damage, including the rigging of the manual steering gear. He left the navy after the war and became a businessman in Nebraska.

Keppler's award was posthumous. That afternoon, when the Japanese torpedo bomber crashed into the after machine-gun platform, his capable supervision of the wounded undoubtedly saved many lives. During the battle, the hangar for the cruiser's scout aircraft was set ablaze. Leading a hose into the starboard side of the hangar, he tackled the blaze without assistance and finally brought it under control, ignoring the risks and the frequent explosion of enemy shells around him. At some stage he received a mortal wound, but he continued to direct fire-fighting parties and assist the wounded until he collapsed.

As fighting continued, the Long Lance torpedoes made their presence felt. *Portland* lost a large part of her stern to one, *Juneau*, struck in the forward engine room by another, was effectively out of the fight, and the destroyer *Barton* was blown apart by a double strike. Against this, many of the American ships had concentrated their fire against *Hiei* and inflicted crippling damage. Admiral Abe, his nerve broken by the sustained assault, limped away, as did the *Nagara*, aboard which fires could be seen raging, the scarcely damaged *Kirishima* and those destroyers that remained operational.

By 02:20 the battle was over. Two Japanese destroyers had been sunk and the *Hiei*, caught floundering north of Savo Island next morning, sustained such serious damage from the Cactus Air Force and aircraft from the carrier *Enterprise* that she was scuttled by her crew. The Americans had lost four destroyers, but further losses were to follow. *Atlanta* was taken in tow but was clearly sinking and was scuttled, while *Juneau* was torpedoed and sunk by a Japanese submarine. *San Francisco*, *Portland* and one destroyer required repairs that would take a long time to complete.

It was said by some that if Callaghan had survived he would have received a court martial. As it was, he received a posthumous Medal of Honor, and it could be argued that, at the cost of his own life, he had prevented a battleship bombardment that would have put Henderson Field out of commission for a critical period. Admiral Scott also received a posthumous Medal of Honor. A force of Japanese cruisers and destroyers did bombard Henderson Field on the night of 13–14 November, firing approximately 1,000 rounds in forty-five minutes, but the results were disappointing. Both sides moved fresh naval units into the area and a second surface action was fought the following night during which the *Kirishima* was sunk by the gunfire of the battleship *Washington*. The naval battle of Guadalcanal marked a turning point in the campaign, aggravating already strained relations between Japanese naval and military commanders.

On the ground, the Americans resumed their outward pressure, slowly but steadily increasing the size of their perimeter. In early December, Major General Alexander Patch and the leading elements of the US XIV Corps, which included the 2nd Marine, 25th and 43rd Infantry Divisions, began relieving Vandergrift and the 1st Marine Division. Many of the latter were so exhausted and ill that they were unable to climb the scramble nets of their transports, about one-third of them being declared unfit for further active service. Vandergrift was awarded the Medal of Honor for his conduct of the campaign and promoted lieutenant general. As commander of I Marine Amphibious Corps he led the landings on Bougainville in November 1943. The following year he returned home to become commandant of the Marine Corps.

The row between the Japanese generals and admirals became increasingly bitter as the month progressed. The generals complained that the Imperial Navy seemed unable to guarantee the delivery of reinforcements and supplies in the required quantities, while the admirals argued that whatever sacrifices the navy made the army seemed incapable of making progress. Although Guadalcanal had become a vast maw that swallowed men, warships and aircraft to no purpose, General Hideki Tojo, Japan's Prime Minister, wished to continue the campaign. However, Admiral Isoruku Yamamoto, the Imperial Navy's Commander-in-Chief, pointed out that the continued rate of attrition could not be maintained, for as well as the warships lost or damaged, 300,000 tons of merchant shipping had been sent to the bottom. Furthermore, in addition to the catastrophic losses incurred at Midway, a further 600 experienced naval pilots had been lost during the Guadalcanal operations. This view prevailed and on 31 December the Emperor sanctioned the abandonment of the island, the news being delivered to General Hyakutake by the Tokyo Express during the night of 14–15 January 1943.

During this period, a Medal of Honor was awarded to Captain Joseph J. Foss, the executive officer of Marine Fighting Squadron 121 (VMF-121). Aged twenty-seven, Foss was regarded as something of an old gentleman by the squadron's young pilots, but he quickly proved himself to be one of the most dangerous fighter pilots in the business. Between 9 October and 19 November he was credited with the destruction of twenty-three enemy aircraft, simultaneously flying escort missions covering bomber and reconnaissance operations. On 15 January he added three more kills to his score. On 23 January, while leading a formation of eight Marine F4Fs and four Army P38s, he tore into an escorted force of enemy bombers, personally shooting down four of the escort and causing the bombers to abandon their mission without dropping a single bomb. After the war he entered politics and served two terms as governor of his native South Dakota.

The Japanese decision to withdraw remained one of the war's best kept secrets. To General Patch, nothing seemed to have changed and the enemy even seemed to be on the point of mounting a fresh offensive. Nevertheless, he maintained the outward pressure begun by Vandergrift, slowly gaining ground against well-entrenched, determined resistance in the area of Mount Austen, to the south of the original perimeter. Here, on 10 January, two soldiers of the 35th Infantry's Company M, Sergeant

William G. Fourner and Technician Grade 5 Lewis Hall, won the posthumous award of the Medal of Honor. Two of Company M's light machine-guns and a squad of riflemen were posted on a knoll to cover Company K while it crossed a tributary of the Matanikau. Suddenly, a Japanese counter-attack swept over the knoll from behind, scattering the rifle squad, killed three of the gun crews and wounded the fourth, then disappeared down the hill to strike Company K in flank while it was strung out to cross the river. Although ordered to withdraw, Sergeant Fournier, who led the company's machine-gun section, ran forward to the guns, accompanied by Hall, and manned one of them. The Japanese were by now well down the slope leading to the stream and it was found that the gun would not depress sufficiently to engage them. Fournier therefore lifted it by its tripod mounting while Hall aimed and fired the weapon. Many of the enemy were mown down before they could mount their attack on Company K. The survivors scattered back into the jungle, but not before their return fire killed both men.

Two days later the II/27th Infantry mounted a two-company attack on a feature designated Hill 53. Some progress was made but the attack was stalled by a concealed enemy strongpoint on an intervening feature known as Sims Ridge. At great personal risk, Captain Charles W. Davis, the battalion's executive officer, located the strongpoint and called down mortar fire, although he was within 50 yards of the target. This, unfortunately, did not solve the problem and when night fell the ridge was still in enemy hands. Dawn found the strongpoint still full of fight. Davis, accompanied by four volunteers, crawled along the reverse slope of the ridge until they were within 10 yards of it. They were then spotted by the occupants, who flung grenades at them. The grenades failed to explode, whereas those thrown by the Americans did. Davis fired one round with his rifle, which jammed, then, drawing his pistol, led his party in a rush that overwhelmed the enemy survivors. Witnessing this, the battalion's Company E, which had hitherto been pinned down, launched a vigorous attack that finally swept the last of the Japanese off the ridge. Davis's act earned him the Medal of Honor.

In this way the battle continued day by day, with the Japanese conducting a fighting withdrawal in the direction of Cape Esperance. On 31 January Lieutenant Jefferson J. Deblanc was leading a six-strong section of Marine Fighting Squadron 112's fighters as escort for dive and torpedo bombers that were to attack enemy shipping. Fourteen thousand feet above the target area, the section became involved in a brawl with a large number of Zero fighters. In the midst of this, Deblanc picked up a call for assistance from the dive bombers, which had come under attack from enemy floatplanes at 1,000 feet. Breaking off, he dived into the Japanese formation, shooting down three of its aircraft and scattering the rest, enabling the dive and torpedo bombers to complete their mission. By now, he had become critically short of fuel and was heading for home when he discovered two Zeros on his tail. In a short, fierce action he destroyed them both, but in the process his own plane had sustained fatal damage. He was forced to bail out at too low an altitude and was killed as he landed among the trees in enemy-held territory. His action, witnessed by many, resulted in his receiving a posthumous Medal of Honor.

This high level of air activity was part of the Japanese deception plan, designed to convince the Americans that fighting was continuing as normal, when the truth was that large numbers of men were being evacuated each night by the destroyers of the Tokyo Express. Patch was simply aware that the enemy was withdrawing doggedly westwards along the coast. To cut off their retreat, the reinforced II/132nd Infantry was landed west of Cape Esperance on 1 February. For a week it was opposed stubbornly by the Japanese as it advanced eastwards, but at the end of that period it seemed as though the enemy had finally been trapped between the battalion and the rest of Patch's troops. However, when the Americans attacked during 8 and 9 February, they found that the last of the Japanese had gone, leaving behind abandoned positions and smashed equipment. The battle for Guadalcanal was over. It had cost the Americans 1,600 killed, 4,200 wounded and 12,000 incapacitated by disease. Japanese losses amounted to 14,000 killed in action, 9,000 dead from disease or starvation, an unknown number of wounded and 1,000 captured.

The entire complexion of the war had changed as a result of Guadalcanal. Having been given a foretaste of what to expect, the Japanese were now firmly on the defensive. Elsewhere, the German Sixth Army had just surrendered at Stalingrad, the last Axis presence in North Africa was about to be eliminated and, later in the year, Italy would be knocked out of the war. The road to final victory would be long and hard, but it was now possible for the Allies to take it with confidence.

Bloody Sunday – The Ploesti Raid

1 AUGUST 1943

In the late summer of 1943 most of the Balkan peninsula still remained firmly under German control. Greece and Albania were occupied, while in Yugoslavia the Wehrmacht was engaged in a bitter war with Tito's partisans. Bulgaria was a special case, for whereas its wily ruler, Tsar Boris, was prepared to grant Hitler certain concessions in return for conquered areas of Greek and Yugoslav territory, he was not prepared to commit himself to a full alliance. On the other hand, aware that he had to retain the Führer's goodwill, he had declared war on Britain and the United States, who were unlikely to do him any harm, but not on the Soviet Union, which could. Romania, however, whose de facto ruler was the fascist dictator General Ion Antonescu, was one of Hitler's firmest allies and of particular importance to the Third Reich as she possessed her own oil supply. By 1943 approximately 60 per cent of Germany's fuel requirements was produced in a complex of Romanian refineries around the town of Ploesti, situated in the foothills of the Carpathian mountains. In 1941 the Red air force had attacked the complex, without seriously affecting its production. The attack did, however, reveal its vulnerability. Under Luftwaffe Lieutenant General Alfred Gertensberg, the area was ringed by balloon barrages and numerous anti-aircraft guns of every type, while fighter squadrons were available to provide a rapid response to any intruders. In addition, dummy refineries were built to the east of the main complex. Subsequent Allied air activity over Ploesti confirmed the strength of the defences. Nevertheless, aware that some bombers might get through, the Germans activated contingency plans to keep the oil flowing, linking the refineries with a grid of pipelines so that if one was put out of action another could continue its work.

Oil being the lifeblood of modern war, the subject of Ploesti had come up at the Casablanca Conference in January 1943, attended by Winston Churchill and President Roosevelt. There it was agreed that to deny the enemy oil was to deny him the means to make war, and the Ploesti complex was, therefore, a natural target. Superficially, it seemed natural that it should be attacked by the Russians, since they were the closest. Against this, the Red air force was essentially a tactical force and did not possess a strategic bombing capability. Furthermore, it had its hands full, for in March the dashing advance that had followed the great Soviet victory at Stalingrad was brought to a costly standstill by von Manstein's brilliant counter-stroke and, for the moment, the Eastern Front had solidified again.

Ploesti lay beyond the range of a strike from the United Kingdom. It could, however, be reached from North Africa, and this possibility became a reality when the fighting there came to an end. The key to such an operation was the Consolidated Vultee B–24 Liberator long-range bomber. With a normal crew of ten, this four-engined aircraft had a longer range than any other land plane of its day, being capable of carrying a 5,000lb bomb load 2,200 miles at 190 mph. Its armament consisted of ten 0.50-inch Browning machine-guns, two in each nose, dorsal, ventral and tail turrets and one on each side of the waist. Its principal disadvantage was that it was something of a handful for the average pilot.

The raid on Ploesti was planned by the US Ninth Air Force under the codename of Tidal Wave. It was decided that the attack would be delivered at low level to achieve surprise and increase accuracy as well as reduce the risks of fighter interception and the time individual aircraft would be exposed to ground fire. Three bombardment groups flew in from England to join the two already in North Africa. Based on airfields around Benghazi, for several weeks they practised low-level attacks on a dummy refinery built in the desert.

After examining the various alternatives, the route selected to the target area left the Benghazi airfields on a northerly heading across the Mediterranean and Ionian Seas as far as the island of Corfu, then swung north-east across Albania, southern Yugoslavia and a corner of Bulgaria to enter Romania, the final run-in to Ploesti being made in a south-easterly direction. The distance on the outward leg was 1,060 miles and on the return leg 1,015 miles, a total of 2,075 miles that lay just within the Liberator's range, assuming all went well.

The Ploesti complex was sub-divided into seven targets – White 1: the Romana Americana refinery – 376th Bombardment Group in four waves of six aircraft; White II: the Concordia Vega refinery – part of 93rd Bombardment Group in three waves of six and one of three aircraft; White III: the Standard Petrol/Urinea Speranta installation – part of 93rd Bombardment Group with four waves of three aircraft; White IV: the Astra Romana/

Urinea/Orion refineries – 98th Bombardment Group with four waves of ten aircraft; White V: the Columbia Aquila refinery – part of 44th Bombardment Group with five waves of three aircraft; Blue: the Creditul Minier refinery – part of 44th Bombardment Group with three waves of six aircraft; Red: the Steaua Romana refinery – 389th Bombardment Group in eight waves of three aircraft.

This gave a total of 154 aircraft for the attack, but it was found that twenty-three uncommitted Liberators were also available, these being distributed among all the target forces save White IV, giving a new total of 177 aircraft. Their total high-explosive bomb load was 623,000lbs. Of this, twenty-four 1,000lb bombs were fitted with one- to six-hour and 364 with one-hour delay fuses, while thirty-six 500lb bombs were fitted with onc- to six-hour and forty-eight with one-hour delay fuses, the intention being to disrupt clearance and repair work and make life difficult for the enemy's bomb disposal teams. Forty-five-second delay fuses were fitted to another 386 of the 500lb bombs so that they would explode after penetrating the refineries' buildings and machinery. In addition, 290 boxes of incendiary bombs and 140 incendiary clusters were to be dropped.

At 05.30 on 1 August aircraft began taking off from Benghazi and the nearby Tocra airfields. One suffered immediate engine trouble and crash-landed, while another crashed into the sea from unknown causes shortly after. The rest assembled into their respective groups and then into two echelons. The lead echelon, consisting of the 376th and 93rd Bombardment Groups, was commanded by Colonel K. K. Compton of the 376th, who was accompanied by Brigadier General Uzal Ent, in overall command of the mission. The second echelon, consisting of the 98th, 389th and 44th Bombardment Groups, was commanded by Colonel John R. Kane of the 98th. As the flight continued, a gap began to open between the lead and second echelons. At various times, a total of thirteen aircraft were forced to turn back because of technical problems, although this still left more than the planners had originally counted upon.

The force climbed steadily until it crossed the northern tip of Corfu at 10,000 feet, then turned to the north-east. There was heavy cumulus cloud above the Albanian mountains, presenting obvious dangers. Colonel Compton decided to lead his echelon through a perceived gap in single file. When the second group reached this point, however, Colonel Kane adopted the textbook solution of circling and passing his aircraft through the gap in formations of three. As a result of this, the second echelon fell even further behind the leaders.

The force began descending above Pirot, in Yugoslavia, down to between 5,000 and 3,000 feet, at which height it crossed the Danube. On reaching Pitesti in Romania it descended to minimum altitude to stay below the enemy radar. Shortly afterwards, Compton made a navigational error that took the White I attack force so far to the right that it was heading for Bucharest. Realising what had happened, Lieutenant Colonel Addison E. Baker, commanding the 93rd, swung his White II attack group to the left, back in the direction of Ploesti. Sitting in his co-pilot's seat was Major John L. Jerstad, who had actually completed more than his share of missions and was no longer a member of the group, but had volunteered for the raid. As they approached the target area it became painfully apparent that surprise had not been achieved. Streams of tracer rose from points too numerous to count, indicating the presence of a large number of automatic weapons ranging in calibre from 20mm to 40mm, including numerous multiple mountings. In view of what followed, both Baker and Jerstad received the posthumous award of the Medal of Honor. Three miles short of the target their aircraft was struck by a heavy shell and soon had uncontrollable fires raging aboard. The terrain below was suitable for a crash landing but Baker was determined not to break up the leading formation. Jerstad therefore flew on straight and level until his bombs were released on the target, then struggled valiantly to gain sufficient height for the crew to bail out. It was to no avail, for the aircraft quickly became unmanageable and crashed in flames.

In addition to the damage caused by bombs, some of the defenders' wild fire, and that returned by the aircrews' gunners, penetrated fuel storage tanks. Soon flames were roaring upwards to a height above which the bombers were flying and a huge pall of smoke was blanketing the scene of destruction, serving as a beacon for the second attack force. Kane was leading this towards Ploesti using a parallel railway line as a guide. Unfortunately a flak train was travelling along the line and it pumped thousands of rounds into the formations passing close overhead, causing damage and casualties. Amid the confusion caused by the smoke and flames above the refineries it was possible to discern that some at least of the bombs from the first attack had hit the wrong targets. Nevertheless, wave after wave of Kane's three groups pressed home attacks on their assigned targets, whether they were burning or not.

At this point an unexpected development took place. Having discovered his navigational error, Compton obtained Ent's permission for the 376th Group to drop its bombs on targets of opportunity. Some of his pilots turned back towards Ploesti and six or more of them dropped their bombs on White II. This created a situation where the path of aircraft approaching from the west was crossed by that of those returning from the south at roughly the same altitude, so that for a while there was the sort of hair-raising cross-over performed by formation flying teams at air shows. To those manning the air defences, and indeed the crews themselves, it seemed little short of a miracle that there were no collisions.

The 389th Group, flying its first combat mission, was the last to attack. By now the scene resembled a medieval painting of hell, with flames belching skywards from the ruptured storage tanks and heavy and accurate flak streaking up from every direction. As it passed through the balloon barrage, one of its pilots, Second Lieutenant Lloyd H. Hughes, became the raid's third member to receive a posthumous Medal of Honor. His Liberator shuddered as it received several hits from large and small calibre anti-aircraft rounds. At once, petrol began to stream in quantity from the port wing and bomb bay. It was obvious to Hughes that if he flew through the towering flames above the blazing refineries, it would ignite. Ignoring the risk, he persevered, dropped his bombs and was last seen crashing into the ground with his port wing ablaze.

With the raid now completed, each pilot had to make decisions as to whether he had sufficient fuel to return to Tocra and whether the damage sustained by his aircraft would permit him to do so. It was appreciated that as they left the target area they would be harried mercilessly by enemy fighters, and indeed the majority of the raiders' losses were from this cause. Those who flew back along the same route they had used to reach the target flew low as long as the terrain permitted, thereby inhibiting their opponents' manoeuvrability, one attacking fighter ending his dive by flying straight into the ground. By now, however, the bombers' formation had been scattered across a wide area. Some, seriously damaged, crash-landed in neutral Turkey, where the crews were interned. Some, including Kane, reached RAF bases in Cyprus. Two were shot down near Sofia, Bulgaria. Twelve were intercepted by fighters based in Greece, three being shot down, and one ditched off the coast of Crete, badly damaged. Others were forced to ditch while crossing the Mediterranean. In return, four German and eight Romanian fighters had been shot down and a further twenty damaged.

It was late afternoon when the aircraft began touching down at the Tocra airfields, some badly shot up and with dead and wounded aboard. After eighty-eight had landed, the time ticked by until no more could be expected. Of those that returned, fifty-five had sustained battle damage and had dead and wounded. Understandably the crews were utterly exhausted, not least the pilots, who had struggled to cope with a demanding aircraft for over nine hours. Finally, when those aircraft that had reached bases in Cyprus were accounted for, it was apparent that fifty-three had been lost. Of the 1,765 men who had flown the mission, 446 were listed as killed or missing, while in excess of 100 had been wounded. So ended 1 August 1943, a date that would be remembered by the USAAF as Bloody Sunday.

Air photo reconnaissance revealed that the raid had produced mixed results. White I and White III seemed to have escaped damage. White II had sustained slight damage. At White IV half the Astra and one-third of the Orion refineries had been destroyed. White V, Blue and Red appeared to have been totally destroyed. The Columbia Aquila refinery was out of action for a year and the Steaua Romana did not come on stream again until 1950. Although the raid did not deliver the knock-out blow that had been hoped for, it did reduce the capacity of the complex by approximately half, so that the Wehrmacht in general, and the Luftwaffe in particular, never had quite enough fuel for their requirements. A further result of the raid was that Romania withdrew all her fighter aircraft from the Eastern Front to strengthen her home defences. For their determined leadership Colonel John Kane, who led the second echelon of the attack, and Colonel Leon Johnson, commanding the 44th Group, both received the Medal of Honor, bringing to five the total awarded for the operation, the most ever awarded for an attack on a single target.

The following year it became possible to launch further raids against Ploesti from airfields in Italy, but these were carried out from high altitude. In August 1944 the Red army overran Romania, which quickly changed sides, and the complex passed into Allied hands.

Anzio

By the winter of 1943–4 the Allied advance up the Italian mainland had been halted by the defences of the German Gustav Line, notably the towering Monte Cassino, which barred all further progress towards Rome. German resistance was dogged in the extreme, the troops having been encouraged in the belief that by tying down Allied troops in Italy, this would assist their comrades fighting on the Eastern Front in the all-important task of keeping the Russians out of the homeland. Furthermore, the Italian terrain itself favoured defensive fighting, consisting as it did of ridges descending to either coast from the central spine of the Apennines, separated by valleys through which ran fast-flowing rivers. In these circumstances it was difficult to employ armour in anything but a supporting role and consequently the burden of the fighting fell upon the infantry of both sides. A state of stalemate existed, and to break this it was decided that an amphibious landing would be made at Anzio, some 30 miles south of Rome and over twice that distance north of the Gustav Line. This, it was hoped, would have the effect not only of cutting the enemy's lines of communication, but also place the defenders of Monte Cassino in a position from which they could only be extricated with difficulty, placed as they were between the main Allied armies to the south and the expanded Anzio beachhead to the north.

The operation, codenamed Shingle, was to be mounted by the US VI Corps, part of Lieutenant General Mark Clark's American Fifth Army. Commanding VI Corps would be Major General John P. Lucas, who was not the ideal choice for the job. Lucas, a fine administrator, admitted to being a tired man who felt more than his fifty-five years. The impression he gave was that he would have been happier retired, smoking his corncob pipe in peace and watching the sun go down. With some justice, he complained that the operation had been too hastily mounted with too few resources. Nor was his relationship with the British troops under his command a comfortable one. His orders required him to land at Anzio and the neighbouring town of Nettuno and secure his beachhead, with the rider that if it seemed safe to do so he was to advance inland across the recently drained Pontine Marshes to the 3,000-feet massif of the Alban Hills, some 20 miles distant, which dominated the two roads and the railway leading south from Rome to the front. The nub of his problem was that, because of preparations for the Allied landings in Normandy, only sufficient landing craft were available in the Mediterranean to transport two reinforced divisions. This meant that if he did advance as far as the Alban Hills before additional formations reached the beachhead, his perimeter defences would be stretched so thin as to be unable to withstand what he regarded as the inevitable German counter-attack. Having already been severely shaken when the earlier Allied landing at Salerno had come close to disaster, he became obsessed with avoiding a repetition at Anzio.

While Lucas's caution was understandable, it was excessive and resulted in Churchill's disappointed comment: 'I hoped that we would be hurling a wildcat ashore, but all we got was a stranded whale.' It also resulted in some of the bitterest fighting of the entire war. Comparisons with Gallipoli were unavoidable and were emphasised by the static conditions prevailing for much of the time. Again, like the Turks, the Germans suffered serious losses from naval gunfire support. For their part, in addition to the normal battlefield hazards, the Allies had to endure the attentions of a huge 280mm railway gun that remained hidden in a distant tunnel. Known to them as Anzio Annie, and to its owners as Slim Bertha, it was capable of firing its 561lb high-explosive shell into the beachhead from a distance of 38 miles. Shipping also found itself at serious risk from the Henschel Hs 293 guided missile, which was launched from a parent aircraft, accelerated with the assistance of a ten-second rocket burst, then glided towards its target under radio guidance. The weapon scored several successes off Anzio, including the sinking of the British destroyer *Janus* and a fully illuminated and marked hospital ship. Rather more of a joke was the German self-propelled 200lb high-explosive charge called Goliath, which resembled a miniature World War I tank and was steered by training wires. This 'wonder weapon' failed to produce any results at all, not only because its tracks were vulnerable to small arms fire, but also because in certain circumstances the machine could be turned round and sent back whence it had come. As far as the human dimension was concerned at Anzio, acts of supreme courage were commonplace on both the American and British sectors, but while many of the former were recognised by the award of the Congressional Medal of Honor, the number of Victoria

Crosses awarded was very small, indicating an even stricter interpretation of the rules than ever before.

The landing took place on 22 January. On the right, Major General Lucian K. Truscott's US 3rd Division, a three-battalion Ranger brigade, the 504th and 509th Parachute Infantry Battalions and the 751st Tank Battalion came ashore at Anzio, Nettuno and the beaches to the south of the town. On the left, Major General W. R. C. Penney's British 1st Infantry Division, the 9th and 43rd Commandos and the 46th Royal Tank Regiment landed on beaches to the north of Anzio. As immediate follow-up reinforcements Clark had provided additional artillery, part of Major General Ernest N. Harmon's US 1st Armored Division and Major General William W. Eagles's US 45th Division, with the promise that the rest of both divisions would be committed if the situation demanded it.

The landings were virtually unopposed. Within twenty-four hours over 36,000 men, 3,000 vehicles and huge quantities of stores were ashore. Their arrival had caught the enemy completely wrong-footed, yet German surprise turned to astonishment when, instead of pushing aggressively inland to the Alban Hills as was expected, the Allies remained passively immobile. With Clark's approval, Lucas simply ordered his troops to dig in and consolidate their hold on the comparatively small area of the beachhead. For forty-eight hours after they had come ashore the Allies remained unmolested, save for some long-range shelling. During that period Field Marshal Albert Kesselring, the German Commander-in-Chief in Italy, orchestrated his response with characteristic energy. Elements of no less than eight divisions began to converge on Anzio, while yet more troops poured into Italy from as far afield as the south of France, Yugoslavia and Germany. By the evening of 23 January some 40,000 Germans had been deployed in a cordon around the beachhead.

The following day Lucas ordered the 1st British Division to patrol in the direction of Campoleone, on the Anzio–Albano road, while the US 3rd Division probed towards Cisterna, both of which could have been taken with minimal difficulty on the first day. The British patrol passed under a bridge carrying a minor road over the main highway, called the Flyover, and then under a second bridge carrying a disused railway line, called the Embankment, at the hamlet of Carroceto. It came under fire from a complex of farm buildings to the right of the road and withdrew. These buildings, which became known as the Factory, were taken by the 5th Grenadier Guards in heavy fighting the following day and held against a determined counter-attack. Likewise, the American probe towards Cisterna revealed that every approach was now covered by for-tified buildings and self-propelled guns. It was now obvious that breaking out of the beachhead was going to be very difficult indeed.

By this time 70,000 men, over 500 guns, 237 tanks and 27,000 tons of stores had been brought ashore. Even Clark was becoming concerned by Lucas's lack of activity and persuaded VI Corps' reluctant commander to take the offensive. On 29 January the British, supported by the US 1st Armored Division, would take Campoleone while the Americans cap-tured Cisterna.

During the preparations for this it became clear that the US 3rd Divi-sion would have to fight for its start line. While so doing, on 28 January Technician Eric G. Gibson won a posthumous Medal of Honor at Isola Bella. Gibson was a company cook, but on this day he was made respon-sible for leading a squad of raw replacements through their baptism of fire. As the open, flat landscape of the former marshland offered little or no cover, the numerous drainage ditches were used as routes forward. Gibson was leading his squad along one of these, the ominously named Fossa Feminamorta (Dead Woman's Ditch) and was some 50 yards ahead of his men when he was fired on and missed by a German with a machine pistol from 20 yards' range. Gibson charged, firing his own sub-machine-gun every few steps, and killed his opponent. At this point he was knocked flat when an artillery concentration landed in the area. Getting up, he continued along the ditch until he was fired on by two of the enemy, one armed with a machine pistol and the other with a rifle, 75 yards distant. Without hesitation, he charged them, killing one and cap-turing the other. During his attack, he became aware that he was also being fired on by a light machine-gun approximately 200 yards further along the ditch. Returning to his squad, he instructed them to give cov-ering fire while he crawled round the enemy's flank. Shells burst around him, showering him with soil, and two machine-guns were also firing across the area. At length he reached a position from which he was able to fling two grenades into the emplacement. Two of the weapon's crew were killed and the third surrendered. When his squad came forward to join him he continued to lead the advance. On reaching a bend in the ditch he went around it alone. An exchange of fire was heard and on rounding the bend the squad found that he had killed a German armed with a machine pistol, and had himself been killed.

The following day's attacks resulted in failure. On the American sector the 3rd Division's attack was spearheaded by the Ranger brigade which hoped to seize Cisterna by *coup de main* after using the cover of the Fossa di Fontana for their approach. Unfortunately, not only had the Germans been heavily reinforced, the Rangers had also been observed. Thus, when they emerged from the ditch they were allowed to get within 500 yards of the town, then ambushed. Their 1st and 3rd Battalions, surrounded and cut off, fought all day against tanks, self-propelled guns and overwhelming numbers but were forced to surrender when their ammunition was exhausted, only six men succeeding in regaining their own lines. The 4th Battalion was also surrounded and incurred serious casualties, but was extracted by a counter-attack.

On the British sector the 1st Division succeeded in reaching a ridge overlooking Campoleone railway station, but sustained heavy casualties in the process. The 2nd Sherwood Foresters twice succeeded in reaching the railway tracks but were cut to pieces in a crossfire that reduced the battalion's strength to eight officers and and less than 150 men. The US 1st Armored Division, which was to have exploited beyond Campoleone towards the Alban Hills, was handicapped from the outset by the numerous drainage ditches and soft going off the road in which tanks and half-tracks bogged down. All that had been gained was a narrow and clearly vulnerable finger of territory 3 miles long.

The Germans continued to mount spoiling attacks against the American sector on 31 January and the night that followed. During these two more members of the 3rd Division won the Medal of Honor. The first went to Pfc Lloyd C. Hawks, a medical orderly serving with the 30th Infantry. At 15:00 Hawks braved an enemy counter-attack to rescue the wounded men, two being riflemen and the third a medical orderly who had gone to their assistance. Under mortar and machine-gun fire, Hawks crawled 50 yards to a small ditch, where he treated his fellow orderly. He then crawled a similar distance to the riflemen, who were lying within 30 yards of the Germans. In the process he was stunned when his helmet was shot off. When he came to he saw that his helmet, lying near by, had been penetrated by thirteen bullets. Undeterred, he reached the casualties, administered first aid to the more seriously injured of the two, then dragged him 25 yards to the cover of a fold in the ground. He returned for the second man, and as he was administering assistance his right hip and left arm were shattered by bullets. Though in agony, he dragged the man back to the cover he had found, then, discovering it was inadequate for three men, crawled back to join the injured orderly.

The second Medal of Honor was awarded posthumously to Sergeant Truman O. Olson of B Company, 7th Infantry. After sixteen hours of continuous fighting, B Company had lost one-third of its strength. At nightfall on 30 January the survivors dug in behind a low bank, on the enemy side of which Olson commanded an outpost containing the only available machine-gun. During the night his detachment all became casualties to the enemy's fire and he was hit in the arm. At daybreak B Company's position was attacked by enemy infantry, estimated to be 200 strong, supported by machine-gun and mortar fire. Manning his machine-gun alone, Olson pinned the attackers down, and although he sustained a mortal wound after thirty minutes' fighting, he carried on for another hour-and-a-half, killing at least twenty of the enemy, wounded many more, and forced the Germans to abandon their assault before he died.

The following day a magnificent solo effort by Pfc Alton W. Knappen-berger disrupted an enemy attack for two hours and earned him the Medal of Honor. Armed with a Browning Automatic Rifle, Knappen-berger crawled to an exposed knoll. Immediately he showed himself an enemy machine-gun, only 85 yards distant, opened fire, kicking up the earth around him. Disregarding this, he rose to a kneeling position, took careful aim and fired back, killing two of the gun's crew and wounding the third. As he did so, he noticed two Germans crawling towards him. One had time to throw a grenade, harmlessly, from 20 yards, before Knappenberger shot them both dead with a single burst. Some time later, a second machine-gun engaged his position from a point 200 yards away. This he also silenced with well-aimed shots. Next, he became the target of a 20mm anti-aircraft cannon, which ceased firing when he wounded one of the crew. Although the knoll was now coming under tank and artillery fire, Knappenberger remained in his precarious posi-tion, making a special target of any of the enemy's infantry armed with automatic weapons. When his ammunition ran out, he obtained fresh clips from the belt of a casualty lying near by. Having expended these in repelling the assault of an enemy platoon, he rejoined his company.

Such German setbacks as these did not unduly concern General Eber-hard von Mackensen, the commander of the Fourteenth Army, who was now responsible for the Anzio front. The events of 29 January had con-firmed that the beachhead was already firmly contained and now he mounted an offensive intended to destroy it. This began on 3 February and, predictably, its main effort was directed at the three sides of 1st Division's salient. For a while a real danger existed that the British 3rd Brigade, holding the tip of the salient, would be cut off. However, as luck would have it, the leading brigade of the 56th (London) Division had just reached Anzio and one of its regiments, the 1st London Scottish, mounted a counter-attack, supported by the Sherman tanks of 46 RTR. This enabled most of the 3rd Brigade to work their way out of the trap. The battle continued with undiminished ferocity the following day, until the British had been forced back to Carroceto. The Germans had paid a heavy price for their success, but by now the 1st Division had been reduced to half its original strength. Lucas reinforced it with the 504th and 509th Parachute Infantry Battalions.

On 7 February Mackensen mounted holding attacks against the American sector of the front, recapturing the village of Ponte Rotto on the Cisterna road, but once again directed his principal effort along the Anzio–Campoleone road. The vital Buonriposo Ridge to the south-west of Carroceto was stormed, outflanking the defenders of the hamlet and the Embankment. Here, amid bitter and confused fighting, Major the Hon. William Philip Sidney, commanding the 5th Grenadier Guards' Support Company, won the Victoria Cross. The company was defending the single crossing point of a deep ditch known as the Fossa di Carroceto between Buonriposa Ridge and the main road. As the Germans came streaming off the ridge towards the road, Sidney charged them, firing his tommy-gun and bringing the enemy advance to a standstill. When the gun jammed he began flinging grenades across the ditch, assisted by two guardsmen. The premature explosion of a grenade killed one of the men and wounded Sidney in the legs. He nevertheless continued to hurl grenades among the enemy while the second man primed them. More guardsmen arrived and assisted in beating off the renewed enemy assault on the crossing, during which Sidney was wounded in the face by an enemy stick grenade. By now, he had become extremely weak from loss of blood but he refused medical treatment until he was satisfied that the position was secure. Sidney, the son-in-law of Field Marshal Lord Gort, VC, later became Viscount De L'Isle. He enjoyed a long and distinguished post-war career, becoming Secretary of State for Air 1951–5, Governor General of Australia 1961–5 and Deputy President of the Victoria Cross and George Cross Association in 1983, a post which he held until his death in 1991.

Counter-attacks against Buonriposo Ridge failed the following day, and, worse still, the Germans captured the Factory, beating off every attempt to retake it, and Carroceto was lost. With some difficulty, the Allied line was re-established some way south of the Embankment. On the morning of 8 February Corporal Paul B. Huff of the 509th Parachute Infantry Battalion won a Medal of Honor while leading a six-man reconnaissance patrol to determine the positions of an enemy unit that was firing into the right flank of his company. The patrol was forced to advance across open, rolling terrain under small arms, machine-gun and mortar fire to obtain the necessary information. When it encountered a minefield, Huff crawled alone through this to a point from which he was able to kill those manning the most advanced enemy machine-gun post with his machine carbine. He then led his men safely back to their own lines, where he accurately reported the enemy's strength and dispositions. During the afternoon he formed part of a fighting patrol that stormed the enemy position, killing twenty-seven of the 122 Germans present and capturing twenty-one more, for the loss of only three casualties.

Following the loss of the Factory, the Embankment and Carroceto, Lucas redeployed his troops on this sector. The US 45th Division became responsible for the Anzio–Albano road and the territory to the right of it while the British 56th Division was responsible for the territory to the left; in reserve south of the Flyover were the British 1st Division and the US 1st Armored Division. Mackensen, believing that he had accumulated sufficient infantry to cut the beachhead in two by driving straight down this axis, launched a fresh attack on the morning of 16 February. Despite the weight of artillery and naval gunfire directed at them, the Germans, believing that victory lay within their grasp, advanced with suicidal bravery. Four days of desperate fighting followed, during which the Allied line bulged, was forced back almost to the Flyover, then stabilised when the reserves counter-attacked. In the face of these, many exhausted Germans, having given their all to the attack without achieving the anticipated breakthrough, surrendered.

The nature of the fighting during these days is graphically illustrated by the manner in which Pfc William J. Johnston, a machine-gunner with G Company, 180th Infantry, won his Medal of Honor near Padiglione. During 17 February he broke up an attack by a German company, inflicting twenty-five casualties and forcing the rest of the enemy to withdraw. Despite artillery, mortar and sniper fire, he manned his weapon for the rest of the day without relief. At one point two Germans crawled forward so close to him that he could not depress his machine-gun sufficiently to engage them. He killed one with a pistol, and the other with a borrowed rifle. Shortly after, a nearby rifleman was killed by a sniper. Realising that the dead rifleman's position possessed a better field of fire, Johnston ignored the obvious risks and moved his machine-gun to it. He volunteered to cover his platoon's withdrawal that night and was the last to leave. Next morning, he inflicted a further seven casualties on the enemy. That afternoon, he again covered his platoon's withdrawal, but while so doing he received a serious wound above the heart. With the assistance of another soldier, he resumed his position behind the machine-gun. The weapon was heard firing for another forty minutes but fell silent when it was overrun by the enemy. Johnston was reported killed but the following morning he crawled painfully into the American lines and was able to give details of the enemy's new dispositions.

Although the crisis of the battle had passed, the Germans still attempted to improve their positions. On the Padiglione sector, First Lieutenant Jack C. Montgomery, peering through the gloom of first light on 22 February, noted that the enemy had established themselves in three new areas in front of his platoon. The first, only 50 yards distant, containing four machine-guns and a mortar, presented an obvious threat to the platoon; the second, 50 yards beyond, seemed to have been entrenched; the third, 300 yards away, was centred on a house. Montgomery's subsequent actions were to earn him the Medal of Honor. Arming himself with an M1 rifle and grenades, he crawled along a shallow ditch until he was within grenade-throwing distance of the first enemy post. He then climbed on to a small knoll to hurl grenades. Eight of the post's occupants were killed and the remaining four surrendered. Returning to his platoon with the prisoners, he called down artillery fire on the second and third positions. Now armed with a machine carbine, he took advantage of the shellfire to crawl towards the second enemy post along the ditch. He was spotted and immediately came under small arms and machine-gun fire. Undeterred, he charged, killing three of the occupants; the rest, seven in number, promptly surrendered. Having seen the prisoners on their way back to the platoon, he continued towards the house, although it was now fully daylight and the flat terrain was devoid of cover. When the artillery strike lifted, he charged the building, from which those within came streaming out to surrender. Altogether, Montgomery killed eleven of the enemy, wounded an unknown number, and took thirty-two prisoners. He was himself severely wounded by mortar fragments that night and evacuated.

By now, although Clark was generally supportive, Lucas had lost the confidence of the Allied leaders and on 22 February was replaced by Truscott as VI Corps' commander, with a British deputy, Major General Eveleigh. The arrangement worked well as the British trusted and liked Truscott and the Americans in turn liked Eveleigh. Major General Gerald Templar assumed command of the British 1st Division when Penney was wounded, and Brigadier General (later Major General) John

W. O'Daniel, known to his men as Iron Mike, took over the US 3rd Division.

Truscott suspected, correctly, that the enemy would mount another attack against the beachhead. In fact, so heavy had been German losses that neither Kesselring nor Mackensen were in favour of the idea, but Hitler insisted that they should deliver a 'final crushing blow'. The attack commenced on 29 February and was delivered on the Cisterna sector, held by the US 3rd Division, the least tired of the Allied formations. After some initial success, in which one of 509th Parachute Infantry Battalion's companies was overrun, the assault foundered amid minefields and accurate artillery concentrations. Further attacks followed the next day but these were not pressed home with any of the enthusiasm that had marked earlier German attempts to crush the beachhead and were easily contained. On 2 March the skies cleared above the battle zone, enabling the Allied air forces to deliver no less than 600 tons of bombs on to the German positions. The offensive, which had cost Mackensen 3,000 casualties and thirty tanks, was called off.

There followed a long period sometimes referred to as The Lull, lasting until the end of May. It was only a lull in the sense that neither side mounted a major offensive, although both conducted local operations. The number of Allied ships lost as a result of Luftwaffe attacks continued to rise, while the British and American air forces struck regularly at targets beyond the perimeter. Artillery activity was almost continuous and as no part of the beachhead lay beyond the reach of the German guns chemical fogs were used to conceal activity. Although it was almost certainly not the intention of the German gunners, even the dressing stations and field hospitals were not immune to shellfire, to the extent that soldiers with minor wounds were sometimes unwilling to go there. The beachhead, 17 miles long and 7 deep, was a wilderness of ruined buildings, wrecked and gutted vehicles, smashed equipment and shell craters. The only improvement was that with the coming of spring the ground began to dry out. The Germans launched a propaganda campaign designed to convince the Allies that their position was hopeless. The most famous product of this was the Beachhead, Death's Head leaflet, showing a skull superimposed on a map of the beachhead. Other leaflets, showing American servicemen taking their pleasure with British women in the safety of the United Kingdom, were intended to provoke a rift between the Allies. There were some changes among the formations within the beachhead. The British 5th Division, commanded by Major General Gregson-Ellis, replaced the exhausted 56th (London) Division, the American-Canadian Special Service Force had already taken over the south-eastern sector of perimeter, and the paratroopers and rangers were replaced by the US 34th Division.

Only one Medal of Honor was awarded during this period. It went to Pfc John C. Squires, a platoon runner serving with A Company, 30th Infantry. On the night of 23–24 April, Squires's company mounted an attack on a series of strongly held enemy positions in and around an area known as Spaccasassi Creek, near Padiglione. During this, Squires's first action, he was sent forward to discover what had happened to the company's leading platoon, which had incurred casualties in a minefield. Braving artillery and mortar fire, he reached the stranded platoon and, seeing that it was unwilling to advance further, carried out a personal reconnaissance that resulted in his discovering a route round the minefield. Having informed the platoon commander, he then formed a group of stragglers into a squad which he led forward. During its approach to Spaccasassi Creek, the platoon suffered serious casualties from automatic fire and grenades, losing many men and almost all its NCOs. On his own initiative, Squires established an outpost, then went back twice under shellfire to bring up reinforcements past the enemy wire and minefield. The outpost was attacked three times, each attack being driven back with loss. During these actions Squires manned a captured light machine-gun to good effect. Later, observing an enemy post some distance away, he crawled towards it and engaged the occupants in a machine-gun duel until all twenty-one of them surrendered. He next collected all the enemy light machine-guns he could find and somehow persuaded a captured officer to instruct him on their finer points, passing on this knowledge to the platoon. The following night he broke up another attack on the outpost, killing several of the enemy and wounding more. As well as winning him the Medal of Honor, Squires's initiative deservedly won him a sergeant's stripes. Sadly, he was to be killed in a subsequent action.

From the beginning, the outcome of the fighting at Anzio had been inextricably linked to the battles being fought by the rest of Clark's Fifth Army to break through the Gustav Line. In planning his spring offensive, General Sir Harold Alexander, the Allied Commander-in-Chief Italy, envisaged the US VI Corps breaking out of the Anzio beachhead once the Gustav Line had been breached. The corps' role would be to advance through Cisterna to Valmontone, thereby cutting the German line of retreat towards Rome and entrapping several enemy divisions in the process. Clark, finding the suggestion unwelcome, decided that the corps would follow his own agenda when the moment came.

The great Allied offensive began on 11 May. The fortress of Monte Cassino was outflanked and rendered untenable, and on 15 May Kesselring ordered a withdrawal to the Hitler Line, which was breached on 23 May. Simultaneously, VI Corps, reinforced with the US 36th Division for the purpose, broke out of the beachhead under cover of diversionary attacks by the British 1st and 5th Divisions at the northern edge of the perimeter. Fully aware of the implications, the German 362nd and 715th Divisions fought themselves to virtual destruction, offering such fierce resistance that the US 3rd Division alone sustained 950 casualties in one twenty-four hour period. During the breakout, no fewer than ten Medals of Honor were awarded to members of VI Corps.

On the 3rd Division's sector, Pfc John W. Dutko won a posthumous Medal of Honor at Ponte Rosso. Clearly possessed with the joy of battle, he left the shelter of a captured trench during an enemy artillery concentration, and continued his platoon's attack alone. Running through the shellbursts, he ducked briefly into a crater, then emerged again with the bullets from three machine-gun posts kicking up the dirt around his heels. From 30 yards' range he flung a grenade into one post, killing both the gunners. Wounded and knocked to the ground by fire from the second post, he scrambled to his feet and, firing his Browning Automatic Rifle from the hip, killed all five of the crew of a nearby self-propelled 88mm tank destroyer. He then tackled the second machine-gun post, killing both gunners. Sustaining further wounds from the third post, he charged it, killing the gun crew before falling dead across the weapon.

Near by, Pfc Patrick L. Kessler of K Company, 30th Infantry, displayed an equally aggressive spirit. When five of his comrades were killed by an enemy machine-gun, he determined to destroy it. Ordering three men to give him covering fire, he left the cover of a ditch and had crawled to within 50 yards of the enemy weapon when he was fired upon. Disregarding the risks, he charged the post, killing the gunner and his assistant from the edge of the weapon pit, into which he then jumped, overpowering a third man in a struggle and wounding a fourth who attempted to escape. While taking his prisoner to the rear, he saw two more of his comrades killed as they attacked another strongpoint that had already taken a toll of his company. Handing over his prisoner, Kessler crawled to one of the casualties and relieved him of his BAR. He then stalked the second strongpoint, which was 125 yards distant, braving the fire of two machine-guns as he crawled through an anti-tank minefield. At one point he was bowled over by an exploding shell, but continued to crawl until he was within 50 yards of the enemy post, upon which he opened fire. Evidently satisfied by the results, he climbed to his feet and walked slowly towards the post, firing his BAR from the hip. Both machine-gunners were killed and thirteen men surrendered. While escorting the prisoners to the rear, he was fired on by two snipers at short range. The prisoners tried to bolt but were discouraged from doing so when he fired into the ground around them. Finally, he engaged both snipers in a firefight and received their surrender, removing the last obstacle to K Company's advance. Kessler was killed in a later action.

The third Medal of Honor to be won by members of the 3rd Division on 23 May went to Pfc Henry Schauer. At about noon, a patrol commanded by Schauer was approaching Cisterna when it was fired upon from behind by four riflemen. Wheeling about, Schauer walked deliberately towards them, killing all four with bursts from his BAR. Spotting a sniper hiding behind a house chimney, he brought him down with another burst. Shortly after, the patrol was forced to take cover by an artillery concentration and two machine-guns. While shells burst near by and bullets cracked past, Schauer calmly knelt in the open and killed the crew of the nearest gun, as well as two more Germans running to man it. He then, in a remarkable piece of shooting, killed the four-strong crew of the second machine-gun at 500 yards' range. The following morning, he and his men were again forced to seek cover when they were fired upon by a Tiger tank and a nearby machine-gun. Although four high-explosive rounds from the Tiger burst around him, Schauer crawled towards the machine-gun and, standing upright 80 yards from the weapon, killed its crew with a burst fired from the shoulder. He survived the battle and later reached the rank of technical sergeant.

Near Carano, a platoon of the 157th Infantry (45th Division), was held up by entrenched positions on high ground. Crawling alone round the enemy flank, Technical Sergeant Van T. Barfoot, knocked out one machine-gun post with a grenade, killing two Germans and wounding three more. Continuing along the enemy's defence line to a second post, he used his sub-machine-gun to kill two of the enemy and capture three. A third post surrendered to him. Sending his prisoners to the rear, he continued to mop up the surrounding area, which yielded a total of seventeen more prisoners. Later in the day, the captured position was counter-attacked by three PzKpfw IVs. Arming himself with a bazooka, Barfoot took up a position in front of the leading tank, which he disabled at 75 yards' range, then killed three of the crew with his sub-machine-gun when they emerged. The two surviving tanks sheered off. Next, having spotted an abandoned enemy field gun in no man's land, he went out and destroyed it by exploding a charge in the breech. Finally, though exhausted, he assisted two of his severely wounded men to reach the aid post, one mile to the rear. Sergeant Barfoot subsequently received a commission.

On the 34th Division's sector, Technical Sergeant Ernest H. Derviskian and four members of his platoon, having advanced rapidly through artillery and sniper fire, suddenly found themselves far ahead of their company. Coming within sight of the railway embankment near Cisterna, they spotted several enemy dugouts near by. While his men gave covering fire, Derviskian charged them, firing his machine carbine, and took ten prisoners. When the platoon came up, a further fifteen Germans emerged from trenches close by. Climbing the embankment, Derviskian saw another nine attempting to make their escape. His platoon opened fire, wounding three, and, accompanied by four men, he dashed out and captured the rest. Continuing the advance, he decided to work around the left of a vineyard, but this move was abandoned when it ran into heavy fire. The platoon then began to move through the vineyard, but was immediately pinned down by close-range machine-gun fire that killed one man and wounded others. Feigning death, Derviskian waited for a lull in the firing, then hurled a grenade at the machine-gun post, which he charged, firing his machine carbine, and forced four Germans to surrender. When the enemy further into the vineyard began to throw grenades, he ordered his men to pull back. They refused and neutralised a second machine-gun post with their fire. At this point the entrance to a dugout was observed just beyond. Derviskian sprayed it with his carbine and more of the enemy came out to surrender. Continuing through the vineyard alone, he spotted a third machine-gun post beside a house. Picking up an abandoned enemy machine pistol, he opened fire on the position. Six Germans emerged with their hands up, joining the platoon's procession of prisoners heading for the rear. Sergeant Derviskian was later awarded a commission.

In a similar action, Staff Sergeant George G. Hall of the 135th Infantry won the Medal of Honor. When his company was pinned down by machine-gun and sniper fire, he crawled forward along a ploughed furrow until he was able to throw four grenades into a machine-gun post, killing two of the occupants and capturing four more, who were sent to the rear. Finding a supply of German 'potato masher' grenades in the post, he commenced a grenade duel with a second machine-gun post, as a result of which five of the enemy were killed and five surrendered. He was crawling along a furrow towards a third machine-gun post when his leg was blown off by an exploding shell. As a result of his action his company was able to outflank the enemy position without incurring excessive casualties.

One of the 1st Armored Division's combat commands was able to exploit the breakthrough, using rocket-propelled explosive 'snakes' to blast gaps for itself in the minefields, but the other sustained heavy casualties and was temporarily halted by a counter-attack near Carano. In the middle of an infantry/tank attack, a tank officer, Second Lieutenant Thomas W. Fowler, came upon two disorganised infantry platoons held up by a minefield. After reorganising the infantry he made a personal reconnaissance of the minefield, which was 75 yards deep, lifting anti-personnel mines by hand until he had cleared a gap. He then returned and led the infantry through, a squad at a time. He next brought up his tanks through the minefield gap and positioned them where they could provide the best support for the infantry. Anxious to get on, he led the way 300 yards ahead of the infantry until he came upon a complex of enemy trenches, the occupants of which seemed to have mixed feelings about continuing to fight. He hauled those who wished to surrender out of their foxholes and sent them to the rear, and flung grenades into the dugouts of those who continued to resist. When the American infantry came up and began to dig in, he went back and brought his tanks forward under fire. Shortly after, the position was counter-attacked by Tiger tanks and during the exchange of fire one of Fowler's Shermans was set ablaze. He ran to the burning vehicle and for the next thirty minutes tried to save the lives of the wounded among the crew. During this time the infantry and the remaining tanks were forced to pull back a short distance. Fowler himself did not join them until the Tigers were on the point of overrunning his position, then administered to nine wounded infantrymen. He was killed later in the campaign, but his action on 23 May won him the Medal of Honor.

The following day two men of the 15th Infantry (3rd Division) won Medals of Honor at Cisterna, where the enemy continued to resist doggedly. That of Sergeant Sylvester Antolak was a posthumous award. When the regiment's B Company was held up by machine-gun and small arms fire, he charged across 200 yards of open ground, being hit and knocked down three times, but always getting up to resume his attack. With his shoulder gashed and his right arm broken, he wedged his sub-machine-gun under his left arm and, halting 15 yards from the nearest machine-gun post, opened fire, killing two of the enemy and receiving the surrender of ten more. When his men came up he refused medical attention and instead led an attack on a second strongpoint, some 100 yards beyond. Having covered most of the distance, he was shot dead but, inspired by his example, his men surged past and took the position.

Private James II. Mills of F Company won the Medal of Honor in what was his first action. He was the leading man of his platoon, which was proceeding along a draw (or ditch) towards a position from which it was to launch an attack against a heavily fortified enemy strongpoint. Suddenly, he was fired on by a machine-gun at point-blank range. He killed the gunner with a single shot and captured his assistant. Next he came upon two men about to hurl grenades at the platoon, killing one and capturing the other. Continuing up the draw, he came under fire from a complete infantry section, which he charged, firing his M1 from the hip, and took six more prisoners. At the top of the draw a machine-gun fired at him from 20 yards. He killed the gunner with one shot, as well as one of two men who attempted to escape, capturing the other. When it became apparent that the platoon's attack on the strongpoint would probably result in heavy casualties, Mills volunteered to crawl along a narrow ditch to within 50 yards of the enemy and distract them. Leaping on to a bank, he shouted, fired his rifle and ducked back into cover, repeating this four times, while rifle, machine pistol and tracer fire zipped past him. With the enemy now thoroughly distracted, the platoon charged, capturing the strongpoint and taking twenty-two prisoners.

By 26 May the German grasp on the Cisterna area had begun to crumble, although pockets of resistance were still encountered. First Lieutenant Beryl R. Newman of 133rd Infantry (34th Division), won a Medal of Honor on one such occasion. While leading his platoon's advance in company with four scouts, two machine-guns opened fire from the crest of a hill 100 yards ahead. The scouts immediately hit the ground, but Newman remained standing until he was able to locate the source of the enemy's fire. He then ordered one squad forward to join him while another worked around the enemy's right flank. When the first squad was pinned down as it tried to move, Newman decided to advance alone, firing his tommy-gun as he did so. He wounded one German in each nest, and the two men with them fled to a house. Almost immediately, three men emerged from the house and ran towards an unmanned machine-gun whose presence was not suspected. Newman killed one as he ran, another as he attempted to bring the weapon into action, and the third fled. Closing in on the house, he fired through its doors and windows, yelling for the occupants to give up. He kicked in the door and immediately received the surrender of eleven Germans who had been so intimidated by his relentless advance that none of them chose to use their own rifles or machine pistols.

Elements of the US II Corps, advancing north along Route 7 from the broken Hitler Line, had already made contact with VI Corps on 25 May. With the breakout now an established fact, Clark turned his attention to fulfilling his private ambition, which was to capture Rome. Clark wanted to enter the Italian capital at the earliest possible moment. Alexander's plan required VI Corps to thrust eastwards through the gap between the Alban Hills and the Colli Lepini to Valmontone on Route 6. In the eyes of Alexander and Churchill, this would achieve the isolation and destruction of several German divisions retreating from the Hitler Line, and was of far greater importance than the immediate capture of Rome, which would fall anyway as a direct result of the enemy's inability to defend it. Clark, however, merely sent the 3rd Division, the Special Service Force and part of 1st Armored Division in the direction of Valmontone, wheeling the rest of VI Corps northwards across the Alban Hills, where little resistance was encountered, and commenced his drive on the capital. Mackensen, well aware of the consequences should Valmontone fall, deployed adequate forces to fend off American attacks until his retreating divisions were out of danger and the golden moment passed.

It was on the Valmontone sector, during the night of 2–3 June, that Private Herbert F. Christian of 15th Infantry (3rd Division), won a posthumous Medal of Honor sacrificing his own life so that his comrades could live. Christian formed part of a patrol that walked into an ambush. When a flare soared aloft it revealed the enemy strength as being some sixty riflemen armed with at least three machine-guns, and three tanks, only 30 yards distant. Christian stood up and shouted for the patrol to pull back. Almost immediately, his right leg was severed above the knee by a tank shell. He crawled forward on his left knee, firing his submachine-gun, killing three of the enemy at once, then a man with a machine pistol. Now the focus of every enemy weapon, he was shot dead, but the rest of the patrol managed to escape from the trap.

Back on the coast, the British 1st and 5th Divisions were advancing northwards towards Rome. On 3 June, Sergeant Maurice Rogers of the 2nd Wiltshire Regiment, already the holder of the Military Medal, won a posthumous Victoria Cross. Rogers's platoon of tracked carriers was held up by barbed wire and intense machine-gun fire only 70 yards from its objective. Crashing his carrier through the wire, he seized his Thompson sub-machine-gun and charged across the minefield beyond, killing the occupants of two machine-gun posts. Inspired by his action, the rest of the platoon joined in the attack. Before they could reach him, Rogers was wounded in the leg, but disregarded this and continued to fight his way into the enemy position until he was shot dead at point-blank range.

Clark entered Rome on 4 May. In fulfilling his personal ambition he had forfeited the chance of the even greater triumph that would have resulted from his following the letter rather than the spirit of Alexander's directive. Two days later the Allied landings in Normandy eclipsed such triumph as there was. The Anzio venture had been initiated with inadequate resources, and Lucas was probably right to consolidate the beachhead rather than go for the Alban Hills, but it is generally agreed that his position would have been strengthened if he had seized Campoleone and Cisterna immediately after the landing, when the enemy lacked the means to defend them. In itself, therefore, Anzio cannot be seen as a victory, although ultimately it did contribute to a victory – one that would have been the greater if Clark had suppressed his desire for personal publicity.

Kohima, Imphal and the Second Chindit Incursion

APRIL–JULY 1944

By the beginning of 1944 the ruling junta in Japan badly needed a victory to report to their people. Such a victory could not be obtained in the Pacific, where the Americans were advancing remorselessly from island to island, nor in China, which was too vast to conquer with the forces available. In Burma, however, there existed a situation where a limited offensive would not only produce the sorely needed good news, but also consolidate the Japanese strategic hold on the area.

Simultaneously, the Allies in Burma were already preparing an offensive of their own. Since the end of the 1942, British Fourteenth Army, commanded by General William Slim, had held the line of the Chindwin River, while in the north the Chinese divisions of the acerbic General Joseph Stilwell occupied the upper reaches of the Hukawng valley. The planned offensive envisaged Stilwell advancing down the Hukawng to capture Myitkyina and Mogaung, the key to reopening the Burma Road land route to China, assisted by Major General Orde Wingate's deep-penetration Chindit brigades, which had proved their value the previous year and would now be landed right on top of the Japanese lines of communications, while the British IV Corps, commanded by Lieutenant General G. A. P. Scoones, advanced across the Chindwin.

In essence, the offensive plans prepared by Lieutenant General Masakuzo Kawabe, commanding the Japanese Burma Area Army, were much simpler. He was confident that he could hold off Stilwell's Chinese without undue difficulty, but felt that the long line of the Chindwin was too vulnerable to be guarded adequately and was looking for an alternative and impregnable defence line. Such a line existed along the crest of the towering Naga Hills, across the Chindwin and beyond the Imphal Plain. Once that line had been obtained, he reasoned, the few routes through the hills could be so guarded that the British would never be able to break out of India proper and resume operations in Burma. The task was entrusted to his Fifteenth Army, commanded by Lieutenant

General Renya Mutaguchi, who had earned numerous laurels during the campaign in Malaya. Mutaguchi possessed three good-quality divisions, to which he allocated missions as follows: the 31st Division (Major General Sato) was to isolate the British IV Corps on the Imphal Plain by cutting the road behind it at Kohima; the 15th Division (Major General Yamauchi) would enter the plain from the north and east; and the 33rd Division (Major General Yanagida), less one column detached to support the 15th Division, would enter it from the south and west, the overall effect being to starve and crush IV Corps where it stood. Mutaguchi was promised all the support that the Burma Area Army could give him, including tanks and as much air cover as possible. His troops would carry one month's food and medical supplies with them, and when these were gone it was confidently anticipated that they would be replaced by captured British stocks, as they had been in Malaya and the first Burma campaign. Furthermore, to make the Fifteenth Army's task even easier, a diversionary offensive would be mounted on the Arakan coast of Burma, designed to draw British troops away from the Imphal Plain before the main offensive began.

It was the Japanese who struck first, but it was quickly apparent that the old free-wheeling days of victory no longer existed. Once, British and Indian troops, devoid of air cover, had been inclined to retreat once the Japanese, using the jungle for cover, began to threaten their rear, and had lost much irreplaceable equipment as they tried to fight their way out. Now, the diversionary offensive in the Arakan quickly came to grief, notably at the Battle of the Admin Box, for a number of unexpected reasons. Recently arrived Spitfire squadrons made mincemeat of the Japanese Zeros, and the Arakan skies became the property of the Allied air forces. This meant that those formations that had been cut off by the Japanese could be supplied by air. Suddenly, the Japanese found themselves heavily engaged with troops who were prepared to fight it out rather than retreat. In addition, the British had begun to use tanks in substantial numbers, to which they had no effective reply. Finally, when their own ramshackle supply system broke down, they began to die in hundreds from starvation and disease and were forced to retreat.

It did not seem to have occurred to Kawabe or Mutaguchi that what had happened in the Arakan could be repeated on a much larger scale at Imphal. For his part, Slim, aware of the Japanese preparations, simply ordered Scoones's divisions to conduct a fighting withdrawal from the Chindwin to the Imphal Plain, thereby concentrating the whole of IV Corps within an area where it could be supplied by air. He also decided that the Chindit penetration should go ahead, as it could be used not only to assist Stilwell in the north, but also to prey upon the supply routes of Mutaguchi's Fifteenth Army when it advanced to Imphal. Subsequent operations, although spread across an immense area, were therefore interlinked and often simultaneous. To avoid confusion, therefore, the Kohima, Imphal and Chindit battles will each be described in turn.

Kohima was situated at a point where the winding road from Dimapur, the railhead for the Central Front, turned sharply south towards Imphal. The town, which was the civil administrative centre for the area in peacetime, lay 5,000 feet above sea level but was dominated by mountains twice that height. The war had turned it into an intermediate-sized base camp, incorporating a hospital, reinforcement depot, supply facilities and workshops. As the road entered the town it wound around a spur on which the hospital had been laid out, then turned south, passing the Deputy Commissioner's bungalow, a tennis court and clubhouse, all constructed on a terraced hillside, on its right. From this point southwards a number of small hills extended southwards, forming a ridge; first, Garrison Hill, then Kuki Piquet, then FSD (Field Supply Depot) Hill, then DIS (Detail Issue Store) Hill, and finally, across the road, Jail Hill.

On 22 March Colonel Hugh Richards arrived as garrison commander with orders to put the town's defences in order. The troops at his disposal were mostly local units, mainly belonging to the 1st Assam Rifles, who had already been in contact with the Japanese, plus a company of Gurkhas, two platoons of 5/27th Mahrattas, and composite British and Indian companies formed from hospital convalescents. Also present were a large number of administrative and non-combatant personnel, some of whom had begun to show signs of panic at the enemy's approach. Richards sent them out at the earliest possible opportunity, while the fighting troops, hindered by a shortage of barbed wire, began digging in. Meanwhile, Slim had activated XXXIII Corps under Lieutenant General Montagu Stopford and directed it to move up to the front through Dimapur. Already present at Dimapur was Brigadier Frederick Warren's 161 Infantry Brigade, belonging to the 5th Indian Division, which had flown in from the Arakan. On 4 April, much to Richards's relief, Warren sent up his British battalion, the 4th Royal West Kent Regiment, to reinforce the Kohima garrison. Originally a territorial unit, the battalion was experienced and battle-hardened, having already served in the Western Desert and the recent fighting in the Arakan, where it had incurred 200 casualties. It was commanded by Lieutenant

Colonel John Laverty, known to his men as Texas Dan, who was fortunately a strong character as the burden of the defence would fall heavily on his battalion.

On 6 April the Japanese isolated Kohima and stormed Jail Hill, reducing the defended area to a triangle measuring 700 by 900 by 1,100 yards. Warren, bringing the rest of the brigade up from Dimapur, sent a Rajput company to reinforce the garrison but recognised that it would not be possible to accommodate his two remaining battalions within the reduced perimeter. Instead, he established a defended box at Jotsoma, two miles west of Kohima, from which three 3.7-inch howitzer batteries of 24th Mountain Regiment, Indian Artillery, were able to bring uncannily accurate fire on the Japanese throughout the siege, directed by observers within Kohima itself. For their part, the Japanese were able to bring every inch of the Kohima defences under artillery and sniper fire.

On the night of 6 April they launched a series of attacks from Jail Hill against DIS Hill. Although they were beaten off with heavy loss, some of them broke through. Those who were not despatched with the bayonet hid themselves in huts and the ovens of a bakery. The huts were burned down around them and the bakery blown up. Others went to ground so that the position was not finally cleared until 8 April. One machine-gun team which had taken cover in an abandoned trench suddenly became active that morning, leading to the first of two acts resulting in the award of a posthumous Victoria Cross to Lance Corporal John Harman, a sniper in the West Kents' D Company. Harman was well educated and came from a wealthy background, his home being Lundy Island in the Bristol Channel. Powerfully built, he was a complex, introverted character and essentially a loner who refused to be considered for a commission and was only persuaded with difficulty to accept a lance corporal's stripe. When the enemy machine-gun opened up, Harman realised that it was capable of doing a great deal of damage unless it was silenced immediately. Asking his section's Bren to give him covering fire, he sprinted 35 yards towards the Japanese position and flung himself down under the bunker's fire slit, from which a continuous stream of bullets passed over his head. Methodically, he released the safety clip on a grenade with a four-second fuse, counted slowly to three, then tossed it through the aperture. Having satisfied himself that both the enemy within had been killed by the explosion, he picked up their weapon and returned to his platoon.

Elsewhere on 8 April, the enemy mounted attacks on Hospital Spur and the DC's bungalow, taking the latter and forcing the defenders back beyond the tennis court above before they were halted. The following day they resumed their attacks on DIS Hill. At a critical moment, Harman was seen tearing downhill through the shattered trees towards a Japanese trench that contained five men armed with automatic weapons. Jumping a rise, he was suddenly among them, shooting his way into the trench. They stood no chance against the big man, who fought with berserk fury, spitting them on his bayonet or smashing them into oblivion with his rifle butt. To the cheers of the West Kents, he emerged holding aloft a captured machine-gun in triumph. As he began to walk slowly back to his platoon he was struck by a burst of fire from behind and mortally wounded. He was brought in by his company commander, Captain Donald Easten, but was beyond help. His last words were, 'I've got to go. It was worth it – I got the lot.'

Harman's attitude mirrored the deep sense of personal loathing with which the British soldier fought against the Japanese in Burma, induced by the latter's numerous atrocities. From the Japanese they knew that no mercy could be expected, whether they were wounded or not, and they were therefore not prepared to grant any. By coincidence, the West Kents had recently been reinforced with a draft of men from the South Wales Borderers, who had inherited the traditions of Rorke's Drift. Now, curiously, the battle took on the form of an enlarged and protracted version of that engagement, for over 8,000 men of Sato's 31st Division had been fought to a standstill by a garrison that never numbered more than 600 unwounded men, while a further 3,000 Japanese were either engaged at the Jotsoma box or were preparing to contest the advance of the 2nd British Division from Dimapur.

As always, the Japanese made the mistake of repeating attacks over the same ground as those that had failed earlier. They also made the mistake of never attacking in more than company strength, when the garrison would have found it difficult to handle battalion attacks. As a result, their losses were immense, and even those of them who broke through, too disciplined to use their personal initiative, chose to hide until they were hunted down. The battlefield itself, shared by the living and the dead in close proximity to each other, became hideous with the sight of multiple decomposing bodies, many of which were blown apart by artillery fire, while the combined stench of decay and human waste that could not be disposed of hung over everything. The garrison remained short of drinking water throughout; tropical rainstorms, welcome at first, quickly soaked and chilled them to the bone. Sleep, lasting only minutes at a time, always ended in a renewal of the nightmare.

Sheer attrition wore down the West Kents' numbers. DIS Hill was abandoned on the evening of 10 April. Three days later the garrison began to receive air-dropped supplies, some of which drifted into the enemy lines. By now, the Japanese had learned from some of their expensive lessons. On the night of 16–17 April, following a heavy bombardment that included phosphorus shells, they attacked in greater numbers than ever before and stormed FSD Hill. The following night, using the same tactics, they took Kuki Piquet. During these days of savage fighting, many of the defenders showed courage and qualities well beyond the expected norm. There was Company Sergeant Major Haines who, though blinded, was guided around the trenches by his minder, encouraging the riflemen with the familiar sound of his voice until he was killed on Kuki Piquet; and Sergeant King, the mortar specialist, who held his smashed jaw together with one hand while he directed the fire of his weapons so effectively that the enemy was unable to advance beyond Kuki Piquet; and Colour Sergeant Eves, the senior cook, and his helpers, who braved every danger to bring the rifle companies hot food and tea; and Captain the Reverend Roy Randolph, the West Kents' chaplain, who always seemed to be available to comfort the sick and the dying; and Colonel Laverty himself, who never seemed to rest, yet was able to spur on his officers and men with a few gruff words of encouragement and a tired smile of appreciation for their efforts; and Colonel Richards, the garrison commander, whose regular visits to the forward trenches were welcomed by the troops, as were those of Charles Pawsey, the civilian Deputy Commissioner, who had preferred to take his chance among them rather than be evacuated, and whose imperturbable figure, accompanied by his companionable dog, were a commonplace sight among the carnage; and many more, whose names have been lost or whose acts have gone unrecorded.

Yet, for all the heroism displayed, when Richards emerged from his command post on the morning of 18 April, there seemed little hope left. The perimeter now measured only 350 yards across, the dressing station contained 600 wounded and no direct assistance could be expected from the Jotsoma box, which was itself surrounded. There was a mood of quiet acceptance that Kohima would fall to the next concentrated Japanese attack unless a miracle occurred. It did. At about 08:00 the Japanese positions were smothered in a welter of bursting 25-pdr and 5.5-inch howitzer shells. This punishment was followed by flights of Hurribombers that roared in to bomb and strafe. This unexpected activity heralded the approach of XXXIII Corps, led by Major General Grover's

2nd British Division, which was itself spearheaded by the Lee medium tanks of 149 Regiment, Royal Armoured Corps. The Lee, while obsolete in other theatres of war, was an ideal tool for jungle warfare, since its 75mm gun, mounted in a limited-traverse sponson, could fire high-explosive rounds ahead while the 37mm in the top turret fired canister rounds that were deadly against troops in the open and could also be used to strip cover from a concealed position.

Soon, those on Hospital Spur could see the tanks fighting their way up the Dimapur road, past the box at Jotsoma. By noon, they had halted below the spur and 1/1st Punjabis arrived from Jotsoma to take the strain off the exhausted garrison. Two days later, the West Kents were relieved by the 1st Berkshire Regiment, some of whom, hardened regulars though they were, found the sights and stench of this most horrible of battlefields so bad that they vomited uncontrollably.

The Kohima garrison might have been relieved, but the battle was far from over. The Japanese had dug themselves securely into all their gains, as well as on other features covering the road to Imphal, and would have to be ejected before the road could be opened. As always, they fought to the death and it took until the middle of May to dislodge them. On 6 May Captain John Randle of the 2nd Royal Norfolk Regiment won a posthumous Victoria Cross when his company was held up by machine-gun fire from an enemy bunker. Although he had already sustained a wound, he charged the bunker single-handed, and in doing so sustained further wounds, which proved to be mortal, but managed to throw a grenade through the fire slit, which he then completely blocked with his body.

In circumstances where the terrain permitted their use, the tanks proved invaluable. On 12 May two troops smashed up no less than twelve bunkers on FSD, DIS and Jail Hills with direct, point-blank gunfire, enabling the British infantry to take possession of the first two. Next day, more bunkers were blown apart on Kuki Piquet. Simultaneously, another Lee, having climbed a track carved by a bulldozer to the summit of Garrison Hill, was deliberately driven over the terrace on to the tennis court below, crushing a bunker and everyone in it, then shooting up every enemy position in sight, including the ruins of the DC's bungalow. At the end of this action, which cost one man slightly wounded, not a Japanese remained alive in the immediate area.

By the end of the month, the remnants of Sato's once proud 31st Division, starving, diseased and shooting their own wounded to prevent capture, was staggering back towards the jungle with the 7th Indian Division in pursuit, and the road to Imphal was open. Sato was bitterly critical of Mutaguchi, his army commander, for not supporting him adequately, and Mutaguchi was equally critical of Sato for not trying harder. Both lost their jobs when their feud became public.

The Imphal Plain covers an area of some 700 square miles and is 2,500 feet above sea level. It is entirely surrounded by mountains up to 8,000 feet in height. Through it, from north to south, runs the Manipur River, draining a marshy area known as Log Tag Lake at the southern end of the plain. If Imphal town lay at the centre of a clock, the road from Dimapur and Kohima would enter it at twelve. At one o'clock is a massive detached feature known as Nunshigum. At two, some 30 miles distant, is the Ukhrul saddle, giving access to the upper reaches of the Chindwin, many miles beyond, by way of primitive tracks. At four o'clock is the Shenam saddle and the road to the Kabaw valley. At six, the Manipur River and Log Tag Lake. At seven, the main road leaves the plain for Tiddim, with the villages of Bishenpur, Potsangbam and Ninthoukong beside it. At nine o'clock a primitive track snaked through the mountains to Silchar in Assam, some 30 miles distant.

The Battle of Imphal started in different places at different times, lasting approximately from late March until the end of June. It was fought around the edges of the plain and on the approaches to Imphal town. At the beginning of the battle, Scoones's IV Corps consisted of the 17th Indian Division (Major General Cowan), the 20th Indian Division (Major General Gracey) and the 23rd Indian Division (Major General Roberts), joined by the rest of the 5th Indian Division (Major General Briggs), which had arrived by air from the Arakan, plus 254 Indian Tank Brigade, commanded by the corps commander's brother, Brigadier Reginald Scoones. The tank brigade contained two regiments, the British 3rd Carabiniers with Lees, and the Indian 7th Light Cavalry with Stuarts.

The Japanese convergence towards the plain, fast and aggressive as it was, was met by sharp local counter-attacks. It was during one such action, at Mapao Ridge, to the north-east of Imphal town, that the battle's first Victoria Cross was won, posthumously, by Jemadar Abdul Hafiz of the 3/9th Jat Infantry (5th Indian Division). When, on 6 April, his platoon was ordered to assault a prominent feature, the only approach to which lay across a bare slope and then up a steep cliff, Abdul Hafiz led the attack personally. Having killed several of the enemy himself, he continued to advance until he was hit twice by machine-gun fire from another feature, the second wound being mortal. By now, however, the sheer determined ferocity of his attack had so unnerved the Japanese that, although they were present in superior strength, they bolted in such numbers that thereafter the ridge became known as Runaway Hill.

Just four days later IV Corps was brought to the brink of disaster. On 10 April Nunshigum, towering 1,000 feet above the plain, was finally taken by the Japanese after changing hands several times. As it dominated the corps' principal airstrips, the supply outlook would be very bleak indeed were it not retaken before the enemy could consolidate. It was decided that on 13 April the 1/17th Dogras, supported by the Carabiniers' B Squadron, would assault the feature in the wake of an artillery bombardment and air strike.

The steep slopes were hard going for an infantryman, but for the tank drivers they were a severe test of skill and nerve. Nevertheless, by 11:15 they had reached the summit of the 7,000-yard long feature, which was composed of small hills joined by hog's-back cols, some only a few yards wide. All went well until approximately halfway along the ridge, when the tanks were forced into single file to negotiate a razor-edged col connecting two features known as the Twin Bumps and the Northern Bump. Because of the precarious nature of the route, all the tank commanders had their heads out so that they could direct their drivers. Suddenly, disregarding the fire of the Dogras on either flank, the tank commanders' tommy-guns and the tanks themselves, the Japanese sprang an ambush. Yelling and screaming, they swarmed towards the tanks from both sides, making their commanders their special target. By the time the attackers had been beaten off, the squadron leader and all his officers had been killed, as had the commanders of other tanks and their replacements. The Dogras had also incurred serious casualties, including both company commanders. A stand-off now existed, with the British attack stalled on the col and the Japanese still in possession of the bunkers dug into the Northern Bump at its far end. Ordered by radio to resume the attack, Squadron Sergeant Major Craddock of the Carabiniers agreed a plan with the senior surviving VCOs of the two Dogra companies, Subadars Ranbir Singh and Tiru Ram. The tanks would close in on the bunkers and suppress their fire, after which the Dogras would go in with the bayonet. First, however, those tanks without commanders had to be moved off the col. This was no easy matter in view of the steep sides of the ridge and one tank even crashed a hair-raising 100 feet down a slope, fortunately without serious injury to the crew. The attack then went in, blasted the bunkers apart, and the Dogras slaughtered every Japanese on the hill. The enemy made an attempt to recapture Nunshigum during the evening, but by then the entire Dogra battalion was in position and they were easily beaten off. The feature was not seriously threatened again.

As SSM Craddock's was not an individual achievement, it did not qualify for the Victoria Cross, although he did receive the immediate award of the Distinguished Conduct Medal. He died shortly after the war, but on each subsequent anniversary of the battle his regiment's B Squadron paraded without officers, and under the command of its sergeant major and NCOs, in commemoration of the event. Subadar Ranbir Singh, who had led the final infantry assault, received the Indian Order of Merit.

Much of the Imphal battle's most ferocious fighting occurred along the Tiddim road, at the western edge of the plain. It took place in ground-saturating monsoon rains, to the accompaniment of violent thunder and lightning storms. Heat, humidity, swarms of flies, mosquitoes, leeches and trench foot added to the troops' permanent discomfort. Here, General Yanagida, commanding the Japanese 33rd Division, was sacked by Mutaguchi for his lack of progress and replaced by the more aggressive Major General Nobuo Tanaka. Yet, for all that he cared so little for his men's lives, at one point ordering his officers to use their swords on anyone showing less than total enthusiasm, he was no more able than his predecessor to overcome the unbelievably stubborn defence he encountered.

On the afternoon of 27 May Havildar (sergeant) Gaje Ghale of the 2/5th Royal Gurkha Rifles (17th Indian Division) won the first of three VCs that would be awarded to members of his regiment during the battle. Gaje Ghale was commanding a platoon of young and inexperienced soldiers to whom he felt he must set an example, although he had never been under fire himself. His platoon was one of two detailed to recapture a stockade at the end of a bare ridge, high in the Chin Hills. The attack, mounted astride the narrow crest, was led by Captain Villiers Dennys, swinging his walking-stick. The Japanese waited until the Gurkhas were only 200 yards from their position, then let fly with everything they had, including artillery, mortars and twelve machine-guns. The Gurkhas surged forward, but stalled short of the knoll on which the stockade was situated. Together, Dennys and Gaje got it moving again, but once more it stalled. At the third attempt it was pressed home, and although Gaje was hit in the arm, leg and chest by grenade fragments 20 yards from the enemy, he led his men's charge in among them, their deadly kukris doing fearful execution in the savage mêlée that followed. Only when the captured position was consididated against counter-attack did he consent to seek medical attention. When Gaje Ghale finally retired from the army, he did so with the rank of honorary captain.

At Ninthoukhong, during the night of 6–7 June, Sergeant Hanson Turner of the 1st West Yorkshire Regiment (17th Indian Division) won a posthumous Victoria Cross. As his battalion's strength had already been seriously eroded by casualties and sickness, Turner had been appointed acting sergeant and was commanding a platoon that contained only twenty men. The Japanese, holding the southern half of the village, launched a series of determined attacks across the stream that divided it. Forced to give a little ground by superior numbers, the platoon held off the enemy with grenades and its one remaining Bren. Turner was wounded twice while fetching more grenades, and, on learning that all the company's officers were down, recognised that he must hold on at all costs. Towards dawn, the enemy were detected trying to work their way round his position. Telling the platoon, now reduced to nine or ten men, to give him covering fire, Turner launched a personal counter-attack, hurling grenades. The explosions were followed by screams, but the sound of Japanese splashing through the stream continued. Returning no less than five times for more grenades, Turner continued to bomb the enemy, but was shot and killed just as the attack began to fade. There was little doubt among the West Yorkshiremen that but for his action, the battalion's defences would have been penetrated and the whole position compromised. His body was found near the stream next morning; thirty dead Japanese were counted in front of his platoon, and many more must have crawled away, wounded. The enemy renewed their attacks during the day, but did not press them fully home.

Five days later, the Japanese mounted another major assault on Ninthoukhong, supported by five of their Type 97 medium tanks. One of the garrison's two anti-tank guns was destroyed, but the second gun knocked out two of the tanks. The remaining three took evasive action and became bogged down, although they continued to give fire support to their infantry. The result was that the defences were penetrated to a depth of 200 yards on a 300-yard frontage before the line was stabilised. Two companies of the 1/7th Gurkha rifles were sent up to mount a counter-attack. With them was Rifleman Ganju Lama, the son of a Tibetan father and a Nepalese mother. Strictly speaking, as a native of Sikkim state, he was not eligible to join a Gurkha regiment, but in wartime this usually strict regulation was relaxed. Tall and strong, he was a natural choice as a PIAT (Projector Infantry Anti-Tank) gunner. This cumbrous weapon threw a shaped-charge bomb by means of a heavy coiled spring mounted in a trough. It required considerable strength to compress the spring, which could only be done by the gunner standing up and pressing with all his weight. It was not accurate beyond 30 yards, but the bomb had tremendous penetrative power when it did connect. The previous month, Ganju had been awarded the Military Medal for knocking out a Japanese tank on the Tiddim road.

When the counter-attack went in, it was stalled by fire from the three bogged-down Type 97s. Ganju crawled forward, intent on their destruction, ignoring the countless bullets that splattered the mud all around, to say nothing of a wound in the leg, further wounds in both arms and a smashed wrist. At 30 yards range, he blasted a hole through the nearest tank's armour, then stood up to recock the PIAT, inserted a fresh bomb, then crawled towards the second tank, which he also knocked out. He would have tackled the third but it fell victim to the garrison's remaining anti-tank gun. Still Ganju was not satisfied. He had seen some of the crews bail out and he wanted them dead. Crawling back to his comrades, he obtained a supply of grenades and returned to finish them off. The counter-attack was resumed and drove the enemy out of their lodgement.

Not surprisingly, Ganju Lama was awarded the Victoria Cross. He recovered from his wounds and after Indian independence joined one of the new Indian Army's Gurkha regiments and was granted the rank of honorary captain while still serving. He also received the appointment of honorary life ADC to the President of India. In 1964 he developed a large boil on his leg; when lanced, the cause was found to be a Japanese bullet, the presence of which had not been suspected.

Elsewhere around the edges of the Imphal Plain, the Japanese were regularly subjected to scientifically planned infantry/tank attacks that ate away at their positions. These, plus the British ability to switch large quantities of artillery fire around the battlefield at will, their growing shortage of supplies, loss of air superiority and lack of progress, all combined to erode their morale. On 22 June, at Milestone 109, 7th Light Cavalry's Stuarts, leading the northwards advance of 5th Indian Division, met the Lees of 149 Regiment RAC, spearheading the drive of 2nd British Division southwards down the road from Kohima. The siege of Imphal was over, but the battle was not.

Unable to make progress at Ninthoukhong, Tanaka decided to try to outflank the position through the hills to the west, only to be fought to a standstill by his old opponents the 2/5th Royal Gurkha Rifles on the

Bishenpur–Silchar track. Here, halfway along the track, at a height of almost 6,000 feet, the monsoon winds had created conditions in which the western slopes of the hills were densely forested but the eastern slopes were bare. The hillsides themselves were punctuated by protruding knolls and bluffs. Having climbed the track from Bishenpur to its halfway point, the 2/5th found themselves facing a long slope to their north, rising several hundred feet to a jungle-clad crest some two miles distant. There were five knolls on the slope, known in ascending order as BP Piquet, Green Dome, Mortar Bluff, Water Piquet and Double Deck. The last two were in Japanese hands and as a preliminary to the capture of Water Piquet a forty-one-strong platoon under a very capable, good-humoured VCO, Subadar Netrabahadur Thapa, was sent up to Mortar Bluff on the evening of 25 June, taking over trenches from men of the 7/10th Baluchi Regiment. At 19:00 a blinding rainstorm descended. An hour later shells exploded in the position and the Japanese materialised out of the pouring rain. They were beaten off with grenades and small arms as well as the fire of the battalion's mortars and a mountain battery, called down over a telephone link.

At 01:30 the enemy attacked again, in greater numbers from a different direction. A section was overrun when one of its Brens jammed and the other was hit and put out of action. Netrabahadur prevented a further advance, but the attacks continued and the knoll was only held because of desperate hand-to-hand fighting. When ammunition began to run low, Netrabahadur called down the fire of the mountain battery on his own position, causing the Japanese to fall back. Unfortunately, at 04:00 the eight-strong party bringing up fresh ammunition was ambushed just as it was about to enter the platoon's position, all being killed or wounded. Wielding his kukri, Netrabahadur charged out, drove off the attackers and retrieved the ammunition. Fifteen minutes later, having distributed the fresh supplies to his platoon, less than half of whom remained alive and unwounded, he led a counter-attack. In the subsequent mêlée he had just cloven the skull of a Japanese with his kukri when he was shot in the face, and was killed a minute later by an exploding grenade. Only six unwounded men now remained of the original platoon. Recognising the impossibility of hanging on any longer, the senior NCO, Havildar Lachimbahadur Thapa, collected as many of the wounded as he could and led them to safety. For tenacious defence of the post during the night, Netrabahadur Thapa received a posthumous Victoria Cross.

On learning that Mortar Bluff had fallen, Lieutenant Colonel N.

Eustace, commanding the battalion, decided that it would be retaken by a company assault that would form up in the lee of Green Dome, and that this attack would be followed through by another company that would take Water Piquet and Double Deck. The rain had now stopped and Mortar Bluff was being hammered by the entire divisional artillery, supplemented by a medium regiment. At 09:50 the company detailed for Mortar Bluff, commanded by Lieutenant J. P. Henderson, swarmed over the crest of Green Dome and attacked across the 250 yards of open hillside separating them from the bluff. They came under fire immediately but Henderson kept them moving despite their losses. Foremost among those of his men to storm up the slippery slopes of the bluff was a young section commander, Naik (corporal) Agansing Rai, who had won the Military Medal in an earlier action. Ripping apart the strands of barbed wire, Agansing led his section in a charge against the machine-gun that had caused most of the company's casualties, firing his tommy-gun. All four of the enemy manning the weapon were killed, three of them by Agansing. Next he led his men in a charge at a 37mm gun that had opened fire from a concealed position just beyond the bluff. Fire from Water Piquet reduced the section to himself and two other men, but could not save the five-man gun crew, three of whom fell to his tommy-gun. At this point the second company, commanded by Subadar Dhirbahadur Gurung, should have passed through Henderson's men, but such was the latter's élan that they charged on towards Water Piquet, some 300 yards distant. They were met by a rain of grenades and intense fire from a bunker which Agansing promptly tackled alone, covered by fire from his Bren gunner. Working his way to the fire slit, he flung in a grenade, then fired his tommy-gun through the opening, killing everyone inside. The rest of the garrison fled. Dhirbahadur's company then came up and, after artillery preparation, drove the Japanese off Double Deck in a ferocious attack. Agansing Rai, who emerged from the battle without a scratch, received the Victoria Cross. He left the army as a subadar major in 1971 and was awarded the rank of honorary captain.

When Dhirbahadur's company took Double Deck, they chased the surviving Japanese over the crest and into the jungle, where the capture of two of the enemy's field guns won the subadar the Military Cross. This was the first time during the entire battle that the Japanese had been seen to abandon their weapons and run, a sure indication that their morale had finally broken. As fighting formations, the Japanese 15th and 33rd Divisions were finished. During the next few weeks they crawled their way back to the Chindwin, leaving the roads and tracks littered with dead. Never in its history had the Japanese Imperial Army sustained such a humiliating defeat. At Kohima and Imphal, Mutaguchi's Fifteenth Army lost 53,000 dead from all causes, including starvation and tropical diseases, as well as all its heavy equipment. British and Indian units sustained 17,000 casualties, including 13,000 wounded evacuated by air.

Here, there is insufficient space to do full justice to the impact of the Chindits' deep-penetration operations on the Japanese. Wingate's strategy was to create fortified defensive boxes in the enemy's rear. These strongholds were supplied by air and from them columns would prey upon Japanese road and rail links, mount ambushes, destroy supply dumps, eliminate isolated garrisons and, as far as possible, sever communications between the Burma Area Army's administrative areas and its troops opposing IV Corps at Imphal and Stilwell's Chinese in the north. Initially, three brigades were employed, two being air-lifted into Burma while the third, starting in February, marched 360 miles into its operational area through some of the worst jungle in the world. These were later joined by three more brigades. Operationally, brigades were subdivided into 300-strong columns, each of which was a self-contained force with its own mule train, heavy weapons and signals detachments. It was appreciated that the Japanese would react violently to the incursion and mount attacks on the Chindit strongholds, but this was all to the good as it would divert strength from their efforts elsewhere. Command of the Chindits passed to Major General Walter Lentaigne when Wingate was killed in an air crash on 24 March. Had Wingate lived, he would have seen his concept of deep penetration fully vindicated, for the Japanese were forced to divert the equivalent of two-and-a-half divisions in an attempt to deal with the Chindits, while in post-war discussions senior Japanese officers frankly admitted that the incursion had been an important factor in their failures at Kohima and Imphal. Latterly, some Chindit brigades were diverted to assist Stilwell's Chinese Army, the advance of which had been stalled by the stubborn defence of Myitkyina. More was probably asked of the Chindits than of any other troops in World War II. When they were finally withdrawn, the health of many had been permanently broken by exhaustion and disease.

Of the Victoria Crosses won by Chindits, the posthumous award to Lieutenant George Cairns is of particular interest since it was the last to be gazetted for World War II. The original recommendation had been among Wingate's papers when his aircraft crashed and it was not possible to reconstitute the file until after the war. On 13 March, as part of the operations leading to the establishment of the White City stronghold, Cairns, serving with the 1st South Staffordshire Regiment, took part in an attack on a pagoda-crowned hill at Henu. The Japanese counter-attacked and a fierce hand-to-hand struggle took place on the summit. During this Cairns came face to face with a Japanese officer whom he shot dead, but not before the latter had slashed off his left arm with his sword. Snatching up the sword, Cairns waded in among the enemy, killing and wounding several before he collapsed and died from loss of blood. The Japanese, forced back behind the pagoda, were finally driven off the hill when several platoons of the 3/6th Gurkha Rifles joined the attack.

When the Chindits were diverted to help Stilwell, they found themselves fighting as conventional infantry rather than in their specialised role, and their casualties rose accordingly. During the battle to capture Mogaung two members of 3/6th Gurkha Rifles won the Victoria Cross. The first went, posthumously, to twenty-year-old Acting Captain Michael Allmand of the Indian Armoured Corps, who was serving with the battalion, for a series of actions. On 11 June his brigade attacked an important road bridge at Pin Hmi, on the approach to Mogaung. Coming under heavy fire and incurring casualties, Allmand's platoon went to ground. Allmand, however, charged on alone, killing three of the enemy single-handed. Inspired by his example, the rest of the platoon renewed their attack and captured the position. Two days later, because of heavy casualties among the battalion's officers, Allmand took over command of his company, which he successfully led to capture a ridge. On 23 June, during the final assault of Mogaung railway bridge, he charged an enemy machine-gun post alone, but was mortally wounded.

The second award went to Rifleman Tulbahadur Pun. During the attack on the railway bridge, fire from an enemy machine-gun post reduced Tulbahadur's section to himself, the section commander and one other rifleman. The section commander immediately led a charge against the position, but was cut down, as was the third man. Undeterred, Tulbahadur, a Bren gunner, charged on alone, killing three of the occupants, putting the remaining five to flight, and capturing two light machine-guns. He then provided the rest of his platoon with accurate supporting fire, enabling them to capture their objective. When he retired from the army he did so with the rank of honorary lieutenant.

Mogaung was captured with the assistance of Chinese troops. Stilwell, whose dislike of his allies verged on paranoia, announced that the town had fallen to the latter alone, and so, to the Chindits' disgust, it was announced to the world. In response, Brigadier Michael Calvert, commanding the Chindit 77th Brigade, which had done most of the fighting, sent a message direct to Stilwell saying: 'The Chinese-American forces having taken Mogaung, 77th Indian Infantry Brigade is proceeding to take umbrage.' Puzzled, Stilwell's intelligence officer, who happened to be his son, reported to the general that he could not find Umbrage on his map!

The last of the Chindit VCs was awarded, posthumously, to Major Frank Blaker, an officer of the Highland Light Infantry serving with the 3/9th Gurkha Rifles. On 9 July his battalion mounted a two-company attack on a feature dominating the main railway line. Near the top of the ridge his company was held up by heavy machine-gun fire. Just as he identified the source of this a grenade exploded near by, wounding him badly in the left wrist. Disregarding this, he got up and advanced through the thick undergrowth, firing his carbine. Only yards from the enemy he was cut down by a burst, being hit three times in the stomach as well as in the arm. His sudden appearance, however, had distracted the Japanese, enabling his men, who were following him, to overrun their objective. Blaker had enjoyed a happy relationship with his company, who were in his thoughts to the end, telling his havildar major to thank them for all they had done for him and recommending two of them for gallantry awards. Gurkhas are not normally demonstrative, but Blaker's death upset them badly, to the extent that they asked one of his officers, Lieutenant J. W. Sweetman, to write to his family on their behalf, saying that he was the most efficient and bravest officer they had ever had.

Shortly after this, the last of the Chindit columns were flown out to India, where they were disbanded. That, however, was not the end of their story, for during the post-war Malayan Emergency their methods were adopted by the Special Air Service Regiment.

The battles of Kohima and Imphal, and those fought by the Chindits and Stilwell's Chinese-American army, marked the turning point of the war in Burma. The back of the Burma Area Army was broken. It could not prevent the reopening of the Burma Road supply route to China and it was driven across the Chindwin to the Irrawaddy. Not even this great river could save it, for in 1945 Slim, having absorbed the enemy's attention with diversionary crossings, suddenly directed an armoured thrust at Meiktila, the hub of the Japanese supply and communication system. Once the town was firmly in British hands, the Burma Area Army disintegrated, to the point that it was unable to offer serious resistance when Slim followed through with a lightning dash to Rangoon.

Market Garden

The business of generals is to win battles, campaigns and wars in the shortest possible time with the minimum loss of life. In September 1944, following the complete rout of the German armies in Normandy and the whirlwind Allied advance across France and Belgium, Field Marshal Montgomery believed that he saw an opportunity to bring an end to the war in Europe within the space of a few months. At the heart of his plan was the capture of the road, rail and pontoon bridges across the Lower Rhine at Arnhem, some 64 miles behind the enemy lines. The effect of this would not only be to outflank the defences of the Siegfried Line, stretching along much of Germany's western frontier, but also to achieve a crossing of the great water barrier presented by the Rhine. This in turn would enable drives to be mounted across the north German plain, or against the industrial heartland of the Ruhr.

The only way such an operation could be mounted was by laying an airborne carpet across Holland. Such a thing had been done before, by the Germans in 1940, during their operations to secure Rotterdam and the Hague, and, while not completely successful, had paid handsome dividends. Now, Montgomery proposed using the three airborne divisions of Lieutenant General Frederick Browning's I Airborne Corps in the same manner. The US 101st Airborne Division (Major General Maxwell D. Taylor) was to secure bridges and canal crossings between Eindhoven and Grave; the US 82nd Airborne Division (Brigadier General James Gavin) was to capture the two major bridges at Grave and Nijmegen, as well as securing the high ground between Nijmegen and Groesbeek to the east; and the British 1st Airborne Division (Major General Roy Urquhart) was to capture the Arnhem bridges and consolidate a bridgehead, into which the 52nd (Lowland) Division, an airportable formation, would be flown when the situation permitted. Appreciating that airborne formations were lightly armed and therefore had a limited endurance in battle, Montgomery planned for each in turn to be relieved by Lieutenant General Brian Horrocks's XXX Corps advancing rapidly northwards from its bridgeheads on the Meuse–Escaut Canal, its flanks covered by VIII and XII Corps. Once XXX Corps had reached Arnhem the advance would be extended to the Zuider Zee, isolating the German formations in western Holland. Market was the codename adopted for I Airborne Corps' part in the plan, and Garden for XXX Corps' concurrent operations.

There were, unfortunately, a number of factors that worked against the concept from the outset. Ultra intercepts, available to Montgomery, indicated that the Germans were clearly aware of the strategic significance of Arnhem and anticipated a thrust in that direction. These were ignored, as were reports that II SS Panzer Corps was refitting in the Arnhem area. This formation had received a fearful mauling in Normandy and its two divisions, 9th SS Panzer Division *Hohenstauffen* and 10th SS Panzer Division *Frundsberg*, were but shadows of their former selves. Against this, they had been rested and were receiving replacement personnel and tanks, whereas British 1st Airborne Division would have none of the latter when it dropped. Ignored, too, was the German Army's ability to cobble together *ad hoc* units with troops drawn from every imaginable source and direct them to crisis points. Again, Montgomery seriously underestimated the time required for XXX Corps to break through and reach Arnhem. The fact was that the corps' 20,000 armoured and soft-skinned vehicles would be confined by marshy, wooded terrain to a single road for most of the way. In several areas the road, of only average width, ran along embankments 4–6 feet high and was flanked by deep ditches, making it impossible for vehicles to deploy off it. Traffic control would be a nightmare as priorities changed in accordance with the tactical situation ahead. Furthermore, as XXX Corps progressed, it would create a long, narrow salient into enemy territory. The inevitable German reaction would be to pinch out the salient from either flank, or at the very least, bring the road under artillery fire. This meant that troops would have to be diverted to keep them at a distance. There were other tactical considerations, too. Insufficient transports and gliders were available to lift the airborne divisions into their drop and landing zones in a single day, which meant that further lifts on the following days would face a thoroughly alerted anti-aircraft defence. This principally affected the British 1st Airborne Division, which was to be dropped west of Arnhem because of RAF concerns, groundless in the event, that strong AA defences near the objectives would inflict unacceptable losses in aircraft. Thus, at the time when the division would need all its strength to fight its way through the town to the bridges, only a portion of it would be available. Having considered all these factors, Browning ventured his opinion to Montgomery that the operation involved taking 'a bridge too far'. Montgomery, however, had obtained the approval and encouragement of General Dwight Eisenhower, the Allied Supreme Commander in Europe, and in his view it was the Arnhem bridges that counted; if they were not the principal objective, there was no point in mounting the operation at all. All of this was quite at odds with his normally thorough and painstaking preparations for a major operation and can only be explained by the euphoria created by the completeness of the Allied victory in Normandy, which was shared by many.

The first drops took place during the afternoon of 17 September. As luck would have it, Field Marshal Walter Model, commanding the German Army Group E, was having lunch in a hotel at Oosterbeek when the 1st Airborne Division's pathfinders began to come down near by. He immediately drove into Arnhem to alert first Major General Kussin, the town's commandant, and then Lieutenant General Wilhelm Bittrich, the commander of II SS Panzer Corps. Such was the speed of the German reaction that when Brigadier Gerald Lathbury's 1st Parachute Brigade, which had a 7-mile march to make from its drop zone, reached the town, it found itself confronted by a strong defensive cordon and under attack from armoured vehicles. Matters went from bad to worse when it was found that the brigade's radios refused to function in the built-up area, thereby inhibiting co-ordinated action and, worst of all, General Urquhart became temporarily cut off from his troops and was forced into hiding. The Germans blew up a span of the railway bridge to prevent its capture and removed the central section of the pontoon bridge, rendering it useless. Nevertheless, most of Lieutenant Colonel (later Major General Sir John) Frost's 2nd Battalion The Parachute Regiment, part of brigade headquarters and elements of other units, a total of less than 700 men, reached the northern end of the road bridge and, having established themselves in the surrounding buildings, held their position for several days against incredible odds.

Meanwhile, to the south, the US 101st Airborne Division had taken all its bridges save that over the Wilhelmina Canal, which it had crossed by an improvised bridge, and was moving into Eindhoven, while the US 82nd Airborne Division had taken the Maas bridge at Grave and the Maas–Waal Canal bridge at Heuven and was advancing on the high ground at Groesbeek. The British XXX Corps had begun its advance but was making slow progress because of stiff opposition.

It was at Best, to the west of Zon, that the operation's first award for supreme courage was won. H Company of the 502nd Parachute Infantry (101st Airborne Division) was fighting for possession of a bridge over the Wilhelmina Canal. In the lead was Pfc Joe E. Mann, armed with a bazooka. Spotting an enemy 88mm gun, he crawled until it was within range of his weapon, then fired bombs into the position, destroying both the gun and its ammunition. He then proceeded to pick off Germans one by one, but received four wounds in return, which rendered both arms useless. Moved into cover, he insisted on taking his turn of guard duty during the night. Next morning, the enemy mounted a counter-attack. A grenade was flung among the group of soldiers he was with. Mann shouted a warning, then, with both bandaged arms strapped to his body, flung himself on top of the grenade, absorbing the entire force of the explosion but saving the lives of his comrades. He received a posthumous Medal of Honor.

On the afternoon of 18 September, XXX Corps, spearheaded by Major General Allan Adair's Guards Armoured Division, broke through to the 101st Airborne and continued along the road to enter 82nd Airborne Division's southern perimeter at 08:20 the following morning. By now it was becoming steadily apparent that at Arnhem something had gone terribly wrong. Urquhart had managed to evade capture and set up his headquarters in the Hartenstein Hotel in the suburb of Oosterbeek, but German reinforcements, including a Tiger battalion, were pouring into the area and, apart from Frost's group at the road bridge, the rest of his division was being pressed steadily back in nine hours of bloody and confused fighting that tested even the nerves of veterans. During this, Captain Lionel Queripel of the 10th Bn The Parachute Regiment, won a posthumous Victoria Cross. Under heavy fire, he carried a wounded sergeant to the regimental aid post and was wounded in the face while doing so. When it became obvious that his battalion would have to fall back, he decided, despite protests from his men, that he would cover their withdrawal. Armed only with a pistol and a few grenades, he remained behind and was not seen again.

The RAF was now dropping desperately needed supplies to the embattled division. Piloting one Dakota was Flight Lieutenant David Lord, an Irishman by birth who had already won the Distinguished Flying Cross, been shot down in the Western Desert and flown numerous unescorted missions in support of the Chindits in Burma. While approaching the supply drop area, his aircraft was heavily hit twice. One engine began to belch flames and a wing seemed to be on the point of collapse. Despite this, he managed to drop most of the supplies aboard. He then discovered that two containers remained and, recognising their importance to the men on the ground, made a second run and dropped them. He then ordered his crew to bale out, but remained at the controls of the juddering, blazing aircraft until it crashed a few seconds later. He, too, received the posthumous award of the Victoria Cross.

On 20 September two more posthumous Victoria Crosses were won at Arnhem, the first by Lieutenant John Grayburn of the Army Air Corps, serving with 2nd Parachute Regiment at the bridge, and the second by Lance Sergeant John Baskeyfield of the 2nd South Staffordshire Regiment, in the long, narrow perimeter, its base resting on the river, into which the rest of the division had been forced. Grayburn had been wounded on the first evening of the operation, and several times subsequently, but despite his pain, lack of food and sleep, had continued to lead his men in aggressive fighting patrols that alarmed the enemy so seriously that they deployed tanks in the area. During one such patrol he had prevented the Germans placing demolition charges on the bridge. He was killed by close-range tank fire. His citation makes it clear that had it not been for his inspiring leadership and personal bravery, the hold on the northern end of the bridge could not have been maintained for as long as it was.

Sergeant Baskeyfield, commanding a 6-pdr anti-tank gun, opened fire on two Tiger tanks and at least one self-propelled gun that he observed moving along a track. He knocked out the leading Tiger with his first shot and badly damaged that behind with his second. At this point return fire wrecked his gun, wounding him and killing or wounding the rest of the crew. Baskeyfield moved to another gun near by, the crew of which had already been killed, and manned it single-handed. He fired twice at the self-propelled gun, knocking it out with his second shot, and was then killed.

At Nijmegen, the 82nd Airborne and Guards Armoured Divisions were forced to fight their way through the town to the river. During the afternoon, Major Julian Cook's I/504th Parachute Infantry, followed by the regiment's 3rd Battalion under Major Willard Harrison, crossed the river in assault boats under intense fire. Browning, who witnessed the crossing, commented, 'I have never seen a more gallant action.' Once ashore, the paratroopers swung right towards the northern end of the railway bridge. This had not been prepared for demolition and its defenders fled, to be cut down in scores as they ran. The Americans pressed on towards the road bridge but had not reached it when it was stormed by the Shermans of 2nd Grenadier Guards' No. 1 Squadron. Here, demolition charges had been laid and the order was given to fire them just as the tanks reached the centre of the bridge. Nothing happened, one possible explanation being that the cables had been cut by a young member of the Dutch Resistance, Jan von Hoof, who was captured and killed during the battle.

It was now common knowledge that 1st Airborne Division was in very serious trouble. Colonel Reuben Tucker, commanding the 504th Parachute Infantry, was furious with the Guardsmen for not pushing on to Arnhem, now only 11 miles distant. His anger stemmed partly from sympathy for fellow paratroopers, and partly from the feeling that his own men's sacrifices during the afternoon were being wasted. In fact, the overall situation did not justify such an advance, for XXX Corps' corridor was under pressure from both flanks and, while the rest of the 82nd Airborne and Guards Armoured Division were fully occupied in holding open their end of it, it was of paramount importance that the Nijmegen bridgehead should be made secure against counter-attack. The Grenadiers were also short of fuel and ammunition and if supplies had been immediately available nothing would have been gained by their pressing on to the north, as no one knew the precise location of 1st Airborne Division. As it happened, at that very moment, Frost's courageous band at Arnhem bridge, which numbered among their achievements the complete destruction of an SS armoured reconnaissance unit that had tried to fight its way across, were firing their last shots amid blazing and collapsing buildings from which friend and foe alike strove to move the wounded of both sides.

During the misty dawn of 21 September, C Company of 504th Parachute Infantry, occupying part of the Nijmegen bridgehead's perimeter near Oosterhout, was attacked by approximately 100 enemy infantry, supported by two tanks and a half-track. Ignoring the enemy's fire, Private John Towle, armed with a bazooka, left his foxhole and ran 200 yards to an exposed position on a raised dike road, from which he was able to obtain flank shots at the tanks. He hit both, and although the skirting plates covering their suspensions prevented penetration of their main armour, they obviously disliked the experience and pulled back. Having seen a squad of enemy infantry run into a house for cover, Towle fired a single rocket at it, killing all nine men inside. Eager to make a clean sweep, he ran 125 yards under fire to get a shot at the half-track, but was killed by an exploding mortar bomb just as he was taking aim in the kneeling position. He received a posthumous Medal of Honor.

At 09:00 that morning a good radio link was established between Horrocks and Urquhart, who was able to report that 1st Airborne's perimeter was at Oosterbeek and that it still controlled the ferry between nearby Heveadorp and Driel, on the south bank of the river. The emphasis now lay on making contact with as much of Urquhart's division as remained. A sortie up the main Nijmegen–Arnhem road by the tanks of 2nd Irish Guards was halted with loss after it had covered 5 miles, and since ditches made it impossible to deploy it was clear that no more progress could be made along that route. However, that afternoon Major General Stanislas Sosabowski's 1st Polish Parachute Brigade was dropped at Driel and secured the southern end of the ferry site. During the evening the leading elements of Major General G. I. Thomas's 43rd (Wessex) Division, the second major formation to pass up XXX Corps' corridor, began entering the Nijmegen bridgehead.

The problem now was how to establish a physical link between Nijmegen and the Poles. On 22 September armoured cars of the 2nd Household Cavalry Regiment took advantage of the early morning mist to slip through the German defences west of the bridgehead. By 08:00, having used secondary roads, they had reached Driel. Later that morning, the 43rd Division, which had relieved the 82nd Airborne in the bridgehead, mounted a two-brigade attack that captured Oosterhout. Supplies and reinforcements were then sent forward to the Poles, using the same route taken by the armoured cars.

Support from XXX Corps' artillery now became available to Urquhart's hard-pressed men, as was a limited amount of resupply and reinforcement by means of assault boat, and this eased their situation a little. However, as 1st Airborne Division's perimeter was now just 2,000 yards deep and 1,000 yards wide, it was apparent that it could not be expanded without a major assault crossing of the river, for which resources were not available. With great reluctance, therefore, Browning and Horrocks agreed that the division should be withdrawn. Under cover of a heavy bombardment, 2,100 men, all that remained of the original ten thousand, were ferried to the south bank during the night of 25–26 September. Montgomery had expected them to hold their ground for two days before relief arrived; Browning had said they could hold it for a maximum of four days; in the event, they had held it for nine.

The last Victoria Cross to be awarded for Operation Market Garden went to Major Robert Cain of the Royal Northumberland Fusiliers, serving with the 2nd South Staffordshire Regiment, for his actions throughout the battle. During the withdrawal into the Oosterbeek perimeter, Major Cain commanded a company formed from stragglers of his own battalion and the 11th Battalion The Parachute Regiment. With this he held a sector of the line near the church in lower Oosterbeek. Using a PIAT, he became the personal scourge of German armour in the area, hunting down and destroying no less than six tanks and several self-propelled guns. Constant explosions perforated an ear-drum, he received numerous wounds, including shards of metal that penetrated his face, and at one stage was temporarily blinded, but considered that none of his injuries justified seeking medical attention. His courage and qualities of leadership not only inspired his own men to continue fighting, but also demoralised the enemy they were facing. It was a measure of his coolness that immediately prior to being withdrawn across the river he took time to shave carefully, commenting to his amazed brigade commander that he had been 'well brought up'. Later in life, while working for the Shell Oil Company, he achieved the unusual distinction of becoming a member of the Nigerian House of Representatives.

If Market Garden had succeeded, both its concept and its execution would have been hailed as one of the most brilliant feats in military history. It failed for a number of reasons that included intelligence and planning errors, insufficient aircraft, bad flying weather, poor radio communications, underestimation of the enemy and a degree of ill-luck. Yet for all that Arnhem is regarded as a gallant struggle against impossible odds, the equally dramatic capture of Nijmegen proved to be of great value in the operations leading to the final crossing of the Rhine in March 1945.

Iwo Jima

19 FEBRUARY – 26 MARCH 1945

Iwo Jima, a small island in the Volcano-Bonin group, is not a place in which one would usually choose to live. Having no natural water source of its own, its few inhabitants rely upon rainwater stored in cisterns. Only by fertilising plots with seaweed can they persuade vegetables and sugar cane to grow, for the sterile, stony soil is otherwise incapable of supporting more than a few stunted trees, gnarled bushes and coarse grass. Their only other source of food is fish. The island's sole natural resource is sulphur, often lying so close to the surface that its heat can be felt.

The island is kite-shaped and lies upon a north-east–south-west axis. The northern and broadest part of the island consists of a dome-shaped plateau about a mile in diameter, consisting of a jumble of shattered volcanic rock, formed by nature into twisted ridges and gorges with occasional level areas. The coastline around the plateau rises steeply from the sea, with few exits from the narrow shore. The central portion of the island is gentler but is flanked on either side by beaches that consist of a deep layer of soft, black, volcanic ash, blown into steep, shifting terraces by the wind. Across these movement on foot is difficult and in some places impossible even for tracked vehicles. At the southern tip of the island is the conical Mount Suribachi, an extinct volcano rising 550 feet above sea level.

By the autumn of 1944 this unattractive speck on the map had become the focus of strategic planning. The war had now reached the Japanese home islands in the form of raids carried out by B-29 heavy bombers flying from the Mariana Islands. The bombers' long haul from the Marianas to Tokyo was unescorted because the American fighters lacked the range for the round trip. Consequently, enemy fighters were able to inflict serious losses above the target area and damaged bombers that had fought their way clear were sometimes forced to ditch in the sea during the flight home. It was immediately apparent that the island of Iwo Jima, lying approximately halfway between the Marianas and the

Japanese home islands, would not only provide an ideal base for fighters that could remain with the bombers throughout, but also a staging post for damaged aircraft returning from raids. Furthermore, Iwo Jima was sovereign Japanese territory and its capture by the Americans would be a tremendous psychological blow.

None of this was lost upon the Japanese themselves. In October 1944 Lieutenant General Tadamichi Kuribayashi was appointed garrison commander with instructions to render the island impregnable. Infantry, tank, anti-tank, anti-aircraft, artillery, rocket and engineer units began to pour into Iwo Jima, together with naval personnel to man coast defence batteries and construction workers. With these assets, the entire surface of the island became a defended area in which every approach to fortified positions was covered by interlocking arcs of fire. Every advantage was taken of the terrain, both Mount Suribachi and the tortuous northern plateau being honeycombed with bunkers and machine-gun posts from which the defenders could retire when they chose into a subterranean warren. Two airfields were also completed, Airfield No. 1 lying to the north-east of Mount Suribachi, and Airfield No. 2 at the southern edge of the plateau. A third airfield, No. 3, was under construction on the plateau itself. Altogether, about 21,000 Japanese were crammed on to Iwo Jima, about 7,000 more than American intelligence sources suggested. The expectation on both sides was that they would fight to the death.

The actual assault on Iwo Jima, codenamed Operation Detachment, was to take place on 19 February 1945. In overall command was Admiral Raymond Spruance with Vice Admiral Richmond Kelly Turner as Joint Expeditionary Force Commander and Lieutenant General Holland M. Smith, USMC, in command of the Expeditionary Troops. The assault landings and destruction of the Japanese garrison would be carried out by Major General Harry Schmidt's V Amphibious Corps, consisting of the 3rd Marine Division (Major General Graves B. Erskine), the 4th Marine Division (Major General Clifton B. Cates) and the 5th Marine Division (Major General Keller E. Rockney), plus corps troops including two medium artillery battalions and several naval construction battalions whose task was to put the airfields in working order. After years of fighting their way from island to island across the Pacific, the Marines had acquired a vast store of experience and were able to prepare for the many contingencies they would encounter. The riflemen of the assault landing divisions, and their heavy weapons, would be deposited above the water-line by armoured amtracs that could also provide local fire support. Vehicle exits from the beach would be cleared by armoured bulldozers and temporary roads laid with sections of Marston airstrip matting laid from trailers. Each division contained its own tank battalion equipped with Shermans, some armed with flamethrowers and some with dozer blades to shovel earth over the enemy's bunker slits. Supplies would be lifted ashore by amphibious DUKWs and Weasels. Because of the arid state of the island, water-condensing equipment would follow so that the troops did not have to rely on supplies from the ships lying offshore.

Starting on 8 December 1944, American bombers had rained thousands of tons of bombs on the island for seventy-two consecutive days, supplemented by naval bombardment from time to time. The preparatory bombardment proper began on 16 February (D-3) when six battleships and five heavy cruisers pounded designated sectors of the island. This bombardment, punctuated by further air strikes, was to last until the landings were made. The planners believed that it would take fourteen days to capture Iwo Jima. Witnessing the bombardment, some thought that ten would be sufficient. Marine riflemen were not impressed, for all too often they had watched bombardments under which it seemed impossible for anyone to survive, then been forced to fight their way ashore amid a blizzard of fire from an enemy who was very much alive.

At 10:45 on 17 February the commander of the Japanese coast defence batteries made a serious error of judgement. He spotted a squadron of LCI(G)s (Landing Craft Infantry (Gun)) lying 1,000 yards offshore and firing at the beach defences with their 20mm and 40mm guns. Believing that the invasion had begun, he ordered his guns to open fire. Every one of the gunboats was damaged, nine of them seriously, thirty-eight seamen were killed and 123 were wounded. Yet in prematurely disclosing the position of his batteries, particularly those at the northern end of the landing beaches, the Japanese commander exposed them to the fire of the battleship *Nevada*'s 14-inch guns. Consequently, many were neutralised before they could fire on the real landings.

The gunboats had simply been providing covering fire for naval demolition teams who were swimming towards the shore to verify beach and surf conditions and dismantle any underwater obstacles they discovered. Other warships put down a smokescreen along the beaches, enabling the demolition teams and the battered gunboats to withdraw. The gunboat squadron, LCI(G) Group 8, was awarded a Presidential Unit Citation, one Medal of Honor and ten Navy Crosses. The Medal of Honor was won by Lieutenant (jg) Rufus G. Herring, USNR, commanding LCI(G) 449. When Japanese shells hit his craft, causing a blaze, Herring was wounded and knocked senseless. Recovering consciousness, he found that he was bleeding heavily, but at that moment another shell exploded on the bridge, killing or fatally wounding the rest of the other officers there, and wounding Herring for the second time. The gunboat, now out of control, began to wallow in the swell. Although in extreme pain, Herring climbed to the pilot house, took the helm, re-established communication with the engine room and carried on until he was able to obtain a relief. By now he had lost so much blood that he was unable to stand, but had himself propped against a stack of empty ammunition boxes, from where he organised treatment for his wounded and brought his 20mm guns into action again. On the return of the swimmers, he conned his craft to safety under cover of the smokescreen.

At 07:30 on 19 February the preliminary bombardment reached its crescendo maintained for the next ninety minutes. It was at this point that the Japanese most missed their coast defence guns, for shortly after 09:00 the first wave of amtracs touched down on the island's south-eastern beaches. Finding the sand terraces too soft and steep to climb, they lowered their ramps and the riflemen charged down them into ankle-deep sand. On the left of the assault landing, one of the 5th Division's regiments, the 28th Marines, was to cross the island, then wheel left to take Mount Suribachi, while on the right of the divisional sector, the 27th Marines would also cross the island, then wheel north to secure the western end of a line of conspicuous features designated the Zero One Line. In the 4th Division's area the 23rd Marines, on the division's left, were to clear Airfield No. 1, part of Airfield No. 2, and tie in with 27th Marines on the Zero One Line; simultaneously, on the right, the 25th Marines would assist in clearing Airfield No. 1, then swing northwards to clear the southern edge of the plateau as far as their Zero One Line objectives. The third regiment of each division would be committed to the fighting as soon as it had landed.

For the first few minutes, no reactions met the eight Marine battalions coming ashore. Then, with growing intensity, the enemy's machine-guns, mortars and artillery opened up until by 09:30 the advancing lines were pinned down and scraping cover for themselves in the sand. All over Mount Suribachi, the muzzle flashes of hundreds of machine-guns sparkled as fire slits were unmasked. Exploding shells erupted along the congested shoreline, setting fire to stalled amtracs and jeeps. Even when tanks began coming ashore they failed to subdue the opposition altogether, an alarmingly high proportion of them falling victim to anti-tank guns, artillery or powerful mines made from buried naval shells or aerial bombs. Nevertheless, by 10:35 elements belonging to two of I/28th Marines' companies had reached the western shore of the island, although they left behind them numerous active and sometimes invisible enemy fire positions. Clearing these occupied the rest of the day, but by nightfall Mount Suribachi had been isolated. Against this, neither division had reached their Zero One Line objectives and a total of 2,420 casualties had been incurred, including 501 killed.

Among the dead was Sergeant Darrell S. Cole of I/23rd Marines, who received a posthumous Medal of Honor. Under fire the whole way, Cole had led his squad from the beach towards Airfield No. 1, personally destroying two enemy posts with grenades. The squad was then pinned down by fire from three more positions. Only one machine-gun remained to the squad, but Cole used it to silence the nearest pillbox until the weapon jammed. The Japanese immediately reopened fire and began hurling grenades. Armed with only a pistol and one grenade, Cole charged it, killing the defenders. Returning twice for more grenades, he killed the enemy in the two remaining strongpoints but was himself killed by the explosion of an enemy grenade. It was largely because of this action that his company was able to secure its objective.

Elsewhere, Corporal Tony Stein of A Company I/28th also won a Medal of Honor. Evidently something of an individualist, Stein preferred to arm himself with a personally improvised, high-output aircraft machine-gun. He used this to provide fire while his platoon, halted by intense machine-gun and mortar fire, sought cover, then deliberately exposed himself so that he could identify the source of the enemy fire. Satisfied, he mounted a lone attack on one Japanese position after another, killing twenty of the enemy. Naturally, his weapon's ammunition quickly became exhausted and he made no less than eight trips back to the beach to replenish his supply, carrying or assisting a wounded man on each occasion. Later in the day, he directed the fire of an armoured half-track against a particularly stubborn position until he was able to close with it and kill those within. During the evening, his platoon was ordered to withdraw into the main company position. This movement was carried out under such heavy fire that Stein's weapon, which he was using to give covering fire, was twice shot out of his hands.

During the day's fighting, Pfc Donald J. Ruhl of E Company II/28th spotted eight Japanese bolting from a nearby blockhouse. Giving chase, he bayoneted one and shot another. The following morning he left cover and, braving mortar and machine-gunfire, brought in a wounded comrade lying some distance ahead of his own trench, then carried him 300 yards along the beach to a dressing station. Later in the day he took possession of an abandoned Japanese 75mm gun emplacement to prevent the enemy returning to it. On 21 February, as his regiment was fighting its way up Mount Suribachi, Ruhl and another Marine climbed on top of a bunker to fire at the Japanese beyond. When a grenade landed between them, Ruhl threw himself on it to smother the explosion and thereby saved the lives of others near by. He received the posthumous award of the Medal of Honor.

Self-sacrificial acts such as this appear regularly in the annals of all elite forces. Tough training and hard battles create a sense of comradeship and mutual respect beyond the norm, the result being that interdependence becomes instinctive. To emphasise the point, during the bitter battle for Iwo Jima, six more Marines (Corporal Charles J. Berry, Pfc William R. Caddy, Pfc James D. La Belle, Pfc Jacklyn H. Lucas, Private George Phillips and Gunnery Sergeant William G. Walsh) all received the Medal of Honor for performing precisely the same act as Ruhl.

Strong leadership and personal initiative combined with courage beyond the call of duty were the driving forces of the American success during the first critical three days of the battle. Lieutenant Colonel Justice M. Chambers of the III/25th landed immediately after the first assault waves to find the momentum of his battalion's attack stalled by intense artillery, rocket, machine-gun and small arms fire. Casualties, especially among the battalion's officers, were mounting rapidly. The supporting tanks were immobilised by a minefield just inland from the shore, but continued to use their guns. Chambers identified the source of most of the enemy fire as coming from cliffs at the southern edge of the plateau, and in particular from a quarry. He calmly reorganised the battalion and then led it in an eight-hour battle to secure this area of high ground and reduced the volume of enemy fire hitting the beach. On 22 February, having again reorganised the battalion because of further casualties, he was seriously wounded by machine-gun fire and evacuated. His leadership was undoubtedly responsible for achieving success on one of the most critical assault landing sectors of all.

Near by, on the high ground to the north-east of Airfield No. 1, a platoon of A Company I/25th was suddenly halted by a shower of grenades. Sergeant Ross F. Gray, the platoon sergeant, pulled the men back out of range and carefully studied the terrain ahead, discovering a network of enemy bunkers connected to one another by covered trenches and protected by a minefield. Under fire, he crawled through the mines, clearing a path as he went, until he reached the nearest bunker. Returning, he informed his platoon commander of the situation and volunteered to attack the position if covering fire could be given. The plan was approved and, armed only with a satchel demolition charge, he again crawled to the bunker under heavy fire, flinging the short-fused charge into the entrance. He then systematically set about the destruction of remaining bunkers in the complex in the same manner, destroying a total of seven in which twenty-five of the enemy were killed.

To the left, Captain Joseph J. McCarthy's company of the II/24th was similarly held up by rifle, machine-gun and 47mm fire as it advanced in the direction of Airfield No. 2. Forming an assault group from men armed with demolition charges and flamethrowers, he laid a charge across 75 yards of fire-swept ground towards one bunker, posting grenades through its fire slit. As his team set about destroying the structure, he shot two of the enemy who were trying to escape. A second bunker was dealt with in the same way, but on entering the smoking ruin he discovered an enemy survivor taking aim at one of his men. Jumping on the man, McCarthy killed him with his own weapon. He then brought up the rest of his company and took the ridge which was his designated objective.

On the extreme left of the Americans' northward advance towards the plateau, C Company I/24th, commanded by Captain Robert H. Dunlap, was pinned down on a slope leading towards a line of steep cliffs. Much of the enemy's fire seemed to be coming from caves high on the cliff face. Taking his radio, Dunlap crawled until he was only 50 yards from the nearest enemy position. There, having taken careful note of the sources of the enemy's fire, he remained alone, and frequently under fire, for the next two days and nights, controlling artillery and naval gunfire support until the position was neutralised. Dunlap, Chambers, Gray and McCarthy all received the Medal of Honor.

On 21 February the Japanese launched a kamikaze air attack on the ships lying offshore, sinking one escort carrier and damaging another, as well as damaging a fleet carrier, a transport and an LST. This was to be the only outside assistance that the garrison would receive. Ashore, the fighting continued to be so severe that General Schmidt committed V Amphibious Corps' reserve regiment, 21st Marines, on the 4th Division's sector. On Mount Suribachi, the 28th Marines continued to fight their way slowly but steadily up the steep slopes. Each cave position had to be dealt with individually under fire. Where direct gunfire support from tanks was available this was reasonably straightforward, but elsewhere the occupants had to be dealt with at close quarters, using grenades and flamethrowers, and sometimes they were simply sealed within when demolition charges were used to blow in the cave entrances. Finally, on the morning of 23 February, the Marines reached the summit. There, the Associated Press photographer Joe Rosenthal took his dramatic picture of the raising of the Stars and Stripes; now translated into an equally dramatic sculpture, it forms the Marine Corps Memorial in Washington.

Far below, Airfield No. 1 had also been captured but the rest of the landing force was still heavily engaged in fighting its way on to the northern plateau. In the centre of the line Corporal Hershel W. Williams, a demolition specialist serving with 21st Marines, won the Medal of Honor on 23 February. Seeing that the regiment's supporting tanks were unable to make headway through a complex of minefields and defensive positions surrounded by soft sand, Corporal Williams volunteered for the extremely hazardous task of reducing the volume of machine-gun fire coming from the enemy bunkers. Covered by four riflemen, he fought a four-hour battle, repeatedly returning to his own lines for demolition charges and refilled flamethrowers, and eliminated one bunker after another. On one occasion he was seen to climb on top of a bunker and insert the nozzle of his flamethrower into the air vent. A squad of Japanese, determined to put a stop to his career of destruction, charged him with fixed bayonets, only to be incinerated in their turn.

Despite such acts, American losses continued to mount. On 25 February, as the advance approached the widest part of the island, General Schmidt committed the 3rd Marine Division, less one regiment, and this entered the line between the 4th and 5th Divisions. Yet, although the Americans had now reached the northern plateau, its multitude of rock-strewn outcrops, ravines, caves and crevices, all interconnected by the enemy's subterranean defence works and galleries made the nature of the fighting even more difficult. The Japanese would emerge from an exit to inflict sufficient casualties to pin down an advance, then vanish into their warren. Sometimes, attacking Marines would find themselves being fired on from hitherto unsuspected enemy position on their flanks or even behind them. In such a battle, with the Americans above ground and the Japanese below, it was inevitable that the former would suffer severely. Progress was slow and piecemeal, with overall daily gains being measured in hundreds of yards.

On 26 February Pfc Douglas T. Jacobson of III/23rd Marines won the Medal of Honor during an attack on a feature designated Hill 382. By any standard, Jacobson's assault on the Japanese possessed a ferocity far beyond the norm. Taking a bazooka and a supply of bombs from a dead comrade, he first destroyed a troublesome 20mm anti-aircraft gun and its crew. He then fought his way upwards, destroying two machine-gun posts, a blockhouse and a pillbox in which the five men inside were killed by an internal explosion. He next blasted five covered rifle trenches, killing ten of the enemy. Conscious that he had only created a narrow breach in the hill's perimeter defences, he decided to assist a neighbouring company, knocking out in turn a second pillbox, a dug-in tank that was firing at the Marines' supporting Shermans, and another block-house. By the end of his rampage he had destroyed one 20mm AA gun, one tank and sixteen prepared positions, as well as killing no less than seventy-five of the enemy.

Some distance to the right, Private Wilson D. Watson, a BAR gunner serving with II/9th Marines, also won the Medal of Honor for a similar berserk attack. When his platoon's advance was halted by fire from a pillbox on a rocky ridge to its front, Watson charged up the slope and fired bursts through its weapon slit until he was able to toss in a grenade. After this had exploded he ran round to the rear of the structure and mowed down several Japanese attempting to escape. The platoon continued its advance but was again pinned down by fire from the next ridge. Accompanied by his assistant BAR man, Watson picked his way up the rocky slope under mortar and machine-gun fire, then charged the summit, firing his weapon from the hip. Often standing erect, he dominated the summit alone for a considerable period until the platoon joined him, cutting down some sixty Japanese who attempted to counter-attack from the reverse slope.

The naval construction battalions were already working hard to put Airfield No. 1 into an operational condition. Airfield No. 2 was overrun by the 3rd Division on 27 February, as were two prominent features on the plateau, Hills Peter and 199 Oboe. Despite this and slow but sustained progress elsewhere, the Japanese continued their fanatical resistance and had not lost any of their capacity to spring unpleasant surprises. First light on 3 March found Sergeant William G. Harrell of I/28th Marines standing guard on the perimeter defence of his company's command post, a duty he carried out alternately with another man. Suddenly, by the light of a star-shell bursting overhead, he saw Japanese emerging from a nearby ravine. He killed two of them with his carbine, but then an exploding grenade tore off his left hand and broke his thigh. He was struggling vainly to reload his carbine when his companion, running from the command post, handed him a pistol. The Japanese then closed in, an officer wounding Harrell with his sword before the sergeant shot him dead. The second Marine had also been wounded in the mêlée and Harrell ordered him to make himself scarce. Shortly after, Harrell, exhausted from loss of blood, was attacked by two more of the enemy, one of whom rolled an armed grenade towards him. Harrell shot one man dead and then used his right hand to roll the grenade towards the second man, who was closing in rapidly. The explosion killed his opponent, but also destroyed his remaining hand. The rest of the enemy disappeared whence they had come. When Harrell was evacuated at dawn, twelve dead Japanese were counted around his position, five of whom he had accounted for personally. He survived his terrible injuries and received the Medal of Honor.

Not all of the supreme awards for valour gained on Iwo Jima were acts carried out in hot blood. That awarded to Pharmacist's Mate Second Class George E. Wahlen, USN, serving with a company of the II/26th Marines, was won by stoic endurance and dogged devotion to duty. Wahlen had received a painful wound on 26 February but chose to remain with his unit and carried a more seriously injured man to safety from well forward of the established front line. At all times he seemed completely tireless in rendering aid to the wounded, whatever the risks involved. He was wounded again on 2 March but refused evacuation and moved out with his company when it carried out an assault across 600 yards of open ground, using his skills wherever they were needed. The following day he received a third wound that left him unable to walk. Ignoring this, he crawled 50 yards to assist another wounded man. He was subsequently evacuated and survived his injuries.

Airfield No. 3 was cleared on 3 March and the 5th Division took another prominent feature, Hill 362B. The following day Iwo Jima began to perform the function for which it was intended when a damaged B-29 bomber landed on Airfield No. 1. Two days later the USAAF's 15th Fighter Group, which would provide escorts for the bombing raids on the Japanese homeland, began touching down.

Between 7 and 9 March, Medals of Honor were won by Second Lieutenant John H. Leims, First Lieutenant Jack Lummus and Sergeant Joseph R. Julian. On 7 March, Leims, commanding B Company of I/9th Marines, directed an attack that captured several cave positions during the afternoon. It soon became apparent that the assault platoons were now in a dangerously exposed position some 400 yards ahead of the main American line. As they lacked communication with his command post, Leims personally braved the enemy's fire to lay telephone lines to them. To his frustration, he was then ordered to withdraw the company, which he did without incident. He was then informed that several casualties had been left behind. Rather than abandon them to the mercy of the Japanese, he went out twice under fire and brought in two seriously wounded men.

The following day First Lieutenant Jack Lummus of II/27th Marines was ordered to advance with his platoon against deeply entrenched and mutually supporting enemy positions. When the platoon, which formed part of E Company, was pinned down by heavy fire he went forward to reconnoitre but was suddenly blown off his feet by a grenade. Recovering, he identified a Japanese pillbox near by, which he knocked out with a grenade. He then came under fire from a supporting pillbox and some rifle pits and sustained a painful shoulder wound from a grenade fragment. Disregarding this, he charged the second pillbox and killed those within. He then returned to his platoon and directed the fire of the supporting Shermans at the enemy strongpoints he had identified. The advance was resumed but soon became pinned down again. Once more, Lummus rushed an emplacement, killing the occupants, and was leading an assault on some foxholes when a mine exploded beneath him, the injuries he sustained quickly proving fatal. He had been a popular officer who was well liked by his men. His death provoked deep anger among the entire company, which surged forward in a furious, no-quarter charge that carried it 300 yards through the enemy positions until it had taken a bluff overlooking the sea.

The award made to Sergeant Joseph R. Julian for acts on 9 March was also posthumous. His company, belonging to I/27th Marines, was attacking a position very similar to that described above and ran into heavy machine-gun and mortar fire. Julian attacked the nearest pillbox alone, throwing demolition charges and phosphorus grenades into the fire slit. Two of those within were killed, but five more bolted into nearby trenches. Snatching up a discarded rifle, Julian hunted them down, one by one. Obtaining more explosives, he and another Marine then blew in the entrances to two cave positions. Finally, armed with a bazooka, he blasted a pillbox to destruction with four rounds, but was then mortally wounded by enemy fire.

By now, the Japanese were being pressed back into a steadily contracting perimeter on the northern coast of the island. Thousands of them had been killed, but those that survived were still determined to die for their emperor and take as many Americans with them as possible. The outcome of the battle was no longer in doubt, for on 14 March, while attacks continued against the remaining enemy positions, General Schmidt ordered the 4th Division to commence re-embarking. It was during one of these attacks that Private Franklin E. Sigler of II/26th Marines won a Medal of Honor. When his squad leader became a casualty he assumed command, leading an attack on a gun position which he reached first and neutralised with grenades. Fire was then directed at the squad from concealed tunnels and caves in the cliff above. Sigler scaled the rocks to ascertain their precise location but was wounded in the process. Rejoining his squad, he refused evacuation and continued to direct fire on the cave entrances, as well as carrying three wounded men to safety. Finally, he was ordered to seek medical attention.

Two days later, on 16 March, Iwo Jima was declared secure after twenty-six days of bitter fighting. On 20 March an army unit, the 147th Infantry, arrived for garrison duty. The last identifiable pocket of resistance was eliminated on 25 March by troops of the 5th Division, which had already begun embarking. Any sense of relaxation, however, was premature, for at dawn on 26 April between two and three hundred Japanese filtered down the island's western coast and charged into the bivouac areas of the 5th Marine Pioneer Battalion and the nearby USAAF units. During the ensuing fight First Lieutenant Harry L. Martin, commanding a platoon in the Pioneers' C Company, won a posthumous Medal of Honor, the last to be awarded for the campaign. When the Japanese first broke into the encampment, Martin organised a firing line that temporarily held them in check. Aware that some of his men were holding out behind the attackers, he made his way through to them, sustaining two severe wounds but killing any of the enemy who tried to stop him, and led them to safety. When some of the Japanese who had taken over an abandoned machine-gun pit began hurling grenades, he charged it, armed only with a pistol, and killed all the occupants. He was organising a counter-attack to drive the enemy out of the bivouac area when he was mortally wounded by grenade fragments. The fight lasted for three hours, at the end of which 196 enemy bodies were counted. The fact that forty of the Japanese carried swords suggests that the attack was made by Kuribayashi's staff, although the fate of the general himself remains unknown. The pioneers sustained the loss of nine killed and thirty-one wounded, and the air force personnel forty-four killed and eighty-eight wounded.

The capture of Iwo Jima cost the Marines a staggering 24,750 casualties, including 5,885 known dead, to which must be added 2,798 naval casualties, including 433 killed and 448 missing presumed dead. Kuribayashi's garrison had not been quite wiped out, for 216 prisoners had been taken by 26 March and many hundreds more were still at large in their subterranean warrens. After the Marines left, the 124th Infantry continued to patrol aggressively throughout April and May, killing another 1,602 and capturing a further 867.

Such was the suicidal nature of the Japanese resistance on Iwo Jima and subsequently on Okinawa that Allied commanders were convinced that an invasion of Japan's home islands could not be undertaken without prohibitive casualties. The decision was therefore taken to end the war by nuclear means.

Epilogue

Since 1945 the Victoria Cross has been awarded only eleven times, six of the awards being posthumous.

Four were awarded during the Korean War, one during the Malaysian confrontation with Indonesia, four to Australians during the Vietnam War, and two during the Falklands War.

A statistical survey carried out in May 1997 showed that 372 awards of the Congressional Medal of Honor had been made since World War II, thereby reflecting the emergence of the United States as a world super-power. Of the 131 awards made during the Korean War, ninety-three were posthumous; of the 239 awards made during the Vietnam War, 150 were posthumous; two awards were made to participants in the fighting in Somalia, both of them posthumous. Since then, a number of awards, retrospective to various periods, have been made, bringing the total number awarded since the medal's introduction to 3,459, including nineteen double recipients.

Every self-respecting nation needs its heroes. Those winners of the supreme award for valour whom I have had the privilege of knowing were invariably modest men possessed of a quiet air of authority. They were conscious that the award brought with it the considerable responsibility of providing role models for present and future generations. It is a sad fact that with the passing of the years the numbers of such men are dwindling fast, for the young instinctively seek heroes. If they are not immediately visible, they will choose idols of their own, including transient celebrities, some of whom are seriously flawed. In such circumstances the disappointments of misplaced admiration can corrode into cynicism, which is itself a milestone on the road to decadence.

Appendix

Only three men have ever won the Victoria Cross twice.

Surgeon Captain Arthur Martin-Leake of the South African Constabulary won his first award at Vlakfontein, South Africa, on 8 February 1902. He attended to wounded men under heavy fire from the enemy, who were only 100 yards distant. Wounded himself, he carried on until he collapsed from exhaustion but refused water until all the other wounded had been served. On the outbreak of the World War I he was working as a doctor with Indian Railways. Travelling to Paris, he enlisted locally and, having been granted the rank of Lieutenant in the Royal Army Medical Corps, attached himself to the 5th Field Ambulance. His second award was made for acts at Zonnebeke, Belgium, between 28 October and 8 November 1914 when, under constant fire, he rescued numerous wounded men lying close to the enemy's trenches. He subsequently rose to the rank of Lieutenant Colonel. After the war he resumed work with Indian Railways. Following his retirement he returned home and commanded a mobile ARP unit in the World War II.

Captain Noel Chavasse, MC, RAMC, the medical officer of the 1/10th Bn The King's (Liverpool) Regiment (the Liverpool Scottish) first won the award on 9 August 1916 at Guillemont, France, for bringing in wounded men from no man's land under fire, having himself been wounded. The Bar was awarded for acts at Wieltje, Belgium between 31 July and 2 August 1917, when, although severely wounded himself early in the action, he refused evacuation and continued to bring in wounded men from between the lines. He received further wounds, which proved fatal, when an enemy shell exploded in his dugout. The award of the Bar was made posthumously.

Details of the first and subsequent award of the VC to Captain Charles Upham of the 20th Bn, 2nd New Zealand Expeditionary Force, (the Canterbury Regiment), can be found in the chapter on the Battles of El Alamein.

By a curious coincidence, there was a family connection between Chavasse and Upham, the latter's aunt-by-marriage being the wife of a second cousin of Chavasse's. A family connection also existed between Chavasse and Lieutenant Neville Coghill of the 24th Regiment, who won the award in the aftermath of the Battle of Isandhlwana, Coghill's maternal aunt having married the Reverend William Chavasse.

Bibliography

Anon, *The Register of the Victoria Cross*, This England Books, Cheltenham, 1997

Axworthy, Mark, Scafes, Cornel and Craciunoui, Cristian, *Third Axis, Fourth Ally – Romanian Armed Forces in the European War 1941–1945*, Arms & Armour Press, London, 1995

Bartley, Lt Col Whitman S., *Iwo Jima – Amphibious Epic*, The Battery Press, Nashville, 1988

Bennett, Geoffrey, *The Battle of Jutland*, Batsford, London, 1964

Bentley, Nicolas, ed., *Russell's Despatches from the Crimea*, Panther, London, 1970

Brooks, Richard, *The Long Arm of Empire – Naval Brigades from the Crimea to the Boxer Rebellion*, Constable, London, 1999

Brown, David, Shores, Christopher and Macksey, Kenneth, *The Guinness History of Air Warfare*, Guinness Superlatives, London, 1976

Calvert, Michael, *Chindits – Long Range Penetration*, Pan/Ballantyne, London, 1974

Carver, Michael, *Tobruk,* Pan, London, 1972

— *El Alamein*, Fontana, London, 1973

Clowes, Sir William Laird, *The Royal Navy – A History from the Earliest Times to 1900, Vols 6 & 7*, Chatham, London, 1997

Colvin, John, *Not Ordinary Men – The Battle of Kohima Re-assessed,* Leo Cooper, London, 1994

Cortesi, Lawrence, *Bloody Friday Off Guadalcanal*, Zebra Books, New York, 1987

Darby, William O. and Baumer, William H., *We Led the Way – Darby's Rangers*, Jove, New York, 1985

Doherty, Richard and Truesdale, David, *Irish Winners of the Victoria Cross*, Four Courts Press, Dublin, 2000

Edwardes, Michael, *Battles of the Indian Mutiny*, Batsford, London, 1963

Farrar-Hockley, A. H., *The Somme*, Batsford, London, 1964

Farwell, Byron, *Queen Victoria's Little Wars*, Allen Lane, London, 1973

Fleming, Peter, *The Siege at Peking,* Rupert Hart-Davis, London, 1960

Furneaux, Rupert, *The Zulu War – Isandhlwana and Rorke's Drift*, Weidenfeld & Nicolson, London, 1963

Gliddon, Gerald, *VCs of the First World War – 1914*, Alan Sutton, Stroud, 1994

— *VCs of the First World War – The Somme,* Alan Sutton, Stroud, 1994

Harclerode, Peter, *Para! Fifty Years of the Parachute Regiment,* Arms & Armour Press, London, 1992

— *Arnhem – A Tragedy of Errors,* Arms & Armour Press, London, 1994

Harris, John, *The Gallant Six Hundred,* Hutchinson, London, 1973

Haythornthwaite, Philip J., *The Colonial Wars Source Book,* Arms & Armour Press, London, 1995

Hibbert, Christopher, *Anzio – The Bid for Rome,* Macdonald, London, 1970

James, Robert Rhodes, *Gallipoli,* Pan, London, 1974

Katcher, Philip, *The American Civil War Source Book,* Arms & Armour Press, London, 1992

Keegan, John, *Opening Moves – August 1914,* Pan/Ballantyne, London, 1971

Kent, Graeme, *Guadalcanal – Island Ordeal,* Pan/Ballantyne, London, 1972

Keown-Boyd, Henry, *The Fists of Righteous Harmony – A History of the Boxer Uprising in China in the Year 1900,* Leo Cooper, London, 1991

Knight, Ian, *Marching to the Drums – From the Kabul Massacre to the Siege of Mafeking,* Greenhill, London, 1999

Lloyd, Alan, *The Zulu War 1879,* Granada, London, 1973

Lucas Phillips, C. E., *Alamein,* Pan, London, 1965

— *Victoria Cross Battles of the Second World War,* Pan, London, 1975

Macintyre, Captain Donald, *Jutland,* Pan, London, 1966

McCarthy, Charles, *The Somme – The Day-by-Day Account,* Arms & Armour Press, London, 1993

Marshall, Brig. Gen. S. L. A., *Crimsoned Prairie – The Indian Wars on the Great Plains,* Macdonald, London, 1972

Mason, David, *Raid on St Nazaire,* Macdonald, London, 1970

Messenger, Charles, *The Unknown Alamein,* Ian Allan, London, 1982

Miller, John Jr, *Guadalcanal – The First Offensive,* Historical Division, Department of the Army, Washington, 1983

Miller, Thomas G., Jr., *The Cactus Air Force,* Harper & Row, New York, 1969

Napier, Gerald, *The Sapper VCs,* The Stationery Office, London, 1998

Neillands, Robin, *By Sea and Land – The Story of the Royal Marine Commandos,* Weidenfeld & Nicolson, London, 1987

Nevill, Capt. H. L., *North-West Frontier – British & Indian Army Campaigns 1849–1908,* Tom Donovan, London, 1992

Nofi, Albert E., *The Gettysburg Campaign, June–July 1863,* Combined Books, Pennsylvania, 1997

Padden, Ian, *US Rangers,* Bantam, New York, 1985

— *US Marines,* Bantam, New York, 1985

Pemberton, W. Baring, *Battles of the Crimean War,* Batsford, London, 1962

— *Battles of the Boer War,* Batsford, London, 1964

Perkins, Roger, *The Kashmir Gate – Lieutenant Home and the Delhi VCs,* Picton Publishing, Chippenham, 1983

Perrett, Bryan, *Tank Tracks to Rangoon*, Robert Hale, London, 1978

— *Desert Warfare*, Patrick Stephens, Wellingborough, 1988

— *Last Stand! Famous Battles Against the Odds*, Arms & Armour Press, London, 1991

— *At All Costs! Stories of Impossible Victories*, Arms & Armour Press, London, 1993

— *Against All Odds! More Dramatic Last Stand Actions*, Arms & Armour Press, London, 1995

— *Impossible Victories – Ten Unlikely Battlefield Successes*, Arms & Armour Press, London, 1996

Pfanz, Harry W., *Gettysburg – The Second Day*, Chapel Hill, N. Carolina, 1987

Rogers, Col. H. C. B., *The Confederates and Federals At War*, Ian Allan, London, 1973

Rooney, David, *Burma Victory – Imphal, Kohima and the Chindit Issue*, Arms & Armour Press, London, 1992

Ross, Graham, *Scotland's Forgotten Valour*, Maclean Press, 1995

Ryan, Cornelius, *A Bridge Too Far*, Hodder & Stoughton, London, 1974

Snelling, Stephen, *VCs of the First World War – Gallipoli*, Alan Sutton, Stroud, 1995

Stewart, Adrian, *Guadalcanal – World War II's Fiercest Naval Campaign*, William Kimber, London, 1985

Symons, Julian, *Buller's Campaign*, White Lion, London 1974

Terraine, John, *Mons*, Batsford, London, 1961

Utley, Robert M., *Bluecoats and Redskins – The US Army and the Indian Wars 1866–1891*, Cassell, London, 1975

Wilmot, Chester, *The Struggle for Europe*, Collins, London, 1952

Young, Peter, *Commando*, Pan/Ballantyne, London, 1974

WEBSITES OF PARTICULAR INTEREST

The **Victoria Cross Reference** site (victoriacross@chapter-one.com) is in a class of its own and not only provides citations but also, in many cases, photographs and much personal detail. It also provides links to many other sites, including the excellent **History of the Victoria Cross**, which contains memorial and other details by county, the **Australian and New Zealand Victoria Cross**, the **Victoria Cross in India** and **Victoria Cross Canadian Recipients**, all of which contain further information regarding the deeds themselves and biographical details of the recipients. Interesting sites relating to specific engagements include **Rorke's Drift** and **Zeebrugge**, both of which are accessible by keyword. Highly recommended is Richard and Doug Arman's **VC Database User's Group** (vcresearch@austarnet.com.au), which possesses an impressive and expanding archive.

There are numerous websites devoted to the **Congressional Medal of Honor**. Of these I found the expanding Congressional Medal of Honor site (http://www.medalofhonor.com) the most helpful. It contains the US Army Center of Military History's full text citations for all services as well as biographical details of the most famous recipients and is subdivided into numerous categories. More specific sites that will reward a visit include **The Great Locomotive Chase** (several), **The Battle of Mobile Bay**, a well-illustrated US Navy Historical Center site, the **Marine Corps Legacy Museum**, the **US Marine Raiders** site, **Ploesti**, a US Air Force site giving full details of the raid, and **Arlington Cemetery**, all accessible by keyword.

Index

Regiments are indexed against their earliest regimental title as it appears in the text

Abdul Hafiz, Jemadar 334–5
Abdullah Khan 131, 132
Adams, Lt. Cdr. Bryan 221
Admin Box, battle of the, 1944
    328
Afghanistan 365
Agansing Rai, Naik 340
Aisne, Battle of the, 1914 171,
    177–81
Aitken, Lt. Robert 69
Alamein
    First Battle of, 1942 273–81
    Second Battle of, 1942 281–6
Allmand, Acting Capt. Michael
    342
Allen, Cpl. Nathaniel M. 92
Allen (Allan), Cpl. William 122,
    124, 125
Alma, Battle of the, 1854
    13–24
American Civil War, 1861-65
    6–7, 78, 83, 98
Amiens, battle of, 1918 236
Andrews, James 79, 80, 81
Anson, Maj. 75
Anson, Gen. Sir George (1797-
    1857) 49
Anstruther, Lt. Henry 17
Antolak, Sgt. Sylvester 323–4
Anzio, 1944 309–26
Argonne, Battle of the 236–9
Argyll 188–90
Armistead, Brig. Gen. Lewis
    (1817-63) 95
Army of India Medal 2
Army of the Potomac 83–97
Arnhem 344, 345, 346, 347–8,
    349, 350, 351
Atherstone, HMS 254, 257, 258,
    264
Atlanta, USS 296, 297, 299
Auchinleck, Gen. Sir Claude
    (1884-1981) 244, 249, 251,
    273, 280

Australian forces 32, 194–5,
    196–7
    9th Australian Division 244,
    279, 285
    Australian and New Zealand
    Army Corps (ANZAC)
    185–6, 192–3, 194–9
Avery, Seaman James 101
Aylmer, Capt. Fenton 131–2,
    132, 134

B11 183
Babcock, Lt. 131, 132
Babtie, Maj. William 149, 150
Bacon, Pte. Elijah W. 96
Badli-ke-serai, battle of, 1857
    49
Bailey, Maj. Kenneth D. 291–2
Bailward, Maj. A. C. 148
Baker, Lt. Col. Addison E. 306
Baker, Quarter Gunner Charles
    101
Balaklava, Battle of, 1854 25–33
Bamford, Capt. Edward 221,
    227
Barfoot, Technical Sgt. Van T.
    321–2
Barnard, Gen. Sir Harry (1799-
    1857) 49, 50
Basilone, Sgt. John 294–5
Baskeyfield, Lance Sgt. John
    348
Bassett, Cpl. Cyril 198–9
Bauer, Lt. Col. Harold W. 293
Beach, Pte. Thomas 37
Beames, Lt. Peter 248–9
Beattie, Lt. Cdr. Samuel 255,
    260, 266
Beatty, Vice Admiral Sir David
    (1871-1936) 163, 201, 202,
    203, 204
Beeley, Rifleman John 247
Bell, Capt. Edward William
    Derr 17, 18, 23

Bell, Capt. Eric 210
Belleau Wood, Battle of, 1918
    231–5
Benedict, Lt. George G. 87
Bensinger, Pte. William 82
Benteen, Capt. Frederick W.
    110, 112, 113, 114
Bentinck, Maj. Gen. H. J. W. 19
Berry, Cpl. Charles J. 357
Berryman, Sgt. John 31, 32
Billyard-Leake, Lt. E. W. 224
Bingham, Cdr. The Hon.
    Edward 203
Blaker, Maj. Frank 343
Boisragon, Lt. Guy 131, 132,
    134
Bonham-Carter, Lt. S. S. 224
Bourke, Lt. Roland 226, 227,
    228
Bourne, Colour Sgt. Frank 122,
    126
Boxer Rising, 1900-01 152–64
Boyle, Lt. Cdr. Edward 193
Bradbury, Capt. Edward 175–6
Bradford, Lt. Cdr. George
    222–3, 227
Bradford, Brig. Gen. Roland
    227
Brewster, Capt. Andre W. 160
Brilliant, HMS 220, 225
Britain, Battle of, 1940 8, 243
British Army 2, 3, 13, 145
    brigades
        1st Cavalry Brigade 175–7
        1st Parachute Brigade 346
        2nd Rifle Brigade, Eighth
            Army 282–4
        Guards 18–20, 34
        the Heavy Brigade 27–8,
            30, 31–2
        Highland 18–19, 20–22,
            25–6, 146
        the Light Brigade 14,
            29–32

The Rifle Brigade 38
British Expeditionary Force
(BEF) 168, 171, 180, 181,
208–9, 229
1st Cavalry Brigade 175–7
18th Division 209–10
30th Division 210
49th Division 213
Cavalry Division 168
I Corps 168, 172
II Corps 168–72, 172–4
XIII Corps 209
cavalry regiments
2nd Household Cavalry
350
4th Dragoon Guards 27–8
4th Light Dragoons (4th
Hussars) 29–32, 33
5th Dragoon Guards 27–8,
175, 176
6th Inniskilling Dragoons
27–8, 32
8th Hussars 29–32
9th Lancers 170
11th Hussars 29–32, 175,
176
13th Light Dragoons (13th
Hussars) 29–32, 33
17th Lancers 29–32, 32
Royal Dragoons 27, 28
Royal Scots Greys 27–8,
32
the Chindits 327, 329, 341–3
commandos 255–6, 261–3,
268–9
Divisions, Crimean War 14,
26
1st 14, 18–19, 26
2nd 14, 15, 16, 22, 34,
36–7
Cavalry 25, 27
Light 14, 15, 34
divisions, Second World War
1st Airborne 344, 344–5,
346, 350
1st Armoured 274, 282,
286
1st Infantry 311, 313, 316,
317, 320, 325
2nd British 332–3
5th Infantry 318–9, 320,
325
7th Armoured 244, 245
52nd (Lowland) 344
56th (London) 314–5, 316,
319
79th Armoured 272
Guards Armoured Divi-
sion 348–9
Eighth Army 244, 273, 280

1st Armoured Division
274, 282, 286
2nd Rifle Brigade 282–4
7th Armoured Division
244, 245
X Corps 281
XIII Corps 244, 249, 250,
281
XXX Corps 244, 245–8,
249, 250, 281
Fourteenth Army 327
IV Corps 327, 328–9, 334,
335
guards regiments
Coldstream Guards 19, 20,
172, 180
Grenadier Guards 19, 20,
39–40, 311, 315, 349
Irish Guards 350
Scots Fusilier Guards 19,
19–20, 21, 23
King's Royal Rifle Corps 246–7
regiments
8th (The King's) 54, 65
19th (The Green Howards)
16, 211–2
23rd (Royal Welch
Fusiliers) 16, 17, 18, 19,
22–3, 65, 159
24th (South Wales Border-
ers) 116, 118–27, 186,
331
30th (the East Lancashire
Regiment) 40
32nd (the Duke of Corn-
wall's Light Infantry)
62
33rd (Duke of Welling-
ton's) 16
41st (The Welch Regiment)
40, 178
42nd (The Black Watch)
20, 21–2
44th (1st Essex) 74, 76, 77,
250
47th (The Loyal North
Lancashire Regiment)
38
49th (1st Bn Royal Berk-
shire Regiment) 40, 333
52nd (Oxfordshire &
Buckinghamshire) Light
Infantry 54, 55, 57
53rd (The King's Shrop-
shire Light Infantry)
65, 66, 67, 68–9
55th (2nd Bn The Border
Regiment) 22, 37
61st (Gloucestershire) 54,
57, 59

64th (North Staffordshire)
77
67th (2nd Hampshire) 74,
76, 77
68th (The Durham Light
Infantry) 37–8
75th (Gordon) Highlanders
54
77th (2nd Bn The Middle-
sex Regiment) 16, 21,
23–4
79th (The Queen's Own
Cameron Highlanders)
20, 21–2, 179
80th (The South Stafford-
shire) 119, 348, 350–51
82nd (South Lancashire)
65
88th (The Connaught
Rangers) 16, 21
90th (the Cameronians) 69
93rd (2nd Bn Argyll and
Sutherland High-
landers) 20, 21–2, 26–7,
65–7, 68, 69
95th (2nd Bn The Sher-
wood Foresters) 16, 313
Hampshire 193–4, 249–50
Highland Light Infantry
178–9, 214
King's Own Borderers 186
King's Own Yorkshire
Light Infantry 173,
173 4
Lancashire Fusiliers 186–8
London Scottish 314–5
The Parachute Regiment
346, 347, 351
Royal Dublin Fusiliers
188–90
Royal Inniskilling Fusiliers
210
Royal Irish Fusiliers
210–11
Royal Irish Rifles 212
Royal Munster Fusiliers
189, 191–2
Royal Norfolk 333
Royal Regiment of
Fusiliers 16–17, 22, 169,
186
Royal Scots Fusiliers 149
Royal West Kent 329–32,
333
Seaforth Highlanders
212–3
Suffolk 173
West Yorkshire 213–4, 337
Wiltshire 325–6
Royal Artillery 38–9, 170,

172, 174, 179, 247, 282–4
Royal Engineers 120,
169–70, 178
Royal Horse Artillery 175–7,
247–8
Royal Tank Regiments
4th Royal Tank Regiment
248–9
40th Royal Tank Regiment
279, 285
44th Royal Tank Regiment
250
46th Royal Tank Regiment
279, 315
50th Royal Tank Regiment
279–80
XXX Corps 344–5, 346, 347
in North Africa 244,
245–8, 249, 250, 281
XXXIII Corps 332–3
Brock, Wing Cdr. F. A. 219, 222
Bromhead, Lt. Gonville 120,
121, 122–3, 124–5
Bromley, Maj. Cuthbert 187
Brooklyn, USS 99, 101
Brown, Capt. Morris, Jr 96
Brown, Landsman Wilson 101
Brown, Pte. Wilson H. 82
Browning, Lt. Gen. Frederick
344, 346, 350
Buckley, John 47
Buffum, Pte. Robert 82
Buller, Gen. Redvers (1839–
1908) 145–6, 146–7,
148–9, 150, 151
Burgess, Cpl. 55–6
Burroughs, Capt. 66, 68
Burslem, Lt. Nathaniel 76, 77
Burtenshaw, Lt. Robert 261–2
Burton, Cpl. Alexander 197
Butler, Lt. Smedley 161, 163–4
Byrne, Acting Storekeeper
Alexander 123, 126
Byrne, Pte. John 37–8

C3 220, 223
Cactus Air Force 288, 288–9,
293, 299, 300
Caddy, Pfc. William R. 357
Cain, Maj. Robert 350–1
Cairns, Lt. George 341–2
Calistan, Sgt. Charles 283, 284
Callaghan, Rear Admiral Daniel
J. 296, 297, 298, 299
Cambridge, Duke of 18, 21, 26
campaign medals 2
Campbell, Lt. 175–6
Campbell, Gen. Sir Colin (1792–
1863) 20–1, 26–7, 64,
65–6, 67

Campbell, Brig. John (Jock)
245–6
Campbell, William 79
Campbelltown, HMS (former
USS *Buchanan*) 253–4,
255, 257, 258, 259–60,
263, 265
Canadian Army 267–72
Carey, Sgt. Hugh 93
Carlisle, Pte. Caspar R. 87
Carpenter, Lt. Cdr. Alfred 227
Carr, Sgt. Frank 262
Casamento, Cpl. Anthony
295–6
Cawnpore 53, 77
Cemetery Ridge 85, 86, 91–2,
94–7
Chamberlain, Col. Joshua L.
90–1
Chambers, Lt. Col. Justice M.
357, 358
Chancellorsville, battle of, 1863
83, 84
Chant, Lt. Stuart 261
Chaplin, Ensign John 76, 77
Chard, Lt. John 120, 121, 122,
122–3, 124, 124–5
Charge of the Light Brigade, the
29–32
Chateau-Thierry, action at, 1918
231
Chavasse, Capt. Noel 367, 368
Chelmsford, Lt. Gen. Lord
(1827–1905) 115–7, 120,
124, 127
Chester, HMS 204–5
Chindits, Second Incursion,
1944 329, 341–3
Christian, Pte. Herbert F. 325
Clark, Cpl. Harrison 93
Clark, Lt. Gen. Mark 8, 309,
312, 317, 319–20, 325, 326
Clifford, Lt. the Hon. Henry 38
Clopp, Pte. John E. 96–7
Coates, Sgt. Jefferson 87
Coghill, Lt. Neville 119, 368
Cole, Sgt. Darrell S. 356
Colenso, battle of, 1899 4,
144–51
commemorative medals 1, 2
Congressional Medal of Honor
5–8, 365
Congreve, Capt. Walter 149,
150
Congreve, Maj. William 150
Cooper, Coxswain John 101
Copland, Maj. William 255–6,
260, 262, 266
Cornwell, Boy First Class John
204–5

Cosgrove, Cpl. William 191–2
Craddock, Sgt. Maj. 335–6
Crete, defence of, 1941 274,
276–7
Crimean War, 1854-56 3, 5, 13,
41–2
Criswell, Sgt. Benjamin C. 113
Croix de Guerre 2
Crook, Brig. Gen. George 106–7
Crutchley, Lt. Victor 225–6,
227
Cunningham, Cpl. Charles 113
Custer, Lt. Col. George Arm-
strong (1839-76) 108–12

D–Day, 1944 272, 326
Daffodil 220, 221–2, 224–5,
228
Dalton, James 120, 121, 122,
124, 125
Daly, Pte. (later First Sgt.) Dan
156 7, 164, 232–3
Davis, Capt. Charles W. 301
de Castro, Cpl. Joseph H. 96
Dean, Lt. Percy 224, 227
Dease, Lt. Maurice 169, 170
Deblanc, Lt. Jefferson J. 301–2
Delhi
Siege of, 1857 49–53
Storming of, 1857 52, 54–61
Delhi Arsenal, 1857 45–8, 59–60
Delhi Field Force 49–53, 54–61
Derviskian, Technical Sgt.
Ernest H. 322
Dieppe raid, Operation Jubilee,
1942 267–72
Distinguished Conduct Medal
5, 126–7, 150, 156
Distinguished Service Order
178, 182
Dobson, Pte. Frederick 180
Donnelly, Ordinary Seaman
John 101
Dore, Sgt. George H. 93
Dorrell, Sgt. Maj. George 176,
176–7
Dorsey, Pte. Daniel 82
Doughty-Wylie, Lt. Col.
Charles 191
Drain, Driver Job 174
Drewry, Midshipman George
188–9, 190
Drummond, Lt. Geoffrey 226,
227, 228
Dunlap, Capt. Robert H. 358
Dunley (Dunlay), L. Cpl. John
66, 68
Dunstan, Cpl. William 197, 198
Durnford, Col. Anthony 116,
117, 118, 119

Durrant, Sgt. Thomas 263–4
Dutko, Pfc. John W. 320

Edson, Col. Merritt 290, 291, 291–2
El Alamein: see Alamein
El Caney, Battle of, 1898 137, 138, 138–9, 141, 142
Elliott, Sgt Keith 274–5
Enderlin, Musician Richard 87–8
Eves, Colour Sgt. 332
Ewart, Lt. Col. 66, 68

Fair Oaks, battle of, 1862 136
Falklands War, 1982 365
Falls, Colour Sgt. Benjamin F. 96
Farragut, Rear Admiral David Glasgow (1801-70) 99
Farrell, Sgt. Joseph 31, 32
Fassett, Capt. John B. 93
Ffrench, Lt. Alfred 66, 68
Finch, Sgt. Norman 222, 227
First World War, 1914-18 167–8, 182–3, 201, 217–8, 229–30, 239–40, 243, 367
Fitzgibbon, Hospital Apprentice Andrew 75, 77
Fitzpatrick, Coxswain Thomas 102
Flinn, Drummer Thomas 77
Flint, Lt. R. B. 178
Flynn, Cpl. Christopher 96
Foote, Capt. John 271–2
Forrest, Lt. George 46–7, 47, 47–8
Foss, Capt. Joseph J 300
Fourner, Sgt. William G. 300–301
Fowler, Second Lt. Thomas W. 323
French Army
    and the Crimean War 14, 14–5, 22, 25, 26, 30, 37, 41
    and the First World War 168, 177, 199, 201, 208, 209, 216, 217
    at the Taku Forts 74, 75, 76
Frost, Lt. Col. John 346, 347, 349
Fuger, Sgt. Frederick 96
Fuller, William 79–82
Fuller, L. Cpl. William 178
Furman, Cpl. Chester S. 93

Gaje Ghale, Havildar 336–7
Galer, Maj. Robert E 289
Gallipoli, 1915 182–200, 310
Ganju Lama, Rifleman 337–8

Gardner, Coal Heaver James 102
Gardner, Capt. Philip 248–9
Garland, Flying Officer Donald 243
Gazala, battle of, 1942 273
Gearing, Lt. Paul 248–9
Geiger, Sgt. George 112
General, The (locomotive) 79-81
German Army
    and the First World War 167–8, 171–2, 177, 181, 216, 229–30, 235–6
    and the Second World War 244, 251, 286
German Navy, High Seas Fleet 201–7
Gettysburg, Battle of, 1863 7, 83–97
Gibbon, Brig. Gen. John 92, 96
Gibbon, Col. John 106, 108, 113
Gibson, Technician Eric G. 312
Giffard, Lt. 175–6
Gilligan, First Sgt. Edward 87
Godley, Pte. Sidney 169, 170–71
Gorman, Seaman James 41
Grant, Lt. Gen. Sir James Hope 51–2, 64, 74, 77
Grant, Pte. Peter 66, 68
Gratwick, Pte. Percival 281–2
Gray, Sgt. Ross F. 357–8, 358
Gray, Sgt. Thomas 243
Grayburn, Lt. John 348
Great Locomotive Chase, 1862 78–82
Green, Capt. John 211
Grenfell, Capt. Francis 170, 171
Grieve, Sgt. Maj. John 28, 32
Grieve, Capt. Robert Cuthbert 32
Grimshaw, Cpl. John 187
Guadalcanal campaign, 1942-43 287–302
Guise, Maj. John 69
Gunn, Second Lt. Ward 247–8
Gurkhas, the 130–32
    in the Second World War 336–9, 342, 343
Gurney, Pte. Arthur 279
Guy, Midshipman Basil 160–61

Haig, Field Marshal Sir Douglas (1861-1928) 168, 172, 180, 209, 214, 215
Haines, Company Sgt. Maj. 332
Hall, Staff Sgt. George G. 322–3
Hall, Technician Grade 5 Lewis 301

Hall, Able Seaman William 68, 69
Halliday, Capt. Lewis 156
Hamilton, Gen. Sir Ian (1853-1947) 185, 193, 199
Hamilton, Pte John 197, 198
Hancock, Pte. Thomas 52
Hancock, Maj Winfield S 92, 94, 96
Hanley, Sgt. Richard P. 113
Harman, L. Cpl. John 330–31
Harrell, Sgt. William G. 360–61
Harrington, Lt. Hastings 69
Harris, Capt. of the Forecastle John 101
Harrison, Lt. Cdr. Arthur 227
Harrison, Leading Seaman John 67–8, 69
Hart, Sgt John W. 93
Hartford, USS 99, 100, 101–2
Harvey, Maj. Francis 202
Hawkins, Pte. Martin 82
Hawks, Pfc. Lloyd C. 313
Hawthorne, Bugler Robert 55, 56
Hazara Singh 131, 132
Hecla, HMS 22
Henderson, Lt. Ian 263
Henry, Sgt. Andrew 38
heroes, need for 365
Herring, Lt. (jg) Rufus G. 355
Hill, Cpl. Raymond W. 92
Hill, Sgt. Samuel 69
Hills (Hills-Johnes), Lt. James 52–3
Hincks, Sgt. Maj. William B. 96
Hitch, Pte. Frederick 122, 124, 125
Hoden, Pte. Henry 113
Hodson, Maj. William 60
Hoffman, Charles F. (also known as Ernest August Janson) 233
Holbrook, Lt. Norman 183
Holmes, L. Cpl. Frederick 173
Home, Lt. Duncan 55–6, 60, 61
Honourable East India Company 2–3, 45–6, 62, 65, 66, 69
Hook, Pte. Henry (Alfred) 123, 124, 125
Hooker, Maj. Gen. Joseph (1814-79) 84
Hope, Capt. Hugh 247
Horan, Sgt. Thomas 92
Horlock, Bombardier Ernest 179
Huff, Cpl. Paul B. 315–6
Hughes, Second Lt. Lloyd H. 307

Huidkoper, Lt. Col. Henry S. 87
Hutchinson, Sgt. Rufus 112–3

Imphal, Battle of, 1944 328, 334–41, 343
Indian Army 3, 274, 329, 333, 335–6, 338
Indian Mutiny, 1857-58 23, 45–6, 49, 53, 77
Indian Order of Merit 2–3, 56, 132
Inkerman, Battle of, 1854 23, 34–42
Intrepid, HMS 220, 224
Iphigenia, HMS 220, 224
Iris 220, 221–2, 222–3, 224–5, 228
Irlam, Seaman Joseph 101
Irsch, Capt. Francis 87
Irwin, Pte. Charles 66, 68
Isandhlwana, battle of, 1879 117–20
Iwo Jima campaign, 1945 295, 352–64

Jacka, L. Cpl. Albert 194–5
Jackman, Capt. James 249–50
Jacobson, Pfc. Douglas T. 360
Janson, Ernest August (also known as Charles F. Hoffman) 233
Japanese Army
  in Burma 327–8, 331, 333–4, 336, 340–1
  on Guadalcanal 288–91, 293–4, 295, 296, 300, 302
  on Iwo Jima 353, 362–3, 364
Jarvis, L. Cpl. Charles 169, 170, 171
Jellicoe, Admiral Sir John (1859-1935) 163, 201, 204, 205–6, 207, 217
Jellison, Sgt. Benjamin H. 96
Jerstad, Maj. John L. 306
Johnson, Seaman Henry 101
Johnson, Col. Leon 308
Johnson, Sgt. Wallace W. 93
Johnston, Capt. William 178
Johnston, Pfc. William J. 316–7
Jones, Quartermaster John E. 102
Jones, Pte. Robert 123, 124
Jones, Pte. William 123, 124, 125–6
Julian, Sgt. Joseph R. 362
Jutland, Battle of 201–7

Kane, Col. John R. 305, 306, 307, 308

Kavanagh, Thomas Henry 64–5
Keneally, Pte. William 187
Keppler, Boatswain's Mate 1st Class Reinhardt 298
Kessler, Pfc. Patrick L. 320–21
Kettle Hill 137, 138, 140–41, 143
Keyes, Lt. Col. Geoffrey 228
Keyes, Vice Admiral Sir Roger 163, 218, 219, 224, 225, 226, 228, 252
Keysor, L. Cpl. Leonard 196, 198
Khudadad Khan, Sepoy 181
Kibby, Sgt. William 285
King, Sgt. 332
Knappenberger, Pfc. Alton W. 314
Knight, Pte. William 79, 81, 82
Knox, Second Lt Edward M. 92
Knox, Sgt. John Simpson 19–20, 23
Kohima, Battle of, 1944 328, 329–34, 343
Korean War, 1950-53 365

La Belle, Pfc. James D. 357
Lackawanna, USS 100, 101, 102–3
Ladysmith, siege of, 1899 145, 151
Lamb, Pte. James 31, 33
Landrecies, action at, 1914 172
Lane, Pte. Thomas 76, 77
Laughnan, Gunner Thomas 69
Laverty, Lt. Col. John 329–30, 332
Lawson, Landsman John 102
Lawton, First Lt. Louis B. 160
Le Cateau, Battle of, 1914 172–4
Lee, Gen. Robert E. (1807-70) 83–4, 85, 88, 94, 95
Légion d'Honneur 1–2, 23, 32, 38, 39, 40, 150, 227, 239, 266
Leims, Second Lt. John H. 361–2
Lenon, Lt. Edmund 76, 77
Leyland, Lt. Cdr. Arthur 222
Lindsay, Capt. Robert James 19–20, 23
Little Big Horn, battle of the, 1876 108–14
Little Inkerman, battle of, 1854 35
Little Round Top 86, 89–91
Loftus Jones, Cdr. William 205
Lonergan, Capt. John 93
Long, Col. C. J. 146, 147, 148, 150

Lord, Flight Lt. David 347–8
Loudoun-Shand, Maj. Stewart 211–2
Lucan, Lord 26, 27, 28, 29, 30
Lucas, Mate Charles 22
Lucas, Pfc. Jacklyn H. 357
Lucas, Maj. Gen. John P. (1890-1949) 309–10, 311, 315, 316, 317
Lucknow, Second Relief of, 1857 62–9
Lucy-le-Bocage, action at, 1918 164, 234
Luke, Driver Frederick 174
Lummus, First Lt. Jack 362

MacArthur, Gen. Arthur (1845-1912) 6
MacArthur, Gen. Douglas (1880-1964) 5
McCandless, Lt. Cdr. Bruce 298
McCarren, Pte. Bernard 97
McCarthy, Capt. Joseph J. 358
McDermond, Pte. John 38
MacDonald, Sir Claude 154–5, 156, 157, 162
McDougall, Pte. John 76, 77
McFadzean, Pte. William 212
McGann, First Sgt. Michael A. 107
McGuire, Sgt. James 57
Mackay, Pte. David 66, 68
McKechnie, Sgt. James 19, 23
McKenzie, Able Seaman Albert 222, 227
Magersfontein, battle of, 1899 146
Maine, USS 135
Malayan Emergency, 1948-60 365
Malleson, Midshipman Wilfred 189, 190
Malone, Sgt. Joseph 31, 33
Mann, Pfc. Joe E. 347
Marne, First Battle of the, 1914 177
Marne, Second Battle of the, 1918 236
Marten, Capt. F. W. 284
Martin, First Lt. Harry L. 363
Martin, Trumpeter John 111
Martin-Leake, Surgeon Capt. 367–8
Mason, Sgt. E. A. 82
Mayberry, Pte. John B. 97
Meade, Maj. Gen. George (1815-72) 84–5, 88–9, 92, 94, 97
Mears, Sgt. George 93
Mechlin, Blacksmith Henry 112

medals 1–3
Meerut garrison 46, 49
Melville, Ordinary Seaman Charles 102
Melville, Lt. Teignmouth 119
Merritt, Lt. Col. Charles 270–1, 278
Messines, 1917 32, 195
Metacomet, USS 99–101, 103
Mexican-American War, 1847 6
MGB 314 254, 255, 257, 259, 260, 264
Midway, Battle of, 1942 287
Military General Service Medal 2
Military Medal 182
Miller, Lt. Frederick 38–9
Miller, Cpl. John 97
Mills, Capt. Albert L. 142
Mills, Pte. James H. 324
Mitchell, Gunner's Mate Joseph 155
Mobile Bay, Battle of, 1864 98–103
Mons, Battle of, 1914 168–72
Monte Cassino 309, 320
Montgomery, Field Marshal Bernard Law (1887–1976) 280–81, 285, 317, 344–6, 350
Montgomery, Capt. Robert 256, 261, 286
Moor, Second Lt. Dallas 193–4
Morris, Capt William 31–2
Morse, Lt Tony 189
Mouat, Surgeon James 32
Mount Suribachi, Iwo Jima 352, 353, 355, 356, 357, 359
MTB 74 254, 255, 257, 258, 260, 263
Mundy, Lt. 175–6
Munro, Signalman 1st Class Douglas A. 292
Munro, Colour Sgt. James 66–7, 68
Munsell, Sgt. Harvey M. 92
Murray, Sgt. Thomas 113

Nagdu, Sepoy 133
Najafgahr, battle of, 1857 50–51
Nasmith, Lt. Cdr. Martin (later Admiral Sir Martin Dunbar-Nasmith) 193
Naval General Service Medal 2
Naylor, Landsman David 102
Nelson, Sgt. David 175–6, 177
Néry, action at, 1914 175–7
Nestor, HMS 203

Netrabahadar Thapa, Subadar 339
New Zealand Army 198–9, 250, 274–8
Newman, Lt. Col. A. C. 255, 258, 260, 262, 266
Newman, Lt. Beryl R. 324–5
Nicolson, Flight Lt. Eric 8
Nicholson, acting Brig. Gen. John 50–51, 54, 58–9, 60
Nijmegen 344, 348–9, 350, 351
Nilt Fort, storming of, 1891 128–34
Noble, Landsman Daniel 101
Nolan, Capt. Lewis 29
North-West Frontier, India 128
Nurse, Cpl. George 149, 150

O'Brien, Cpl. Henry D. 93
O'Connor, Sgt. Luke 17, 18, 22–3
Olson, Sgt. Truman O. 313–4
Operation Crusader 243–51
Operation Jubilee, 1942 267–72
Operation Market Garden, 1944 344–51
Ord, Lt. Jules 140, 142
Osborne, Lt. (jg) Weedon E. 234
Ostend Raid, 1918 218, 220, 225–7, 227–8

Paige, Sgt. Mitchell 295
Palmer, Pte Anthony 39
Park, Gunner James 69
Park, Sgt. John 23–4
Parker, Lt. John 141, 142
Parkes, Pte. Samuel 31, 33
Parrott, Cpl. Jacob 82
Passchendaele, Battle of, 1917 216, 217, 218
Paton, Sgt. John 68
Pawsey, Charles 332
Peel, Capt. Vincent 67–8
Peking 77, 152–7, 161, 162
Pelham, Landsman William 102
Percy, Col. the Hon. Henry 39–40
Pershing, Gen. John (1860–1948) 230–31, 233, 239
Petty, Lt. Orlando H. 234
Phillips, Pte. George 357
Pike, Leading Seaman F. C. 255, 259, 260
Pinney, Maj. Bernard 247–8
Pipes, Sgt. James 93
Pittinger, Cpl. William 82
Ploesti raid, 1943 303–8
Porteous, Capt. Patrick 268–9

Porter, Pte. John 82
Postles, Capt. James Parke 92
Pour le Mérite 1, 171
Preston, Sgt. J. E. 156
Preston, Landsman John 102
Prettyjohn, Cpl. John 41
Price, Coxswain Edward 101
Pritchard, Capt. William 254, 256, 262
Purcell, Pte. John 52
Purdon, Lt. Corran 261, 262
Purman, Lt. James J. 92–3
Purple Heart, the 5–6
Pye, Sgt. Maj. Charles 68–9

Queripel, Capt. Lionel 347
Quigg, Pte. Robert 212

Raglan, Field Marshal Lord Fitzroy Somerset, 1st Baron (1788–1855) 14, 15, 26, 29, 35, 37
Ramage, Sgt. Henry 28, 32
Randle, Capt. John 333
Randolph, Revd. Roy 332
Ranken, Capt. Harry 180
Ravenhill, Pte. George 149, 150
Raynor, Lt. William 46, 47
Reade, Surgeon Herbert 57, 59
Reddick, Pte. William 82
Reed, Bugler Charles W. 92
Reed, Capt. Hamilton 149, 150–1
Reed, Pte. Oliver P. 97
Reeves, Seaman Thomas 41
Reisinger, Cpl. J. Monroe 87
Renny, Lt. George 60
Reno, Maj. Marcus 108, 110–1, 113, 113–4
Reynolds, Capt. Douglas 174
Reynolds, Surgeon Major James 120, 122, 124, 125
Reynolds, Pte. William 19–20, 23
Rice, Maj. Edmund 96
Richards, Sgt. Alfred 187
Richmond, Pte. James 97
Ritchie, Drummer Walter 212–3
River Clyde, HMS 188–90, 191
Roberts, Lt. the Hon. Frederick 4, 149, 150, 151
Robertson, Pte. Samuel 82
Robinson, Pte. John H. 96
Robinson, First Sgt. Joseph 107
Rogers, Sgt. Maurice 325–6
Rogers, Lt. Robert 76, 77
Rommel, Field Marshal Erwin (1891–44) 244, 245, 249, 250–51, 252, 273, 280–81, 286

Rooper Khan 51–2
Roosevelt, Col. Theodore (1858–1919) 138, 140, 142–3
Rorke's Drift, 1879 116, 120–7
Rose, Seaman George 158
Rosebud River, battle of the, 1876 106–7
Ross, Sgt. Maj. Marion 82
Roush, Cpl. J. Levi 93
Rowlands, Capt. Hugh 40
Roy, Pte. William 126–7
Royal Air Force 5, 8, 243, 256, 258, 347–8
Royal Marines 41, 74, 75, 156, 186, 220
Royal Navy 2, 3, 40–41, 73–4, 201–7
    Naval Brigade, Indian Mutiny 64, 67–8, 69
Ruhl, Pfc. Donald J. 356–7
Russell, Brevet Maj. Sir Charles 39
Russian Army 25, 41, 129
    at the Alma 14, 16–18, 19, 20, 21–2
    at Balaklava 26–8
    at Inkerman 35–7
Rutter, Sgt. James M. 87
Ryan, Drummer Miles 57
Ryder, Cdr. R. E. D. 255, 257, 257–8, 258, 260–1, 266

Salkeld, Lt. Philip 55, 56
Salmon, Lt. Nowell 67–8, 69
Samson, Able Seaman 189, 190
San Francisco, USS 296, 297–8, 299
San Juan Hill, Battle of, 1898 135–43
Sanders, Cpl. George 213–4
Sandford, Lt. Richard 223, 227
Santiago, siege of, 1898 141–2
Sasse, Capt. Cecil 198
Savage, Able Seaman William 259, 261
Scarlett, Brig. Gen. the Hon. James 27, 28, 29
Schauer, Pfc. Henry 321
Schiess, Cpl. Ferdnand 123–5
Schlick, Pte. Robert von 160
Schmidt, Maj. Gen. Harry 353, 358, 359, 363
Schofield, Capt. Harry 149, 150, 151
Scholefield, Seaman Mark 41
Schonland, Lt. Cdr. Herbert E. 298
Scott, Pte. John 82
Scott, Rear Admiral Norman 296–7, 299

Scott, Gen. Winfield (1786–1866) 6
Scully, Conductor 47, 48
Seach, Ordinary Seaman William 158–9
Second Boer War, 1899–1902 4, 144–5, 146
Second World War, 1939–45 243, 252, 303
    Far East theatre of operations 327–9, 343
Secundrabagh, attack on, 1857 65–7, 69
Sellers, Maj. Alfred J. 87
Sevastopol 3, 13, 22–3, 24, 25, 41
Seymour, Vice Admiral Sir Edward 157–9
Shadrack, Pte. Perry 82
Shafter, Maj. Gen. William R. (1835–1906) 136, 137, 138, 139, 141
Shah Najaf, attack on, 1857 67–8
Shark, HMS 205
Shebbeare, Capt. Robert 58
Sheridan, Quartermaster James 102
Sherman, Pte. Marshall 97
Shingle, First Sgt. John H. 107
Shout, Capt. Alfred 198
Sickles, Maj. Gen. Daniel E. (1825–1914) 88, 91–2
Sidney, Maj. the Hon. William Philip 315
Sigler, Pte. Franklin E. 363
Sikh Wars, 1845–46 & 1848–49 45
Sioux War, 1876 104–14
Sirius, HMS 220, 225
Slavens, Pte. Samuel 82
Slim, Gen. William (1891–1970) 327, 328–9, 329, 343
Smalley, Lt. Christopher 261
Smith, Revd. George 120, 121, 122, 126
Smith, L. Cpl. Henry 57
Smith, Pte. J. 66, 69
Smith, Sgt. John 55–6, 56
Smith, Capt. of the Forecastle John 101
Smith, Capt. John Lucian 289
Smith, Lt. John Manners 133, 134
Smith, Cpl. Thaddeus S. 93
Somalia 365
Somme, Battle of the, 1916 150, 195, 208–16, 227
Spanish-American War, 1898 135–6

Squires, Pfc. John C. 319
St George Cather, Lt. Geoffrey 211
St Nazaire Raid, 1942 252–66
Stacey, Pte. Charles 93
Stanley, Shell Man William A. 102
Stein, Cpl. Tony 356
Stephenson, Capt. George 120
Stewart, Capt. William 67, 68
Stilwell, Gen. Joseph (1883–1946) 327, 342–3
Stockham, Gunnery Sgt. Fred W. 235
Stormberg Junction, battle of, 1899 146
Stubbs, Sgt. Frank 187
Suvla Bay 192–3, 199
Symons, Second Lt. William 196–7, 198

Taku Forts, the, 1860 73–7
Taylor, Lt. 133
Taylor, Armourer George 103
Taylor, Coxswain Thomas 103
Tecumseh, USS 99–100, 101
Tennessee, CSS 99, 100–101
Terry, Maj. Gen. Alfred J. 105–6, 108, 113
Texas (locomotive) 80–1
Thackeray, Second Lt. Edward 60
Thetis, HMS 220, 223–4
Thomas, Armourer's Mate J. T. 155
Thompson, Sgt. James H. 97
Thompson, Pte. Peter 113
Tibbits, Lt. Nigel 254, 260
Tientsin 158, 159–61
Tirpitz, the 266
Tisdale, Sub-Lt. Arthur 190
Tobruk, Operation Crusader, 1941 243–51
Tollerton, Pte. Ross 179
Tombs, Maj. Henry 52–3
Toms, Lt. J. E. B. 283
Towle, Pte. John 349
Townsend, Charles 134
Tozier, Sgt. Andrew J. 90–91
Tubb, Lt. Frederick 197, 198
Tulbahadur Pun, Rifleman 342
Turkish army 14, 25, 26–7, 34–5, 41
    and the First World War 182–3, 184, 185, 199
Turnbull, Sgt. James 214
Turner, Sgt. Hanson 337
Turner, Lt. Col. Victor 282–4
Tynedale, HMS 254, 264

Unknown Warrior, tomb of the, Arlington National Cemetery 7, 240
Unknown Warrior, tomb of the, Westminster Abbey 5, 7, 240
Unwin, Cdr Edward 188–90, 190, 193, 200
Upham, Capt Charles 275–9, 367–8
Urquhart, Maj. Gen. Roy 344, 346, 347, 350
US Army 6, 7, 135–6; *see also* Army of the Potomac
1st US Ranger Battalion 268
American Expeditionary Force 230–40
divisions
  1st Armored Division 311, 312, 313, 316, 323
  3rd Division 311, 312–3, 313–4, 318, 320
  34th Division 319
  36th Division 320
  45th Division 311, 316
  82nd Airborne 344, 346, 348–9
  101st Airborne 344, 346, 347
regiments
  1st US Volunteer Cavalry (the Rough Riders) 136, 138, 140, 141, 142–3
  2nd Cavalry 106
  2nd Massachusetts Volunteer Infantry 139
  3rd Cavalry 106, 107
  4th Infantry 106
  6th Infantry 141
  7th Cavalry 106, 108–14
  7th Infantry 106, 313–4
  9th Infantry 106, 160
  15th Infantry 323–4, 325
  16th Infantry 141
  17th Infantry 106, 142
  20th Infantry 106
  24th Infantry 141
  27th Infantry 301
  35th Infantry 300–301
  71st New York Volunteer Infantry 139
  132nd Infantry 302
  133rd Infantry 324–5
  135th Infantry 322–3
  147th Infantry 363
  157th Infantry 321–2
  164th Infantry 294
  328th Infantry 237–8
VI Corps 309, 319–20, 325
XIV Corps 299

US Army Air Force
44th Bombardment Group 305
93rd Bombardment Group 304–5, 306
98th Bombardment Group 305
376th Bombardment Group 304, 305, 306–7
389th Bombardment Group 307
US Marine Corps 156–7, 163–4
1st Marine Division 287–8, 290–93, 299
1st Marine Raider Battalion 290–92
2nd Marine Raider Battalion 296
4th Marine Brigade 231–5
5th Marines 292, 295–6
7th Marines 292–3, 294–5, 296
9th Marines 360, 361–2
21st Marines 358
23rd Marines 356, 360
24th Marines 358
25th Marines 355, 357–8
27th Marines 355, 362
28th Marines 355, 356–7, 360–1
V Amphibious Force 353–64
3rd Marine Division 359
4th Marine Division 353, 355, 363
5th Marine Division 353, 355, 361, 363–4
US Navy 6, 7, 99

Vandergrift, Maj. Gen. Alexander A. (1887–1973) 287, 290, 292, 296, 299–300
Veazey, Col. Wheelock G. 96
Victoria, Queen of Great Britain and Ireland, Empress of India (1819–1901) 3
Victoria Cross 4–5, 7, 365, 367–8
forfeitures 4, 57, 77, 150
Vietnam War, 1956–75 365
Vincent, Col. Strong 89, 90
Vindictive, HMS 219–20, 221–2, 224–6
Voit, Saddler Otto 112

Wahlen, Pharmacist's Mate Second Class George E. 361
Walford, Maj. Garth 191
Walker, Lt. Mark 40
Wall, Pte. Jerry 96

Waller, Cpl. Francis A. 87
Walsh, Gunnery Sgt. William G. 357
Walters, Sgt. George 40
War of 1812 6
Ward, Quarter Gunner James 103
Washington, George (1732–99) 5
Wassall, Pte. Samuel 119
Watson, Pte. Wilson D. 360
Webb, Capt. 31
Weir, Capt. Thomas 112
Western and Atlantic Railroad raid, 1862 78–82
Wheeler, Maj. Gen. Joseph P. (1836–1906) 136, 137, 138, 141
Wiley, Sgt. James 97
William R. Smith (locomotive) 80
Williams, Cpl. Hershel W. 359
Williams, Pte. John 123, 124, 126
Williams, Pte. Joseph 123
Williams, Capt. Lloyd 231
Williams, Leading Seaman William 189
Willis, Capt. Richard 187, 187–8
Willoughby, Lt. George 46, 47, 48
Wilson, Col. Archdale 49, 50, 51, 59
Wilson, Pte. George 82, 178–9
Wilson, Pte. John Alfred 82
Windolph, Pte. Charles 112
Wingate, Maj. Gen. Orde (1903–44) 327, 341
Witt, Otto 120, 121
Wollom, Pte. John 82
Wood, Pte. Mark 82
Wooden, Cpl. Charles 31–2, 32–3
Woodfill, Lt. Samuel 238–9
Wright, Maj. Alexander 170
Wright, Capt. Theodore 169, 178
Wyatt, L. Cpl. George 172
Wynne, Sub-Lt. R. C. 255

Yate, Maj. Charles 173 4
Yonah (locomotive) 80
York, Sgt. Alvin C 237–8
Young, Lt. Thomas 68, 69

Zeebrugge Raid, 1918 163, 217–25
Zulu War, 1879 115 6, 127, 145